HENRY FIELDING: THE CRITICAL HERITAGE

THE CRITICAL HERITAGE SERIES

GENERAL EDITOR: B. C. SOUTHAM, M.A., B.LITT.(OXON)
Formerly Department of English, Westfield College, University of London

---

Volumes in the series include

JANE AUSTEN	B. C. Southam
BROWNING	Boyd Litzinger *St. Bonaventure University* and Donald Smalley *University of Illinois*
BYRON	Andrew Rutherford *University of Aberdeen*
COLERIDGE	J. R. de J. Jackson *Victoria College, Toronto*
DICKENS	Philip Collins *University of Leicester*
THOMAS HARDY	R. G. Cox *University of Manchester*
HENRY JAMES	Roger Gard *Queen Mary College, London*
JAMES JOYCE (2 vols.)	Robert H. Deming *University of Miami*
D. H. LAWRENCE	R. P. Draper *University of Leicester*
MILTON	John T. Shawcross *University of Wisconsin*
SCOTT	John O. Hayden *University of California, Davis*
SWINBURNE	Clyde K. Hyder
TENNYSON	J. D. Jump *University of Manchester*
THACKERAY	Geoffrey Tillotson and Donald Hawes *Birkbeck College, London*
TROLLOPE	Donald Smalley *University of Illinois*

HENRY FIELDING

THE CRITICAL HERITAGE

Edited by

RONALD PAULSON

Professor of English, The Johns Hopkins University, Baltimore

and

THOMAS LOCKWOOD

Assistant Professor of English, University of Washington, Seattle

LONDON: ROUTLEDGE & KEGAN PAUL

NEW YORK: BARNES & NOBLE INC

Published in Great Britain, 1969
by Routledge & Kegan Paul Limited
and in the United States of America
by Barnes & Noble Inc
© Ronald Paulson and Thomas Lockwood 1969
No part of this book may be reproduced
in any form without permission from
the publisher, except for the quotation
of brief passages in criticism
SBN 7100 6282 6

Printed in Great Britain
by W & J Mackay & Co Ltd, Chatham

General Editor's Preface

The reception given to a writer by his contemporaries and near-contemporaries is evidence of considerable value to the student of literature. On one side we learn a great deal about the state of criticism at large and in particular about the development of critical attitudes towards a single writer; at the same time, through private comments in letters, journals or marginalia, we gain an insight upon the tastes and literary thought of individual readers of the period. Evidence of this kind helps us to understand the writers' historical situation, the nature of his immediate reading-public, and his response to these pressures.

The separate volumes in the *Critical Heritage Series* present a record of this early criticism. Clearly for many of the highly productive and lengthily reviewed nineteenth- and twentieth-century writers there exists an enormous body of material; and in these cases the volume editors have made a selection of the most important views, significant for their intrinsic critical worth or for their representative quality— perhaps even registering incomprehension!

For earlier writers, notably pre-eighteenth century, the materials are much scarcer and the historical period has been extended, sometimes far beyond the writer's lifetime, in order to show the inception and growth of critical views which were initially slow to appear.

In each volume the documents are headed by an Introduction, discussing the material assembled and relating the early stages of the author's reception to what we have come to identify as the critical tradition. The volumes will make available much material which would otherwise be difficult of access and it is hoped that the modern reader will be thereby helped towards an informed understanding of the ways in which literature has been read and judged.

B.C.S.

Contents

CONTENTS

Pasquin
The Historical Register (21 March 1736–7)
Eurydice Hiss'd (13 April 1737)

CONTENTS

Joseph Andrews

Joseph Andrews in France

Joseph Andrews

Joseph Andrews in France

Joseph Andrews

Tom Jones (28 February 1748–9)

Joseph Andrews and the Jacobite's Journal

Tom Jones

Tom Jones and Joseph Andrews

Tom Jones

CONTENTS

Tom Jones

Fielding's 'New Species of Writing'

The Enquiry, Tom Jones, etc.

Tom Jones

Tom Jones in France

Fielding's 'New Species of Writing'

The Scurrilous Plays of the 1730s

Amelia (18 December 1751)

CONTENTS

CONTENTS

Amelia

Fielding's 'New Species of Writing'

Fielding's Art

Tom Jones

Elizabeth Canning and Tom Jones

The Novels of Richardson and Fielding

Amelia and the Domestic Novel

CONTENTS

CONTENTS

Fielding's Art

ERRATUM

Due to limitations of space, only Fielding's literary works have been dealt with in this collection. An error in the publisher's editing of the essays dealing with Fielding's social tracts has inadvertently left two items, Nos. 96 and 97, among the criticisms of the fiction.

Preface

The reactions to a literary work extend from sales (number of editions) to translations, imitations, parodies, illustrations, remarks of casual readers, reviews, and critical essays. Within this range we have tried to present Fielding's contemporary reputation and also catch that often elusive phenomenon, criticism. The limitations of the subject are best shown by admitting at the outset that the most enlightened contemporary criticism of Fielding's fiction was written by Fielding himself—in his prefaces and in his periodicals. And not only the best but the most influential; for most criticism of Fielding's works that was at all sympathetic or methodical derived from, in fact largely restated, his own explanations of what he was doing. Fielding's most important statements of intention, while hovering in the background, are not reprinted, since they are readily available in the novels themselves. We have reprinted two or three unavailable pieces and, for convenience of reference, the *Covent-Garden Journal* replies to the critics of *Amelia*. The prologues and prefaces to the plays are less helpful; unlike those to the novels, they are usually puffs or comic-ironic defences. For example, in the preface to *The Tragedy of Tragedies* 'Scriblerus Secundus' examines the tragedy through the formal method of Richard Bentley and Professor Burmann of Leyden, and while he is in some sense explaining what Fielding has done, the weight of the preface falls on the satire on pedants and heroic tragedies. Also omitted are ironic criticisms like the one of *The Tragedy of Tragedies* by 'Sir Simple Coblecraft' in the *Daily Post*, 29 March 1742, which, ostensibly attacking the play for its scurrility, in fact draws attention to its anti-Walpole allegory.

Another fact to be noticed is that Fielding criticism by contemporaries became most alert and lively when Fielding impinged in one way or another upon political controversy. The most brilliant pieces were personal attacks which only occasionally deviated into criticism of his works. Even when stimulated by a work, the replies were most often to Fielding the place-hunter and menial hack; and Fielding, when replying to the attack, answered the personal accusations first, and often solely, and even when answering the charges against his work he slipped into self-defence: a defence of his play's morality became hinged on his own good character, and ultimately a criticism of his style and grammar might be answered with a gesture in the direction of his gentlemanly background and education at Eton.

This would have been a very bulky book indeed if it had included the criticism of Fielding the man, or even left unedited the attacks and panegyrics that teeter back and forth from the man to his works. Only when the man was serving as a metonymy for his literary work, or when the biographical fallacy was being employed in a meaningful way, does Henry Fielding himself appear in these pages.

From Johnson's philosophic criticism, which places Fielding's novel in the context of moral principles and didactic and psychological effect, we descend to the opposite extreme of particular criticism that deals with specific passages, retells the plot or discovers errors, in one egregious case proceeding chapter by chapter through *Tom Jones*. It is another sad fact about Fielding criticism—and the criticism of prose fiction at mid-century—that the only attempt to examine a whole work systematically (the *Examen of Tom Jones*) is one of the most wrong-headed pieces of criticism on record. Besides the published criticism of evaluative essays and reviews, there was also the large body of letters which sometimes carried the most perceptive comments recorded; besides these, Fielding attracted (as he created) much indirect criticism through imitation and parody. Finally, many of these criticisms shade off into the criticism of Richardson's novels, in which Fielding is almost always the unstated 'other' which helps to define Richardson (as Richardson is the 'other' in many discussions of Fielding).

We have then a body of writing, little of which is great criticism and much of it opinion rather than criticism at all, and a collection which, we hope, will make up in comprehensiveness and typicality what it lacks in genius. It presents from all angles the problem of how to fit Fielding's transitional works into the critical categories available at the time, especially when there was a great rival who managed to satisfy some (though not all) of the old prejudices and was himself in the process of being fitted in. This problem is of interest itself, as well as illuminating the context in which Fielding shaped his novels.

The effective cut-off date is 1762, when the first collected edition of Fielding's works was published, and with it Murphy's *Essay*, which adequately if not brilliantly sums up both Fielding's reputation and the critical attitudes that helped to define this reputation. Beyond this date we have included a review of *The Fathers* and a few pronouncements by 'survivors' like Johnson and Horace Walpole of opinions that had not been modified by changing tastes. The collection, though comprehensive, is not exhaustive: however, we hope that every critical pronouncement on Fielding's literary works that is known has been checked and at least recorded; many hitherto unlisted have been collected. What has seemed most important, significant, and (sometimes a determining factor) substantial has been numbered and placed in the text. Quotations peripheral to some major utterance, or views that can more clearly be stated by summary, along with samples of personal abuse, have been salvaged in the introduction or in the notes to the text. References to the social tracts have been included only when they bear on the literary works.

There are no checklists or bibliographies of Fielding criticism for the eighteenth century. The most helpful guide is still Wilbur Cross's *The History of Henry Fielding* (3 vols., 1918). Frederic T. Blanchard's *Fielding the Novelist. A Study in Historical Criticism* (1926) adds a few citations, but in general reverently follows Cross's references and conclusions; like most subsequent writers, including F. Homes Duddon (*Henry Fielding, His Life, Works, and Times*, 2 vols., 1952), Blanchard quotes Cross's citations rather than going out to find the original. We would, however, recommend (though our conclusions are somewhat different) Blanchard's excellent summary of Fielding's reputation and the reasons for it (Chap. V, pp. 126–39).

We wish to thank Martin C. Battestin, always generous in his advice and suggestions, and George Rousseau, John Feil, Homer Johnson, Ira Gruber, and Kathleen Williams for their assistance on various matters. In particular we are indebted to Alan D. McKillop, who shared with us his unrivalled knowledge of Fielding and suggested several sources otherwise unknown—as did also his careful study of Richardson's reputation in *Samuel Richardson, Printer and Novelist* (1936). He has also kindly given us permission to adapt his notes from his Augustan Reprint edition of the *Essay on Mr. Fielding's New Species of Writing*.

For permission to reprint manuscripts from their collections we would like to thank the Bodleian Library, the University of Chicago Libraries, the Edinburgh University Library, the National Library of Scotland, the Victoria and Albert Museum, and Professor Austin Wright. We are also grateful to the Clarendon Press, Oxford, for permission to reprint material from *The Correspondence of Jonathan Swift* (2nd ed., 1958) and *Swift's Poems*, ed. Harold Williams; *The Collected Works of Oliver Goldsmith*, ed. Arthur Friedman (1965); *The*

Complete Letters of Lady Mary Wortley Montagu, II, ed. Robert Halsband (1966); *The Selected Letters of Samuel Richardson*, ed. John Carroll (1964); *The Correspondence of Thomas Gray*, ed. Paget Toynbee and Leonard Whibley (1935); and Boswell's *Life of Johnson*, ed. G. B. Hill and L. F. Powell (1934). Thanks also to the Yale University Press for permission to reprint passages from Fielding's *Covent-Garden Journal*, ed. G. E. Jensen (1915) and *Horace Walpole's Correspondence*, ed. W. S. Lewis; the Macmillan Company, New York, for permission to reprint a passage from Helen S. Hughes, *The Gentle Hertford* (1940); and the University of Minnesota and the Oxford University Press, London, for permission to reprint letters from *The Letters of William Shenstone*, ed. D. Mallam (1939).

RONALD PAULSON
THOMAS LOCKWOOD

Introduction

An irony runs through the criticism of Fielding's plays. He and his adherents claimed they were farces parodying and satirizing the debased entertainments of the time; his less sympathetic critics saw them as debased entertainments themselves. Fielding's explanation of his comedies was conventional: 'The Comick Muse, in Smiles severely gay,/Shall scoff at Vice, and laugh its Crimes away.' He insisted that the comic 'was not for low farce designed,/But to divert, instruct, and mend mankind', but when he employed farce, it was, like a magnifying-glass, 'To raise the object larger to the sight,/And shew her insect fools in stronger light.'[1] Throughout the plays he stressed his satiric intention by employing mouthpieces within the action and commentators, pre-faces, and footnotes without. His formal aim was to present folly in its own attire, a strategy which Shenstone recognized when he commented on those people who 'mistake burlesque for the very foolishness it exposes' (below No. 41).

If Fielding saw himself continuing, as 'Scriblerus Secundus', Pope's war on the dunces, Pope's *Grub-street Journal* saw him producing profitable Hurlothrumbo entertainments.[2] It seems likely that the sheer popularity of *Tom Thumb* combined in the critics' minds with the idea that, whatever its claims, it was subverting proper drama. The lines from a satire called *The Candidates for the Bays* (December 1730) are typical: '*Tom Thumb* and such stuff alone tickle this Age,' bewails the poet, and, adding *The Author's Farce*, he continues: 'While H——y of Bantom, and Doodle's respected,/Othello and Hamlet are wholly neglected.'[3] Fielding's plays, to some, appeared in the same category with Rich's harlequinades and Heidegger's masquerades, performances satirized in Hogarth's *Masquerades and Operas* and Pope's *Dunciad* for having driven true drama from the stage.

These criticisms demonstrate that Fielding was making his audience laugh. He himself later referred to *Tom Thumb* as 'a Tragedy that makes me laugh' and to its author as one 'who dealt so much in ghosts that he is said to have spoiled the Haymarket stage, by cutting it all into trap-doors'; as Swift's laughter seems to indicate, the ghost scenes must have been especially popular.[4] But these criticisms also point to the question of whether one's laughter at the Marplays and Bookweights, let alone at the more ambiguous Lucklesses and Tom Thumbs, was a laughter of censure or of imbecile delight.

The Grub-street Journal, it should be noted, concentrated attention on Fielding only after he returned to Drury Lane in the 1731-2 season, associating himself with Colley Cibber (a subject of the Journal's attacks since he became laureate) and with a patent theatre that would not attack the Ministry, and, indeed, dedicating The Modern Husband to Sir Robert Walpole. Whatever the motive, the Journal's complementary aims were to fit Fielding into the Dunciad and to judge his plays by neo-classical criteria. As the author of The Candidates for the Bays had remarked, 'Church Canons are few to the Rules of the Stage;/For in suiting the Plot to the Players good Grace,/They banish the Sense for Time, Action, and Place.' Decorum was the rule violated by Fielding. In his review of The Modern Husband (No. 9), 'Dramaticus' refuses to accept the characters of Lady Charlotte (a fantastic), the Moderns ('a pair of monsters most entirely new'), or Lord Richly (all bad)—each, in its way, a violation of propriety. Lady Charlotte is singled out as one of those characters Jeremy Collier found objectionable in Restoration comedy because it is never clear whether they are to be ridiculed or taken as models. Dramaticus argues that these faults show Fielding ignoring 'the true end and design of Comedy' to demonstrate merely 'the affectation and inordinate desire of saying something new' ('new' is frequently repeated), though this does not preclude his having stolen most of his devices from other plays. Removing the strait-jacket categories of the Dunciad, we find the real criticism to be of Fielding's subject-matter and the ambiguous reaction that some of his characters elicit; and these two will be the essential objections aimed at all his later works.

In extreme cases like The Modern Husband and The Covent-Garden Tragedy, where high behaved like low and low behaved like high, the public seems to have shared the critics' outrage. The Covent-Garden Tragedy, laid in a bawdyhouse, focused the Journal's attack. 'Prosaicus' (No. 13) argues that 'nature must be the basis of humour, . . . [and] humour is to represent the foibles of nature, not its most shocking deformities', and 'Publicus' (No. 10) notices Fielding's assertion (made with less mitigating charm than Gay's similar one in The Beggar's Opera) 'that there's no difference' between the best ladies in the boxes 'and the bawdy-house trulls they had been seeing on the Stage; and that, pretend what they would, they were all a parcel of downright errant *whores'*. Within limits, of course, this was Fielding's point—not the 'respect and decency' which Publicus thinks should be their due; Fielding's real game was the vice of high society. But Publicus argues that these low characters are dangerous rather than edifying (though not mentioning Gay, he uses the same arguments used against *The Beggar's Opera* in 1728): when criminals are allowed to get off scot-free on the stage, and when the blame is pushed off on to the 'great' in the audience, ' 'tis no wonder there are so many Whores and Pickpockets in the streets'.[5] Poetic justice is seen as a function of both decorum and good rhetoric.

The satirist treads slippery ground. The *Journal* accused Fielding of presenting evil people and failing to punish them, in fact making models of them; Fielding and his supporters replied (No. 11) that obviously these are not models but the objects of attack—even though the attack may be upward to their betters who are even worse; and, of course, irony, in the heat of controversy, can be taken either way, and the ironist can be accused of wishing to boil babies. Nevertheless, the truth lies between these extremes; Fielding is rationalizing a form that is indeed producing a new and unsettling effect. The Mother Punchbowls and Kissindas do emerge as more complex figures, eliciting a more complex reaction, than bawds and trulls ordinarily do. This is part of the characteristic effect Fielding was to develop in his fiction, and—as the *Journal's* critics seemed to sense—it led from persuasion to representation as an end in itself. The issue is stated as early as the epilogue to Fielding's second play, *The Temple Beau*, in 1730; our bard, the Epilogue says,

> forsooth, will argue that the Stage
> Was meant t'improve, and not debauch the Age.
> Pshaw! to improve!——the Stage was first design'd,
> Such as they are, to represent Mankind.

The second phase of the criticism of Fielding's plays followed from his return to the Little Theatre in the Haymarket and the politically inspired satires that began with *Pasquin* in March 1736 and ended a year later with *The Historical Register* and the closing of his theatre by the Licensing Act. Anticipating the usual objections to such a play, Aaron Hill pointed out in *The Prompter* (No. 22) that not Religion, Law, and Physick but rather their abuses were being attacked. He greeted this immensely popular play on its own terms as a return of common sense to the London theatre. But, showing signs of the Richardsonian he was to become, he admitted that Fielding's welcome restoration of English drama was still in its initial stage—it had the strength and force, the crudeness, of satire; the next stage, for which his satire prepares, would be 'the *Pathetick* and *Delicate*'.

Hill saw Fielding's new plays in terms of theatrical rebirth; 'Marforio' and 'An Adventurer in Politics' saw them in strictly political terms. Indeed, the plays linked literary and political abuses, but with *The Historical Register* the latter predominated, and the criticism became warm, dividing along party lines. Fielding was attacked by *The Gazetteer*, the official ministerial organ, and defended by *Common Sense: or, the Englishman's Journal*, an opposition paper founded in February 1736-7 by Chesterfield and Lyttelton, taking its name from *Pasquin's* Queen Common Sense.

The main critical emphasis now was on the function of satire, and instead of Jeremy Collier the source of arguments was the *Tatler* or *Spectator*. The two criteria for satire, according to such influential documents as *Tatler* No. 242, were the generality of the object ridiculed and the motive (good nature) of the satirist. Anticipating the former, Fielding had in the prologue of his very first play insisted that 'Our bard at vice, not at the vicious, throws'.[6] Though contemporaries might note allusions to Walpole's domestic irregularities, Rich's illiteracy, and Lord Hervey's effeminacy, it is evident from their silence that most of the critics accepted this definition until the political aim was unmistakable and the play's popularity undeniable.

Accordingly, the 'Adventurer in Politics' (No. 29) argues that any work attacking Sir Robert Walpole or other particular individuals in the Ministry was not only demoralizing and dangerous to the State but was 'false' satire and bad art. Second, he expresses the view that vice is too evil to to be jested about and that in practice discriminations are difficult and a touch of pitch on one priest defiles the whole clergy.[7] To these arguments he adds the practical consideration that the stage is a much more excitable, even inflammatory, medium than the printed page, and appeals to the need for political and social security. The reply of 'Pasquin' (Fielding, No. 30) was predictably the Shaftesburyian defence that such wit is a test of false gravity, and for sanction he cites Aristophanes, who demonstrates 'that the gravest Matters have been try'd in this Way'.[8] Exactly, replies the Adventurer, pointing to the results of Aristophanes' irreverence. All in all, the Adventurer, whoever he was, offers a strong example of one practical argument against political satire, which, however stultifying to the cultural life of a country, has had its adherents in our own day; and Fielding offers the counter-arguments.

The practical outcome was the suppression of the theatre by the Government, and from warnings the *Gazetteer* proceeded to justifications (No. 31). Introduced 24 May 1737, the Licensing Act was quickly pushed through both Houses and passed its third reading in Lords 6 June, received the royal assent on 21 June, and on the 24th the Little Theatre, among others, closed.

Fielding's defeat earned him a complimentary allusion in the 1742 *Dunciad* (No. 36), and his subsequent turning to the law for a livelihood was met equally with panegyric and lampoon. *An Epistle to Mr. Fielding, on His Studying the Law* (1738) praised his resolve: 'While Others feel the drowsy Pow'r of *Coke*,/Thy Antidote shall be some well-tim'd Joke' (p. 17). This poet predicts a great future for Fielding in the law and hopes he will become a Lord Chancellor. On the other hand, twelve lines in *The Church Yard. A Satirical Poem* (1739) are devoted to Fielding (p. 14), explaining that while the hydra head of Fielding the dramatist is cut off, it now sprouts the hydra head of the lawyer. *The Satirists. A Satire* (n.d.) also turns to Fielding (p. 8):

> Tell F—— that— But F—— is no more—
> Betaken now Reports and Coke to Pore—
> The scurril Jest, all the licentious Rage,
> Behold! absorpt in the dry cumbrous Page.

Fielding's unsavoury reputation as a joker and a scurrilous playwright who brought about the Licensing Act—repeated in Cibber's *Apology* and years later in Mrs. Haywood's *Betsy Thoughtless* (Nos. 35, 105)—was the legacy of these years to the anti-Fielding moralists. Depiction of the low was linked with a low-living author, a hasty and facetious scribbler.

As he remained in the public eye—as periodical writer, pamphleteer, and Bow Street magistrate—the majority of references to him remained attacks and of a personal nature. When the *Champion* began to appear in 1738 he was described by the *Gazetteer* as 'a little, low creature, whose utmost extent of politick has been employ'd in over reaching managers of play-houses and actors' and who is now presumptuous enough to discuss great matters of state. This 'parrot', 'a hireling, and a mercenary', began by writing satirical plays that ridiculed 'all government and all religion whatever' and justly led to the Licensing Act, as his present journalism will lead to a similar restraint upon the press.[9]

With the myth of haste, carelessness, and prolific output went the myth of profligacy and poverty.[10]

The hostile criticism of the plays was not without its effect on Fielding's writing—on his inserted justifications, of course, and perhaps on the high moral tone often adopted in *The Champion*, but, more importantly, on his conscious dissociation from the burlesques and farces of his earlier career in the preface, and to some extent in the body, of *Joseph Andrews* (1742). The evidence suggests that the most influential criticism was that which laboured the generic distinction between farce and comedy, and that Fielding concluded (agreeing with Aaron Hill) that farce was useful for one fairly crude end, but not for a more serious and ambitious undertaking like *Joseph Andrews*. While he repudiated the caricatural elements of farce, he retained the association between comedy and ridicule, and comedy's moral purpose.

Shamela (1741) had offered no serious crux for the critics, who had not, in fact, made up their minds about the novel it was parodying.[11] But *Joseph Andrews* presented an alternative with critical justifications, explanations, and the outline of a 'new species of writing', which posed the whole generic question of the long realistic prose narrative. It is a pity that no one but Fielding seemed very much aware of the issues at stake. Richardson understood what he was doing himself, but had nothing but jealous and vindictive oversimplifications to utter about his rival; yet even he was strangely silent on *Joseph Andrews*. The scarcity of public comments after publication is perhaps explained by the scarcity of journals that reviewed such an anomalous and doubtfully reputable form. Richardson, as Professor McKillop has noted, was shrewd 'in dissociating *Pamela* as far as possible from current fiction, and in taking his position with the moralistic opponents of romance'.[12] Fielding, however, while dissociating himself from French romances as from farces, defined his work in literary terms, taking his terminology from the criticism of epic and romance—fable or plot, characters, sentiments, diction, etc.—but adjusting the neo-classical doctrines to conform to his idea of realism. Even *Pamela*, though awarded a long review in the *History of the Works of the Learned*, had received only puffs in the friendly *Gentleman's Magazine*, presumably because of its genre. Only the French periodicals reviewed such forms of fiction with any consistency. Rather than reviews there were reactions: letters from readers to each other or, in the case of Richardson (who saved them), to the author.

Much of *Joseph Andrews*'s favourable reception must be inferred from its sale and from the speed with which some of its characters passed into the language. The negative response of the critical intelligence was registered by Thomas Gray (No. 40), who enjoyed the delicate psychological nuances of Marivaux and Crébillon *fils* (and Richardson); thus in *Joseph Andrews* 'the incidents are ill laid and without invention; but the characters have a great deal of nature, which always pleases even in her lowest shapes'—and he singles out Adams and Slipslop. Elizabeth Carter, one of the most perceptive of contemporaries writing on Fielding, and herself a member of the Richardson circle, commended the work's plenitude (No. 45): 'such a surprizing variety of nature, wit, and morality, and good sense, as is scarcely to be met with in any one composition'. She grasped Fielding's sense of 'epic' and, unbothered by the lowness of his protagonists, detected 'a spirit of benevolence that runs through the whole' and noticed that Fielding 'has touched some particular instances of inhumanity which can only be hit in this kind of writing'—a very suggestive phrase. Her remarks indicate that some readers had already extended lowness in *Joseph Andrews* to immorality and seen a 'most dangerous tendency'.

Gray and Miss Carter express the basic conflict that runs through the reactions to Fielding's novels between the distrust, based on classical criteria of decorum, of Fielding's 'lowness' and the praise of his truth to real life and 'nature'. The problem now is more complex than in the plays, for here the low comic characters—who were ostensibly ridiculed in the plays, though they were, in fact, sometimes reflectors of a greater evil off-stage—are presented as good; in the plays they could be laughed *at*, but in *Joseph Andrews*, as the more perceptive readers uneasily realized, the response was more difficult to formulate. One group tended to emphasize the moral value (or lack of it) in such representation, and another concentrated on Fielding's ability to represent true 'nature'. Fielding's own uncertainty as to both what he was writing and how it should be defended in terms of the neo-classical categories is evident in his preface. He gives *Joseph Andrews* a respectable genealogy, ties it into the criticism of romance and epic, attempting to assimilate old terms to his new concept, but the essential apologia for his novel, followed by his supporters, (1) defended the moral utility of ridicule as it operated on affectation; (2) argued that the reader's enjoyment and happiness were as legitimate ends as moral correction; and (3) praised its 'nature' as more important than the adherence to a simple didacticism.

7

Indeed, it says something about the critical problems *Joseph Andrews* raised that many writers persisted in treating its characters as real people and either extended their existences beyond the bounds of the novel, sought to identify their prototypes, or used them as descriptive analogues. John Mulso, in a letter of 18 July 1744, wrote an extended description of a clergyman he knew who, he said, was 'quite Parson Adams', and a few years later Colley Cibber unexpectedly referred to the 'fearless, open honesty of a poor Parson Adams'.[13] Adams, the character that made the novel's reputation, was also the crux of its critical problems. Was Adams ridiculed? And was ridicule a legitimate tool for a sensitive writer? The second question seemed, when Adams was the character, to follow from the first.

William Whitehead, in his verse essay *On Ridicule* (1743), argued that man is such a complex of subtle goods and evils that to laugh at a vice 'May hurt some virtue's intermingling ray'. He agreed that Fielding's 'affectation' is a true object of ridicule, 'Yet oh, repress them, wheresoe'er they rise—/But how perform it?—there the danger lies.'[14] Others, agreeing with Whitehead that ridicule was cruel, tried to defend Fielding, and writers like him, by refining the idea, and distinguishing the different kinds, of ridicule. In his *Essay on Ridicule* (1753), Allan Ramsay placed Fielding under what he called representative ridicule, though there are also, he admits, 'strokes of the argumentative Ridicule in the character of Parson Adams, and other characters in those instructing novels written by Mr. Fielding'. In general works in which representative ridicule appears are 'pictures of life and manners' rather than tendentious and perhaps destructive 'tests of truth'.[15] But as Arthur Murphy showed in his *Gray's-Inn Journal* essays of the next year, ridicule still meant essentially that Adams was laughed at (No. 146).

It is this impression that Sarah Fielding attempted to correct in *The Cry* (1754, No. 144) by arguing that a central figure like Adams, innocent and basically good, is not an object of ridicule. She expressed a feeling that had not yet found expression in critical terminology: that 'ridicule' itself was an inappropriate word. It is indicative of the detachment of critics that Corbyn Morris did not take Adams as an example in his *Essay towards Fixing the True Standards of Wit, Humour, Raillery, Satire, and Ridicule. To Which is added, an Analysis of the Character of an Humourist, Sir John Falstaff, Sir Roger de Coverly, and Don Quixote* (1744). A humorist as he defines one is 'obstinately attached to sensible peculiar *Oddities* of his own Growth. . . . The Guardian of Freedom, and Scourge of such as do wrong. . . .'[16] It was some time before the critics caught up with Adams. As the distinctions were worked out by Lord Kames and James Beattie and laughter was subdivided into 'ridicule' and sympathetic laughter, laughter *at* and laughter *with*, laughter of censure and of incongruity, Parson Adams became a proverbial figure of incongruous simplicity and learning, a true fourth to Morris's Falstaff, Sir Roger, and Quixote. Faced with a certain kind of man, one described him, as Cowper did, as 'a man of learning and good sense, and as simple as parson Adams'.[17] And Richardson's editor, Mrs. Barbauld, summed up Adams's independent existence in 1810, when she said of *Joseph Andrews*:

> The most striking figure in this piece is that of Parson Adams, an original and most diverting character, in which the lights and shades are so admirably blended, and estimable qualities with foibles and eccentricities, that we love and laugh at him at the same time.[18]

It is another symptom of the times that the French were sometimes better able to accept Fielding's novels than the English—though always with much talk about excusing the Englishness of the work. The most thoughtful published comment on *Joseph Andrews* came in the Abbé Desfontaines's preface to his French translation (1744, No. 49). Desfontaines had praised *Pamela* (though he preferred *Joseph Andrews*), but he was most closely associated with Swift and the English satirists, and so contrasts Fielding's manly English work, which he links to the tradition of *Don Quixote* and the *Roman comique*, with the insipid, delicate French novels of his day. Most of all, he admires the honesty ('l'honnêteté') of Fielding's representation and the tact with which he treats subjects that could become licentious—for example, the passion of a lady of quality for her servant. He praises the excellent characters ('un caracter vrais, & peint d'après nature') and recommends *Joseph Andrews* as a book that will show accurately the manners and customs of the English (and so spends much of his preface explaining these strange customs).[19]

To justify to the French Fielding's sense of 'nature', Desfontaines connects both *Joseph Andrews* and the picaresque tradition with Dutch painting. Fielding himself had connected his 'comic epic in prose' with the genre of painting in his preface; and early as the *Prompter* essay of 1736 (No. 22) Hill had applied the poetry-painting analogy to *Pasquin*: while he detected Michelangelesque touches in the tragedy half, there was clearly much of the '*Flemish* Touch, for the sake of the vulgar', and noticeable lacking was 'the *Correggio Manner*'—delicacy and sweetness. The Abbé du Bos' suggestion that prose romances were to poetic romances as a print was to a painting—lacking the colouring, but in its own way as good[20]—tended to support the analogy between Fielding's works and Dutch drolls, and also made natural Fielding's own analogy with Hogarth's prints. Both writer and artist, however, were trying to raise their genre above the droll, as above the burlesque, and Hogarth's own response to *Joseph Andrews* was the print *Characters and Caricaturas* (1743), in which 'character' is contrasted to caricature on the one hand and to the idealization of history painting (Fielding's epic) on the other.[21]

As both Fielding and Hogarth learned, the 'comic epic in prose' and the 'comic history painting' were talked of more than they were understood. James Hulett's illustrations for *Joseph Andrews* (3rd ed., 1742-3, and repeated in many subsequent editions) were closer to Hogarth's small, grotesque *Hudibras* illustrations than to his heroic *Hudibras* plates or his 'comic history paintings', and about as remote from the spirit of *Joseph Andrews*[22]. They portray the scenes of most violent burlesque action: a small, grimacing figure of Adams being chased by the hounds or dragging the squire after him into the tub of water. At the opposite extreme, Thomas Uwins's illustrations for the 1809 edition sentimentalized Adams, choosing the scenes of Adams's benevolence and filling the picture space with his large, kindly, static figure.[23]

Of the *Miscellanies* (1743) there is virtually no criticism except what Fielding himself had to say in his preface.[24] Nor is there anything but personal praise and vituperation in the following years of journalism before the publication of *Tom Jones*.[25] In 1746 Joseph Warton recorded an evening spent with Fielding and his sister Sarah: 'I find he values, as he justly may, his Joseph Andrews above all his writings.'[26]

Tom Jones was published in February 1748-9 and had a wide sale—10,000 copies printed in the first year. Its great success with the public and its own pronounced critical dicta, perhaps combined with its heroic ambitiousness, forced the critics to comment, and at the same time to reconsider the earlier novel. The hero of 'mixed character'—the further complicating of the 'nature' in *Joseph Andrews*, and of course, a reaction against the paragons of Richardson—served as the main subject of hostile criticism, but it needs to be remarked that the large range of attacks, while developing a genuinely controversial aspect of the novel (Fielding shows that he was aware of this by his own polemics in the introductory chapters), were still personally directed if not inspired.

In the political context, Fielding went out of his way within *Tom*

Jones to praise Lyttelton and the Duke of Bedford and associate himself in general with the Pelham ministry. The opposition accordingly used him as a convenient focus of attack, and found chastising immorality in *Tom Jones* a useful strategy for suggesting the same in Fielding's patrons. The attacks of *Old England* and the *Examen of Tom Jones*, when they were not personal, settled on inaccuracies and the old accusation that his novel is prejudicial to religion and offensive to chaste eyes, with Thwackum and Supple educed to prove the first and Molly Seagrim in various scenes to prove the second (Nos. 66, 82, 83). But, as behind all the attacks on the novel, there was the admission that it was 'greedily swallowed' by the public.[27]

The literary context was the recent (1747-8) publication of *Clarissa*. Richardson himself saw at once that (however much Fielding may have praised *Clarissa*) Tom was an anti-Richardsonian hero, and moreover a decidedly popular one, overshadowing *Clarissa* in sheer sales.[28] Richardson very soon began to plot a novel that would produce both a male equivalent of Clarissa and an anti-Tom Jones. In this sense, not his correspondence but *Sir Charles Grandison* carries Richardson's criticism of *Tom Jones*. Initially at any rate, Richardsonians were pitted against Fieldingites.

The first account of *Tom Jones* in print was the *London Magazine's* long review of February 1748-9 (No. 57)—its first long review of a novel. Thomas Astley, the publisher, certainly a political and perhaps a personal friend of Fielding, was presumably responsible.[29] Like the run-of-the-mill reviews of the time, this one criticizes (in this case praises) by retelling the plot: interpretation emerges only through the perhaps unconscious emphases of the retelling, through what is included and what omitted. For example, the reviewer gives almost no emphasis to the crucial incest situation or to the significance of Tom's testing. He omits the motive for Sophia's disdain of Tom after Upton and after reading Lady Bellaston's letter. His recounting does indeed treat the novel as a 'prose epick composition', listing many unsubordinated adventures, but makes no demonstration of its other assertion, that it shows 'the bad consequences of indiscretion' and 'sets several kinds of vice in their most deformed and shocking light'. The *Monthly Review*, the first review periodical published in England, began in May 1749, just too late to review *Tom Jones*; but in the December issue it defended Fielding's novel against the attack of the *Examen* (No. 82).

The Richardsonian correspondence offers both an epitome of the anti-*Tom Jones* camp and a comical interlude in which are demonstrated

Richardson's inability to control the responses of all his admirers and the mode of criticism that is based on a non-reading (or possibly a surreptitious reading) of the text. Whether or not he in fact read the novel, Richardson's own criticism is based on the biographical fallacy: he fancies Fielding (who after all wrote *Shamela*) as a debauched and profligate rake, sunk in 'Evil Habits': 'Do Men expect Grapes of Thorns, or Figs of Thistles?' (No. 73). Thus we have, first, the reactions of the Richardson faithful: that instead of portraying paragons like the beautiful and good Clarissa, Fielding represents unchaste and immoral characters and actions in a facetious light.

Second, there are those members who have the temerity to suggest that there may be something more to it. Miss Carter makes as strong claims for *Tom Jones* as she did for *Joseph Andrews* (No. 67), and, best of all, the daughters of Aaron Hill show the reaction of two sophisticated yet fresh girls, not quite browbeaten by the author of *Clarissa* (No. 72). Gently and self-deprecatingly, they point out to Richardson that *Tom Jones* 'endeavors rather at ironic satire, than Encouragement of Folly'. They still cannot see comedy as other than 'a Fool's Coat' thrown over Virtue, and yet 'it *seems* wantoner than It was meant to be'. Accepting the mode on its own terms, they go on to praise the famous plot (taking exception to the Man of the Hill digression): 'All the changefull windings of the Author's Fancy carry on a course of regular Design; and end in an extremely moving Close, where Lives that seem'd to wander and run different ways meet, All, in an instructive Center.'

Outside the coterie, but within the assumptions of the Richardsonians, were the reactions of Shenstone and Lady Luxborough, who regretted that there were no characters as strikingly comic and central as Parson Adams, but rather characters 'but too like those one meets with in the world'. Squire Western is the only character in the Adams range who made Shenstone laugh, and Lady Luxborough sees the novel as too satiric, showing too many blemishes and lacking the good humour of the earlier novel (Nos. 60, 62).

The Richardsonians bustled with letters exchanged, but in Samuel Johnson Richardson had also a powerful public critic on his side. Presumably because of his influence on the *Gentleman's Magazine*, that periodical not only ran no review of *Tom Jones* (in itself not strange) but showed its unfriendliness in asides and uncomplimentary allusions from time to time.[30] On the emblematic frontispiece for the year *Tom Jones* appears at the bottom of a pile of the year's books, under *Clarissa*. Only in March 1750, in a review supposedly written by a Frenchman of

La Place's French translation (No. 90), did the *Gentleman's* begin to admit favourable comments. Here it was called an 'ingenious work of imagination' and both its characters and plot praised in terms that anticipate Coleridge's of nearly a century later.[31]

Johnson made his own feelings clear in a *Rambler* of 1750 and, in later years, in conversation (by which time he had to defend his opinion against Boswell). Not surprisingly, *Rambler* No. 4 (below, No. 91) best sums up the hostile critique of *Tom Jones*, warning that 'when an Adventurer is levelled with the rest of the World' (as opposed to being a romance hero 'remote from all that passes among Men'), 'young Spectators fix their Eyes upon him with closer Attention, and hope by observing his Behaviour and Success to regulate their own Practices, when they shall be engaged in the like Part'. Because of this immersive power, the novelist must present only 'the best Examples'. Probably as outraged by Fielding's defence of 'mixed character' as by Tom himself, Johnson attacks the idea that such a character should be presented simply because he is an accurate representation. Such writers

for the sake of following Nature, so mingle good and bad Qualities in their principal Personages, that they are both equally conspicuous; and as we accompany them through their Adventures with Delight, and are led by Degrees to interest ourselves in their Favour, we lose the Abhorrence of their Faults, because they do not hinder our Pleasure, or perhaps, regard them with some Kindness for being united with so much Merit.

The reader's unconscious imitation of a mixed hero and his inability to judge him are both at stake in the work of those 'who confound the Colours of Right and Wrong, and instead of helping to settle their Boundaries, mix them with so much Art, that no common Mind is able to disunite them'.

Of course, Fielding himself was aware of the problem of immersion, but saw the solution not in an impoverishing of his fiction and realism by using idealized characters but in authorial control—in the commentaries, essays, and irony, lacking in *Pamela* and *Clarissa*. But in *Tom Jones* he was also dealing with the problem of judgement and demonstrating a profound difficulty that did not bother him in *Joseph Andrews*— which was also to some extent present in *Clarissa*, but not articulated by the author for all to read.

There was much vague talk of both Richardson's and Fielding's works as a species new and yet undefined.[32] But, probably because of his own writing on the subject, Fielding was much more frequently discussed in these terms. Dr. John Hill asserted that he was the inventor of a new form, and Warburton and Coventry said much the same (Nos. 103, 104, 134). In 1751 an *Essay on Mr. Fielding's New Species of Writing* (No. 99) appeared, spelling out what this new genre was thought to be. Predictably, the author defines it much as Fielding did in his novels: as a reaction to the fantasy of romances, Fielding produced 'Characters which really existed' and were as entertaining as the romances' characters were chimerical; and so *Joseph Andrews* was 'not a mere dry Narrative, but a lively Representative of real Life. For chrystal Palaces and winged Horses, we find homely Cots and ambling Nags; and instead of impossibility, what we experience every Day.' As a contrast to Dr. Johnson, this author states his approval of Fielding's 'thorough Insight into Low-life'.

This particular kind of reality as subject is one defining feature, although the writer does not attempt to contrast Fielding's 'lively Representative of real Life' with Richardson's different but no less real representation. The difference, we might infer, is the style, which 'should be easy and familiar, but at the same time sprightly and entertaining; and to enliven it the more, it is sometimes heightened to the Mock-heroic, to ridicule the Bombast and Fustian which obtain'd so much in the Romances'. Such devices, he adds, are used 'when the Story is least interesting'. And to the style the 'new species' adds many formal characteristics: the essays, chapter titles, as well as the complicated mechanics of the plot. *Tom Jones* did much to counteract the reputation for haste and carelessness; in December 1752, *The Inspector's Rhapsody . . . on the Loss of his Wig*, an attack on Dr. John Hill (no longer an admirer of Fielding), has the doctor say

> For fame let *Fielding* scratch his pensive head,
> Fame I despise, I scribble but for bread;
> Let him his labours polish and retouch,
> He may write better, but not near so much!

We need not go into all the imitations of *Tom Jones* except to remark the general characteristics adopted—partly an expression of the author's idea of what Fielding was doing, and partly of his own limitations. The author of the *Essay on Mr. Fielding's New Species* tended to judge the imitations on their rendering of externals, and the Author of *Charlotte Summers*, pointing out that Fielding forgot to serve drink in his ordinary, employs the metaphor of food, the friendly rambling conversation with his reader; he divides his narrative into books and chapters, to which he refers the act-scene, traveller-inn metaphors and gives facetious titles; he delights in digressions, in mock-heroic interludes, and in assertions of his authorial power.[33] These imitators seemed to think that the wit, as Shenstone said, is 'ty'd up in Bundles at ye beginning of every Book' (No. 63), and when they were not playing with chapter titles they were producing infinite repetitions of Adams and Western and scenes like Joseph with the coachload of respectable folk. The *Monthly Review* remarked of one of the earliest of these imitations, *The History of Tom Jones the Foundling, in his Married State,* that it bore no marks of Fielding's 'spirit, style, or invention', [34] but two years later it was complaining of Mrs. Haywood's *Betsy Thoughtless* that it lacked 'those entertaining introductory chapters, and digressive essays, which distinguish the works of a *Fielding*'.[35] At bottom, the idea grasped by the imitators of Fielding was that an author can, in various ways, communicate with his readers, telling them how they should read his book, and that this 'voice' can be as important as the actions and voices (thoughts and emotions) of the characters.

While on the whole, *Tom Jones* was a success with critics as well as readers, *Amelia* (1751) fell short with both. The novel was so naked— so unprotected by the ironic intellect that held *Tom Jones* in line—that hostile critics began and ended with the most trivial aspects. The autobiographical fallacy began early and was not altogether unfounded if we consider Colonel James's description of Booth as having 'a nose like the proboscis of an elephant'.[36] Then there were the errors. The generally favourable *London Magazine* review pointed out inconsistencies, errors in chronology, anachronisms, and Amelia's nose ('That vile broken nose never cured,' remarked Dr. Johnson, 'ruined the sale' of *Amelia*).[37] Blemishes were remarked, like the puffs of Fielding's own Universal Register Office, which was also, having been but recently founded, an anachronism.[38] Bonnell Thornton's witty exercises at the expense of *Amelia* began with the first number of *The Drury-Lane Journal,* 16 January 1752, and followed in parodies that treated Fielding to the same satire he had delivered to Richardson, emphasizing the grossness of Booth or Mrs. Atkinson's tippling, and Amelia's violent agitations in emotional crises, which Fielding seems to gloss over much as Richardson did certain qualities of Pamela. Fielding revised and corrected errors, style, and lapses of taste (though leaving in the error concerning Ranelagh pointed out by the *London Magazine* reviewer).

But the second edition was not called for, and so remained in manuscript until Murphy used it in his collected edition of 1762.

Cleland's friendly review in the *Monthly* (December 1751, No. 109) reveals something of the basis for dissatisfaction: 'from the choice of his subject, [Amelia] appears to be the boldest stroke that has been yet attempted in this species of writing'. By this he means that Fielding 'takes up his heroine at the very point at which all his predecessors have dropped their capital personages', *after* marriage. Cleland thinks it in general a success in inculcating the conjugal virtues and dramatizing the pains of vice, but significantly objects to too many low characters.

It was objected to *Amelia* that the characters had indeed reached a nadir of lowness—in social status and behaviour, but also in the behaviour of the highest social class in a manner indistinguishable from the lowest. Second, it was not contradictory to add that Fielding had also attempted to rise above comedy to the Richardsonian sublime and failed. Mrs. Donnellan's comment is typical (No. 119): 'Poor Fielding, I believe, designed to be good, but did not know how, and in the attempt lost his genius, low humour.' Thomas Edwards remarked that both Fielding and Hogarth—both of whom had in a sense attempted higher flights (Hogarth with his recent history paintings)—should stick to Dutch drolls (No. 117). Samuel Johnson, however, whose requirements were simpler, later said he had 'read Fielding's *Amelia* through without stopping' and thought Amelia 'the most pleasing heroine of all the romances'.[39]

Possibly the very experimental nature of the novel was responsible: its beginning in *medias res* and dealing with the situation of a couple after marriage. But more basically, it defeated expectations, lacking much of what Mrs. Donnellan called Fielding's 'low humour'. This was Fielding's own explanation for the reaction,[40] and it was perhaps reflected also in Sarah Fielding's remark in *The Cry*:

Comic authors have difficulty in escaping from their prison. The public desires nothing but laughter and jests from them. Let them paint the most agreeable images of human nature, let them ever so accurately search the inmost recesses of the human heart, there is a general outcry up against them, that they are spiritless and dull.[41]

The realism unlightened by comedy, the evil characters and the good relatively untouched by humour, the pessimism and the Juvenalian satiric exposure: all of these recall the effect (and the reception) twenty years before of *The Modern Husband*, one of *Amelia's* models.

The *Covent-Garden Journal* and the pamphlets of those years produced personal and ideological criticism (the pamphlets generally well received), but nothing that altered Fielding's literary reputation. When he died in 1754 and his last work, *The Voyage to Lisbon*, appeared the next, the reviews were strangely brief and apologetic—perhaps, as Blanchard thinks, due to the humility of the 'Dedication' attached posthumously to the book, which says:

If in this little work there should appear any traces of a weaken'd and decay'd life, let your own imaginations place before your eyes a true picture, in that of a hand trembling in almost its lastest hour, of a body emaciated with pains, yet struggling for your entertainment; and let this affecting picture open each tender heart, and call forth a melting tear to blot out whatever failings may be found in a work begun in pain, and finished almost at the same period with life.[42]

There were no memorials published when Fielding died (there were a few when Richardson died, though quite a stir followed Sterne's death). Arthur Murphy's edition and essay, published in 1762, sums up Fielding's reputation in his lifetime. Murphy's limitations, dwelt on by Wilbur Cross, were less serious in the critic than in the biographer.[43] Part of his usefulness as a gauge of the time derives from his lack of original insights; on the other hand, his view was strictly of the 1750s, when he first became acquainted with Fielding, and lacked sympathy with the earlier works. The selections in his edition tell as much as his *Essay*: the novels are all there (including the revised *Amelia*), on which he felt Fielding's fame must rest. Most of the plays were reprinted, but they are dismissed in the *Essay* as hasty products in which Fielding let his wit run away with his judgement—and as equally dated by historical particulars and by the freedom of speech and ridicule exercised in the pre-Licensing Act days. A light sampling of the periodicals was included (nothing from the *Covent-Garden Journal*, because, he said, Fielding's contributions were unidentifiable), and only one poem ('An Epistle to the Right Hon. Sir Robert Walpole', used in the *Essay*), the rest being rejected because they were hastily written and showed no talent for poetry.[44] Murphy included the true version of *The Journal of a Voyage to Lisbon*, but, of the social pamphlets, only the *Charge to the Grand Jury* and the *Enquiry*.

To the extent that Murphy did not utter the commonplaces of his day, he adapted Fielding's own pronouncements. He had entered journalism with the *Gray's-Inn Journal* in 1752, which was so close to

Fielding's *Covent-Garden Journal* in manner and matter that some thought Fielding was writing two papers at once. Christopher Smart commended it as an imitation of Fielding and remarked 'that 'tis a certain Test of true Humour to be delighted with the Writings of Mr. *Fielding*'.[45] Murphy's essays on comedy and related subjects (below, Nos. 145-8) took their ideas from the *Covent-Garden Journal* and Fielding's other essays. The same derivative quality is evident in the *Essay*. Finally, Murphy tended to criticize by metaphor: *Tom Jones* is like a river, Fielding's career is like a body growing old or the journey of the sun on a bright summer's day, setting with *Amelia* and *The Voyage to Lisbon*.

But if Murphy promulgated an image of Fielding as a genius addicted to vices and follies, to haste and carelessness, and a tendency to let wit have its way, he also transformed this image into a critical view of Fielding's development, very close to the one we have followed in contemporary criticism. He saw Fielding directed by two separate tendencies: toward political satire, which is at best general ridicule, at worst wit run wild; and toward the fulfilment of his talent for 'imitation', for 'just and faithful copies of human life', which begins to appear in some of the plays, but, of course, emerges triumphantly in the novels. Murphy's conclusion about the direction of Fielding's development requires a modification of his earlier view of Parson Adams, who is no longer seen as ridiculous or in any sense contemptible: '. . . the humanity, and benevolence of affection, the goodness of heart, and the zeal for virtue, which come from him upon all occasions, attach us to Mr. Adams in the most endearing manner'.

Nevertheless, Murphy distinguished Fielding and his 'just and faithful copies of human life' from the psychological novelists like Marivaux (and implicitly Richardson) whose 'copies' were of internal structures: Fielding, he believed, 'was more attached to the *manners* than to the *heart*'. Sarah Fielding, in *The Cry*, had expressed a prevalent feeling of the 1750s and 1760s when she observed that the 'motives to actions, and the inward turns of mind, seem in our opinion more necessary to be known than the actions themselves'.[46] As Murphy considered Fielding inferior to Marivaux in this respect, Dr. Johnson considered him inferior to Richardson, because, as he put it, Fielding created only 'characters of manners', while Richardson created 'characters of nature'. Here, rather than in the *Rambler's* contrast of good and mixed characters as the proper and improper hero of a novel, lies the distinction that has survived to our own times between the two great novelists.

Blanchard indicates perhaps too distinct a cleavage between the Richardsonians and the advocates of Fielding. Even in their lifetimes the examples of accommodation were common enough: *Charlotte Summers* (1750) was by an admirer of Fielding who also had a good word for Richardson, and Miss Smythies in *The Stage-Coach* (1753) was an admirer of Richardson who also praised Fielding (Nos. 87, 142). James Ridley in *James Lovegrove* (1761) praised Fielding's 'inimitable Works' as well as Richardson's 'System of Ethicks'.[47]

The popularity of *Pamela* probably outdid anything by Fielding, but the rest of Richardson's novels were equalled in popularity by Fielding's (excepting *Amelia*). If Richardson appears to have had the better critical press, there were reasons: he collected all the testimonial letters sent him by well-wishers and published many of them; his 'System of Ethicks' lent itself better than Fielding's 'inimitable Works' (a significantly vague designation) to the known critical categories and to the piety of the most vocal readers. Fielding's controversial personal reputation also played a part in his reputation as a writer: he was in the thick of things—a political pamphleteer, a journalist, a playwright, and a magistrate in constant contact with the lowest classes; and his writing was largely concerned with this same subject. Richardson, however, was out of it all, insulated by his little circle of adoring females, literarily-inclined clergymen, and conservative critics. That he was praised by the literary great from Pope and Johnson to Young and Gray is evidence of a deep-seated moral if not literary orthodoxy in his works that was missing in Fielding's, however much he tried to tie them into the great literary traditions.

Richardson wrote in the area of tragedy and the sublime; again and again the lesser quality of Fielding's genre is emphasized: he is 'of facetious memory', or 'the witty and ingenious author of *Tom Jones*', and when a comic or low-life novel was attempted the authors invoked were always Cervantes and Fielding, and perhaps Smollett.[48] Fielding was the 'most celebrated' writer of romance since the 'Days of old Cervantes', but Richardson was compared to Shakespeare.[49] However ingeniously Fielding treated his subject, it was low; he was always the best 'in his way', the designation used by contemporaries for Hogarth —in so many ways bracketed with Fielding then and since. Fielding's reputation was for wit and, at best, superior craftsmanship; Richardson's was for moral purpose and profundity of thought; in an age of growing sentimentalism the latter was bound to be spoken of more often in print and with greater encomia.

By the time of Fielding's death he and Richardson, however ranked in relation to each other, were established in an unofficial pantheon, and comments like that of the *Monthly* reviewer of *The History of Amanda* (1758) were typical: the heroine, he said, 'must not think herself qualified to keep company with Madam Clarissa, or Miss Western: ladies of the first distinction in the records of romance'.[50] In Sarah Fielding's *Lives of Cleopatra and Octavia* (1757) she lists as characters in fiction who have made a vivid impression, 'the wonderful Atchievements of *Don Quixote*', the 'rural Innocence of a *Joseph Andrews*', and 'the inimitable Virtues of *Sir Charles Grandison*' (p. iii). Although they continued to be compared and contrasted, they had become twin norms by which later novelists were judged and placed.

Fielding's reputation abroad is only very revealing on the Continent. In America he was read much as he was in England. To take one example, the Quaker John Smith read *Joseph Andrews* in 1748 and *Tom Jones* in 1749—the latter only a few months after publication, borrowing it from a cousin who had just brought it over from England. The day he received it he sat up late into the night reading it, and later secured a copy for himself.[51] He also read Richardson and, being a Quaker, was particularly concerned with the bad influence the novel might have on the young. But his conclusion was very un-Johnsonian:

Those of *Fenelon, Fielding,* and *Richardson* ought unquestionably to be considered as excellent in their kind, and cannot be read to any bad purpose, unless there are minds, like some sorts of spiders, which are supposed to increase their venom by sucking the sweetest flowers.[52]

In France, the usual intermediary between England and the Continent, and with more thorough review coverage than in England, Fielding's fortunes were mixed. There was some truth in Mrs. Calderwood of Polton's assessment in 1756:

All Richardson's books are translated, and much admired abroad; but for Fielding's, the forreigners have no notion of them, and do not understand them, as the manners are so intirely English.[53]

Gravelot's *Tom Jones* illustrations (for La Place's French translation, 1750), with gracefully genteel figures in impeccable French interiors, show the French attitude and what their translators did to Fielding.

They abridged Richardson's novels, too, but the mutilation of Fielding's was more damaging, for the essays, the digressions, much of the dialogue, the 'reality of assessment' and the author-reader relationship, all went; what remained was hardly distinguishable from a novel of Smollett. Even so reviewers suspected that not enough had been cut. As Mrs. Polton indicates, they needed Desfontaine's apologetic explication of English manners, and then, with *Tom Jones* they were unable to understand the English acceptance of Sophia's flight and Tom's unpunished and forgiven infidelities (see No. 90). It was at first thought that these immoralities contributed to the novel's prohibition in France. The Marquis d'Argenson, however, read it and found 'rien que de vertueux dans ce petit roman anglais' (nothing but virtue in this little English novel) and explained (28 March 1750) that the French printer was merely the victim of a private quarrel. When the book did reach the French public, 'After "Gulliver" and "Pamela" here comes "Tom Jones", and they are mad for him'.[54] In fact, in spite of the temperamental and sociological differences, the reviewers tended to end by admitting that they were completely won by the novel (No. 102).

Despite Fielding's Englishness, which was always commented on, his novel fitted into a French tradition, the *roman comique* or *satyrique* of Sorel, Scarron, Furetière, and Le Sage; just as Richardson's, with their moralizing ignored, were fitted into the psychological tradition of Mme de Lafayette and Marivaux. Neither, the French reviewers realized, quite fitted, and if Richardson received the greater praise it was because the extension of psychology into sentimentality appealed to the new generation and earned the enthusiastic admiration of men like Diderot and Rousseau. A more accurate estimate may emanate from the next generation and the Marquis de Sade, who, at the very end of the century, saw both Fielding and Richardson as offering 'robust and manly characters' rather than the 'fastidious languours of love or the tedious conversations of the bedchamber'; they portrayed man not just as he is or pretends to be but 'as he is capable of being when subjected to the modifying influences of vice and the full impact of passion'.[55]

For the remainder of the century in England Fielding survived popularly through delight in his comic characters and critically through admiration for his structure and a carefully qualified toleration of his 'nature'. Lord Monboddo disliked his digressions into mock heroics, but said he had read no other book ancient or modern so alive with comic characters as

Tom Jones—'an extraordinary effort both of genius and art'.[56] *Tom Jones*'s independent reputation was very great: 'le premier roman du monde', as one French critic called it, or 'a work of the highest merit', as Sir Joshua Reynolds remarked in one of his *Discourses*.[57]

Stage adaptations give the most conservative attitude of the years following Fielding's death. In George Colman's revision of *Tom Jones* in his play *The Jealous Wife* (1761), the Fielding characters contributed to its 'prodigious success', but Blifil's hypocrisy and Tom's intrigue with Lady Bellaston were excised. In 1768 Joseph Reed turned *Tom Jones* into a comic opera at Covent Garden: Squire Western was very popular, but now his strongest oath was 'Zounds'; Parson Supple was changed into a country squire and married to Diana Western instead of to Mrs. Waters; and Tom, 'stripped of his libertinism' (as Reed noted in his preface) was now Bridget Allworthy's legitimate son. Thus did Reed make *Tom Jones* conform to 'the refined taste of the present age'. It was the 'lowness' of Fielding's 'nature' that led to the excisions in the dramatized versions and made Vicesimus Knox remark that Fielding's scenes of real life were true and entertaining, but that some might corrupt 'a mind unseasoned by experience'.[58]

Edward Gibbon was probably thinking of the scope and structure as well when he remarked in *The Decline and Fall of the Roman Empire* that *Tom Jones* is 'the romance of a great master, which may be considered as the history of human nature'.[59] As Fielding himself intimated in his essays, 'nature' in his sense has a much greater scope than most of his contemporary defenders (as well as detractors) would admit; and this was the line of argument taken by his greatest nineteenth-century defender, Coleridge.

There is some truth to the generally held view that Fielding and Richardson were polarized as the great structuralist and technician *v.* the great moralist. Except for Johnson, who would have awarded Richardson the palm for both, in general Fielding was praised for a careful, finished work of art, but was thought to be in one or more senses morally questionable. But as we have tried to show, for Fielding's more perceptive contemporaries the dichotomy was rather between a portrayal of true life and of ideal life, and—not entirely contradictory— of action and analysis of the heart, and of manners and 'knowledge of the human mind'. Coleridge made the first of these dichotomies predominate when he undermined Richardson's morality by pointing to its morbidity and awarded Fielding highest honours in both structure and morality. This remained the distinction through the gradual decline of Richardson's reputation in the nineteenth century, until the revaluations of the 1950s brought both novelists again to a parallel eminence.[60]

NOTES

[1] Prologue, *The Temple Beau;* prologue, *The Modern Husband;* prologue, *The Lottery.*

[2] See the *Grub-Street Journal,* 15 April 1731.

[3] Quoted, James T. Hillhouse, ed., *The Tragedy of Tragedies* (1918), pp. 16, 17. For authorship of the poem, see pp. 188–9. In 1731 Orator Henley's *Hyp Doctor* (15, 22 June 1731) based its personal attack on Fielding on the same grounds; Henley, of course, had been satirized in *The Author's Farce.*

[4] *The Letters Writers,* I. iv; *Champion,* 27 November 1739; below, No. 18. For details of the reception of *Tom Thumb,* see Hillhouse, pp. 12–23.

[5] Mr. Hint the Candle-Snuffer (a role in which Fielding probably had a hand) first brings up *The Beggar's Opera* as a sanction for *The Covent-Garden Tragedy,* and A.B., and the *Grub-street Journal* in general (No. 8), let the point go—perhaps because they were unable to dissociate Fielding's play from Gay's except as brothel from prison, and do not wish to extend their indictment to a fellow Scriblerian.

[6] *Love in Several Masques.*

[7] Cf. the *Grub-street Journal's* attack on *The Old Debauchees,* Nos. 9, 10.

[8] A witty and ironic reply to his critics also appears in the 'Dedication to the Publick' of the first edition of *The Historical Register.*

[9] See the *Gazetteer,* 4, 29, 30 July, 2, 12, 17, 19 September, 9, 17, 20 October 1740; 31 July, 5, 7 August, 2, 7, 23, 30 September, and 20 October 1741. The only notices of the *Champion* worth mentioning are articles and letters in the *Gazetteer* signed Hercules Vinegar, which burlesqued the *Champion* (30 March and 18 September 1741); also, for a counter-history of the Vinegar family, see the issue for 24 July 1740. A letter in the *Gentleman's Magazine* (March 1741), xi. 141–2, produces an allegory on the *Champion* which suggests that Fielding-Hercules is in fact a Sisyphus. See also *An Historical View of the Principles, Characters, Persons, &c. of the Political Writers in Great Britain* (1740), pp. 49–50.

[10] For his 'industry', see No. 20; for his impecuniousness, see, e.g., *Seasonable Reproof: A Satire in the Manner of Horace* (1735), ll. 46–52:

> F——g who yesterday appear'd so rough,
> Clad in *coarse Frize,* and plaister'd down with *Snuff.*
> See now his *Instant* gaudy Trappings shine;
> What *Play-house* Bard was ever seen so fine!
> But this, not from his *Humour* flows, you'll say,
> But mere *Necessity;*—for last Night lay
> In *Pawn,* the *Velvet* which he wears to Day.

Or, from a few years later, *The Seventh Satyre of Juvenal Imitated* (1745), p. 7:

> Would you have F—— match what Congreve writ?
> Oh, give him Cloaths, e're you deny him Wit!

[11] See Nos, 37, 38.

[12] A. D. McKillop, *Samuel Richardson, Printer and Novelist* (1936), p. 50.

[13] *Letters of Gilbert White of Selborne from the Rev. John Mulso,* ed. Rashleigh Holt-White (1907), p. 2; Cibber, *The Character and Conduct of Cicero considered from the History of his Life by Dr. Middleton* (1747), p. 2. Fielding himself carried Adams's existence over into *A Journey from this World to the Next* (Introduction); *The True Patriot,* 17 December 1745 and 28 January 1746; *The Jacobite's Journal,* 9 January 1747–8; and *Tom Jones,* Bk. XVIII, Chap. 13.

14 Whitehead, in *Plays and Poems* (1774), ii, 102–4; the quotation, p. 103.

15 Ramsay, *Essay on Ridicule*, pp. 78n., 79.

16 *Essay*, pp. 15, 20–21, 23; see Stuart Tave, *The Amiable Humorist* (1960), pp. 140, 142.

17 William Cowper, letter to Joseph Hill, 25 October 1765, *Correspondence*, ed. Thomas Wright (1904), i. 53; cited, Tave, p. 145.

18 *The British Novelists* (1810), xviii, xiv.

19 See below, No. 49. His reviewer responded: if these are the customs of the English, *tant pis* for the English, and rehearsed all the dangers of presenting the low and the imperfect.

20 *Critical Reflections on Poetry, Painting, and Music* (1719), tr. Thomas Nugent (1748), Pt. I, Chap. 48.

21 See R. Paulson, *Hogarth's Graphic Works* (1965), ii, Pl. 174.

22 Ibid., ii, Pls. 77–105.

23 Tave, op. cit., Pl. 1 and 2 and p. 291.

24 There are only perfunctory comments like Pope's in a letter of 12 April 1743, stating that Ralph Allen's copies had arrived, and adding, 'In one Chapter of the second vol. he has payd you a pretty Compliment upon your House' (*Correspondence*, ed. George Sherburn, 1956, iv. 452). For a somewhat later comment on *Jonathan Wild*, see below, No. 169, and for still later comments on the *Miscellanies*, see William Creech, on the *Essay on the Knowledge of the Characters of Men, Edinburgh Fugitive Pieces, with Letters* (1815), p. 150; *Memoirs of Richard Cumberland, Written by Himself*, ed. Henry Flanders (1856), p. 101; and Edward Gibbon, on the *Journey from this World to the Next*, in *Decline and Fall of the Roman Empire*, ed. J. B. Bury (1897), iii. 363 n.13.

25 However, see Nos. 53, 54.

26 Joseph Warton, from a letter to Thomas Warton, 29 October 1746, in John Wooll, *Biographical Memoirs of the late Revd Joseph Warton, D.D.* (1806), p. 215.

27 See *Old England*, 27 May 1749; also *Gentleman's Magazine* (1750), xx. 177.

28 See McKillop, *Richardson*, p. 171.

29 Cross, ii. 129. Cross asserts that a 'friend' wrote the review, but does not identify him, and presumably bases his contention on the speed with which the review was published. This is possible, but reviews were often published with equal dispatch, and the review in question required nothing more than a quick reading. If it is true that the reviewer 'could see no fault whatever in the book', it is because he only recounted the plot.

30 In the February 1748–9 issue, which would have carried a review, the literary article treated Johnson's own *Irene*, then being performed at Drury Lane. Edward Cave, the editor, was mildly opposed to the Pelham ministry, but his political bias seldom appeared in his magazine. For the fact that Johnson was 'frequently, if not constantly' supervising the contents of the *Gentleman's* by 1747, see John Nichols, 'Prefatory Introduction' to the 'General Index' of the *Gentleman's Magazine* (1821), iii. xlii. For the *Gentleman's Magazine*'s subsequent digs at *Tom Jones*, see below, Nos. 61, 75, 76. Nevertheless, by December 1750 (xix. 547–50) it was printing a dialogue between Allworthy and Thwackum on the *Book of Common Prayer*, which if nothing else shows the popularity of these figures.

31 See, e.g., 'Table Talk', 5 July 1834, *The Complete Works*, vi. 521.

32 For references to Richardson, see, e.g., Aaron Hill, *Works* (1753), ii. 228, 269; and Edward Young, *Conjectures on Original Composition* (1759), p. 78.

33 The last derives from Fielding's assertion of the novelist's power as law-giver of this 'new species' (Bk. II, Chap. 1).

34 *The Monthly Review* (November 1749), i. 25–6. Other examples of early imitations include Edward Kimber, *The Life and Adventures of Joe Thompson* (1750); Dr. John Hill, *The Adventures of Mr. Loveill* (1750); anon., *The Adventures of the Rd. Mr. Judas Hawke, the Rd. Mr. Nathan Briggs, Miss Lucretia Briggs, &c. Late Inhabitans of the Island Querumania. After the Manner of Joseph Andrews* (1751; in fact, an imitation of *Tom Jones*); W. Goodall, *Adventures of Captain Greenland* (1752); W. Chaigneau, *History of Jack Connor* (1752);

W. Guthrie, *The Friends* (1754); John Shebbeara, *Lydia* (1755); anon., *The History of Sir Harry Herald and Sir Edward Naunch, by Henry Fielding, Esq.* (1755); anon., *The Life and Adventures of a Cat, by the late Mr. Fielding* (1760).

35 *Monthly Review* (October 1751), v. 394.

36 Cf. Cross, ii. 328–35, esp. 335.

37 See also *Old England*, 21 December 1751, which predicts poor Amelia's approaching death, and Hill's *Inspector* in the *London Daily Advertiser and Literary Gazetteer*, 8 January 1752; on 15 January, *Habbakkuk Hilding*, in which Amelia is 'a draggle-tailed bunter, who had lost her nose in the exercise of her occupation' (p. 19); Thornton, in a 'Covent-Garden Journal Extraordinary', in the *Drury Lane Journal*, 20 January, 1752 runs a facetious obituary for Amelia. Fielding's reply in the *Covent-Garden Journal* appears below, No. 114.

38 See Cross, ii. 337–8; 'Criticulus' in *Gentleman's Magazine*, xxii. 103 (No. 131).

39 *Life of Johnson*, iii. 43; G. B. Hill, *Johnsonian Miscellanies*, i. 297.

40 *Covent-Garden Journal*, 26 January, below, No. 131.

41 Sarah Fielding, *The Cry*, pp. 169–70 (not included in the passages quoted in No. 145).

42 Blanchard, p. 116; 1755 ed., pp. ii–iii.

43 Cross, iii. 125–50.

44 Cf. the review of Murphy's edition in the *Monthly Review* (May 1762), xxvi, 365, which remarks that the poetry had all 'been disapproved by Mr. Fielding himself' as 'crude and unfinished'.

45 *The Midwife*, iii. 137.

46 *The Cry*, p. 65.

47 i, 171; cited by McKillop, *Richardson*, p. 231; for McKillop's account of the relative reputations of Fielding and Richardson, see pp. 226–31.

48 See the *Critical Review* (May 1760), ix. 420; or Edward Moore, *The World*, 12 June 1755, who refers to 'the witty and ingenious author of *Tom Jones*'; and *The Life and Real Adventures of Hamilton Murray* (1759), i. 4.

49 *Letter IV. Relating to the Memoirs* [by the Earl of Orrery] *of . . . Dr. Swift* (1753), p. 100.

50 *Monthly Review* (1758), xviii. 182.

51 MS. Diary, vol. viii, entries for 26, 27 September 1749. See Frederick B. Tolles, *Meeting House and Counting House* (1948), pp. 198–9.

52 *Pennsylvania Chronicle*, 24 October 1768.

53 *Letters and Journals of Mrs. Calderwood of Polton from England Holland and the Low Countries in 1756* (1884), p. 208. *Joseph Andrews* was translated into French in 1743, German in 1745, Danish in 1749; *Tom Jones* into Dutch in 1749, French and German in 1750, and Italian in 1757; *Amelia* into German in 1752, Dutch in 1758, French in 1762; *Jonathan Wild* into German in 1750, French in 1763; *Journey from this World* into German in 1759 and French in 1784; *Voyage to Lisbon* into German in 1764. The Dutch translation of *Amelia* (1758) has a foreword and address to the reader by the translator, P. A. Verwer, which discusses Fielding as a delineator of men and women as they are.

For Fielding's contemporary reputation in Germany, see Laurence M. Price, *English Literature in Germany* (Berkeley and Los Angeles, 1953), pp. 180–92; and 'The Work of Fielding on the German Stage, 1762–1801', *Journal of English and Germanic Philology* (1942), xli. 257–78. There were a few contemporary reviews, like Haller's of *Tom Jones*, in the *Göttingische gelehrte Anzeigin* (1750), 123–4. Lessing was familiar with Fielding, but his remarks are cursory: see his *Samtliche Schriften*, ed. Lachmann-Muncker (Stuttgart and Leipzig, 1886–1924), ix. 212; xv. 62. For Fielding's influence on German literature, see Augustus Wood, *Der Einfluss Fieldings auf die deutsche literatur* (Heidelburg diss., Yokahama, 1895).

54 *Journal . . . du Marquis d'Argenson* (1864), vi. 182; *Mémoires et Journal inédit du*

Marquis d'Argenson (1857), v, 'Remarques en lisant', No. 1832; quoted, J. Jusserand, *The English Novel in the Time of Shakespeare* (1890), p. 24.

[55] 'Reflections on the Novel' (publ. 1800), in *The 120 Days of Sodom and other Writings*, ed. Austryn Wainhouse and Richard Seaver (New York, 1966), p. 106.

[56] *Of the Origin and Progress of Language* (1776), iii. 134–5, 298.

[57] Jean-François de la Harpe, 'Discours sur l'état des lettres en Europe' (1797), in *Cours de littérature ancienne et moderne,* xvi, 110; *Discourses,* ed. Helen Zimmern (1887), pp. 222–3.

[58] *Essays, Moral and Literary* (1782), i. 69.

[59] *Decline and Fall,* ed. J. B. Bury (1898), iii. 363.

[60] The development of Fielding's reputation in the nineteenth and twentieth centuries can be traced in the following works: Cross, Chaps. 32–35; Blanchard, Chaps. 10–17; Frank Kermode, 'Fielding and Richardson', *Cambridge Journal* (1950), iv. 106–14; and R. Paulson, *Fielding: A Collection of Critical Essays,* in the Twentieth-Century Views series (1962).

NOTE ON THE TEXT

The texts are uncorrected from the originals, and contemporary spelling and punctuation have been retained. The order of the documents is chronological except in the one or two instances where this would have broken a series. Annotation has been limited to the criticism and does not ordinarily extend to the works criticized. The editors' footnotes are numbered; footnotes that are part of the text are asterisked, daggered etc. Three stars indicate that material has been omitted.

THE AUTHOR'S FARCE

30 March 1730

TOM THUMB

24 April 1730

1. John Perceval, first Earl of Egmont, from diary entry

24 April 1730

From *Diary of the First Earl of Egmont* (*Viscount Perceval*), ed. R. A. Roberts, Historical Manuscripts Commission (1923), i. 97.

. . . I went to the Haymarket playhouse, and saw a play called 'The Author's Farce and the Pleasures of the Town,' with an additional piece called 'The Tragedy of Tom Thumb.' Both these plays are a ridicule on poets, and several of their works, as also of operas, etc., and the last of our modern tragedians, and are exceedingly full of humour, with some wit. The author is one of the sixteen children of Mr. Fielding,[1] and in a very low condition of purse.

[1] Colonel Edmund Fielding, Henry's father, who is known to have had ten children, but may have had more (see Cross, i, 15–40).

2. [John Martyn]
The Grub-street Journal No. 23
11 June 1730

Letter signed 'Bavius'. Martyn, a botanist, was one of the original editors of the *Grub-street Journal*. See James T. Hillhouse, *The Grub-street Journal* (1928), p. 40.

The Comical Tragedy of *Tom Thumb* having had so great a run (this being the 33d day) he raised the envy of some unsuccessful Poet against the Author, and occasioned the following Parody.

Act. 1. Sc. 1, pag. 1,

Dood. When Good { y Thumb first / man F——g } brought this *Thomas* forth,

The *Genius* of { our Land / the Bard } triumphant reign'd:

Then, then, O { Arthur / F——g } did thy genius reign.

Nood. They tell me it is whisper'd { in / from } the { books. / mouths. }

Of all our Sages, that this mighty { Hero, / Piece, }

By Merlin's art / On Folly's self } begot, has not a { bone / joke }

Within { his skin, / its leaves, } but is a lump of { gristle. / non-sence. }

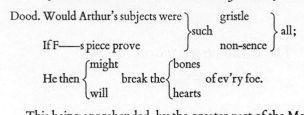

Dood. Would Arthur's subjects were ⎫
⎬ such   gristle ⎫
                      ⎬ all;
If F——s piece prove ⎭   non-sence ⎭

He then ⎧ might ⎫ break the ⎧ bones ⎫ of ev'ry foe.
        ⎩ will ⎭   ⎩ hearts ⎭

This being apprehended, by the greater part of the Members present, to be design'd as a Satire upon the Author, for whom they have a great value; they were against the inserting of it in our Journal. But I observed to them, that let it be design'd as it would, it was in reality a Panegyric; which the last 2 lines evidently shewed. And that even the 2 preceding lines, which seemed to carry in them the greatest reflection, had really none upon this performance, but upon the Plays which were ridiculed by it. The Collection of those Plays is *Folly's self*, upon whom our Author *begot* this *mighty Piece;* which, being more like its mother, than Father, is consequently *a heap of Nonsense.* Mr. CURIOSO was wonderfully taken with the art of *whispering in books* which it seems was known to the *Sages* in K. Arthur's days; an art as ingenious as that of painting a sound.

BAVIUS.

3. *The Grub-street Journal No. 98*

18 November 1731

From 'The Modern Poets. A Satire in allusion to the 10th Satire of the first Book of Horace. By a young Gentleman of Cambridge.' The poem begins with censure of Cibber, and then continues:

> That he's incomparable, yet must we own,
> Because he chanc'd to please the fickle Town?
> Then fiddling J——[1] might some merit claim,
> And *Huncamunca* rival him in fame.
> 'Tis not enough, to gain a wild applause,
> When crouded Theatres espouse your cause.
> 'Tis not enough, to make an audience smile;
> But write a strong, correct, yet easy stile.
> No balmy slumbers shou'd describe a fear;
> Nor dull descriptions load the wearied ear.
> But aim to soar in SHAKESPEAR's lofty strain;
> Or nature draw in JOHNSON's[2] merry vein.
> To F—— names unknown—to him have come
> The fame of *Hickathrift*, and brave *Tom Thumb*:
> The brave *Tom Thumb* does all his thoughts engage:
> See! with what noble port, what tragic rage,
> His Lilliputian Hero treads the stage.
> How nice the Judgment, and the toil how great,
> To make our nervous language soft and sweet:
> From WALLER and from DRYDEN phrases chuse,
> To smooth the roughness of your Highland muse.
> Thus the skill'd Tapster to the harsher stale,
> To please the palate, adds the milder ale.

* * *

[1] Samuel Johnson of Cheshire, author of *Hurlothrumbo*.
[2] i.e. Ben Jonson.

THE MODERN HUSBAND
14 February 1731–2

4. 'Dramaticus'

The Grub-street Journal No. 117

30 March 1732

Letter signed 'Dramaticus' (probably Sir William Yonge, politician and occasional writer [d. 1755]). See Hillhouse, pp. 14n. and 184.

Sir,

The favourable reception *The Modern Husband* has met with from the Town, having given me some occasion to doubt of the justness of the judgment I had framed of that Piece, from seeing it the last night of its representation,[1] I resolved to give it a careful and unprejudiced reading. You know, Mr. BAVIUS, tho' it be possible to form a pretty tolerable idea of the goodness or badness of a Play from seeing it acted once; it is certainly the surer way to judge rightly of it, to examine it carefully in one's closet. An Author may, indeed, fare worse from this examination, than from an immediate sentence delivered from the benches in the Boxes or Pit. The good humour with which the Play-house generally inspires one; the beautiful appearance of the Ladies, who never fail to croud at a first night; the action of the Players; their cloaths, scenes, and other theatrical decorations, help very much a good, as well as a bad Play; and contribute not a little to byass us in our opinions. The tryal of the Play is, when we see it divested of all these exterior helps; and take it, as we would a fine woman, naked of all its ornamental drapery; then it is either really beautiful or not.

[1] 18 March 1731–2.

Having examined *The Modern Husband* in this manner, without seeing any reason to alter my first judgment, I shall, with your good leave, Mr. BAVIUS, lay before you such reflections as occurred to me during this examination. You must not expect a formal piece of criticism from me, deduced with method and order; all that I pretend to, is only to give you my reasons for disliking a performance that had been so cried up, both within and without the House, before its appearance in print.

The design and end of Comedy, Mr. BAVIUS, is, as I take it, to divert and instruct mankind. We may then lay down as a maxim, That no Comedy that wants this fundamental point can be good. Now, I presume, it will not be thought, that the diverting of mankind is properly done by the jokes of a Pickled-herring, the grimaces of a Scaramouch, or the agility of a Tumbler: at least it must be allowed, that these methods of diverting mankind come not within the province of Comedy; nay, that they are even below Farce. What then does come within that province? To divert mankind, *Comedy chuses such characters, as having nothing absolutely ill in them, render themselves nevertheless ridiculous by their follies*. This then we may lay down as a general rule in this point.

As to the instruction of mankind, the second end of Comedy, this may be done either by drawing characters that may serve for models for our conduct in life; or else by shewing the inconveniences, under which the vicious bring themselves, and opening a gate for them to escape. People that find themselves in the circumstances of such a Drama, are by this means instructed, and very often reformed.

Thus Comedy, Mr. BAVIUS, may be either serious, or merry, or both. Our best Comedies are those that mix the serious and merry together: of this kind are *The Careless Husband, The Conscious Lovers, The Journey to London,* &c. The decency of polite life is preserved in these pieces; and the whole interspersed with characters that enliven the scene, and feast the mind with an agreeable mixture of light and solid meats. The Fable likewise ought to be such, as suits with these two ends; and this will necessarily exclude characters not seen in common life, or at least very rarely. For no Poet ought to rake into human nature, and compound characters from the excesses of each of our passions, or the intemperance of some of our humours, in order to entertain his Audience with something new; which would rather prove an inlet to vice and folly than an exlusion of either. Such a thing were scarce allowable, even if there were not follies and vices enow practiced by the polite part of both sexes, that require an immediate cure. A Poet therefore that neglects these, to expose others that as yet are only theoretic, and are introduced into life by his prolific brain, does a very absurd thing, and falls very short of the true end and design of Comedy. But to come to the Play now before me.

The Author of *The Modern Husband* does not appear to have had a true notion of Comedy. He seems to have thought, that the assembling of a certain number of characters together, under the titles of Husbands and Wives, Sons and Daughters, is sufficient to preserve the relation that ought to be kept up between the persons of the Drama; and that the making of them talk together, is enough to form the dialogue part of it. Thus with the addition of a popular scene or two, such as a great man's levee, which he thought could not fail of pleasing, and therefore clapt it in without enquiring whether it was necessary to the Play or not, and some other accidental chit-chat, which filled up a certain quantity of paper, having artfully tacked the whole together, he calls this motly composition a Comedy.

Now if half the persons of the Drama, and the conversation that passes between them, might all be entirely left out, without hurting the main action of the Play, all good judges will condemn the performance; unless there is something exceeding beautiful and entertaining in the conversations of these persons, that may justify their unaccountable introduction. I would fain ask this Author, what business Capt. BELLAMANT and EMILIA, Mr. GAYWIT and Lady CHARLOTTE have with the main design of the Play? What business Lord RICHLY and his levee have? What is there in their conversation to justify their introduction? What variety is there in their characters? Mr. GAYWIT is only EMILIA drest in mens cloaths; and EMILIA, GAYWIT in womens. Capt. BELLAMANT and Lady CHARLOTTE need only change cloaths to appear each the other, we have the Captain's word for it.

Capt. BELLAMANT. You dear agreeable creature! Sure never were two people so like one another as you and I are; we think alike, we act alike, and some people think we are very much alike in the face. p. 64.[1]

But what are their characters? Never was any thing more impertinent than Lady CHARLOTTE, or more silly than her conversation. She is supposed to be a young Lady of great life and vivacity, whose sallies are to be both witty and agreeable. Hear her speak.

Lady CHARLOTTE. Oh! dear MODERN, I wish you had seen

---

[1] Act V, scene ii, in *The Complete Works of Henry Fielding, Esq.*, ed. W. E. Henley (1903), x. 78. Subsequent citations to act and scene and to this edition appear in brackets.

EMILIA's dressing-box; such japaning——he! he! he!——she hath varnished over a windmill ten several times, before she discover'd she had placed the wrong side upwards. P. 26. [II. viii. Henley, x. 39]

Mrs. MODERN answers her in the same style.——Oh! my Dear, I have had just such another misfortune; I have laid out thirty pounds on a chest, and now I dislike it of all things.

Wonderful indeed!——But she has not done yet.

But you have not heard half my misfortune; for when I sent my chest to be sold, what do you think I was offer'd for my thirty pounds worth of work? P. 27. [II. viii. Henley, x. 39]

Lady CHARLOTTE. I don't know, fifty guineas, perhaps.

Mrs. MODERN. Twenty shillings, as I live.

Lady CHARLOTTE. Oh! intolerable! Oh! Insufferable!

Intolerable, insufferable indeed!——After the Hazard, they re-enter, and Lady CHARLOTTE is as bright as ever.

Lady CHARLOTTE. Oh, my Dear, you never saw the like.—— MODERN has held in nine thousand mains in one hand, and won all the world. P. 29. [II. x. Henley, x. 41]

Oh heaven and earth! but this is wonderful!

Lady CHARLOTTE [speaking of GAYWIT in a rallying way] Oh! the most agreeable creature in the world.——He has more wit than any body: he has made me laugh five hundred hours together. P. 30. [II. x. Henely, x. 42]

Gods! is't possible! sure she exaggerates: Oh BAVIUS! Oh! CONUNDRUM! Can this be true?—The 5th, 6th, 7th and 8th scenes of the third Act are full of the same redundancies of wit, too numerous to point out here: but I cannot omit some strokes of fire in the 5th Act.

Capt. BELLAMANT. Sister, good-morrow; Lady CHARLOTTE abroad so early! P. 63.

Lady CHARLOTTE. You may well be surpris'd: I have not been out at this hour these fifty years. P. 64. [V. ii. Henley, x. 77]——Smart indeed!

Lady CHARLOTTE [Speaking of the Capt.] Well, he has such an excessive assurance, that I am not really sure whether he is not agreeable. Let me dye, if I am not under some sort of suspence about it; ——and yet I am not neither;——for to be sure I don't like the thing; ——and yet methinks I do too;——and yet I do not know what I should do with him neither.——Hi! hi! hi!——This is the foolishest circumstance that ever I knew in my life. P. 72. [V. x. Henley, x. 86]

Hi! hi! hi! thou art the foolishest creature I ever saw in my life.

Lady CHARLOTTE. What can the creature mean? I know not what to think of him. Sure it can't be true! but if it should be true——I can't believe it true;——and yet it may be true too. P. 75. [V. x. Henley, x. 89]——Lack-a-day, lack-a-day.

But to be a little serious. Either Lady CHARLOTTE's character is designed as a model for young Ladies of fashion to imitate, or quite the reverse; and she is some impertinent character the Author intended to ridicule. Which of the two he meant, I really can't tell. If it be an original of his own invention, which he has compiled out of the intemperance of female vivacity, he has been led away by that false notion so prevalent among modern Poets, of shewing something new; and, as I observed before, fallen very short of the true end and design of Comedy. If he had any particular person in his eye, whose folly he intended to expose, in order to prevent other young Ladies from falling into the same errors; he has indeed succeeded in expressing that character, but wit will hardly cure either that person, or save any others of the like turn. For as throughout the whole Play, Lady CHARLOTTE does not shew one grain of understanding, the real Lady CHARLOTTES that tread the grand Theatre of the world (if such there be, which I much question) must be supposed as void of understanding (for if they had any, they would not be what they are) and if they are void of understanding, what hopes of amendment or cure? Lady CHARLOTTE's vivacity arises from her want of understanding. Had he therefore given this Lady a little understanding, to temper this immoderate vivacity of her nature; he would have drawn a better character, and a more useful one.

As to EMILIA and GAYWIT, they are but faint sketches after Lady GRACE and Mr. MANLY in *The Journey to London;* as Mr. and Mrs. BELLAMANT, are of Lord and Lady EASY in *The Careless Husband,* with an alteration of some few circumstances.[1]

I know not why he has made Lord RICHLY a great man, unless it be for the sake of describing a levee; nor why this great man should be the greatest rogue that ever lived: I don't conceive but that the Play had gone on full as well without it. The making of a great man absolutely and totally bad, both in the public and private station, in his morals and behaviour, is so poor, so scandalous, so vulgar, and so mean a piece of satire, that (fools, malicious or discontented persons, may indeed laugh, but) all good and wise men will despise the odious picture.

---

[1] Sir John Vanbrugh's fragment, *A Journey to London,* was expanded and performed by Colley Cibber in 1728 as *The Provok'd Husband.* Cibber's *The Careless Husband* was first performed in 1704.

As to the *Modern Husband* and his Lady, they are such wretches, that they are as much below Comedy, as they are our pity: he calls them, very justly, in the *Prologue*, a pair of monsters *most entirely new*.

> To-night (yet strangers to the scene) you'll view
> A pair of monsters most entirely new!
> Two characters scarce ever found in life,
> *A willing Cuckold*———sells his *willing Wife*! [Henley, x. 9—10]

Thus the affectation and inordinate desire of saying something new, has made our Author draw some of the vilest characters that ever yet entered into Comedy, and honour them with the title of *Modern;* implying (in contradiction to what the *Prologue* says) by that title, not only, that there are such characters, but that they are common too: for what can the *Modern Husband* mean, but a character actually come into fashion? else it is theoretic, as observed above, and introduced into life only by his prolific brain. But what instruction or pleasure can be gathered from this heap of absurdity? those parts from which instruction may be reaped, (viz.) the reformation of Mr. BELLAMANT, the prudent conduct of his Wife; and the marriage of GAYWIT and EMILIA, being imitations from much better Plays than this; and those parts from which we are to expect pleasure, being a most monstrous kind of wit, consisting in an affected invention of ridiculous names, such as the *Dutchess of* SIMPLETON, *Lady Betty* SHUTTLECOCK, Mrs. SQUABBLE, Mrs. WITLESS, Lady BARBARA PAWNJEWELS, &c, and a more affected choice of very extraordinary similes and surprising chit-chat.

These, Mr. BAVIUS, are the reflections that occurred to me in reading the *Modern Husband*. I found indeed, here and there, but very sparingly scattered, a touch that implied good sense and reflection; but, like an April sun, it only shews itself, and away; bad weather returns, and we have a great deal of filth to struggle through. I am,

Mr. BAVIUS,

March 7, 1731.   Your unknown friend and admirer

DRAMATICUS.

5. [Thomas Cooke], 'Reflections on some modern Plays', *The Comedian, or Philosophical Enquirer*

June 1732

From *The Comedian*, No. 3, June 1732, pp. 11–15. An unsigned reply to *The Grub-street Journal*, 30 March 1732 (No. 4).

I Lately payed a Visit to a Yorkshire Gentleman, just come to Town, who told me that several in the Country entertain a Suspicion of the Booksellers presuming to publish bad Plays which were never performed on any Stage, and to print them as acted at the Theatres in *Drury-Lane, Lincoln's-Inn-Fields,* &c. with the Names of the Players opposite to the Names of the Characters; and this Art, say'd he, they are supposed to use as an Imposition on their Customers who live at a great Distance from *London*; some of which buy every Play that is acted. I wonder, continues he, why the Managers of the Theatres will suffer themselves to be abused, in such a Manner, by the Chicane of Booksellers, if the Law has any Redress for them.

He was going on in the same invective Strain, taking the Facts for granted, till I interrupted him by asking his Reasons for suspecting the Booksellers guilty of such Frauds.

My Reasons! says he. Can any Man of common Sense (and here he began with a Tone of Indignation and Contempt) read the dramatic Pieces which have been printed within these few Years, such as the Tragedy of *Timoleon, Periander, Medea,* the Ballad-Operas of *Sylvia* or the *Country-Burial,* the *Devil to pay*[1], and the long Catalogue of Rubbish published these last three Winters; under the Denominations of Tragedys, Comedys, Farces, and Ballad-Operas, and suppose the

---

[1] Benjamin Martyn, *Timoleon* (1730); John Tracy, *Periander* (1731); Charles Johnson, *The Tragedy of Medaea* (1730); George Lillo, *Silvia; or, The Country Burial* (1730); Charles Coffey and John Mottley, *The Devil to Pay; or, The Wives Metamorphos'd* (1731).

Managers of the Theatres would affront their Audiences with the Representation of such Stuff? Can any one read the comical Incidents in the Tragedys of *George Barnwell*, and *Injured Innocence*,[1] and the dismal Passages in some late Comedys not to be rival'd and imagine that the two *Cibbers*, who are reputed Judges of Something more than Action, and the few other good Actors of that House, would ever burden their Memorys with such an Heap of indigested Trash, or condescend to be the Spokesmen of such Nonsense?

Here I interrupted him again, and assured him notwithstanding his great Surprise, that all the Plays which he had named had been performed in *Drury-Lane*, and *Lincoln's-Inn-Fields*; but, as I have been neither a Spectator nor Reader of any of them, I told him I could not judge of the Justness of his Censure; and that my Opinion of his good Taste and Understanding will keep me from reading them. One Play I mentioned to him as not liable to the Censure which he had passed on the rest; which is *the modern Husband*. I own, says he, that is a Comedy which gave me Pleasure, tho it is not entirely conformable to the Rules of the Drama.

By the Rules of the Drama, says I, you mean, I presume, the Rules of Critics, who have no Right to impose Rules: the antient Writers of Tragedy and Comedy divided their Plays into five Acts, in which we have generally followed their Example; and I know no other stated Rule to be observed; and that may be departed from sometimes without any Disadvantage. Unerring Reason is the only Guide in Tragedy and Comedy, tho a Man who is merely a reasonable Man, and no more, is not qualifyed to write either, particular Talents being requisite for both, under the Conduct of Reason; and that Poet who wants any other Rule besides Nature or Reason mistakes his Province when he attempts to write. The *modern Husband* I acknowledge to have some Scenes independent on the main Busyness of the Play, and some Expressions the Omission of which would be no Detriment to the Work; yet it has Wit, Humour, Satire, and moral Reflections not unworthy the Pen of the Stoic. If indeed the Author had made every Scene conductive to the principal Design, to the Plot of the Play, and as dependent one on the other as every Link in a Chain, and every Expression as necessary as every Scene, he would have produced a more perfect Piece than it now is: and I doubt not but that he, who is capable of writing so entertaining a Play as it now is, is ingenuous enough to confess these Truths, and to

[1] George Lillo, *The London Merchant: or, The History of George Barnwell* (1731); Fettiplace Bellers, *Injur'd Innocence* (1732).

acknowledge that his Intent was to expose particular Vices and Follys, to make these ridiculous and those odious, to give his Audience Pleasure and himself Profit, and that he had not Leisure to make it otherwise than it now is,[1] and that he laughs, without Anger, at those who expose themselves by a fruitless Endeavour to expose him.

My Friend, who now thought it his Turn to speak again, asked me what I thought of the Character of *Lady Charlotte*, some Objections to which he had seen, he sayed, in a paultry weekly Journal in March last, the Title of which he had forgot. I own the Possibility, continued he, of such a Character, tho I never met with one like it, which I attribute to my living chiefly in the Country, and not conversing much with Ladys in Town. To whom I replyed, you speak like a reasonable Man; and the ignorant *Thing*, who published his Objections in the paultry weekly Journal of which you before spoke, discovered himself to have no Notion of Humour, and that his Conversation was not among Persons of superior Rank, especially the Ladys; for, if it was, he must have met with more than one *Lady Charlotte*, or at least with some who partake of that ridiculous foolish Alertness, and Volubility of talking Nonsense, joined to an extraordinary Opinion of themselves, and a Fondness for Gaming and every fashionable Folly, all which constitute the Character of *Lady Charlotte:* so whether the Folleys represented in her meet in one real Person, (as I am certain they often do) or are divided among several, and she made a Compound of them all, she is a proper Character for Comedy. As I was proceeding in my Remarks on this Character a young Lady came in, and, immediately addressing herself to my Friend, occasioned the following Dialogue.

Lady. Mr. *Manly*! Where have you been these fifty Years since last Summer?

Manly. Where, Niece, have you learn'd this Manner of talking within these few Months? Who do you keep Company with?

Lady. My Companions, Sir, are all Persons of the *Beau Monde*, who have not their Equals at Hazard, and who never stay from a Masquerade or Opera.

Manly. I hope, Madam, the Masquerade has no Charms to you.

Lady. The Masquerade! I have been at a hundred this Winter. Ha'n't you seen the *Oratorio*, Sir?

Manly. I have read it.

[1] In fact, the play had been circulating in manuscript among Fielding's friends for more than a year prior to the first performance (Cross, i, 95, 118–19).

Lady. Read it! But the Music! O! I cou'd sit a thousand Years to hear it!

Manly. I wou'd not be a Slave, Cousin, to what ought to be the Amusement of but a few Minutes.

Lady. And ha'n't you really been at the *Oratorio*? All the World is fond of the *Oratorio*.

Manly. Then all the World is fond of Nonsense.

Lady. Well, you are the strangest Man still that ever was. I have five hundred Visits to pay this Morning, and have made but fifty of them yet. Mr. *Manly*, your Servant.[1]

---

[1] Cooke also printed a pro-Fielding epigram in No. 6, September 1732, p. 32:

> When *Grubs*, and *Grublings*, censure *Fielding*'s Scenes,
> He cannot answer that which Nothing means:
> Scorn'd by the wise, and in their Filth secure,
> How should he damn the damn'd, or soil th' impure?
> When unprovok'd, and envious of his Fame,
> The Wretches strive to blast his honest Name,
> To such, if known, such slander-howling Men,
> The Cudgel should reply, and not the Pen;
> But from their Holes their Dirt the Vermin throw,
> And to Obscurity their Safety owe.

6. 'Prosaicus'

The Grub-street Journal No. 127

8 June 1732

From the PEGASUS *in Grub-street.*

Sir,

As Dramatical performances come under the cognizance of your Society, I hope, without any apology, you'll give this letter a place in your next.

The depravity of modern taste has been long complained of; and several Dramatic performances have been instanced to prove that depravity. I thought this only the bigotted opinion of some peevish old Gentlemen, who commend every thing of the last age, and condemn every thing of the present. I entered into a dispute on this subject the other evening with a Gentleman of the Temple, who esteems it a more amiable Character to be a man of wit and pleasure, than a great Lawyer. After I had urged all the common arguments against our present theatrical taste, and he had spoken as strenuously in the defence of it. Sir, says he, there is a fine burlesque Piece to be played to night at Drury lane; which, for pointed satire, true humour, and mock heroick, will exceed any thing that ever appeared on the stage. It is founded on as good a subject as the *Beggars Opera*; and I assure you, the moral is as instructive. In short, he urged our theatrical taste was rather improved than depraved; and engaged me to go with him to see it the next evening.

But, Mr. BAVIUS, how was I surprized to see the most notorious Bawds, Pimps, and Whores, brought on the stage to please as polite an audience as I ever saw for the time of the year. My Man of pleasure was not only very busy in explaining the beauties of the language, but the secret history, the reality of the characters, and some personal scandal. I observed there were several young fellows in the pit and boxes smiling, and mightily pleased at some passages; which, tho' they knew the meaning of them, were entirely misunderstood by three parts of the audience. It gave me some satisfaction to see so many too ignorant to relish the archness of the Poet, and dull enough not to applaud the wit they did not understand.

After an *Epilogue* entirely adapted to the Play, and listening to some different whispers in the pit, of Critics, Wits, Men of pleasure, &c. as my companion and I were returning to his Chambers, coming along the Play-house passage, a Lady of his acquaintance trip'd out of an adjoining Coffee-house, and clapping him on the shoulder, accosted him with two lines of this new Piece. He replied in two others, which, tho' I've forgot, were in the character of LOVEGIRLO; and then they very lovingly hurried into the Rose.

I had seen too much in the Play-house to follow them, and went to a Coffee-house to examine, whether there was any thing in this *Covent Garden Tragedy*, that could lay the least claim to wit, or deserve any encouragement from the Town. I must submit it to all men of sense, whether that can pass for humour, which is only the dull representation of the most obscene characters in life; and humour is the only thing the Poet can pretend to boast. Were it so, I doubt not but every Drury-lane Bully might make a humourous Poet: for surely he could very naturally describe a scene of life in which he was always conversant; nor is there the most stupid wretch but might pass for a Wit, would he gain that name at the expence of all decency, as well as innocence.

Where is the humour of the Bawdy-house scene to any but a Rake? Or that of HACKABOUTA[1] and STORMANDRA to any women, but those of the Town? These indeed, may smile to see how naturally the Poet enters into their characters; but the joke is entirely lost to all others.——As to the mock Heroic, the lines are bad, nor any thing to

---

[1] An allusion to M. Hackabout, the protagonist of Hogarth's *Harlot's Progress*, which had been published in April 1732. No character named Hackabouta appears in the printed version of Fielding's play; it is possible that 'Prosaicus' simply used the name to allude to the obvious debt *The Covent-Garden Tragedy* owed to the *Harlot's Progress*; or perhaps there *was* a character named Hackabouta in the play, whose name was changed before publication.

recommend the numerous similies. The success of this Piece will determine whether the age is fallen to the lowest ebb; for I should entertain but a bad opinion of the intellects of that Man, or chastity of that Woman, who would give the least encouragement to the most dull obscene Piece, that, I may venture to say, ever appeared on any public stage.

Tom's Coffee-house, Covent-Garden, June 3.　　　　PROSAICUS.

7. 'Dramaticus'
The Grub-street Journal No. 128
15 June 1732[1]

From the PEGASUS *in Grub-street.*

Sir,

I did not think I should have troubled you before next winter, as *Censor of theatrical performances*, little dreaming I should have been call'd upon to exercise that Office sooner. But the horrible profanation of the Stage at present is such, that unless some stop be put to it, no man of any taste, or woman of common modesty must dare henceforward to appear there.

For the truth of this, Mr. BAVIUS, I appeal to last night's new Entertainment, and particularly to that part of it, called, *The Common Garden Tragedy*, written, as is said, by the Author of *The Modern Husband*. Such a scene of infamous lewdness, was never brought, I believe, before on any Stage whatsoever! For my part, if I had any interest in the present *young Managers*, who copy, but too well, the old in their choice of (I presume) *theatrical* Pieces, I would advise them, instead of acting this Play again, to invite the audience to some noted

---

1 For this, and subsequent references to 'Dramaticus', see No. 4.

Bawdy house in Drury-lane, giving the old Lady timely notice to have her Whores, Bullies, Cullies, &c. in readiness. There would be no difference in the Entertainment I assure you. Sir JOHN GONSON[1] might indeed interrupt the action there, and send the Actors to Bridewell, which he cannot so well do, where the thing is *theatrically* represented. In every respect else it would do full as well.

If these, Mr. BAVIUS, are *theatrical* Pieces; these the only fit Entertainments for the Town; these such only as can be undertaken to be acted; I despair indeed of ever making mine fit for the Stage, or seeing it there. God forbid I should ever attempt it.

It would be ridiculous to aim at any sort of criticism upon so shameful a Piece; for which reason I shall drop it, and only add, that if I had not a greater regard for the public, than I have for my own self, I should be overjoyed to see such monstrous Pieces received in a House where mine had been rejected; which certainly must be the most consolatory thing that could happen to me, as it necessarily implies, that the true reason for rejecting mine, was because it was not *bad* enough for the Stage.

If any body should be foolish enough to alledge in justification of such proceedings, that this being a dead time of the year, most of the Company being either gone, or going out of Town, any Play will go down; I will go so far as to agree, that the best Plays ought indeed to be kept for the best Company, and the best time of the year: but no Company, nor any time of the year can justify the turning the Stage into a rank Bawdy-house, and the Actors into arrant Bawds, Pimps, Whores, Rogues, Rakes, and Cullies. I am, Mr. BAVIUS,

Your admirer, and old correspondent,

Friday, June 2, 1732.   DRAMATICUS.

---

[1] Sir John Gonson (d. 1765), a Westminster Magistrate, was notable for his zeal in apprehending prostitutes. See, e.g., Hogarth's *Harlot's Progress*, Plate 3.

THE MODERN HUSBAND
THE COVENT-GARDEN TRAGEDY
THE OLD DEBAUCHEES

1 June 1732

THE MOCK DOCTOR

23 June 1732

8. 'Prosaicus' and 'A.B.'
The Grub-street Journal No. 130

29 June 1732

Following Dramaticus's attack of 15 June, a letter signed 'Mr. Wm. Hint, Candle-Snuffer' (probably Theophilus Cibber in consultation with Fielding), appeared in the *Daily Post* on 21 June, replying to 'Dramaticus, alias Prosaicus, alias Bavius, alias &c. &c. &c.' Hint challenged the *Grub-street Journal* to produce 'some quotations' or 'some particular scene or incidents' to substantiate their accusations of indecency. His only point of critical interest is quoted by A.B. below, most of his essay being a personal attack on the *Journal*. Bavius replied in a personal vein in the *Journal* No. 129 (22 June). Then in No. 130 Prosaicus and A.B. both returned to the attack, A.B. replying specifically to Hint.

> *This is thy Province this thy wondrous way,*
> *New humours to invent for each new Play:*
> *This is that boasted byass of thy mind,*
> *By which one way to dulness 'tis inclin'd.*
> DRYDEN's Mac Flecknoe.[1]
>
> [1] ll. 187–90.

45

Sir,

As some observations on our Dramatic performances may be useful, as well as entertaining, especially to your Readers in the Country, I intend to send you some remarks on each new Piece, as it shall appear, during this summer season at Drury-Lane. I undertake not this office, as instituting myself sole Critic, and invading the known liberties of the Pit; but rather as a task imposed on me by a young Templar, whom I have lately had occasion to mention, to give him an account of the progress of theatrical poetry in his absence. How far he may agree with my sentiments, I know not; but he is very well assured, that I shall not be biassed by partiality or prejudice. He was the more earnest to engage me in this correspondence, as he had been assured, that the Manager of the young Company had several good Pieces, which were every way *theatrical.*—*Theatricality* is sure something of which the Drury-lane Managers only can form an idea. There have been so many expositions of its sense, that it seems to me almost impossible accurately to define it. But whatever it be, this I have observed, that those Pieces, which were said to be most theatrical, were least consistent with the rules of Dramatic writing. I could prove the truth of this assertion in an examen of the *Modern Husband*: but as Mr. DRAMATICUS hath given already a critique on it in your 117th *Journal*,[1] I shall at present only observe, that there is scarce a scene in the whole, but what betrays want of judgment, or, to use softer terms, manifests at least the Author's hasty way of writing. The latter I believe, he himself will most readily own, as thinking it a sufficient plea for whatever his most fertile Muse may produce.[2] But I must beg leave to dissent from him: no hasty productions should be imposed upon the Town; a constant flow of which is no better proof of a fruitful brain, than a numerous, sickly, short-liv'd off-spring is of a fruitful womb. In either case, such a course of barren fruitfulness is but one degree beyond frequent abortion.—Besides, this Gentleman has the least excuse for hasty writing of any Author. The vast encouragement he met with last winter, might sure have enabled him to take due time to finish any Piece he intended to bring on the Stage since; unless he has agreed with the Managers to furnish them with so many annual Pieces. Besides his *Lottery* and *Modern Husband* in the winter, he has produced two more, his *Covent-Garden Tragedy* and *Old Debauchees* within four months after.[3] But the former of these twins being in a dying condition

---

[1] See No. 4.
[2] See *The Comedian*, No. 5 above.
[3] *The Lottery* (1 January 1731–2).

under the just censure of the Town, he publicly made a sort of a voluntary sacrifice of it to their resentment, in order to preserve the life of the latter. This was a fairer piece of policy, than that, which perhaps may by custom become truly THEATRICAL; I mean an endeavor to puff a favourite Piece of a favourite Author into reputation; so that its character is not to depend on the reception the Town gives it at the Theatre, but on the figure it makes in a *theatrical* paragraph in a *Daily Post*. In that Paper, of June 2, and 5, *The Old Debauchees* was said to have met with *universal applause*; and tho' the 3d night's audience on June 13th was dismissed, as not being sufficient to pay half the charges, yet in the *Daily Post* of the 16th a paragraph was inserted, affirming that it had *met with great applause*. The Author, I dare say, had no hand in any of these Puffs; he has been too well approved by the Town to endeavour to delude them into an approbation of any Piece of his, by descending to as low and mean artifices as Mr. Orator and Hyp-Doctor almost daily stoops.—But lest he may think himself any way injured by my general censure of *The Old Debauchees*, I will next week send you some observations on it; and continue the same course on all the new productions at Drury-lane, in letters to my Friend of the Temple: not that I am resolved to condemn every thing, but to examine impartially, and give promiscuously the praise or censure they may deserve. One thing before I conclude, I would advise the Manager of the young Players, that, as he seems to stand in favour with the Town at present, he would not foist that on them which they may not be willing to receive; but if he finds one thing not go off well (as he has such variety of new Pieces) to bring on another. By this conduct, he can't fail of considerable success this summer vacation, and may prepare the way for something more diverting and instructive the ensuing winter.

Tom's Coffee-House,   I am, Mr. BAVIUS, yours,
June 17.   PROSAICUS.

Mr. BAVIUS,

AS *in this age there needs no great apology for commencing Author*, I hope you'll give this a kind reception, tho' it is dated from a place, where I believe you have but few correspondents. As to my character, let it suffice, that I have been a constant spectator at Drury-lane Play-house these 10 years, and am well known in this place for keeping up a decorum, and being an impartial Critic. I think, Sir, from so long an attendance, I may be as good a judge of Dramatical performances as Mr. HINT the *Candle-snuffer*; whose letter in the *London Evening Post* of last night I have now before me, and on which I send you these observations.

In the second paragraph Mr. HINT alledges in vindication of Mr. F. from the charge of indecency, that *Bullies, Bawds, Rakes, Whores, are in themselves characters not improper to be shown on the stage, if they were, you must quarrel with half our Plays, and particularly with the Beggars Opera*. I own, those characters have been brought on the English stage: nay I'll go farther, and give a sanction to it by the example of TERENCE. This is certainly allowable, as to the characters in *themselves*: but then, Mr. BAVIUS, is a Poet to have nothing in his Play but such characters? Is he in drawing such a character to pick out the most profligate wretches in it? Is he to correct lewdness by almost shewing the commission of it? Did TERENCE to ridicule the tricks of a *Whore*, exhibit to a Roman audience a brothel? No, he could represent the vices in low characters of life in a language not unbecoming the Roman dignity, nor offending against the rules of decency. I don't doubt but he might have found in Rome among the dregs of the people, characters as vicious as those of our modern Author; but his *Thais's* and *Lenones* betray their several artifices in a pleasing inoffensive humour. I know not whether in reality they were more decent than the HACKABOUTA'S and BILKUM'S of the present age; but this I affirm, that the Roman Pagan was far more modest than our English Christian.

Neither *envy*, nor *malice*, nor *provocation* has *inhumanly animated* me against the Author, or Theatre; I am disinterested and impartial, I have no enmity to the man, but to his Tragedy: no *exclamation* from a *Bawd* to a *Porter* has given me any disturbance: nor indeed can I see that those against whom the little satyrical line was levelled, have any occasion to complain; for however keen the rage of the Author might be, his wit was too dull to wound. Mr. HINT in the next paragraph declares, he thinks *it is incumbent on every man who affirms a Play to be bad, indecent, and infamous to give some quotations from it, or mention some particular scene or incident which are so*. It cannot be supposed, that quotations could be given from the action only; and it was unneccessary to mention any *particular scene*, when there was not one scene through the whole but would make the accusation good; which will be obvious to every one, if the Author proceeds to print his incomparable Piece, faithfully as it was acted.

The rest of this letter is a retort on DRAMATICUS's Play and your *Journal*. As to the first, I know nothing of it, nor will I pretend to vindicate any thing on the hearsay only. As to the latter, you are the best judge, what answer to give to it. I am now impatiently waiting to see another production of the Author of the *Covent-Garden Tragedy*, translated from MOLIERE; and to shew my envy to the Poet, I only wish he has kept up to the spirit of the original.

Theatre Royal in Drury-lane: I am, Mr. BAVIUS,
  First row in the upper Gallery.   Yours,
  Friday, June 23.   A.B.

9. 'Dramaticus' and 'Miso-cleros'
The Grub-street Journal No. 132
13 July 1732

A reply to *The Comedian* of June 1732 (No. 5).

> *Shall we, you cry, learn writing ill by Rule;*
> *And have we need to study to be dull?*
> Harlequin-Horace, pag. 35.[1]

To Mr. BAVIUS, Secretary of the Society of Grub-street.

Monday, June the 26th, 1732.

Sir,

I have just dipt in a monthly *thing* called the *Comedian, or Philosophical Enquirer:* in which the Author, who seems very desirous to be thought an *acquaintance of persons of superior rank,* as well as a man of a considerable share of understanding, has attacked me for some reflections on *The Modern Husband.*

As I never publish any thing but what I think right, (not having any view of interest to answer which might oblige me to write) I was rather surprized, than concerned, at an attack from so unexpected a quarter. And indeed, were it not for the contempt, which from the

---

[1] [James Miller], *Harlequin-Horace, or the Art of Modern Poetry* (1731).

height of his understanding, he insolently bestows on those he quarrels with, I should have taken no manner of notice of him, nor drawn him from the peaceful state of obscurity, in which he lies, from one month to another, by placing him in so conspicuous a light, as he will henceforth appear in, by being known to be an opposer of the GRUBEANS.

Under an article which he calls *Reflections on some modern Plays*, he tells us, he made a visit lately to a Yorkshire Gentleman just come to town, who told him, that some persons, who lived in the Country, and himself among the rest, could not believe, that several Plays printed within these 3 years, had ever been really acted: and therefore they looked upon them to be no other than impositions of the Booksellers upon their customers in the country. He instanced in *Timoleon, Periander, Medea, George Barnwell, Injured Innocence, Sylvia* or *The Country Burial, The Devil to pay*, and a long catalogue of rubbish. (This, by the way, I conceive is what he means by *Reflections on some modern Plays*; for I don't find in the whole article any other *reflection* on them: nay, our Author expressly declares he had been *neither a spectator nor reader of any of them*). Upon this our *Comedian* mentioned *The Modern Husband*, as not liable to the censure which our Yorkshire Critic had passed upon the rest. This Comedy, the Gentleman owns, 'gave him pleasure, tho' it is not entirely conformable to the rules of the Drama.'

From the mention of the rules of the Drama, our Philosophical Critic takes an opportunity to talk in the following most profound, unintelligible manner about Plays, and the rules for writing them. 'By the rules of the Drama, says I, you mean, I presume, the rules of Critics, who have no right to impose rules: the antient writers of Tragedy and Comedy divided their Plays into five Acts, in which we have generally followed their example; and I know no other stated rule to be observed, and that may be departed from sometimes without any disadvantage.' —Thus, Mr. BAVIUS, there is no rule to be observed in writing of Plays, but to divide them into five Acts, and even that rule may be departed from: so that in fact there is no rule at all absolutely necessary to be observed. What direction then is a Poet to follow in composing a Dramatical Piece? Why,—'Unerring reason is the only guide in Tragedy and Comedy, tho' a man, who is merely a reasonable man, and no more, is not qualified to write either, particular talents being requisite for both, under the conduct of reason; and that Poet who wants any other rule, besides nature or reason, mistakes his province when he attempts to write.' If *unerring reason is the only guide to Tragedy and Comedy*, it is no wonder that we have so many bad ones: nay, I fear it

is impossible that there should be a good one, of either kind. For what
Poet ever had this guide; which must make him as infallible in poetry,
as the old Gentleman at Rome pretends to be in religion? But it seems a
merely *reasonable man and no more,* tho' he has this *unerring reason, is not
qualified to write,* because *particular talents* are *requisite under the conduct of*
[this unerring] *reason.* By these *talents,* I suppose, he means invention,
wit, humour, &c. which a man who wants cannot write a Play: but no
other rule is necessary besides nature or [unerring] reason: so that *nature
and unerring reason* are the same. Now the whole meaning of this
sublime period, if it has any, is no more than this, That a man of good
sense without a genius cannot write a Play; and that *nature* or *reason* is
the only guide which a Dramatic Poet is to follow. But how does this
set aside the rules of the Critics? which I affirm are agreeable to nature
or reason, and consequently, according to this Author's own concession,
ought to be observed.

He then goes on: '*The Modern Husband* I acknowledge to have some
scenes independent of the main business of the Play, and some expressions, the omission of which would be no detriment to the work; yet
it has wit, humour, satire, and moral reflections in it, not unworthy
the pen of the best Stoic. If indeed the Author had made every scene
conducive to the principal design, to the plot of the Play, and as dependent one on the other as every link in a chain, and every expression as
necessary as every scene, he would have produced a more perfect piece
than it now is: and I doubt not but that he who is capable of writing so
entertaining a Play as it now is, is ingenuous enough to confess these
truths, and to acknowledge that his intent was to expose particular vice
and follys, to make these ridiculous, and those odious, to give his
audience pleasure, and himself profit, and that he had not leisure to make
it otherwise than it now is, and that he laughs without anger at those
who expose themselves by a fruitless endeavour to expose him.'———
That is to say, *The Modern Husband* is defective in the principal con-
stituents of a good Play, but has some very entertaining things in it,
(at least the Comedian tells us so) which make amends for the want of
the rest: so that all things considered, the Author's *want of leisure,* not
ability, to make it better; *his intent* of giving *pleasure to his audience* and
profit to himself; his ingenuity to *confess these truths, his intent to expose
particular vices and folleys, in order to make these ridiculous and those odoius;*
all this put together plainly proves, what the *Philosophical Comedian*
undertook, which was to shew, that this Play was *not liable to the
censure,* which his Yorkshire friend has *passed upon the rest,* which he

owns he himself had neither seen, nor read, and consequently must be a very proper person to make *reflections upon modern Plays,* and to give one the preference before all the others. As to the Author's *laughing without anger at those who expose themselves by a fruitless endeavour to expose him,* I have received an account of a transaction at a certain Bookseller's shop near Temple-bar, which directly contradicts this: for there two celebrated Captains quarrelled about this affair, and were likely to have come to blows; at which it was thought the Bookseller, as usual, would have had the advantage of the Tragedian.

Upon the whole, I think, Mr. BAVIUS, till this *Philosophical Comedian,* or *Comical Philosopher,* or his friend the Author of *The Modern Husband,* or *Mr. Wm. Hint,* the Candle-snuffer, shall be more explicit in their justification of this Play, I may even set down without anger, and content myself with refering them once more to the *Grub-street Journal,* No. 117.[1] without giving myself any further trouble to defend a Paper which has been so lamely attacked by this Dramatical *Enquirer.*

This Gentleman, who has so short a memory that he could not, or was so ill natured that he would not, tell his country friend the name of that *paultry weekly Journal* he mentioned to him, concludes very affirmatively that 'The *ignorant thing,* viz. DRAMATICUS, discovered 'himself to have no notion of humour, and that his conversation was not among persons of superior rank, especially the Ladies'. But how has he made this discovery of himself? Why, because he has questioned whether there are any real Lady CHARLOTTES in the world; and therefore he *can't be supposed to have any notion of humour,* or *conversation with Ladies of superior rank.* A pretty genteel compliment, upon my word, for which the *Ladies of superior rank* he frequents, are infinitely obliged to him. Instead of answering such a ridiculous surmise, or giving him a list of the Ladies of my acquaintance, I must once more beg leave to say, that I both believe and hope, that there is no such character among the Ladies as Lady CHARLOTTE; and as for the *Comedian's young Lady that came in* while he was in conversation with his Yorkshire friend, if she is a real person, she clearly proves the truth of what I advanced in that Paper about Lady CHARLOTTE, viz. *that such Ladies as answer this character can never be cured.* I am, Mr. BAVIUS, your most humble servant,

DRAMATICUS

★   ★   ★

1 See No. 4.

Sir,

An ingenious and learned Writer has lately informed us,★ that both
in Athens and Rome the Stage was 'an engine of the State; that the
wisest Statesmen have esteemed it of admirable use in amusing the
people, and keeping them from too strict an enquiry into Politics and
Religion; and that formerly if ever Players meddled with Politics it
was in favour of the power governing.' He then complains, 'that some
pragmatical Players of the present age, forgetting both their duty and
interest, have under pretext of declaiming at vice in general exhibited
state lampoons'; but, in the conclusion, assures us, that 'the conduct of
those in Drury-lane has been as decent as the general licentiousness of the
age would admit of.' In confirmation of the *decent conduct* of these
Gentlemen, I think it will be of some service, Mr. BAVIUS, to produce
a famous instance of a Comedy, or rather a Farce, lately acted several
times by them, called the *Old Debauchees*.

The story of Father GIRARD and Miss CADIERE had been treated
with great variety, both in prose and verse; and yielded a comfortable
subsistence to several of your Members during the last winter. At the
same time the Drawers and Engravers went to work upon it, and exhibited several lively pictures to the view of all persons who passed the
streets. When the subject seemed quite exhausted, and the discourse
about it was almost ceased, a Gentleman of a surprizing genius wrought
it into a Play, under the title mentioned above, and brought it upon
the Stage with success. I may take another opportunity to point out
the several beauties of this Piece; at present I shall only take notice of the
principal design, and shew how happily it has been executed.——The
principal design is to expose the Clergy; and, since in opinion of all
wise and honest men, they are the teachers of such doctrines as tend to
introduce popery and arbitrary power, can there possibly be a more
justifiable design?——Nor has the manner of executing it been liable
to the least censure, the Author having employed no other weapon
against them but the keenest wit, and treated them with all the good
manners and politeness imaginable: of which the following instances
are an evident demonstration.

Old LAROON, before he knows any thing of the villainy of *Father*
MARTIN, says to him, 'It were happy for such Rascals as you, Sirrah,
&c.' *pag.* 23 calls him 'a roguish Priest' *p.* 34. 'a rascal.' *p.* 35. says he has
seen 'a damn'd rogue of a Priest riding an old honest whoremaster to

★ See *Daily Courant* of May 9.

the Devil.' *p.* 10. and under a curse declares, 'I'll carbonade the villain: I'll make a ragout for the Devil's supper of him.' *ibid.*

JORDAIN says, 'I once committed a Priest to Newgate for picking pockets.' *p.* 12.

All this indeed particularly relates to one Priest; but that which follows strikes in general at the whole order. *Old* LAROON says, 'Peace cannot stay long in any place where a Priest comes.' *p.* 5. 'Judgment cannot be far off when a Priest is near.' *p.* 23. 'I no more rely on what a Woman says out of a Church, than on what a Priest says in.' *p.*10. To *Father* MARTIN, 'Exert thy self in thy proper office, and hold the door.' *p.* 23. 'Thou art the Devil's footman, and wearest his proper livery.' *p.* 22. 'Death and the Devil, another Priest.' *p.* 16. 'You are possessed with a Priest, and that's worse'. [than being possess'd with the Devil.] *p.* 21. The Priests in general are called, wild beasts. *p.* 36. a set of dirty Priests. *p.* 2. 'of greasy Priests'. *p.* 25. 'of rescally Priests.' *p.* 4. 'of black locusts.' *p.* 23. and 'a regiment of black guards.' *p.* 10.

You may imagine perhaps, Mr. BAVIUS, that much the greatest part of this fine language being spoken by *Old* LAROON, a vicious Character, and only of the Popish Clergy, it can have but very little efficacy in exposing ours. But there are two maxims which you are to take as a key to the whole: That whatever scandalous thing is said of a Priest, you are to regard only what is spoken, and not the person who speaks it; and that

Priests of all religions are the same.

Yours MISO-CLEROS.

10. 'Publicus'

The Grub-street Journal No. 133

20 July 1732

> 'Tis then, and then alone, the point you gain,
> If no one precept in your works remain,
> But ribaldry, and scandal, lawless reign,
> Thus shall all Drury in your praise combine,
> And distant Goodman's Fields their Peans join:
> So far Barbadoes shall resound your fame,
> And ev'n transported Felons know your name.
>
> HARLEQ. HOR. p. 46[1]

To Mr. BAVIUS.

Sir,

As in my younger days I was a great frequenter of Dramatic Entertainments, so I have been ever since a strenuous advocate for the Stage. I have been always particularly warm against any who declared for a total demolition of it; and looked on them as persons employed to introduce popery and arbitrary power, as many other honest people have thought. I used to offer in its behalf, that, however it might be perverted in particulars, it was still wholesome in the general; that from thence our youth might not only acquire a good address, and just elocution, but likewise, by seeing vice punished, and folly corrected, the particularities of caprice and affectation exposed, and honour and honesty come off triumphant, they might be induced to chuse the good, and refuse the evil. This, and much more, Mr. BAVIUS, have I hitherto urged against the enemies of the sock and buskin. But, alas, I can now stand my ground no longer; for, as the Stage is at present directed by the *Drury-Lane-Managers*, and supply'd by their *Farce-Writers*, I must acknowledge it to be so far from being useful, that 'tis not tolerable; and that the extirpation of it is more necessary, and would be of more publick service, than of *night-cellars, brothels*, and common *gaming-tables*. Surely the *Masters* of that house procured the renewal of their

---

[1] See No. 9, note 1.

Patent, with a design of insulting the common sense, and common modesty, of mankind; and they have very happily pitched on *Authors*, who were fit to execute such a design. I think the first new Entertainment they gave us, after the confirmation of their *Grant*, was a *concert of cats, dogs, monkeys, goats,* &c. and the first new Plays were the *Covent-Garden Tragedy*, and the *Old Debauchees*. The two last performances, Mr. BAVIUS, having meritoriously met with the *universal detestation* of the Town (instead of their *universal applause*, as some of our pander News-writers had impudence enough to assert,) I was excited to look into them, that I might see what grounds there were for such a general outcry; when I was soon convinced, that they were so far improper for an *English Stage*, or to be exhibited to a *polite*, an *honest*, and a *christian* people, that, (unless Sodom and Gomorrah had been now undestroyed) they were only fit for the hangman's flames. But, notwithstanding the just abhorrence the Town has shewed to this imposition, these performances were too good, it seems, in the opinion of their promoters, to be given up; a formal defence of them has been published in the papers, and a challenge to their opposers to produce a single passage which can be wrested into *indecency* or *profaneness*.[1] This challenge, however disagreeable, I accept; holding myself obliged to do a little dirty work, rather than suffer others to be suffocated with the mire.

To begin then with the Tragedy. The scene of this Piece lies in a *bawdy-house*, and the characters of it, as the Author informed us in his Prologue, are *bullies, bawds, sots, rakes,* and *whores*; a very pretty collection to entertain the Boxes; tho', to their honour be it told, many that were there had neither so much taste, nor so little modesty, as to be able to sit it out, but quitted their places in the middle of the performance. But, to come to particulars, (and yet I'm ashamed to come to them too) observe the following speech of LOVEGIRLO, Page 13. [I. ix. Henley, x. 121].

> *Oh! I am all on fire, thou lovely wench;*
> *Torrents of joy my burning soul must quench,*
> *Reiterated joys!*
> *Thus, burning from the fire, the washer lifts*
> *The red hot iron to make smooth her shifts;*
> *With arm impetuous rubs her shift amain,*
> *And rubs, and rubs, and rubs it o'er again;*
> *Nor sooner does her rubbing arm withhold,*
> *'Till she grows warm, and the hot iron cold.*

[1] See again *The Comedian*, No. 5 above.

Abominable! sure a man must wrest with all his might to make any thing else of this but the most gross obscenity. I don't know whether the impudence or the nastiness of another speech in the same scene is most to be wondered at.

> LOVEG. *Who but a fool would marry that can keep?*
> *Sounds less the scolding of a vertuous tongue?*
> *Or who remembers, to increase his joy,*
> *In the last moments of excessive bliss,*
> *The ring, the licence, Parson, or his clerk?*
> *Besides, whene'er my mistress plays me foul,*
> *I cast her like a dirty shirt away.*
> *But oh! a wife sticks like a plaister fast,*
> *Like a perpetual blister to the pole.* [Henley, x. 120]

Here's instruction! here's delicacy! a dirty shirt, and a blister are most entertaining images! why this turns my stomach, as well as shocks my understanding. This is language more gross than even goats and monkeys, if they could speak, would express their brutality in. And as this writer, in the foregoing quotations, exposes matrimony and recommends whoredom, so, in the next, he is as strong an advocate for *drunkenness.*

> *And were it not for wine, I would not be;*
> *Wine makes a Cobler greater than a King;*
> *Wine gives mankind the preference to beasts, &c.*
> [I. vii. Henley, x. 118]

Here the end of a man's being, and the excellency of his nature, are placed in debauchery; and, lest the audience should forget to league lewdness and intemperance together, the writer joins and enforces them in the following reflection.

> BILK. *Wine is a good, and so is woman too,*
> *But which the greater good, I cannot tell;*
> *Either to other to prefer I'm loth,*
> *But he does wisest who takes most of both.*
> [I. viii. Henley, x. 119]

The wit and burlesque of this Piece is likewise very uncommon, the following lines I suppose are meant for ridicule.

> *Oh! I am mad, methinks I swim in air,*
> *In seas of sulphur, and eternal fire;*
> *Methinks I'm mad, mad as a wild march-hare;*

> *My muddy brain is addled like an egg,*
> *My teeth, like Magpies, chatter in my head;*
> *My reeling head! which akes like any mad.*
>
> [II. xii. Henley, x. 132]

It must be an *addled brain* indeed that such stuff as this could come from. Is this *burlesque*? Where is the similitude? Where is the point? No, 'tis downright toothless, tasteless, *original nonsense*; there never was any thing like it, and, I hope, never will be. Methinks the writer tho' might as well have left *seas of sulphur*, and *eternal fire*, out of the mad joke, for fear he should meet with them in sober sadness.

And now, Mr. BAVIUS, I must beg pardon for soiling your paper with such smut, and loading it with the language of Billingsgate and the stews; but, as I told you before, 'tis by absolute force, much against stomach or inclination. But, that we may get out of the kennel as soon as possible, we'll take a skip at once as far as the Epilogue, not doubting but the Reader has got enough of the Play. Now this bravely carries on the business of the Piece, and clenches its *moral*; here the Author leaves fiction and the Stage, and addresses himself in *propria persona* to the Boxes. What had been said before by the different characters, might probably have been mistaken: the audience might have looked on it as false and ridiculous when it came from such speakers; but, to prevent this, the Poet appears in the *Epilogue*, and informs us, that 'tis nothing but solemn truth. Pray observe him.

> *The Priest makes all the difference in the case,*
> *Kissinda's always ready to embrace,*
> *And* Isabel *stays only to say grace.*
> *For several prices ready both to treat,*
> *This takes a guinea, that your whole estate:*
> *For prudes may cant of vertues, and of vices;*
> *But, faith, we only differ in our prices.* [Henley, x. 134]

A very decent complement to the Boxes, in truth, and the Ladies will, I hope, reward him for it his next benefit night. He tells them, without any ceremony, that there's no difference betwixt the best of them, and the *bawdy-house trulls* they had been seeing on the Stage; and that, pretend what they would, they were all a parcel of *downright arrant whores*. Here is respect and decency with a vengeance, a most elegant dessert to regale the Ladies at the close of the Entertainment; we are mightily obliged to him for the good opinion he has of our wives and daughters;

and, in good truth, were we to suffer them to frequent his Entertainments, the opinion might soon become just enough too.

But now, Mr. BAVIUS, let us take a slight look on the other of these performances, and have done; for I'm both tir'd and sick of the employment. The *Old Debauchees* is the Author's favourite, it seems; for, in the preface to a piece of MOLIERE's,[1] which he has most *execrably murdered*, he modestly compares it with the *Misanthrope* of that Author. This writer then makes no distinction between the most chaste, moral, witty performance, and the most coarse, vicious, insipid trumpery that ever was hatched. Just so much difference is there between the *Misanthrope* of MOLIERE, and the *Old Debauchees*. However, it must be said for the writer, that in this piece he has made most violent attempts to be witty; and how he has succeeded may be best seen by setting a few of his flowers to view. Old LAROON says, *p.* 3. [I. ii. Henley, ix. 284–5] *I remember the time when I could have taken a hop, step, and jump over the steeple of Notre Dame.* To which the fine Lady ingeniously makes answer, *I fancy the sparks of your age had wings, Sir.* Which answer was contrived, I suppose, to introduce the following wonderful witty reply. O. LAR. *Wings, you little baggage, no, but they had limbs like elephants and as strong they were as Sampson, and as swift as——Why, I have myself run down a stag in a fair chace, and eat him afterwards for dinner.* Certainly, when the Poet penn'd this speech, his *brains were* in a *wild goose chace* after wit, and the Reader's stomach must be as coarse as the writer's fancy, that can digest this *stag*. But he kindles, you'll find, as he runs, and grows wittier and wittier. O. LAROON advises the young Lady, *not to let a sett of rascally Priests put strange notions in her head, for that there are no raptures worth a* LOUSE, *but those in the arms of a brisk young Cavalier.* [I. ii. Henley, ix. 284–5]. He says to his son, *At your Devotions! Nay, then you are no son of mine; I believe you are the son of some travelling English Alderman, and must have come into the world with a custard in your mouth.* [I. iii. Henley, ix. 286] Here's wit! here's imagery! was ever any thing like this spoke out of a sculler? but this is decent to what follows in almost every page; observe the next. O. LAROON says, *The Devil is a great lover of Musick: I have known half a dozen Devils dance out of a man's mouth at the tuning of a Violin, then present the company with a Hornpipe, and so dance a Jig through the key-hole.* MARTIN very justly makes answer, *Thou art the Devil's son.* To which the other replies, *Thou art the Devil's Footman, and wearest his proper Livery.* [II. vi. Henley, ix. 303]

This is delightful jesting indeed! could the Writer imagine, that any

---

[1] i.e. *The Mock Doctor*. For Preface see Henley, x. 139–40.

above Draymen and Scavengers would laugh at this? But we have more of such pleasantry. O. LAROON assures JOURDAIN, *That Purgatory is a very warm place, for he had called there to take lodgings for him, that 'twas not above a mile and a half there, and every step of the way down-hill.* JOURDAIN says, *Is it possible that you can have seen the dreadful horrors of that place.* O. LAROON. *Seen 'em, Ay, ay, I have seen 'em, and a pretty tragical sort of a sight they are; if it was not for the confounded heat of the air——Then there's such a fine consort of groans, you would think your self at an Opera; some spirits are shut up in ovens, some are chained to spits, some are scattered in frying-pans——And I have taken up a place for you on a grid-iron.* [III. iv. Henley, ix. 312]. The Scripture has given us too frightful a description it seems of Hell, and painted the Devil and his Angels in too formidable colours; our Poet therefore, in order to prevent any ill effect such dismal ideas might have on the mind, is perpetually drolling throughout this piece upon Hell and Damnation, and representing the *Devil* as a *Bugbear* fit only to fright children. This must be an admirable entertainment for the Ladies, as well as excellent instruction to our youth. When such things as these are suffer'd on the Stage, 'tis no wonder there are so many *Whores* and *Pickpockets* in the streets. And now, since he makes so free with the Bible, no wonder if the Priests are splashed with his mud. I'll give you, Mr. BAVIUS, one or two of his genteel reflections upon them, and so wash my hands, and meddle with him no more.

The fine Gentleman of the Play [i.e. Young Laroon] says, That *if you once attack a hornet, or a Priest, the whole nest of hornets, and the whole regiment of black guards, are sure to be upon you.* [I. viii. Henley, ix. 291]. O. LAROON, being asked the cause of his mirth, answers, *'Tis the sight of an old honest whore-master in a fit of despair, and a damn'd rogue of a Priest riding him to the Devil.* Two speeches after he says, *Well, I have never tapp'd a Priest yet; but if I don't let out some reverend blood before the sun sets,——I'll make a ragout for the Devil's supper of him.——*'Tis a pity but the Poet was to serve for *sauce* then, tho' 'twould be very *insipid.* But he goes on, *I no more rely on what a woman says out of a Church, than on what a Priest says in it.* [I. ix. Henley, ix. 291-2]——*Hearkee, old Gentleman, set the young couple together, and they'll sacrifice their first fruits to the Church.* [II. ii. Henley, ix. 297] *What the Devil are you possessed with?——I am possessed with the Devil.——You are possessed with a Priest, and that's worse,* [II. vi. Henley, ix. 303]——*I'll disband such a sett of black locusts,* [II. vii. Henley, ix. 304]——*wild beasts,* [III. viii. Henley, ix. 317]——*rascally Priests,* [I. ii. Henley, ix. 285]——*greasy Priests,* [II. viii. Henley,

ix. 306] &c. &c. &c.——He compliments *England upon every man's believing what religion he pleases, and most believing none at all.* [III. ix Henley, ix. 317–18] His belief of the last is indeed the only apology he can make for his way of entertaining them; but then he ought to have taken away their modesty too. And this he really does in the character of his fine Lady [i.e. Isabel] in the two last lines of the Play, where she concludes the piece with the following chaste and instructive moral. *The fears of a lover are very unreasonable, when he is once assured of the sincerity of his mistress:*

> *For when a woman sets herself about it,*
> *Nor Priest, nor Devil, can make her go without it.*

[III. xiv. Henley, ix. 322]

Soh!——I've done, which the Reader, I dare say, will be glad of as well as myself. This writer can't accuse me of wresting any thing, since I have done little more than quoted from him; and this can't offend him, because 'tis what he demanded. If I had either leisure, or inclination, I could go a little farther with him; and make it appear, from all his performances, that his pen is not only void of *wit, manners,* and *modesty,* but likewise of the most common *rules* of *Poetry,* and even *Grammar.* But this, Mr. B A V I U S, I leave to you, and your correspondents; I shall only observe at present, that the *managers* of the *Theatre* are more in blame than the writers, by giving encouragement to such writings, and such Authors, and to none but such. I am, Sir, your most obedient,

P U B L I C U S.

P.S. I would advise this writer, that, if he does any thing more from M O L I E R E, as he threatens us, he would forbear to *adulterate* it with any thing of his own, or to mix it with such *Debauchee-Songs,* and *Covent-Garden Ribaldry,* as he has done in the *Forc'd Physician* of that Author; which he has mangled and misunderstood from the very *Title-Page* to *Finis.* He might as well have translated, *Medecin malgré lui,* the *Mock-Poet* as the *Mock-Doctor,* nay, better; for that had been applicable to the Translator, if not to the Piece; but the other suits nothing but the Person to whom he dedicates it.

11. From 'Philalethes'

The Daily Post

31 July 1732

'Philalethes', probably Fielding, answers the *Grub-street Journal's* personal and factual allegations against Fielding, and then turns to the accusation of immorality against *The Old Debauchees*.[1]

. . . why should any Person of Modesty be offended at seeing a Set of *Rakes* and *Whores* exposed and set in the most *ridiculous Light*? Sure the Scene of a Bawdy-house may be shewn on a Stage without shocking the most modest Woman; such I have seen sit out that Scene in the *Humorous Lieutenant,* which is quoted and commended by one of the finest Writers of the last Age.[2]

The Author is said to recommend *Whoring* and *Drunkenness*; how! Why a Rake speaks against Matrimony, and a Sot against Sobriety: So Moliere in Don Juan recommends all Manner of Vices, and every Poet (I am sure every good one) that hath exposed a vicious Character, hath by this Rule contributed to debauch Mankind.

. . . he proceeds to *the Epilogue*, where he says the Author tells the Ladies, without any Ceremony, *that there's no Difference betwixt the best of them, and the Bawdy-house Trulls they had been seeing on the Stage; and that pretend what they would, they were all a Parcel of Errant Whores*: This is *a most infamous Lye*, as any one who reads the Epilogue to the Covent Garden Tragedy must see, where nothing more is asserted, than that it is natural for one Sex to be fond of the other,

> *In short you* (Men) *are the Business of our Lives,*
> *To be a Mistress kept the Strumpet strives,*
> *And all the modest Virgins to be Wives* [Henley, x. 134].

---

[1] The first part of this letter is reprinted by Cross, i. 135–6.

[2] John Fletcher's *The Humorous Lieutenant* (1619) was commended by Steele in *Spectator* No. 266 (4 January 1712).

But he is not contented with representing the Poet as having abus'd the Ladies, (which I believe the Poet is so much a Gentleman as to think the worst Thing could be said of him) the Critick, after having terribly mangled the Play by tearing out several Passages, without inserting the whole Speeches, or making the Reader acquainted with the Character of the Speaker, accuses the Author with being free with the Bible; how free with the Bible? Why he has given a ridiculous Description of Purgatory: Well, and hath Purgatory any Thing more to do with the Bible than a Description of the Infernal Shades or Elisian Fields of the Heathens, or of the Paradise of the Mahometans. If the Critick had shewn as much Sense as Malice, I should have imagin'd the *Popish Priest* had peep'd forth in this Place; for sure *any Protestant, but a Nonjuring Parson, would be asham'd* to represent a Ridicule on Purgatory as a Ridicule on the Bible, or the Abuse of *Bigotted Fools* and *Roguish Jesuits* as an Abuse on Religion and the English Clergy.

Not having vented enough of his Malice on these two Pieces, he adds, *Had I either Leisure or Inclination I could go a little farther with this Writer, and make it appear from all his Performances, that his Pen is not only void of Wit, Manners and Modesty, and likewise of the most common Rules of Poetry, but even Grammar:* This is a most barbarous Assertion; how true it is I shall leave to the Opinion of the World: As for the strict Rules which some Criticks have laid down, I cannot think an Author obliged to confine himself to them; for the Rules of Grammar, the Education which the Author of the Debauchees is known to have had, makes it unlikely he should err in those, or be able to write such wretched Stuff as, *I used to offer in its Behalf,* &c. a Sense wherein that Verb is never found in any good Writer of the English Language; nor indeed will its Derivation from the Latin *Utor* at all admit of it. Again, *Trulls they had been seeing,* Expressions a Boy in the second Form at Eaton would have been whipt for: As for the other Part of the Charge, I must tell our Critick, there is a Vein of Good Humour and Pleasantry which runs through all the Works of this Author, and will make him and them amiable to a good-natur'd and sensible Reader, when the low, spiteful, false Criticism of *a Grub-street Journal* will be forgotten.

Yours,

PHILALETHES.

P.S. Whether his Scurrility on the *Mock Doctor* be just or no, I leave to the Determination of the Town, which hath already declared loudly on its Side. Some Particulars of the Original are omitted, which the

Elegance of an English Audience would not have endur'd; and which, if the Critick had ever read the Original, would have shewn him that the chaste *Moliere* had introduced greater Indecencies on the Stage than the Author he abuses: I may aver he will find more in *Dryden, Congreve, Wycherly, Vanbrugh, Cibber,* and all our best Writers of *Comedy,* nay in the Writings of almost every Genius from the Days of *Horace,* to those of a most *Witty, Learned, and Reverend Writer of our own Age.*[1]

12. 'Epigram' by 'Maevius'

The Grub-street Journal No. 135

3 August 1732

Charg'd with writing of bawdy, this was F——'s reply:
Tis what DRYDEN and CONGREVE have done as well as I.
Tis true——but they did it with this good pretence,
With an ounce of rank bawdy went a pound of good sense:
But thou hast proportion'd, in thy judgment profound,
Of good sense scarce an ounce, and of bawdy a pound.[2]

[1] i.e. Jonathan Swift.

[2] A second epigram by Maevius to the same effect, 'On a Poet's pleading the example of Congreve, Wycherly, &c. for writing of bawdy', appeared in No. 141, 10 September 1732.

13. From 'Prosaicus'

The Grub-street Journal No. 138

24 August 1732

Besides Maevius's epigram, No. 135 of the *Journal* had contributed an answer by Publicus to the defence of Fielding in the *Daily Post* which was largely debators' points and slurs at Fielding's concern to prove his gentility. Then in No. 136 (10 August) Bavius reviewed the controversy, with references to Fielding as 'a venal and venereal Poet' and 'one . . . conversant with strumpets', and published an ironical defence of *The Covent-Garden Tragedy* with a scurrilous plot summary by 'B.B.' In No. 137 Bavius commented on Fielding's Prolegomena to the printed text of *The Covent-Garden Tragedy*, and (except for Bavius's defence of the *Journal* against Philalethes's 'slanders' and another epigram by Maevius in No. 141) the quarrel came to an end with Prosaicus's letter in No. 138:

Dear NED,

The province you assigned me of giving you an account of our Dramatical Poetry, is more irksome than I at first imagined. And as a paper war seems to be commenced between the favourite Poet of Drury-lane and the Grub-street Journal, I should upon no account enter the lists, but to gratify your unaccountable whim, and keep my promise. There is much more pleasure to be found in rural than theatrical scenes; and I envy you the natural and innocent amusements you have in Salop, whilst I am doing penance, in seeing those, which are opposites to nature and innocence at Drury-lane. My Remarks upon *The Old Debauchees* and *Covent-Garden Tragedy* will be very short, several having been already published by others. The Author from his first appearance in the world as a Poet, has always aimed at humour: which, if founded on a right basis, is the chief support and life of all comic writing. But as that basis is nature only, he has often succeeded ill, when he had great hopes of pleasing well. Humour, when embellished by the assistance of wit, still grows more diverting; and hence it is, that CONGREVE is generally more admired than JOHNSON;[1] a great deal of the humour of the latter being found in the former, with that charming additional beauty of wit, of which JOHNSON was not a master. This assertion may not be so readily agreed to by many; but a further defence of it here is foreign to my subject.

There runs through *the Old Debauchees* a continued conatus both at wit and humour: but the Poet, like TANTALUS in the fable, is ever aiming at what is ever deceiving him. His wit is nothing but a few forced common-place strokes against Priestcraft; and the whole character of *Father* MARTIN is but DRYDEN's GOMEZ and SHADWELL's *Teague o' Divelly* curtailed, and divested of their native beauties.[2] I accuse him not for having said any thing against Priestcraft, but for having said nothing new. The characters of old JORDAIN and LAROON are as far from being humorous, as they are from being natural; they might have passed in a Farce; but are altogether inconsistent with Comedy. 'Tis true, there are such things as Priest-ridden and debauched old men; but the Poet has not drawn them with a just humour. The superstition of the one consists chiefly in a deep groan; and the ranting of the other in the natural rodomontadoes and descriptions, such as *leaping over Notre Dame Steeple,* [I. ii. Henley, ix. 284] *and an Opera in purgatory, and Opera of groans, &c.* [III. iv. Henley, ix. 312] If this is what he is pleased to call his *ridiculum acre,* I must ingenuously confess it is stronger than any I have ever met with among the antients or moderns; and is much beyond my taste.

As to the *Covent-Garden Tragedy,* I shall pass by the moral part, which has been attacked by other hands; and consider it only in the Author's own way, whether 'tis a piece of just humour; and as such to be tolerated on the stage. I should not have entered on this subject, since the Author so prudently gave this Piece up the first night, had not his defence of it since (which shews his submission to the Town was not voluntary) required it. As I layed it down before, that nature must be the basis of humour, Mr. F——may say this is just humour, as being a just imitation of nature; and that the characters are drawn from known realities. But humour is to represent the foibles of nature, not its most shocking deformities; and when any thing becomes indecent, it

---

[1] i.e. Ben Jonson.

[2] Dryden, *The Spanish Fryar* (1680); Shadwell, *The Lancashire Witches, and Tegue o' Divelly the Irish Priest* (1681).

is no longer humour, but ribaldry. BEN JOHNSON, the greatest humourist, I believe, of any age, never makes any infringement on morals or good manners: That would be only to pretend to an excellence in which a Poet might be equalled if not excelled, by any rake or bawdy-house bully.

These observations were not occasioned by spleen or malice; I am ignorant of Mr. F——, even as to his person, nor do I envy him his interest with the Managers at Drury-lane. I am not of a party against him, nor the same with DRAMATICUS, PUBLICUS, &c. I have not used any scurrility, but have censured his writings, not him: I pay a deference to his birth, but cannot think it a title to wit, any more than it is to a fortune; nor that every man who has had the honour of being scourged at Eaton or Westminster is a man of sense: this I mention only that I would have no Poet pique himself on his family or his school.

I should now give you some account of the *Mock Doctor*, about which you are so very earnest. 'Tis done from MOLIERE by Mr. F——g. The Town has receiv'd it well; but some Critics say, he has not done justice to the French Poet, nay, that he has translated the very title itself wrong. As I am ignorant of the original, I shall not pretend to pass my judgment upon the Translation: but here, to show my freedom from all prejudice against Mr. F——g, I must confess, that I think it an entertaining Farcical Piece; but whether the pleasure is owing to him, or MOLIERE, I know not. Some say it is owing only to *young* CIBBER's playing his part so well: but tho' a Player may set off and give life to a part, yet action only would not divert, where there was not some original pleasantry. . . .

It has been said *young C——*[1] *was esteemed a judge of something besides acting*: but his management this vacation has not increased his reputation as a judge. If I am not misinformed he apes his father, and must not only judge, but correct. Whatever pretensions the father has to such a liberty, I am sure the son can have none as yet. And even his judgment has been called in question for bringing the *Covent-Garden Tragedy* on the stage, and afterwards pretending to defend it in a public Paper. I am glad, Dear NED, that Bartholomew Fair relieves me from my engagement; tho' I might as well have promised to have sent you an account of the Drolls there, as of those at Drury-lane.

I am, Dear NED, yours,

PROSAICUS

[1] Theophilus Cibber, about whom 'Prosaicus' has been writing in the preceding (deleted) paragraph.

14. John Perceval, first Earl of Egmont, diary entry

20 February 1732–3

From *Diary of the First Earl of Egmont (Viscount Perceval)*, i. 333.

*   *   *

After dinner I went to the new play called 'The Miser', which is well translated from Molière by Mr. Fielding, and well acted.

15. 'Cynick'

The Auditor

23 March 1732-3

This review was reprinted in the *Gentleman's Magazine*, March 1733, iii. 138-9.

Ah! MISER! Quantâ laboras in CHARYBDI![1]

The Miser, a Comedy, having been taken, as the Author confesses, from *Plautus* and *Moliere*, Mr CYNICK bestows some Remarks on it.

In *Poetry*, as in Painting, there are Pieces for the *Judges*, and Pieces for the *Many*. The *first* are satisfied with one *Figure drawn to the Life*, and *of a Piece* with itself. The other require gay Colourings, and Variety of Figures; no matter whether there be any Relation to each other. *Plautus* has drawn the Character of a *Miser*, naturally, as he is; *Moliere* has a little left the Character of a *Miser*, by giving him Thoughts of marrying one in *mean Circumstances*. Our *English* Poet, the Impetuosity of whose Genius allows him not time to consider *Nature*, has given his *Miser* not only Thoughts of Marriage with one whose Wealth he has but an indifferent Account of, but makes him very much *in Love*, and contrary to his Interest; an Absurdity *Moliere* avoided.

The Character of *Mariana* (which in *Moliere* is most beautiful) is no more of a Piece than that of *Lovegold* the Miser. In the first Act *She is a most intolerable Coquette*, and eternally at Cards;—This, it seems is the Reverse of the Medal; *the right side contains Beauty, Wit, Genteelness, Politeness.* But, where is the Difference between the *Right* and the *Reverse*? Beauty, Wit, Genteelness, Politeness, are all Ingredients of a Coquette. In the second Act she declares Love for *Frederick*. In the third she disclaims it, and consents to marry the Miser. In the fourth the Contract is signed, and *Frederick* dismiss'd and laugh'd at. In the fifth

---

[1] 'Poor wretch! How great the Charybdis you have been struggling in!' Horace, *Odes*, I. xxvii. 18-19.

she enters as Mistress of *Lovegold*'s Family; and a wonderous Discovery is made, *viz.* the Forfeiture of the Bond is to be bestowed on *Frederick* whom *Mariana* marries. If she really loved *Frederick*, why did she consent to marry the Miser? If not, why bestow on him the 8000*l.* and herself?

The principal Plot of the Play is as ridiculous as the rest. A *true Miser*, if he had been foolish enough to have signed a Bond of 10,000*l.* as he did, to marry *Mariana*, would have married, rather than pay the Forfeiture. When she was once his Wife; he might have govern'd her as he pleas'd.

A young Girl that really loves, would not have ventur'd so far, tho' she was a Coquette. But it's to be question'd, whether a Coquette can *really love*; and if she *can*, whether she would so easily give up her *Love* to her *Coquetry*, when nothing obliges her to do it; which is the Case of *Mariana*.

These are the two principal Characters in the *English* MISER, and are contrary to the Maxims laid down by the best Criticks, as well as Poets,

Servetur ad imum
Qualis ab *incepto*, processerit, & sibi constet.[1]

Notwithstanding, the *Auditor* allows it to be the only Play deserving the Name of Comedy, this long while, except the *married Philosopher*.[2]

---

[1] '[A character] must be kept to the end the same as he has been from the beginning, and must be consistent.' Horace, *Ars poetica*, ll. 126–7.

[2] John Kelley, *The Married Philosopher* (1732).

16. 'Belvidera'

The Gentleman's Magazine

April 1733, iii. 172

A reply to the criticism of *The Miser* in *The Auditor*, 23 March 1732–3 (No. 15):

Mr AUDITOR

I am surprized, Sir, that in your Criticism on the *Miser* (See p. 138.) you talk so insensibly of Love! Why do you think it strange a *Miser* at threescore should be *in Love*? If you think the Love of Gold has so lin'd his Soul, that no other Love can make an Entrance, you are mistaken; for, if he were made up of that rich Metal, the Heat and Force of Love would soon dissolve and melt him, till he were as free and generous, as if he had never known a covetous Thought.

BELVIDERA.

Belvidera should consider, that the Poet was to draw the Character of a *Miser*, and not of a *Miser in Love*.

Q.C.

17. Jonathan Swift, *On Poetry: A Rapsody*

(1733), ll. 393-400

Swift's Poems, ed. Harold Williams (2nd ed., 1958), ii. 654. These lines, reprinted in the Swift-Pope *New Miscellany* of 1734, place Fielding in the company of the Dunces. However, the Dublin edition of 1734 changed 'That Feilding' to 'The Laureat Hyde', and George Faulkner (certainly as Swift's spokesman) added a note in his edition of 1735: '*In the* London *Edition, instead of* Laureat, *was maliciously inserted Mr.* Fielding, *for whose ingenious Writings the supposed Author hath manifested a great Esteem.*' Harold Williams (ibid.) accepts Faulkner's word that Swift did not himself write 'Feilding'—in which case Pope, Swift's London coadjutor, seems a likely candidate.[1]

> For Instance: When you rashly think,
> No Rhymer can like *Welsted* sink.
> His Merits balanc'd you shall find,
> That *Feilding* leaves him far behind.
> *Concannen*, more aspiring Bard,
> Climbs downwards, deeper by a Yard:
> Smart JEMMY MOOR with Vigor drops,
> The Rest pursue as thick as Hops:[2]

[1] Cf. his influence on the *Grub-street Journal* and his revision of the London edition of Swift's *Verses on the Death of Dr. Swift* (see *The Correspondence of Alexander Pope*, ed. George Sherburn [1956], iv. 130).

[2] For Welsted, Concannen, and Moor, see Williams's notes (p. 654) and Pope's *Dunciad* ii. 207; iii. 169; ii, 299–304; ii. 35–50

18. Jonathan Swift, in conversation

c. 1733

Reported in the *Memoirs of Mrs. Laetitia Pilkington* (1754), iii. 155.

★   ★   ★

The Dean [Jonathan Swift] told me he did remember that he had not laughed above twice in his life—once at some trick a mountebank's merry-andrew played, and the other time was at the circumstance of Tom Thumb's killing the ghost;[1] and I can assure Mr. Fielding the Dean had a high opinion of his wit, which must be a pleasure to him, as no man was ever better qualified to judge, possessing it so eminently himself.

★   ★   ★

19. From *The Connoisseur. A Satire on the Modern Men of Taste*

n.d. [c. 1734], p. 20

★   ★   ★

F——with Comedy now best can please,
England's Moliere! he writes and charms with ease;
Tho' Careless, every Thought is bold and new,
His Beauties many, and his Faults are few.

★   ★   ★

[1] Mrs. Pilkington is mistaken: the ghost of Tom Thumb is killed by Grizzle.

20. From 'An Author's Will'

The Universal Spectator

6 July 1734

This mock testament refers to Fielding's prolific output, his haste, and his negligence of composition (alluded to in Cooke's defence of *A Modern Husband*, above, No. 5):

*   *   *

Item, I give and bequeath to my very *negligent* Friend *Henry Drama*, Esq; all my INDUSTRY. And whereas the World may think this an unnecessary Legacy, forasmuch as the said *Henry Drama*, Esq, brings on the Stage *four Pieces* every Season; yet as such Pieces are always wrote with uncommon *Rapidity*, and during such fatal Intervals only as the *Stocks* have been on the *Fall*, this Legacy will be of use to him to revise and correct his Works. Furthermore, for fear the said *Henry Drama* should make an ill Use of the said *Industry*, and expend it all on a *Ballad Farce*, it's my Will the said Legacy should be paid him by equal Portions, and as his Necessities may require.[1]

*   *   *

[1] Cf. a verse satire called 'The Dramatic Sessions: or the Stage Contest of 1734' by 'Scriblerus Theatricus', published in August 1734, which attacked 'F—ld–ng . . . with his heavy Quixote' and stressed his idleness as the chief cause of his dullness. *The Grub-street Journal* attacked this scurrilous poem in Nos. 241, 242, and 243, the issues for 14, 22, and 29 August 1734.

AN OLD MAN TAUGHT WISDOM: OR, THE VIRGIN UNMASK'D

17 January 1734–5

THE UNIVERSAL GALLANT

10 February 1734–5

21. Aaron Hill

From *The Prompter*

18 February 1734–5

Hill includes *An Old Man Taught Wisdom: or, the Virgin Unmask'd* and *The Universal Gallant* in a survey of the season's dramatic offerings in London:

*   *   *

I pass by the *Virgin Unmasked*, and *Plot*,[1] as Things that do not deserve any Notice at all. . . .

The last Piece brought on the Stage, this Season, was the UNIVERSAL GALLANT; or, DIFFERENT HUSBANDS, wrote by the prolifick Mr. *Fielding*.—And, as in the *Toy-shop*,[2] I had the Pleasure of remarking, that the good Taste of the Town wanted only to be *awakened* to become as *strong* as ever, so here I had an Opportunity of making an Observation very much in Favour of the Town, *viz.* That the Accusation of BAD TASTE is very *falsly* and *unjustly* brought against them, since if the *Town* had really the bad Taste, they are represented to have, this

---

[1] John Kelley, *The Plot* (22 January 1734–5).
[2] Robert Dodsley, *The Toy Shop* (3 February 1734–5).

Play would have run the remaining Part of the Season, in an *un-interrupted* Course of *Applause*. I had likewise an Opportunity of observing much more *Impartiality* than I expected, in the Behaviour of the *Audience*, for till almost the third Act was over, they sat very quiet, in hopes it would mend, till finding it grew still *worse* and *worse*, they at length lost all Patience, and not an *Expression* or *Sentiment* afterwards passed without its *deserved Censure*.

★   ★   ★

PASQUIN

5 March 1735-6

22. Aaron Hill

The Prompter

2 April 1736

The very great Run *Pasquin* has already had, and is still like to have, is the severest Blow, that cou'd be given to our Theatres, and the strongest Confirmation of an Opinion, I have ventured, *singly*, to advance, *viz. That the Stage may,* (and as it may, ought to) *be supported without* PANTOMIME. While our Theatrick Sovereigns, with the best Actors the Age can afford, are forced to call in the Assistance of *wonderful Scenary, surprising Transformations, beautiful Landscapes, Dancers,* (the very best, both in the graceful and humourous Manner) and in short, all the attendant Powers of *inexplicable Dumb Shew,* at a very great Expence; a Gentleman, under the Disadvantage of a very bad House, with scarce an Actor, and at very little Expence, by the single Power of *Satire, Wit,* and *Common Sense,* has been able to run a Play on for 24 Nights, which is now, *but* beginning to *rise* in the Opinion of the Town.

BUT this is not all; *Farinelli's* Benefit has pass'd,[1] without an Article mentioned in any Paper, of a single Present made him; nay, I have been told, some of the Subscribers *used* their Tickets; yet every body can remember last Year, what an Epidemical Madness was diffused all over the Town, caught by a Poison he communicated to every body within the Reach of his Breath, against which there cou'd then be found no *Antidote,* nay, not even a *Preservative.*

ENTERTAINMENT is now a Word out of Fashion, and wou'd be quite forgot, were it not kept in use by the *Play-bills,* but even here, I observe

---

[1] Carlo Broschi, called Farinelli, the Neapolitan castrato who had made his début in London in 1734, was customarily showered with expensive gifts by his English admirers.

a very considerable Difference of *Stile*, as well as *Effect*; for not only the *Advance Money* is publickly declared to be returned to those, *who find no Entertainment* after the Play is over, but it is *actually done*, as I was a pleased Eye Witness of the other Night myself. And to what shall we ascribe this unexpected, sudden Change? Why, COMMON SENSE has appeared in Person on the Stage.

In my Paper, NºVI. so long ago as *Nov.* 29, 1734. I published, but not at the Request of the Managers, who, I discover'd since, had turned her out themselves, a Hue and Cry after COMMON SENSE, who had quite left the Theatres of this great City. About a Month after I received Advice, that she was retired into the Country, and was protected, till the Day of his Death, by an honest Vicar, who, in taking her into his Care, shew'd a Charity, not generally practised by the rest of his Brethren, who, for the most Part, are as hard-hearted against any Thing, that bears the Shew of *Common Sense*, out of the PALE, as the *merciless* Banishers of her, from the abovesaid Theatres. When this good Man died, a Gentleman out of the Country sent me a Letter, signed *Verax*, to acquaint me, that he was resolved, in Imitation of the Deceased, to keep COMMON SENSE with him, till the Theatres were (once more) worthy to receive her. I little thought then, that *Verax*, and Mr. F——d——g, were one and the same Person: For tho' this latter has always appeared inclinable to an Alliance with COMMON SENSE in the main, yet he has at Times taken such Liberties with her, that for a while I looked upon him as a Person in open War with her. —But, to do him Justice, I now think he quitted *Common Sense*, in Compliance to the vicious Taste of the Town, and not his *own*; that he reserved shewing the Regard he had for her, in some of his Pieces, till he knew he shou'd not be laughed at, for daring to shew himself a Friend to her. I am the more inclined to this Belief, as about the Time COMMON SENSE left the Theatres, the abovesaid Gentleman retired into the Country, where he has continued ever since, till this Winter, that he returned, the professed Friend to COMMON SENSE, whom he brought up with him, and breathing nothing but Revenge against the vile Usurpers of her lawful Empire, THE STAGE. An Example worthy Imitation, and which I venture to recommend to the *Practice*, not the *Approbation*, (for barely to approve, is negative) of such GENIUS'S, as are left in *England*, in whose Power it will be, by seconding this first Attempt, and accustoming the Stage to the Sight of COMMON SENSE, to make her at last, the only loved *Entertainment* there.

BUT I would not advise any, YET, to venture her NAKED on that

Ground, but to arm her, like the Porcupine, *all round*, with the SHARPS of *Wit, Satire,* and *Humour,* of the *strongest,* and most *piercing* Kind. Let it, at first, like Pictures bigger than the Life, command Admiration by the Force of its Appearance: By Degrees the *Colouring* may be *taken down,* and the *Terrible* softened. It may afterwards be brought nearer Life, and deal in *beautiful Proportion,* and *graceful Attitude,* instead of *forcible Muscling,* and *bold Posture.*

THE *Pathetick* and *Delicate,* in Dramatick Common Sense, (which nevertheless is the highest Effort Human Genius can reach) would, at present not be felt. Like a Picture of *Correggio,* where Grace and Nature delicately represented, shew all the Art of the Painter, and fill the *true, tasting* Connoisseur with inexpressible Delight, yet scarce draw the Eye of the *Vulgar,* or the *Many;* while *Michael Angelo, rough, grand, bold,* that makes Nature in every Composition stronger than she is, never fails of attracting the most indifferent Eye. But to come nearer the present Test of publick Taste for Poetry, I would recommend the *Dutch* and *Flemish* Schools, where Nature is every where either *low,* or *burlesqued.* Here the common, injudicious Gazer, justifies by his own Example the Pencil of the Painter; the Pleasure he expresses in looking, putting him in the very *outrageous* Attitudes of Joy he is laughing at.

THE ingenious Author of *Pasquin,* conscious how dangerous it might be, to venture *Common Sense* in the Stile of *Correggio* at first, has, in Imitation of some of the best of Painters, form'd to himself a Manner, out of different Stiles, which (tho' the Particulars may be traced) is, in the whole, *Original.* Thus in the Tragedy we see the bold, daring Pencil of *Michael Angelo.* Satires start out of every Line; they are *seen* and *felt.* Even when they *smile,* they look *terrible,* and *strike* with *Force.* He has here and there given them a *Flemish* Touch, for the sake of the *Vulgar.* He has been rather too sparing of the *Correggio Manner;* for tho' in some Parts his Allegory is delicate in the highest Degree, he has heightned the Colouring so much, that it comes too *full* and *gross* upon us. We lose the Beauty of *Simplicity,* in the Strength with which *it* is lay'd on; but he is justifiable; for, as I observed before, the *Pathetick* and *Delicate* is not to be ventured yet. *Wit, Humour,* and *Satire,* on a *Substratum* of COMMON SENSE, *warmly coloured,* must be preparatory, and have a due Course of Admiration. I cou'd have wish'd he had been a little less *Flemish* in his Comedy; for tho' the *Corruption* he strikes at would not have been *felt,* had it been less *coarsely hit,* than it is *practised* in the *World,* I question, whether so dangerous a vice as *Corruption* will not lose of the *Disgust* it ought to inspire, by being laugh'd at with so much Wit: A Thing we laugh at only, is no longer terrible. If he had dipped his Pencil in the Colours of *Michael Angelo*; and shewn the terrible Effects of Corruption, in the Ruin of a Borough or Corporation, he had render'd the State a publick Service; but *Trapwit* will tell us, *It would not have been a true Picture of Life, for Boroughs thrive by Corruption*.

SOME Persons have injudiciously thought, the Poet levels his Satire, (not against the Abuses of, but) against Religion, Law, and Physick, themselves; but if they would attend to the Characters of the Speakers, they would find, all that is said is only against the *Abuse*, and not the *Foundation* of each.

I CAN'T help observing here, with a good deal of Mortification, tho' quite in Favour of the Poet's Skill in judging, what will, or will not, succeed, that it was a considerable Time, before the Tragedy, (tho' by much the finer Performance of the two) made its Way. I have heard it called, *stupid, dull, nonsensical*, with other Appellations, modern Criticks give to what they don't understand, and that the Comedy supported it. A short, humourous Advertisement engaged a close Attention, and set it a going, and now I believe it supports the Comedy, at least it loses nothing by coming after it.

I AM told *Pasquin* is preparing to attack *Pantomime*, and is to begin with the *Fall of Phaeton*.[1] I heartily wish him Success; he is so much in Vogue with all Sorts of Persons, that I believe, if the Thing is practicable, he alone can compass it. But I wish his Burlesque of *Pantomime* may not be formed upon the Model of *that*, of Tumblers, to introduce it on his little Theatre. But let him reflect, that his first Step towards that, is a *Remove* from *Common Sense*; to whose Friendship he owes so much already, and whom, without the blackest Ingratitude, he can never forsake. Besides, has it not appeared, that the very first Attempt of *Common Sense* has done more in one Instant, than *Pantomime* ever since its Introduction, and during its long Continuance, has been able to effectuate, PLEASED EVERY BODY!

BUT what I now mention, arises more from my own Fears, than any Reason I have to believe it intended. Interest is a very prevailing Argument, especially with Poets; he has shewn in his *Election* the Power of Gold; let him that knows it so well, arm himself against it, and continue, in all he undertakes, as he has so happily begun, to carry *Common Sense* along with him, and never lose Sight of her one Instant.

---

[1] Fielding parodied William Pritchard's *The Fall of Phaeton* (28 February 1736) in *Tumble-Down Dick; or, Phaeton in the Subs* (29 April 1736).

23. From 'A Letter to a Friend in the Country. . . .'

The Old Whig

8 April 1736

These remarks on *Pasquin* conclude a political article, which was reprinted in the *Gentleman's Magazine*, April 1736, vi. 200

$\star$ $\star$ $\star$

The pacific Disposition of *Europe* has had no small Influence on our Parties here; and the Press itself has almost had a Cessation of Arms. Papers come out as formerly; the *Craftsman* on *Saturdays*; and the *Gazetter* (as Miss calls it in *Pasquin*) every Day in the Week. But the Wit, Satire, and new Sentiments in either, would be far from crowding a political *Index.*—You'll ask me, perhaps, Whence I fetch the Quotation? And what I mean by *Pasquin*? 'Tis a *Dramatic Satire* now upon the Stage, that bears that Title; and is full of Sarcasm from one End to the other. The Humour is very Popular at least, tho' not all equally delicate. It is a Representation of a Rehearsal of a Comedy and Tragedy. The Latter is principally pointed at the Abuses of the *Law* and *Physick*; and *Priestcraft* is delineated under the Character of *Firebrand Tartuffe*, Priest of the *Sun*. You would be greatly pleas'd with the *Panegyrick*, as Mr *Fustian* calls it, on our Clergy, who act with Views so different from this Heathen Priest! I cannot omit observing the Delicacy of the Poet, in not introducing the Minister of the *Queen* of *Common Sense*, who must be suppos'd to have advis'd the Checking the Ambition and Insolence of this Priest: Tho' I must at the same Time own to you, that the avoiding this Complement to Great Men, led a dull Fellow of my Acquaintance to fancy that *Common Sense* made use of no Minister at all. There are such strong Strokes in this *Satire*, that if it continues to be follow'd with the crowded Audiences it has now had for above 40 Nights together; some Gentlemen will feel its Influence more effectually, and be more hurt in the Esteem of Mankind, than by a Thousand *Examinations*, tho' ever so well writ, to expose their *Schemes*.

24. Mary Granville Pendarves (later Delany), letter

22 April 1736

From a letter to Jonathan Swift, *The Correspondence of Jonathan Swift*, ed. Harold Williams (1965), iv. 475.

* * *

When I went out of Town last autumn the reigning madness was Faranelli, I find it now turn'd on Pasquin a dramatick satire on the times, it has had almost as long a run as the beggars Opera, but in my opinion not with equal merit, though it has humour.

* * *

25. 'Marforio'

The Grub-street Journal Nos. 330 and 332

22 April and 6 May 1736

Review signed 'Marforio', probably by Richard Russel, a non-juring clergyman and editor of the *Grub-street Journal*. See Hillhouse, p. 184. In No. 229, 15 April, the *Journal* had published a sharply worded note that Pope had not, as rumour had it, been present at a performance of *Pasquin*: 'we think it very probable that a person of his uncommon sense and wit will not have any curiosity to see it acted at all.' This was followed in the next issue by Marforio's long review. It is to be noted that since the attacks on Fielding in 1732, the *Journal* had only made passing allusions to him, as in the verses addressed 'To a Gentleman who had bound up some of Swift's and Pope's poems with one of F——'s plays' (No. 179)—

> In this position be assured
> He's more conspicuously undone,
> For Mercury's but more obscured
> By being placed too near the sun

—and in a character sketch of a flirt (No. 268), which notes that 'there is not a woman in England of this character but what has ruined more young ladies than either the Charitable Corporation or Beau Fielding.'

When a Nation is divided into two opposite Political Parties, and almost all the Learned exercise one or other of three different Professions, the generality of the people, consisting of unlearned and undesigning persons, are very liable to be imposed upon by the pretences and practices of the most eminent in those Parties and Professions. It is therefore expedient at all times, that they should be advised to stand upon their guard against such ill designing persons. But it is absolutely necessary, at a time, when corruption has so far infected all Parties and Professions, that the most considerable persons in every one of them are guided only by self-interest, having no other aim, but to advance and inrich themselves by the simplicity and credulity of the rest of the world. To make this advice the more effectual, and to set all these deceivers in a true light, it must needs be very proper to represent the Candidates for any place in Parliament, of either Party, as void of all public spirit, honour, and integrity; and the Gentlemen of the three Professions, Law, Physic, and Divinity, as exercising them in direct opposition to COMMON SENSE. And as Theatrical representations strike the senses most forcibly, and leave the deepest impression upon the mind; the surest way to render all such persons ridiculous, and consequently despised, is to introduce them personated upon the stage, and there openly acting those vile parts, which they dayly act in a more clandestine manner upon the stage of the world. This the Author of *Pasquin* has done: and if success be a certain sign of the goodness of a Dramatic Piece, as it is generally taken to be; the prodigious success of this has fixed it secure beyond the attaques of any malicious Critic. A few impartial Observations upon it however may be of some use, to manifest the goodness of the design, and the ingenuity of the execution; from both which it may be inferred, how justly it has been received with *universal applause* for so many nights together.

The design of the *Comedy* is to ridicule the late Election of members of Parliament, by representing the Candidates of both Parties as bribeing their Electors. Those on the Court side are dignified with the titles of *Lord* PLACE and *Colonel* PROMISE, to denote that the gentlemen in that interest aim at nothing but *places*, and have little or no regard to their word and *promise*. The names of the Country Candidates, *Sir Henry* FOX-CHACE and *Squire* TANKARD, plainly intimate, that the chief busi[ness] of their lives is hunting and drinking; to which they are as much addicted as the Courtiers to gaming and whoring. *Sir* HENRY and the *Squire* are chosen by *a majority of two or three score*; but the honest *Mayor*, at the instigation of his wife, returns the two former. Such qualifications in the Members, and the occasion and manner of returning them, must needs excite a proper regard and reverence for laws enacted by such Senators.

Lord PLACE, in his first conversation with Mrs. *Mayoress* and her Daughter, tells them he 'does not question but *Miss* (if she come to Town) will be soon taken into keeping by some man of Quality.' Pag.

14. [II. i. Henley, xi. 179] With this they both seem very well pleased; and *Mrs. Mayoress*, like a good *Mother*, in the Drurian signification of the word, advises her daughter to go into *keeping*. Pag. 16, 30. [II. i, III. i. Henley, xi. 181, 195]

To justifie *Lord* PLACE's asking *Mrs. Mayoress*, 'Whether she was at the last *Ridotto?*' Poet TRAPWIT says, 'She had been woman to a Woman of Quality.' Pag. 13, 14. But there is a greater difficulty which he leaves uncleared, and of which even *Poet* FUSTIAN takes not the least notice, and that is, How it came to pass, that *the wife of a poor Country tradesman*, (as she calls herself, Pag. 15.) to whom she had been married long enough to have a daughter ready to be *taken into keeping*, should have been absent from the Town no longer than a year. Which it is plain she had not, from her answer to Lord PLACE, Pag. 14. 'Oh, my Lord! mention not those dear *Ridotto's* to me, who have been confined these twelve long months in the country'. But TRAPWIT's solution on another occasion, Pag. 15. may serve as well on this, 'Gad that's true; I had forgot. . . . it's a fault I sometimes fall into——a man ought to have the memory of a Devil to remember every little thing'. [II. i. Henley, xi. 179–80]

At Pag. 28. Poet TRAPWIT swears *Oons and the Devil* [III. i. Henley, xi. 193], i.e. by the wounds of Christ, and by the Devil: and Poet FUSTIAN, to shew he has as much religion as his brother, swears in the same manner, Pag. 59. [V. i. Henley, xi. 222]

Drams are generally used as a remedy in lowness of spirits, in order to raise them: but *Lord* PLACE, upon hearing the joyful news, that the *Mayor* intended to return him, says, 'Madam, this news has so transported my Spirits, that I fear some ill effect, unless you instantly give me a Dram'. Pag. 31. Immediately upon which TRAPWIT says, 'If it had not been for that Dram, my Play had been at an end'; and yet in the very next words, adds, that his 'Plot, which has hitherto open'd itself like the infant Spring, will display itself, like a ripe Matron, in its full Summer's bloom'. [III. i. Henley, xi. 196] A poet of a less extraordinary genius, according to the more common way of thinking, would have compared this *ripe Matron* rather to the *ripe* fruit than to the *full bloom of Summer*.

At Pag. 34. [III. i. Henley, xi. 199] the *Colonel* and *Miss Mayoress* enter as just married; which cannot but be very surprizing to the audience, since at Pag. 30. [III. i. Henley, xi. 194–5] *Miss* had dutifully complied with her Mama's advice, and seemed determined to go *into keeping*.

The Moral of the whole *Comedy*, in order to *set our judgments right*, is beautifully summed up in the two last lines. Pag. 35.

> Nor like our Misses, about Bribing quarrel.
> When *better Herring* is in *neither Barrel*.
>   [III. i. Henley, xi. 199.]

In the two Parties, it seems of Court and Countrey, the Elected and the Electors are both equally corrupt, the one bribing and the other bribed; and therefore it is foolish and ridiculous, for a person out of love to his country, to ingage himself in any dispute about the Election of Members of Parliament. An admirable moral!

The design of the *Tragedy* is to expose the Gentlemen who profess either Law, or Physick, or Divinity, as carrying on the business of each Profession directly in opposition to *Common-Sense*.——In the first Act, Pag. 42. *Firebrand*, Priest of the Sun, addresses himself thus to *Law*, *Physick* being present.

> *Fireb.* Speak boldly; by the Powers I serve, I swear
> You speak in safety, even tho' you speak
> Against the Gods, provided that you speak
> Not against Priests.

To incourage *Law* to *speak* out, *Firebrand* swears secrecy by *the Gods he serves*; at the same time letting him know, that he may *safely speak even against* those very *Gods*. Such an Oath must needs create in *Law* a great degree of trust and confidence, and induce him to speak his mind freely in the following words.

> *Law.* What then can the Powers
> Mean by these Omens, but to rouze us up
> From the Lethargic Sway of *Common-Sense*?
> And well they urge, for while that drowsy Queen
> Maintains her Empire, what becomes of us?

Here the Gods are piously and rationally supposed by their *Omens* to design to *rouse up Divinity, Law,* and *Physick*, that they may throw off the Empire of *Common-Sense*, and in confederacy with them impose upon mankind. This is somewhat extraordinary and surprizing; as is the representing of *Common-Sense* to be a *drowsy Queen* governing with a *lethargick sway*; but still more so are the instances of her *lethargick sway*, produced immediately by *Physick* and *Law*.

Phys. Yes, by Heav'n
She stops my proud ambition! keeps me down
When I would soar upon an Eagle's wing,
And thence look down and dose the world below.
    Law. Thou know'st, my Lord of *Physick*, I had long
Been privileg'd by Custom immemorial,
In Tongues unknown, or rather none at all,
My Edicts to deliver thro' the Land;
When this proud Queen, this *Common-Sense*, abridg'd
My Power, and made me understood by all?

So that the *stopping* of the *proud ambition* of *Physick*, and the *abridging* of the *power* of *Law*, are instances brought to prove the *drowsiness* of *Common-Sense*, and her *lethargick* government.

Law and *Physick* having declared their disaffection [with] Queen *Common-Sense*, *Firebrand* makes an open confession of his hypocrisy, and of the real design of all his actions. Pag. 43.

> Know, thro' this Mask,
> Which to impose on vulgar minds I wear,
> I am an Enemy to *Common-Sense*;
> But this not for Ambition's earthly cause,
> But to enlarge the worship of the Sun:
> To give his Priests a just degree of Power,
> And more than half the Profits of the Land.
>   [IV. i. Henley, xi. 206–7]

Here he disclaims all *earthly Ambition*, and in consequence of his renouncing it, declares he aims only at *a just degree of Power*, and above *half the profits of the Land*. This declaration seems a little too free and open; and might probably have occasioned some dissention betwixt these three Conspirators. For being all three upon a level, an equal division of all *the profits of the Land* amongst them, might justly have been insisted on by *Law* and *Physick*. But they have so great a regard for *Divinity*, and pay her so just a deference (instances of which we meet with every day) that they acquiesce in this Partition Treaty, and are satisfied with less than *half the profits of the Land.*—The justness of this representation of the ambition and avarice of the English Clergy cannot but be evident to all, who observe how much they have increased in wealth and power for above these last forty years. How by receiving only part of the tenth part *of the profits of the land*, (settled on them by Law) so freely pay'd by the Laity, without the least deduction, they have been incouraged to grasp at *more than half the profits of all the Lands* in the kingdom.

At Pag. 44. *Firebrand* speaks thus to *Queen Common-Sense,*

> The Gods are angry, and must be appeas'd:
> Nor do I know to that a readier way
> Than by beginning to appease their Priests,
> Who groan for Power, and cry out after Honour.

This speech seems fitter to have been spoken to *Queen Ignorance*; and might well provoke *Queen Common-Sense* to return a cross answer. But we must suppose it spoken to her as a *drowsy Queen*; and that being suddenly awaked by it, she was a little peevish.

In Pag. 45. An *Officer* enters, and tells *Queen Common-Sense* this strange piece of news:

> *Queen Ignorance* is landed in your Realm,
> With a vast Power from *Italy* and *France*
> Of Singers, Fidlers, Tumblers, and Rope-dancers.
>   [IV. i. Henley, xi. 208-9]

This *landing* is after the *mighty Deluge*, which, as *Law* just now very poetically expressed it, s w a m *into our Hall*; which happened on Feb. 17. but this *vast power of Singers,* &c has been coming hither from time to time for several years. And if Q. *Ignorance* had not presided here before this time, how could Q. *Common-Sense* complain of the abuses of *Law* in Pag. 44. [IV. i. Henley, xi. 208] and how could my Lord of *Law* in Pag. 43, say, that by *custom immemorial* he *had been privileg'd to deliver* his *Edicts in tongues unknown,* 'till Q. *Common-Sense abridg'd his power*? [IV. i. Henley, xi. 207] By this, one would rather imagine, that Q. *Ignorance* had reigned here from time *immemorial;* and that Q. *Common-Sense* was but newly *arrived.*—But it is to be supposed, that the former had been dethroned, and forced to abdicate, by the latter; and was now returned with a foreign *power*, in order to recover her dominations.

⋆   ⋆   ⋆

The Remarks *on* Pasquin, *begun in* No. 330, *continued.*

QUEEN *Common-Sense,* upon receiving the news, that *Queen Ignorance* was just landed, with *Singers, Fidlers, Tumblers,* &c orders

Law and *Physick* to *join* her *with* their *utmost levies straight*: concluding with this direction to *Firebrand,*

> Go, Priest, and drive all frightful Omens hence;
> To fright the Vulgar they are your Pretence,
> But sure the Gods will side with *Common-Sense.*

Upon his informing her of *strange Omens,* just before the news of this invasion came, she owned to him, that

> The Gods, indeed, *had* Reason for their Anger,

And promised that

> Sacrifice *should* be offer'd to them.

But here under the very first surprize of this invasion, when it had actually happened, she ridicules all those *Omens,* as being only his *pretence to fright the Vulgar,* and bids him *drive* them *all* away; but says not one word of performing, in this time of danger, the promise she had made just before of *offering sacrifices* to the Gods.—But her conduct is consistent enough, if we suppose her *sure,* that they would *side with* her, as she declares in the last line of her speech to *Firebrand;* tho' she happened to be as much mistaken, as if she had been Q. *Ignorance.*

As soon as she is off the stage, *Firebrand* says to *Law* and *Physick,*

> They know their interest better; or at least
> Their Priests do for 'em, and themselves.

The *Gods,* whom these *Priests,* the Clergy of the Church of England, pretend to worship, *know their interest better,* or their Priests for them, than to *side with* Common-Sense.

He goes on——

> Oh! Lords,
> This Queen of *Ignorance.* . . .
> Is the most gentle, and most pious Queen,
> So fearful of the Gods, that she believes
> Whate'er their Priests affirm. And by the Sun
> Faith is no Faith, if it falls short of that.
> I'd be infallible. [IV. i. Henley, xi. 209]

And in the 2d Act, at Pag. 50. he asserts directly that he is *infallible,* to Q. *Common-Sense* herself.

> *Fireb.* Why I, his Priest infallible, have told you.
> Q. C. S. How do I know you are infallible?
> *Fireb.* Ha! do you doubt it? nay, if you doubt that,
> I will prove nothing. [IV. i. Henley, xi. 214]

In these places, the generality of the English Clergy are represented as claiming *infallibility* to themselves, and a blind obedience from all the Laity in *believing* whatever they *affirm*. This is declared to be the onely proper meaning of that *Faith* which they require.——This is a great discovery, which our Poet must have made by his intimate acquaintance with the Clergy; there being neither any such claim, nor any such account of *Faith*, to be found in any of their writeings.

Firebrand concludes his speech to *Law* and *Physick*, begun in Pag. 45. with this advice to the latter:

> And you, my good Lord *Physick*, to the Queen;
> Handle her Pulse, potion and pill her well.

The *Queen*, in the hearing of *Firebrand*, had but this very minute commanded *Physick* to *join* her *with* his *utmost levies*, in order to oppose Q. *Ignorance* by force of arms. Here *Firebrand* advises him to *repair* immediately to her, in order to feel her *pulse*, and plie her with *pill and potion*. This advice must necessarily be grounded upon one or other of these suppositions: either that *Firebrand* had forgotten what she had just now said to *Physick*; or that *Physick* had forgotten it; or that this *Queen* of *Common-Sense*, would so far forget herself in this imminent danger, as, instead of taking arms and going to fight, to take a dose of physick and go to sh——.

Lord Physick in his answer, among other things, complains, that Q. *Common-Sense* had publickly *averr'd*,

> That *Walter Cruel* is the best Physician.

Since this was her Majesty's opinion, it is a wonder that she had not dignified this physician with knighthood; the conundrum upon the name would have been much improved by the addition of *Sir*.

Firebrand then concludes the First Act in this exulting manner,

> Yes, by the Sun, my Heart laughs loud within me,
> To see how easily the World's deceiv'd;
> To see this *Common-Sense* thus tumbled down
> By men, whom all the cheated Nations own
> To be the strongest Pillars of her Throne.
> [IV. i. Henley, xi. 210]

So that all *the World*, it seems, *all Nations* are *deceiv'd* and *cheated* by the generality of Lawyers, Physicians, and Divines; and it was consequently a generous, public-spirited undertaking in our Poet to endeavour to undeceive them.

In the Second Act, in Pag. 49. the *Ghost* of *Comedy* speaks thus to
Q. *Common-Sense* asleep,

> ———— ———— Think not to survive
> My Murder long; for while thou art on Earth,
> The Convocation will not meet again.
> The Lawyers cannot rob men of their rights;
> Physicians cannot dose away their Souls.
>   [IV. i. Henley, xi. 212–13]

That what has been, maybe, has been hitherto generally allowed to be
a true saying: but our Author, a great opposer of ancient errors, here
asserts the contrary. For it is evident from the discourse between *Law,
Physick,* and *Divinity* in Pag. 42, 43. [IV. i. Henley, xi. 205–07] and from
the complaint of Q. *Common-Sense* concerning the abuses of *Law,* in
Pag. 44, and those of *Divinity,* Pag. 45, 51 [IV. i. Henley, xi. 209, 214–
15]; that they are all three represented as having imposed upon mankind, during the life of *Common-Sense,* and of *Comedy* too; and the
Convocation, no doubt, sate within that period. But our Poet's prophetic
spirit, speaking through the mouth of a *Ghost,* foretells, that these, and
several other things, which had been done, while Q. *Common-Sense*
was *on earth, will not,* and *can not* ever happen again while she continues
here.

The opinion of the appearance of Spirits being ridiculed, as never
seen *unless in sleep,* the English Clergy are represented at Pag. 50, as
violent enemies to all *Toleration,* and furious promoters of sanguinary
persecutions; and that for this surprizing reason, in order to hinder the
apparition of *Ghosts. Firebrand* says to Q. *Common-Sense,*

> Make a huge Fire, and burn all Unbelievers,
> Ghosts will be hang'd ere venture near a Fire.

In which lines, three great discoveries are made as in the person of a
Divine: that murder is the way to prevent all apparitions; that the
murder of those who do not believe there are any apparitions is the
way to prevent the belief that there are; and that a Ghost had rather be
hang'd than burn'd.

Firebrand insults the Queen in the next page thus,

> ———— ———— Madam, you yourself
> Are a most deadly Enemy to the Sun,
> And ALL his Priests have greatest Cause to wish
> You had been never born. [IV. i. Henley, xi. 214]

ALL the Clergy in general, without any exception, *have the greatest cause to wish*, that *Common-Sense* had never been in the world: and consequently the Christian Religion, as taught by ALL PRIESTS, is directly contrary to *Common-Sense*. This declaration would have been put by a poet of a more common genius into the mouth of a professed enemy to *Priests*: but to make it the more surprizing, it is pronounced here by a *Priest* himself.

Nor less surprizing is the account which he gives of the origin of Ecclesiastical Power.

> *Fireb.* Madam, our Power is not deriv'd from you,
> Nor any one: 'Twas sent us in a Box
> From the great Sun himself, and Carriage paid:
> *Phaeton* brought it when he overturn'd
> The Chariot of the Sun into the Sea.
> Q.C.S. Shew me the Instrument, and let me read it.
> *Fireb.* Madam, you cannot read it; for being thrown
> Into the Sea, the Water has so damag'd it,
> That none but Priests could ever read it since.
> Q.C.S. And do you think I can believe this Tale?
> *Fireb.* I order you to believe it, and you must.
> [IV. i. Henley, xi. 215]

The Scriptures are the *Box*, which *the great Sun* (by which throughout this *Tragedy* God is represented) *sent* by *Phaeton, carriage paid*: and *Phaeton*, who represents those by whose hands the Scriptures were first conveyed to the world, by *overturning the chariot*, threw them *into the sea*; by which accident they were rendered unintelligible ever since, to all persons, except *Priests*. A generous discovery this of the original of Priestcraft, in a beautiful Allegory, deliver'd by a Priest, at the very time when he is struggling with the Laity, in order to promote Priest-craft.

In the Third Act, *Law* and *Physick*, with the approbation of *Divinity*, agree to desert Q. *Common-Sense*, and to go over to the side of Q. *Ignorance*, and join her army, consisting of foreign *Singers, Fidlers, Tumblers*, and *Rope-dancers*. By this part of the Allegory is shadowed out as great a truth as most of those represented by any other part of it, *viz*. That Lawyers, Physicians, and Divines have been the greatest encouragers of the late foreign senseless Entertainments which have been exhibited in our Theatres.

But to give the finishing stroke to the Clergy, our Author represents them as the murderers of *Common-Sense*, and as disguised villains and assassins: for at Pag. 61. *Firebrand* meets the *Queen*, who had been just defeated, and stabs her to the heart. Upon which she delivers this dying prophecy:

> Oh! Traytor, thou hast murder'd *Common-Sense.*
> Farewel vain World! to *Ignorance* I give thee,
> Her leaden Sceptre shall henceforward rule.
> Now, Priest, indulge thy wild ambitious Thoughts;
> Men shall embrace thy Schemes, 'till thou hast drawn
> All Worship from the Sun upon thy self:
> Henceforth all things shall topsy turvy turn;
> Physick shall kill, and Law enslave the World. &c.
>
> [V. i. Henley, xi. 224]

In which two last lines there is a particular beauty; for, *all things turning henceforth topsy turvy, Physick shall* first *kill the world*, and *Law* afterwards *enslave* it.

To make this murder of the *Queen* pass for self murder, *Firebrand* lays the *dagger by her side*, and resolves to *preach her Funeral sermon, and deplore her loss with tears.* But by a sudden turn in the Catastrophe, the Poet brings her *Ghost* upon the stage, which frightens away Q. *Ignorance* and all her forces, &c. recovers the day, and gains a complete victory; and then triumphantly utters the following prophecy, directly contrary to that at the time of her death.

> The Coast is clear, and to her native Realms
> Pale *Ignorance* with all her Host is fled,
> Whence she will never dare invade us more:
> Here, 'tho' a Ghost, I will my Power maintain, &c.
>
> [V, i. Henley, xi. 226–7]

Q. *Common-Sense*, just before her death, foretold, that *Ignorance should henceforward rule with her leaden sceptre*: her *Ghost* now foretells, that *She will never more dare invade us.* The contrariety of these prophecies leaves us under great difficulties, whether we should believe *Common-Sense* alive or dead, her person, or her ghost. And tho our desires and hopes may strongly incline us to give credit to the latter; yet the doctrine concerning *Ghosts* inculcated in this Piece, and the probablity that the great success of it will determine the author to write again for the Stage, over-ballance that inclination.

To do him justice, it will be now proper to add all that he has alledged to obviate the objections which might possibly be made against the severity of this *Dramatick Satire.* His apology with respect to all three Professions together, is put into the Mouth of Q. *Common-Sense,* Pag. 51. and is in as general terms as the Satire itself.

Religion, Law, and Physick were design'd
By Heaven the greatest Blessings on Mankind;
But Priests, and Lawyers, and Physicians made
These general Goods to each a private Trade;
With each they rob, with each they fill their Purses,
And turn our Benefits into our Curses.

[IV. i. Henley, xi. 215]

As to that part of the *Satire* which concerns the Clergy in particular, he introduces the following dialogue between *Fustian* and *Sneerwell*, Pag. 46.

Fust. I think the Panegyrick intended by it is very plain, and very seasonable.
Sneer. What Panegyrick?
Fust. On our Clergy, Sir, at least the best of them, to shew the difference between a Heathen and a Christian Priest. And as I have touched only on generals, I hope I shall not be thought to bring any thing improper on the Stage, which I would carefully avoid.

There is no *difference* pointed out between *Heathen and Christian Priests* throughout the whole *Tragedy*; but these are all in general, without exception, represented as acting like Heathens; which *touching only on generals* is here pleaded in justification of the Poet's conduct. Which is somewhat different, with regard to *Law* and *Physick*; concerning which Professions *Sneerwell* and *Fustian* thus continue their dialogue,

Sneer. But is not your Satire on Law and Physick somewhat too general?
Fust. What is said here cannot hurt either an honest Lawyer, or a good Physician; and such may be, nay, I know such are: if the opposites to these are the most general, I cannot help that; as for the Professors themselves, I have no great Reason to be their friend, for they once joined in a particular conspiracy against me.
Sneer. Ay, how so?
Fust. Why, an Apothecary brought me in a long Bill, and a Lawyer made me pay it.

[IV. i. Henley, xi. 210–11]

There *may*, it seems, *be an honest Lawyer*, and *a good Physician*, nay, our Author *knows*, there *are such*: but as to an *honest* and *good* Divine, he does not so much as say there *may be* any *such*, much less does he pretend to *know* one: for the omission of which pretence, the Clergy will, no doubt, think themselves in some measure obliged to him.——

The ludicrous complaint of the *particular conspiracy* against our Poet may serve as a key to let us into the true original cause of his indignation against Lawyers and Physicians; and from that we may easily account for his animosity against Divines.

This Piece is set in a very different light by the *Prompter*, in his Paper of *Apr.* 2[1] where, among other great things say'd of the whole, the following character is given of the latter part of it. 'In the Tragedy (much the finer Performance of the two) we see the, daring Pencil of *Michael Angelo*. Satires start out of every Line; they are *seen* and *felt*. Even when they *smile*, they look *terrible*, and *strike* with *force*. He has here and there given a *Flemish* Touch, for the sake of the *Vulgar*.——— Some Persons have injudiciously thought, the Poet levels his Satire, (not Against the Abuses of, but) against Religion, Law, and Physick, themselves; but if they would attend to the Characters of the Speakers, they would find, all that is said is only against the *Abuse*, and not the *Foundation* of each'.———If this *judicious* Critic, who has lately displayed his judgment so conspicuously, in recommending Plays and Players to the Town, will undertake to shew the truth of this assertion; one may venture to promise him, that more notice will be taken of it, than was of his laboured Defence of the *Double Deceit*,[2] a Play and a Criticism which very few would give themselves the trouble to read.

MARFORIO.

---

[1] See above, No. 22.
[2] William Popple, *The Double Deceit, or, A Cure for Jealousy* (1735).

26. 'To the Author of *Pasquin*', in

A Collection of Miscellany Poems, Never before
Publish'd

n.d. [*c.* 1736], p. 69

Tho' Folly reigns, rise thou by Wit inspir'd,
And shew the Town how *ancient Bards* were fir'd;
To *Wycherly*'s strong Sense, join *Congreve*'s Art,
And while you lash, correct the vicious Heart.
Let plodding Scriblers toil with Grief and Pain,
And write whole Quires of Scurvy Rhimes in vain;
Those Sons of Farce, who court obsequious Sound,
And run, O Dulness, they eternal Round!
Be thy bold Muse, still free and unconfin'd,
To lash the Coxcombs of the Age design'd;
Fix'd to no Party, censure all alike,
And at the undistinguish'd Villain strike.
Pleas'd we behold the Great maintain thy Cause,
And *Court* and *Country* join in thy Applause.
Tho' disappointed Authors damn the Town,
And tax 'em with a Fault too much their own;
From thy Success let Bards on this depend,
If they *write* well, the *Town* will still commend.

27. [Philip Dormer Stanhope, fourth Earl of Chesterfield] from a leader in *Common Sense: or, the Englishman's Journal*

5 February 1736–7

An ingenious Dramatick Author has consider'd Common Sense as so extraordinary a Thing, that he has lately, with great Wit and Humour, not only personified it, but dignified it too with the Title of a *Queen* . . .

PASQUIN
THE HISTORICAL REGISTER
21 March 1736–7
EURYDICE HISS'D
13 April 1737

---

28. John Perceval, first Earl of Egmont, from diary entry
22 March 1736–7

Diary of the First Earl of Egmont (Viscount Perceval), ii. 375.

. . . I went to the Haymarket Playhouse to see *The Historical Register,* wrote by Mr. Fielding. It is a good satire on the times and has a good deal of wit.

29. 'An Adventurer in Politicks'
The Daily Gazetteer
7 May 1737

From a letter which gives the general case for regulation of the stage by the Government, and then focuses on *Pasquin* and *The Historical Register:*

      ★   ★   ★

THE ELECTION, (a *Comedy in Pasquin*) laid the Foundation for introducing POLITICKS on the Stage; but as the Author was general in his

Satyr, and exposed with Wit and Humour, the Practices of *Elections*, without coming so near, as to point *any Person* out, he was not then guilty of the Fault he has since committed; tho' I cannot think him *Praiseworthy*, for turning into Ridicule and making slight of one of the *gravest* Evils our Constitution is subject to: 'Twas as ill judged, as the late Mr. *Gay's* turning *Highwaymen, Pickpockets*, and *Whores*, into *Heroes* and *Heroines*, which (tho' done with all the Wit and Humour, conceivable in Man) served only to increase the Number of those *corrupt* Wretches, who encouraged one another, from the Example of the Stage, which exposed with *Wit*, what ought to be punished with *Rigour*.

The great Success which *Pasquin* had, encouraged the Author to give his Genius unlimited Scope, in this Vein; in which it has been made evident since, he was secretly *buoy'd up*, by some of the *greatest Wits* and *finest Gentlemen* of the Age, who letting their Passions get the Better of their more mature Reflections, have patronized a Method of Writing, themselves, were they in the Administration, would be the first to discountenance.

THE HISTORICAL REGISTER then, appeared to the Town, under the *Patronage* of the *Great*, the *Sensible*, and the *Witty*, in the Opposition, and contains a History of the Transactions of the Year 1736.

This witty Writer, in order to insinuate *Ignorance in the Ministry, and want of Intelligence of the Affairs of other Nations*, and to shew, that nothing has been produced in that Year, makes the Troubles in *Corsica*, the only known Transaction. Now tho' there is something most *ridiculously pleasant*, and apt to excite Laughter, in this Conception, yet to make it *genuine Humour*, no Event of Consequence ought really to have been brought about in that Year; whereas, perhaps, Events, as great as any recorded in History, have come to a definitive CRISIS in it. We have seen a War terminated, and three PRINCES established in DOMINIONS, the Discussion of whose Rights finally, by the *Lex ultima Regum*, had, perhaps, been attended with all the Fatalities that accompany the most *obstinate* and *bloody* War. The settling the Interests of a *Twice* King of *Poland*, a *Duke* of *Lorain*, and an Infant of *Spain*, are EPOCHAS, that hereafter may be thought very Considerable in History.

I have mentioned this, only to shew that the very Point, on which the greatest *Stress* of the Humour lies, is founded on a Falshood; and I would from hence infer, how much it is in the Power of such Exhibitions, to make a *Minister appear ridiculous to a People*; and if the Humour spreads, as possibly it may, and should take in *Home-Affairs*, how much and how unjustly he might be exposed to publick Resentment, from such humourous and poetical Colouring of Things.

It may be said here, in favour of the Author, that in the Close of his *Register*, he has treated the PATRIOTS no better than the POLITICIANS: But this, instead of *extenuating* only *doubles* his Crime, for, I think, to turn *Patriotism*, the noblest of Characters, into a Jest, equally blameable, and that neither should have any *Place* on the Stage. But perhaps these Patriots have consented to have themselves play'd, only to *exhibit that* IMPUDENT FELLOW, *who can stand their* HISSES, *and laugh in his Sleeve at them.*

The *Auri sacra fames*, from which the Poet, no more than the private Man is exempt, had been so plentifully gratify'd by the Success of these two Pieces, that the Author (since he had gone so far with Impunity) was resolv'd to try his Vein further, and in EURYDICE *hiss'd*,[1] very impudently compares *Government* to a *Farce*, and carries the Allegory throughout. (I shall not pursue him in his particular Satyr, it not being to my immediate Purpose.) Now to insinuate to the *Vulgar*, who must ever be *led*, that *all Government is but a Farce* (*perhaps a damned one too*) in just as bad to *Society*, as it would be to tell the *People*, that their *Religion* is a *Joke*. There are Things which, from the Good they dispense, ought to be Sacred; such are *Government* and *Religion*. No Society can subsist without 'em: To turn either into Ridicule, is to unloose the fundamental Pillars of Society, and shake it from its *Basis*.

If it be said here, that it is not comparing Government in general to a *Farce*, but only the present Managers, to *Farce-Actors*, I would then ask the *high Patronizers* of this *new* Method, what Good they propose to the State from encouraging such Licenciousness? Will the exposing the Ministry before the Eyes of the REPRESENTATIVES of all the Princes in EUROPE, give their Masters a *higher* Idea of the *Court of England*? Will it give Us a *greater* Weight Abroad? Is it then, the Part of a *true Patriot*, one actuated by the Love of his Country, to spread its Weakness thro' all the *foreign* Courts, by publickly favouring such ridiculous Representations of its Government? I talk upon their own Principles, and suppose the absurd Charge on the Ministry true. No true Patriot would endeavour to render his Country contemptible: He would rather strive to hide its Weakness. He would try at a Cure, but by such Means as would not lay the Wound too open.

[1] *Eurydice* was first performed on 19 February 1737 and *Eurydice Hiss'd* on 13 April as an afterpiece with *The Historical Register* (the last two subsequently published together on 12 May).

The Stage has a large Field in the *Follies*, *Vices*, and *Passions* of Mankind. It has nothing to do with POLITICKS or RELIGION. The Press is open to detect any Imposition from either of these, without the Help of the Stage; and as it has such Liberty, it does not use it sparingly, but lays on Ministers most abundantly.

To encourage then Politicks on the Stage, is not only *unjust* in itself, and *improper*, but of a most pernicious Tendency to the Stage itself, which instead of being a general Mirrour, where the Beauties and Deformities of human Nature are represented Impartially; whence we either *copy* or *reject*, as we find our Resemblance *good* or *bad*, becomes a private Looking-Glass, where Spleen, Resentment, and inconsiderate Levity, displays Objects without any Regard to Truth, Decency, Good Manners, or true Judgment. If such Attempts are suffered to go on, and Poets tolerated to pursue such *unpoetick* License, the very Gentlemen themselves, who now personally support it, tho' perhaps, in their own Minds they can't justify their Conduct in so doing, may themselves, in process of Time, be the Objects of such Exhibitions, and afford themselves as publick Spectacles of Derision on a Stage to the lowest of Mankind. And whom then can they blame? For the VERY POET that now prostitutes the Muses to their Private Passions, may serve those of a future Opposition to a future Ministry.

———*nec Lex est justior ulla*
Quam Necis Artifices, arte perire, sua.[1]
I am, SIR,

An ADVENTURER in POLITICKS.

[1] 'There is no more fitting law than for artificers of death to die by their own arts.' Ovid, *The Art of Love*, I. 655–6 (misquoted).

30. 'Pasquin'

Common Sense: or, the Englishman's Journal

21 May 1737

'Pasquin' was probably Fielding.

To the Author of COMMON SENSE.

Sir,

As I have yet no Vehicle of my own, I shall be obliged to you if you will give the following a Place in the next Stage, and am,

Your humble Servant.

To the Author of the Gazetteer of May 7.

Sir,

Though the Paper you have attack'd me in be so little read, that should you print a Libel in it, you could scarce be said to have published it; yet as you are pleased to style yourself an Adventurer in Politicks, and as I know a certain Person whom that Appellation will exactly fit, I shall take a little Notice of what you have advanced. This I undertake, not with Regard of what is written, but out of Respect to the Person whom I suppose the Author. And here; if I should happen to mistake you, I hope I shall not offend: For my Lord *Shaftesbury* well observes, that a judicious Beggar, when he addresseth himself to a Coach, always supposeth that there is a Lord in it; seeing, that should there be no Lord there, a private Gentleman will never be offended by the Title.[1]

You set out, Sir, with a pretty Panegyrick on the Lenity of the Administration, whence you draw this Conclusion, That it is ungenerous to attack it, because it will not crush you for so doing. *To abuse the Lenity of Power, when Men know it will not hurt them* (say you) *is like talking Obscenity to a Woman who will not defend herself, and* MUST *hear*

[1] Anthony Ashley Cooper, third Earl of Shaftesbury, *A Letter concerning Enthusiasm* (1708), in *Characteristics*, ed. J. M. Robertson (1900), i. 26.

it. The Comparison between the Attack of a Ministry, and that of a Woman, might afford some pleasant Remarks; I shall only say, I suppose you do not mean an old Woman, seeing, that to talk a little smuttily to such, would be no great Insult, if the common Saying be true, which however I do not believe, that all old Women love B——y.

You are pleased to say, Sir, that *no Argument whatever can be alledged to support the bringing of Politicks on the Stage*. If you mean by Politicks, those Secrets of Government which, like the *Mysteries* of the *Bona Dea*, are improper to be beheld by vulgar Eyes, such as Secret Service, &c. I must answer, your Caution is unnecessary, at least to me, who cannot expose to others, what I have not found out myself. But if by your Politicks, you mean a general Corruption (one of the greatest Evils (you are pleased to own) our Constitution is subject to) I cannot think such Politicks too sacred to be exposed. But *Pasquin* was not (as you insinuate) the first Introducer of Things of this Kind; we have several Political Plays now extant: And had you ever read *Aristophanes,* you would know that the gravest Matters have been try'd this Way. A Method which a great Writer (I think Mr. *Bayle*) seems to approve; where he represents Ridicule as a kind of Fiery Trial, by which Truth is most certainly discovered from Imposture.[1] Indeed, I believe, there are no Instances of bringing Politicks on the Stage 'in those neighbouring Nations' where, you say, that 'we may see disguised Informers in almost every publick Place, with blank *Lettres de Cachet*, ready to fill up with the Names of such as dare barely inquire, in a Manner different from the Sense of the Court, into the State of Affairs, and a *Bastile* always open to receive them:' Nor where you tell us, that 'a Holy Inquisition, and the Gallies, offer their Service to the *State*, as well as to Religion'.

But pray, Sir, what do you intend by mentioning these? I hope not to threaten us, nor to insinuate that any Thing will make it *necessary* to introduce such damned Engines of Tyranny among us.

But you seem to think, Sir, that to ridicule Vice, is, to serve its Cause. And you mention the late ingenious Mr. *Gay*, who, you say, in his *Beggars Opera* hath made Heroes and Heroines of Highwaymen and Whores. Are then Impudence, Boldness, Robbery, and picking Pockets the Characteristicks of a Hero? Indeed, Sir, we do not always approve what we laugh at. So far from it, Mr. *Hobbes* will tell you that Laughter is a Sign of Contempt.[2] And by raising such a Laugh as this against

[1] Pierre Bayle, note 'O' in article on 'Achillini', *Dictionnaire critique et historique* (1697).
[2] *Leviathan*, I. vi, and *Human Nature*, ix. 13.

Vice, *Horace* assures us we give a sorer Wound, than it receives from all the Abhorrence which can be produced by the gravest and bitterest Satire.[1] You will not hardly, I believe, persuade us, how much soever you may desire it, that it is the Mark of a great Character to be laughed at by a whole Kingdom.

I shall not be industrious to deny, what you are so good to declare, that I am buoy'd up by the greatest Wits, and finest Gentlemen of the Age; and patroniz'd by the Great, the Sensible, and the Witty in the Opposition. Of such Patrons I shall be always proud, and to such shall be always glad of the Honour of owning an Obligation. Nor is it a small Pleasure to me, that my Heart is conscious of none, to certain Persons who are in the Opposition, to those Characters by which you have been pleased to distinguish my Patrons.

The *Historical Register*, and *Eurydice Hiss'd*, being now publish'd, shall answer for themselves against what you are pleas'd to say concerning them; but as you are pleased to assert, that I have insinuated that all Government is a *Farce*, and perhaps a damn'd one too, I shall quote the Lines on which you ground your Assertion; and, I hope, then you will be so good as to retract it.

> ——Wolsey's *Self, that mighty Minister,*
> *In the full Height and Zenith of his Power,*
> *Amid a Crowd of Sycophants and Slaves,*
> *Was but (perhaps) the Author of a* Farce,
> *Perhaps, a damn'd one too.*
>
> [*Eurydice Hiss'd*, Henley, xi. 298]

I am far from asserting that all Government is a *Farce*, but I affirm that, however the very Name of Power may frighten the Vulgar, it will never be honoured by the Philosopher, or the Man of Sense, unless accompany'd with Dignity. On the contrary, nothing can be more Burlesque than Greatness in mean Hands. Mr. *Penkethman* never was so ridiculous a Figure, as when he became* *Penkethman the Great*.

I shall only make a Remark or two, and conclude.

First, I have not ridiculed Patriotism, but have endeavoured to shew the several Obstructions to a proper exerting this noble Principle; and that Corruption alone is equal to all the rest. I have endeavoured to

---

[1] *Satires*, I. x. 14–15.

* In the Burlesque of *Alexander* [William Pinkethman, Jr. (d. 1740), son of the famous comedian, acted burlesque 'tragic scenes' from serious plays as 'entertainments'. The play referred to here is probably Nathaniel Lee's *The Rival Queens* (1677), which had been revived in 1735. Ed.]

represent the Consequence thereof, and to shew, that whoever gives up the Interest of his Country, in Fact gives up his own.

Secondly, I must observe, Sir, that if we are not (as you say) to expose evil or weak Measures, for fear of informing our Neighbours, this Argument will extend in its full Force to the Press; and I think I remember to have seen it formerly used on that Occasion. But it will not hold in either Case; for I do not believe foreign Ministers to be so weak, as to remain in an entire stupid Ignorance of what we are doing; nor do I think, if well considered, a more ridiculous Image can enter into the Mind of Man, than that of all the Ambassadors of *Europe* assembling at the *Hay Market* Play-house to learn the Character of our Ministry.

Lastly, you insinuate, that the *same Poet*, who (you say) *now prostitutes the Muses* (that is, by laughing at Vice and Folly) may hereafter attack future Administrations (tho', by the by, I am far from owning that he hath attacked the present.) To this, Sir, I must beg Leave to say, without any Reflection on our present Ministry, that, I believe, there are now amongst those Gentlemen who are stiled the *Opposition*, Men in Genius, Learning, and Knowledge so infinitely superior to the rest of their Countrymen, and of Integrity so eminent, that should they, *in process of Time*, be in the Possession of Power, they will be able to triumph over, and trample upon all the Ridicule which any Wit or Humour could level at them: For Ridicule, like *Ward*'s Pill, passes innocently through a sound Constitution; but when it meets with a Complication of foul Distempers in a gross corrupt Carcase, it is apt to give a terrible Shock, to work the poor Patient most immoderately; in the Course of which Working, it is ten to one but he bes——ts his Breeches. I am, Sir,

Your humble (tho' not obliged) Servant,

PASQUIN.

31. From 'An Adventurer in Politicks'

The Daily Gazetteer

4 June 1737

A reply to 'Pasquin's' letter in *Common Sense*, 21 May 1737 (No. 30). The Licensing Act was at this time pending in the House of Lords:

★   ★   ★

There is something peculiarly absurd (excuse the Freedom of the Phrase) in your quoting *Aristophanes* in your own Justification; whose licentious Abuse of the State, put the *Athenians* upon the very Thing our Legislature is now passing into a Law. Every Body that has the least Acquaintance with Literature, knows what the *Vetus Comoedia* was; and that the Licentiousness of it took in not only Private Life, and as near as was possible, the very exact Figure of Persons; but exposed on the Scene, the Principal Men of the Republick by Name. *Aristophanes* carry'd this so far, that in a Piece of his, in which he brought the Person of *Cleon* on the Stage, who was a leading Man in *Athens*, the Actor refusing to play the *Roll*, He himself went on and performed it. He afterwards brought *Lampsacus* [i.e. Lamachus] and *Brasidas*, nay, *Alcibiades* and *Pericles* on the Scene, and treated their Ministerial Characters, as well as their Private ones, with the same Licentiousness. Such was the Intemperance of this, your Model, Sir, that the very *best*, as well as the *wisest*, Man of all *Greece*, no less than *Socrates*, was exposed by him, and thro' his Sides, *Morality* and *Government* radically struck at. This Abuse of Comedy at length stirr'd up the Indignation of the *Athenians*, who thought the *Minister* as well as the Private Man accountable to them for his Actions, and not to the Poet; and finding, as Horace tells us, the Grievance *fit to be restrained by Law, they did restrain it by Law*.[1]

★   ★   ★

[1] *Ars poetica*, ll. 283–4.

I believe, and am confident, the Government had no Thought of
vesting any Power in any Great *Officers* Hands for this Purpose, had not
you *pav'd* the Way for the Subversion of the Stage, by introducing
on it Matters quite foreign to its true Object; and by making yourself a
Tool to the indiscreet Mirth of some great Men, put Others upon keeping the Stage within its proper Bounds; which is all that is now *aim'd*
at, or really done.

I do not think, that *to ridicule Vice is to serve its Cause*, as you are
pleased to make me think. But I say, that to represent Vice in Colours,
more amiable than its natural ones, is to *serve its Cause*. And I dare say,
there is not one single Person that ever went to the *Beggars Opera*, but
who *thought* of the Characters there represented, with much *less Horror
and Aversion*, than the same Person would, and actually does, of the
Wretches that go to *Tyburn*, or the Plantations, tho' there is no Difference *but the Poet's Colouring* between them. Is this then ridiculing Vice,
to make it less shocking? Surely, the greatest Advocate for Mr. *Gay*
will not pretend to clear him of this Imputation. Is this ridiculing Vice,
to shew Corruption, as you have done in *Pasquin*? This is a familiarizing
Corruption, just as Mr. *Gay* familiarized *Vice*, by taking away all the
ODIUM of it.

I shall not pretend to make you believe, that *it is the Mark of a great
Character to be laugh'd at by a whole Kingdom*. But I rather think 'tis
your Vanity that makes you believe the Case was so; for by the Moral
with which you sum up your *Election*, at which the whole Kingdom
laugh'd, as you say, you plainly tell us, that

> Better Herring is in neither Barrel.
>
> [*Pasquin*, III. i. Henley, xi. 199]

So that your Great Men and Patrons may have the same Pretence to
the same Greatness of Character, by having been equally laugh'd at,
in *Pasquin*, the *Historical Register*, and *Eurydice hiss'd*; as, if necessary,
might be shewn by Quotations from the two last.

★   ★   ★

. . . But of what Advantage to you is all this? Does it reflect any
Lustre on you? Alas! my Friend! Don't you see you are nothing but the
Cat's Paw! No Office surely to be proud of! An Engine, supported by
them, to bespatter with! Were you chosen by them for any other Reason
but because your *licentious Satire* pleas'd their *Spleen*, I would allow the
Choice, marking you out as an Object of Merit. But to be singled

out for a *Squirt* to throw Filth about—How ill does this suit *Horace's* Idea of a Poet,

> Ingenium cui sit; Cui Mens divinior atque os
> Magna sonaturium—Des nominis hujus honorem.[1]

I will not cavil with you about Words; you may not perhaps have expressly said, *All Government is but a Farce*; but you should have carry'd your Quotation a Word further, and you would have found——

> ————'TIS ALL A CHEAT;
> *Some Men play little Farces, and some Great.*
> [Henley, xi. 298]

But the Drift of the Allegory throughout, is too plain to be mistaken; and you may, if you please, deny what every Body else is convinced of.

Your Ideas are, for the most Part, Ludicrous, and I cannot help smiling with you, at your Conception *of the Ambassadors in Europe assembling all at the Haymarket House, to learn the Character of the Ministry.*——But the Misfortune is, you had rather say a *witty* Thing at any time, than a *true one*; for you should have said, To see the *Ministry exposed.*

★   ★   ★

---

[1] 'If someone has genius, an inspired mind and a way of expressing noble ideas, give him the honor of the name [i.e. of poet].' Horace, *Satires*, I. iv. 43–4.

FIELDING AND THE LICENSING ACT

32. Philip Dormer Stanhope, fourth Earl of Chesterfield, as reported in
The Gentleman's Magazine
July 1737, vii. 409

This version of Chesterfield's speech of June 1737 in the House of Lords against the Licensing Act should be compared with that in his *Miscellaneous Works*, ed. Matthew Maty and John O. Justamond (1779), ii. 323.

★ ★ ★

My Lords, I apprehend it to be a Bill of a very extraordinary, a very dangerous Nature, and tho' it seems designed only as a Restraint on the Licentiousness of *the Stage*, I fear, it looks farther, and tends to a Restraint on the Liberty of the *Press*, a Restraint even on *Liberty itself*. ——I have gather'd from common Talk, while this Bill was moving in the House of Commons, That a Play was offer'd the Players, which if my Account was right, is truly of a most scandalous, a most flagitious Nature. What was the Effect? Why they not only refused to Act it, but carried it to a certain Person in the Administration, as a sure Method to have it suppress'd. Could this be the Occasion of the Bill? Surely no, the Caution of the Players could never occasion a Law to Restrain them, it is an Argument in their Favour, and a material One, in my Opinion, against the Bill, and is to me a Proof that the Laws are not only sufficient to deter them from Acting what they know would offend, but also to punish 'em in Case they should venture to do it.—— My Lords, I must own I have observed of late a remarkable Licentiousness in the Stage. There were two Plays acted last Winter, that one would have thought, should have given the greatest Offence, and yet were suffer'd without any Censure whatever;[1] in one of these Plays the Author thought fit to represent *Religion*, *Physick*, and the *Law*, as inconsistent with *Common Sense*. . . . The Stage *may* want Regulation, the Stage may have it, and yet be kept within Bounds without a *new Law* for the Purpose. I cannot but think, that Great Men are generally more sollicitous to guard their own Characters from publick Contempt, than to maintain the Principles and Practice of public Virtue, Decency and Order.

★   ★   ★

33. From *Common Sense: or, the Englishman's Journal*

28 October 1738

The writer, deploring the Licensing Act, has suggested that even if the professional stage were ruined by it, 'Gentlemen and Ladies would, in this Case, act some of the best Plays themselves, for their own Entertainment and that of their Friends. . . .' This practice, moreover, would have its own advantages:

★   ★   ★

It would be a very honourable Way of a Gentleman's keeping up his Interest among his Inferior Neighbours, by conveying good Sentiments into their Minds and mending their Morals.——I should therefore think it adviseable, that the Play of *Pasquin* should be acted in every Borough in *England*, a little before the next Elections.—I think it might caution the People against the Artifices of those who come to corrupt their Honesty with adulterate Wine, and more adulterate Promises.

★   ★   ★

[1] The other play was William Havard's *King Charles the First*.

34. From *Observations on the Present Taste for Poetry*

1739, pp. 16–21

The author is discussing poets who thrive by attacking other poets (or dramatists).

★   ★   ★

But what can we say for being pleas'd with an Abuse of all our finest Performances together! an Attack, at once, on all the Great Geniuses *England* has produced, for a Couple of Ages! whose best Endeavours, and some of their greatest Beauties were selected, to provoke our contemptuous Mirth, by being set in a ridiculous Light: And this was done, with wonderful Applause, by *H——y F——d——g*, Esq; *alias, Scriblerus secundus*. For whom a Friend of mine wrote, many Years ago, the following Lines, *viz*.

> Go on, Scriblerus, make our Britons see,
> Their Country ne'er produced a Wit but Thee.
> Persuade them *Fenton* scribed out of Rule,
> That *Addison* was mad, and *Rowe* a Fool!
> That *Congreve's* Merit was a mere Pretence,
> That *Lee* and *Dryden* wanted common-Sense!
> That Fame in their Applauses should be dumb!
> Your End, no Doubt, in Writing labour'd Thumb.
> Such Spleen, base Scribler, makes the Learned laugh!
> Who gladly give thee★ *Boccalini's* Chaff.
> Is *Fenton* low? let thy more manly Scene
> Display a Dame beyond his *Hebrew* Queen:

★ *See the Story in the* Spectator, *No. 291.*

N.B. *All the Poets and Pieces mentioned here were censured by this Paltry Scribler; the best of whose Writings were below the Worst of those he ridiculed.*

Than *Zara*'s Rage by Fury higher borne,
Below *Almeria*★ teach the sad to mourn!
Surpass the† World-Subduer's tender Woes,
And Struggles more than *Anthony*'s expose!
Make *Tamerlane* his moral Glory yield,
And *Cato* quit to thee the Patriot Field!
Then shall the World thy Right to Censure own,
And on thee Envy's Taint to more be blown!
But now, with honest Scorn, the Wise regard
The Statesman‡ *Noodle,* and his noodle Bard,
Whose baneful Morals are a Peoples Jest,
His Life a Scandal, and his Works a Pest.
I've shown the Bards whose Praise you'd take away,
The Tribe who 'scape you let me now display!
Shadwell, who once usurp'd the Laureat's Bays,
And *D'Urfey* famous long for vulgar Plays;
Settle, who fathom'd Dulness, thy Profound,
And taught Heroic *Fustian* high to sound!
Ev'n *Dennis* scarcely feels the lashing Lay!
But *Dennis* is§ alive and might repay,
Who never patient takes the Lash or Joke,
But gives assailing Authors Stroke for Stroke.
All these were Poets dimly doom'd to shine,
Whose humble Glories have with Ease been thine!
What Wonder then to them thy Satires blind?
The Worst of Brutes but seldom hurt their Kind.
At length, dull *F——d——g*, give thy Labours o'er,
And shew thy Spleen, and plague the Town no more!
No more to Wit by Libels make Pretence,
But grub thy Pen, and shew a Grain of Sense:
To aid which pious Resolution, I
Will tell a Tale, I need not to apply.
An envious Peasant saw, with venom'd Eyes,
Beside his Cot a splendid Palace rise!
That Bulk, he cry'd, the Stone, the Glass, the Lead,
Reproach the Meanness of my plaister'd Shed:
I have not Means to make my House so fine,
Then down shall that descend to suit with mine.
And, thus resolv'd, he goes, at Dead of Night,
When scarce a Star affords its glimm'ring Light,

★ Zara *and* Almeria: *Characters in Mr.* Congreve's Mourning Bride.
† Mark Anthony *in* Dryden's *Tragedy call'd,* All for Love, or the World well lost.
‡ *A Character in the Tragedy of Tragedies, or* Tom Thumb.
§ *The Authors principally lash'd were all dead.*

And, delving deep, a dreadful Cavern makes,
The Timbers crack, and all the Fabric shakes!
When lo! a heavy Part, unskilful plac'd,
That useless hung, and all the Pile disgrac'd,
From the strong Wall, the forceful Shock unbound,
It fell! and quash'd the Miner to the Ground.

And let my Reader determine if this Tale did not prove a true Prophecy, for Mr. F——d——g is since crush'd by his Labours, and for ever damn'd as a Poet: A Fate which I hope every Libeller of their betters will find.

★   ★   ★

35. Colley Cibber

From *An Apology for the Life of Mr. Colley Cibber*

1740

Edited by Robert W. Lowe (1889), i. 286–8. By way of accounting for the passage of the Licensing Act, Cibber refers to the increasing number of small theatrical companies:

. . . these so tolerated Companies gave Encouragement to a broken Wit[1] to collect a fourth Company, who for some time acted Plays in the *Hay-Market*, which House the united *Drury-Lane* Comedians had lately quitted: This enterprising Person, I say (whom I do not chuse to name, unless it could be to his Advantage, or that it were of Importance) had Sense enough to know that the best Plays with bad Actors would turn but to a very poor Account; and therefore found it necessary to give the Publick some Pieces of an extraordinary Kind, the Poetry of which he conceiv'd ought to be so strong that the greatest Dunce of an Actor could not spoil it: He knew, too, that as he was in haste to get Money, it would take up less time to be intrepidly abusive than decently entertaining; that to draw the Mob after him he must rake the Channel and pelt their Superiors; that, to shew himself somebody, he must come up to *Juvenal's* Advice and stand the Consequence:

> *Aude aliquid brevibus Gyaris, & carcere dignum*
> *Si vis esse aliquis——*

Juv. Sat. I.[2]

[1] i.e. Fielding.

[2] 'If you want to be somebody important, dare to do something that merits exile or prison.' ll. 73–4.

Such, then, was the mettlesome Modesty he set out with; upon this Principle he produc'd several frank and free Farces that seem'd to knock all Distinctions of Mankind on the Head: Religion, Laws, Government, Priests, Judges, and Ministers, were all laid flat at the Feet of this *Herculean* Satyrist! This *Drawcansir* in Wit, that spared neither Friend nor Foe! who to make his Poetical Fame immortal, like another *Erostratus*, set Fire to his Stage by writing up to an Act of Parliament to demolish it. I shall not give the particular Strokes of his Ingenuity a Chance to be remembered by reciting them; it may be enough to say, in general Terms, they were so openly flagrant, that the Wisdom of the Legislature thought it high time to take a proper Notice of them.[1]..

36. Alexander Pope

The New Dunciad

March 1742, iv. 41–44

P. 345 in the edition of James Sutherland (1943). Pope, alluding to the state of drama at the time of the Licensing Act, implies approval of Fielding's satiric plays and praises Chesterfield's opposition to the Act (see No. 32):

> There sunk Thalia, nerveless, cold, and dead,
> Had not her Sister Satyr held her head:
> Nor cou'd'st thou, CHESTERFIELD! a tear refuse,
> Thou wept'st, and with thee wept each gentle Muse.

---

[1] Cibber's view that Fielding's activity caused the Licensing Act was perpetuated in Benjamin Victor's *History of the Theatres* (1761), i. 50–1 (see also *Monthly Review*, 1761, xxv. 45), Arthur Murphy's *Essay* (see below, No. 166), and *The Life of Mr. James Quin* 1766), p. 42.

37. 'To the Author of Shamela'

The London Magazine

June 1741, x. 304

Admir'd *Pamela*, till *Shamela* shown,
Appear'd in every colour—but her own:
Uncensur'd she remain'd in borrow'd light,
No nun more chaste, few angels shone so bright.
But now, the idol we no more adore,
Jervice a bawd, and our chaste nymph a w——
Each buxom lass may read poor *Booby*'s case,
And charm a *Williams* to supply his place;
Our thoughtless sons for round-ear'd caps may burn,
And curse *Pamela*, when they've serv'd a turn.

38. Thomas Dampier, letter

30 July 1741

See Historical MSS. Commission, Twelfth Report, Appendix, ix. p. 204. Dampier is replying to some English gentlemen in Geneva on 'the state of learning in England', and after commenting on *Pamela* and Middleton's *Life of Cicero*, he remarks of the latter:

The dedication to Lord Hervey has been very justly and prettily ridiculed by Fielding in a dedication to a pamphlet called 'Shamela' which he wrote to burlesque the forementioned romance.[1]

* * *

[1] Cf. Aaron Hill's letter to Richardson of 13 April 1741 where he rejoices in 'the justice that is done to your Pamela; and the oblique reputation weaker writers endeavour to draw, from a distorted misuse of her name, for a passport to malice and faction' (*Correspondence*, ed. Barbauld, i. 68.)

39. Dr. George Cheyne, letter

9 March 1741-2

From a letter to Samuel Richardson (Letter LV in the Laing MSS. III, 356, University of Edinburgh Library); printed in Alan D. McKillop, *Samuel Richardson* (1936), p. 77. Dr. Cheyne, a physician of Bath, and a friend of Richardson, had no reason to like Fielding, who had taken his *Philosophical Conjectures* (1740) 'into custody' and tried it before the 'Court of Censorial Enquiry' as an example of worse gibberish than Cibber's *Apology* (*Champion*, 17 May 1740). In February, Cheyne wrote to Richardson, 'I beg as soon as you get Fielding's Joseph Andrews, I fear in Ridicule of your Pamela and of Virtue in the Notion of Don Quixote's Manner, you wou'd send it to me by the very first Coach' (McKillop, p. 77). After reading it he writes again:

I had Feilding's [*sic*] wretched Performance, for which I thank you. It will entertain none but Porters or Watermen.

40. Thomas Gray, letter

[8] April [1742]

From a letter to Richard West, *Correspondence of Thomas Gray,* ed.
Paget Toynbee and Leonard Whibley (1935), i. 191–2.

West, who apparently enjoyed *Joseph Andrews,* lent Gray his
copy. After reading Gray's opinion, recorded below, West replied, *c.* 12 April: 'I rejoice you found amusement in Joseph
Andrews. But then I think your conceptions of Paradise a little
upon the Bergerac.' West is alluding to Cyrano de Bergerac's
fantastic *Histoire comique des états et empires de la Lune* (1656) and
Histoire comique des états et empires du Soleil (1661). (Toynbee and
Whibley, i. 195).

. . . I have myself, upon your recommendation, been reading Joseph
Andrews. The incidents are ill laid and without invention; but the
characters have a great deal of nature, which always pleases even in her
lowest shapes. Parson Adams is perfectly well; so is Mrs. Slipslop, and
the story of Wilson; and throughout he shews himself well read in
Stage-Coaches, Country Squires, Inns, and Inns of Court. His reflections upon high people and low people, and misses and masters, are
very good. However the exaltedness of some minds (or rather as I
shrewdly suspect their insipidity and want of feeling or observation)
may make them insensible to these light things, (I mean such as charac-
terize and paint nature) yet surely they are as weighty and much more
useful than your grave discourses upon the mind, the passions, and
what not. Now as the paradisaical pleasures of the Mahometans consist
in playing upon the flute and lying with Houris, be mine to read
eternal new romances of Marivaux and Crebillon.

★   ★   ★

41. William Shenstone, letter

[17 or 18 May 1742]

From a letter to Richard Graves, *Letters of William Shenstone*, ed. Duncan Mallam (1939), p. 38.

. . . You cannot conceive how large the number is of those that mistake burlesque for the very foolishness it exposes (which observation I made once at The Rehearsal,[1] at Tom Thumb, at Chrononhoton-thologos;[2] all which are pieces of elegant humour. . . .

JOSEPH ANDREWS

42. Catherine Talbot, letter

1 June 1742

From a letter to Elizabeth Carter, *A Series of Letters between Mrs. Elizabeth Carter and Miss Catherine Talbot* (1808), i. 11.

*   *   *

I want much to know whether you have yet condescended to read Joseph Andrews, as I am well assured the character of Mr. Adams is

[1] George Villiers, Duke of Buckingham, *The Rehearsal* (1671).
[2] Henry Carey, *The Tragedy of Chrononhotonthologos* (1734).

drawn from one in real life:[1] if the book strikes you as it did me, you will certainly come up to town next winter, that you and I may join in contriving some means of getting acquainted with him, I have known you throw away your contrivance upon people not half as well worth it. . . .

43. William Shenstone, letter

[1742]

From an undated letter to Richard Graves, *Letters of William Shenstone*, ed. Mallam, p. 44.
Graves had sent Shenstone some 'little parody', and in this letter Shenstone takes Graves to task for being reluctant to have it printed:

. . . —Indeed, as to the little parody you send, it would fix your reputation with men of sense as much as (greatly more than) the whole tedious character of Parson Adams. I read it half a year ago; the week after I came to town: but made Mr. Shuckburgh[2] take it again, imagining it altogether a very mean performance.—I liked a tenth part pretty well; but, as Dryden says of Horace (unjustly), he shews his teeth without laughing:[3] the greater part is *unnatural* and *unhumourous*. It has some advocates; but I observe, those not such as I ever esteemed tasters. Finally, what makes *you endeavour* to like it?

★   ★   ★

[1] i.e. the Rev. William Young (1702–57).
[2] A London bookseller and publisher.
[3] *A Discourse concerning the Original and Progress of Satire* (1693), in *Essays of John Dryden*, ed. W. P. Ker (1900), ii. 84.

44. Andrew Michael (André Michel) Ramsay, letter

1 September 1742

From a letter signed 'The Chevalier Ramsay', to 'Monsieur de Ramsay' (probably Michael Ramsay), printed in John Hill Burton, *Life and Correspondence of David Hume* (1846), i. 12, note 1. Ramsay (1686–1743) was part of the Pretender's entourage.

*   *   *

I have read the first book of 'The History of Joseph Andrews,' but don't believe I shall be able to finish the first volume. Dull burlesque is still more unsupportable than dull morality. Perhaps my not understanding the language of low life in an English style is the reason of my disgust; but I am afraid your Britannic wit is at as low an ebb as the French. . . .

45. Elizabeth Carter, letter

1 January 1742-3

From a letter to Catherine Talbot, *A Series of Letters*. . . , i. 16.

★   ★   ★

I must thank you for the perfectly agreeable entertainment I have met in reading Joseph Andrews, at it was your recommendation that first tempted me to enquire after it. It contains such a surprizing variety of nature, wit, morality, and good sense, as is scarcely to be met with in any one composition, and there is such a spirit of benevolence runs through the whole, as I think renders it peculiarly charming. The author has touched some particular instances of inhumanity which can only be hit in this kind of writing, and I do not remember to have seen observed any where else; these certainly cannot be represented in too detestable a light, as they are so severely felt by the persons they affect, and looked upon in too careless a manner by the rest of the world.

It must surely be a marvellous wrongheadedness and perplexity of understanding that can make any one consider this complete satire as a very immoral thing, and of the most dangerous tendency, and yet I have met with some people who treat it in the most outrageous manner. . . .

46. From a letter to Caleb D'Anvers

The Craftsman

1 January 1742–3

Reprinted in the *Gentleman's Magazine*, January 1742–3, xiii. 25. Fielding's preface is cited to support a general attack on satire.

★   ★   ★

I Honour the Author of that facetious Work, *The History of* JOSEPH ANDREWS, for what he saith in his Preface, by Way of Explanation of the *Ridiculous, viz. What could exceed the Absurdity of an Author, who should write the* Comedy *of* Nero, *with the* merry *Incident of ripping up his Mother's Belly?* Nor do I know any one Piece of Criticism better worth the Study (if they study at all) of those Critics, or Orators, who endeavour to divert their Audience, or Readers, with pleasant Images of the public Calamities, and arch Charactures of those Persons to whom they are thought to be owing.

★   ★   ★

The *Outré*, or Extravagant, requires but a very little Portion of Genius to hit. Any Dauber, almost, may make a shift to portray a *Saracen*'s Head; but a Master, only, can express the delicate, dimpled Softness of Infancy, the opening Bloom of Beauty, or the happy Negligence of graceful Gentility.

47. Charles Macklin, from the Prologue to *The Wedding Day*

17 February 1743-4

Macklin, who also delivered the Prologue, is addressing Fielding ironically:

---

*   *   *

Ah! thou foolish Follower of the ragged Nine,
You'd better stuck to honest Abram Adams, *by half.*
He, in spight of Critics, *can make your Readers laugh.*

*   *   *

48. [Pierre François Guyot Desfontaines], review of *Joseph Andrews*[1]

1743

In *Observations sur les écrits modernes* (1743), xxxii. 189–91. The Abbé Desfontaines had praised *Pamela* in 1742 (*Observations,* xxix. 70–1, 193–214), and a *Lettre à Monsieur l'Abbé Des Fontaines sur Pamela* (1742) had taken him to task for his anglophilia. *Joseph Andrews* turned him into a Fieldingite who first wrote the following laudatory review and then translated the novel (see. No. 49).

Last summer a work appeared in England which the English rank above all the novels that have ever been written, or at least place on an equal eminence with *Don Quixote* and the *Roman comique* of Scarron. It is called *The History of the Adventures of Joseph Andrews, and his Friend Mr. Abraham Adams, Written in imitation of the manner of Cervantes,* London 1742, in 12° 2 vols. It is a judicious and moral novel full of salt and pleasures, without the least touch of libertinage either of spirit or of heart, which exalts virtue and is infinitely interesting. Its cruxes and episodes are charming. The denouement, prepared for since the very beginning, is only perceived in the last chapter, and cannot be guessed earlier; so that up to that point the uncertain reader does not know what will be the issue of the ingenious imbroglio. Moreover, nothing is so simple as the contrivance. The style is comic throughout, excepting the passages where it is a tender and lawful love that creates the interest. Joseph Andrews is the brother of Pamela, who appears on the scene near the end of the second volume with the English nobleman who has married her; the most agreeable situations result. Finally, I have no fear in assuring you that England has not hitherto produced such a per-

[1] Translated from the French.

fect example of this genre. More, this is not a vain and frivolous fiction; it instructs the reader in the customs of the English, which are completely unknown in France, and carries a hundred particulars worth the attention of the gravest person. The author is Mr. Fielding, one of the best comic poets of England. The dialogue is another excellent part of the book. Everywhere are strokes that are lively, naïve, fine, even delicate, always pleasant, and sometimes burlesque. This is the judgment I dare make from the original English version, which has been sent me, and which I have read with very great pleasure. If this excellent work should appear in French, as may be the case, the public should hope that this service is not rendered by some ignorant refugee who will disfigure it, as happens with the greater part of translations of English books. To avenge the authors of their nation, the English often render us the same service.

49. [Pierre François Guyot Desfontaines] 'Lettre d'une Dame Angloise . . . '[1]

1744

Prefixed to his translation of *Joseph Andrews, Avantures de Joseph Andrews* (Amsterdam, 2nd ed., 1744), i. i–xxiv.

FROM AN ENGLISH LADY
TO MADAME ★ ★ ★
WIFE OF MR. ★ ★ ★
HEAD ACCOUNTANT
OF MONTPELLIER

In recognition, Madame, of all the favours you have bestowed upon me during my stay at Montpellier, and in order to reinforce your memory of me (fully convinced that you never forgot me, as I shall never forget you) I am honoured to send you my translation of the most clever and pleasing Book that our England has produced. This is

[1] Translated from the French.

The Adventures of Joseph Andrews and Parson Abraham Adams. This Novel, in its briefness, is the equal here of *Don Quixote*, and is considerably superior to all of your French Novels, especially the Novels of this century and of the most recent times, which are (I confess) quite scorned by our Experts. For is there any resemblance to *The History of Cleveland* and *The Dean of Killerine*?[1] What a tissue of insipidities and trifles is *La Vie de Marianne*! *Le Paysan Parvenu* is worth a little more: but what coarse features! what lowness! what descriptions! *Les Confessions du Comte de* . . . are of a man of spirit, and they portray well the corrupt manners of all Europe; but the women there are treated with too little respect for my liking, and this clever book from start to finish breathes only sensual corruption, and teaches only emotional licentiousness. Your *Madame de Luz* smacks of the same. I never refer to certain sordid and infamous Novels which would dishonour the French Nation in our minds, if we did not treat you justly, knowing that they horrify good people in your country as they have in ours.

The novel that you are going to read is somewhat in the same vein as your *Roman comique* by Scarron, which is considered to be a masterpiece in England as well as in France. The Author is Mr. Fielding, one of our good dramatic authors, who is at his best mainly in the comic scene. You will judge his skill in this genre by a large number of features prevalent in his book, and especially by the dialogues, for which he possesses talent of the highest order. But you will value most highly the honesty of all his descriptions and of all his expressions, and the wisdom with which he treats a subject which could have drawn him into licentious descriptions. With what propriety he characterizes a lady of quality's amorous inclinations for her servant, whom she is tempted to marry! How well he paints the battle between love and pride! How effortlessly he sustains the trait of pride in this lady, who condemns her own foolishness without however renouncing her designs, and who is punished at the end, not for having executed them, but merely for having conceived them. Should some critic find some basic fault in this excellent fiction, which is the love of a lady for her servant whom she has considered marrying, a thought which she nevertheless condemns and never executes, I would ask him if the history of Potiphar's wife

---

[1] The works referred to in these paragraphs are Prévost's *Le Philosophe anglais ou les mémoires de Cleveland* (1732–9) and *Le Doyen de Killerine* (1735–40); Marivaux's *Vie de Marianne* (1731–41) and *Le Paysan Parvenu* (1735–6); Charles Pinot Duclos, *Les Confessions du Comte* . . . (1742) and *Histoire de Madame de Luz* (1741); Pierre-Charles Roy, *Les Anonymes* (1724); Etienne-François Avisse, *Le Valet embarrassé ou la vieille amoureuse* (1742); Pierre-Charles Fabriot, *Les Amants déguisés* (1728).

with regard to the young Joseph of the Scriptures, injures his sense of decency. Now the English Joseph has here the same feelings as the Hebrew Joseph, the same wisdom, the same discretion; and the lady is not impudent like the wife of the Egyptian lord. If someone is scandalised by this history, he must therefore erase all the paintings of the greatest masters who describe it. But does not your theatre, as well as ours, treat such subjects every day? Your *Comédie des Anonymes*, your *Valet embarrassé*, your *Amans déguisés* (it was an English 'Bright-light' who is often in Paris and frequently attends your theatre there, who told me the names of these plays that I have never read) do they not offer valets who are objects of benevolence and of tender affection either from their mistresses or from persons of rank who have occasion to see them? I am ashamed to subject you to this ridiculous objection, which I have heard one perhaps presumes to make in France. But I refuse to believe this of a judicious nation. Besides, this servant was a gentleman. I do not want to apprise you of the merit of the characters in this work, who are perfectly drawn from beginning to end. Joseph is the hero of it and Fanny is the heroine. Lady Booby is the rub; she is the Dido of the *Aeneid,* or, if you wish, the Juno, by the persecutions which she heaps upon our two lovers. Mr. Adams, friend and adviser of both, is an admirable man. His is a genuine character, drawn from nature. For we have a vicar in one of our provinces who resembles him perfectly, and there is no one in England who would not recognise him. Such faith! such piety! such erudition! such philosophy! But at the same time what simplicity of manners, what ignorance of the world! I nearly said what a fool, this sensible man!

   The remarkable thing about this work is that just as *Don Quixote* is the picture of Spanish customs, the work at hand is the picture of English customs, which are hardly known in France in spite of the large number of *Englishmen* that one sees in Paris, at Montpellier, and elsewhere. This is certainly not a Book of simple pleasures for the crowd: this is a Book of science and of unadorned morality, available to every one; and in addition it is a book in which one comes to understand how we live in *England.* You will see there our principles, our virtues, our vices, city life and country life. Because this is a comic and homely novel, many low characters are introduced: as in Comedy, chiefly innkeepers, male and female, copied from existing originals whom those who travel often see. Mrs. Slipslop, chambermaid of Lady *Booby*, plays an important role here: she is the 'Soubrette' of the Comedy. I am now going to clarify certain aspects of the work for you.

FIRST BOOK

Colly Cibber is the most famous comic actor that we have. He seldom acts, now that he has been decorated by the Court with the glorious title of Poet Laureate, or Poet of the King. This title, or office, obliges him to compose yearly odes in praise of our king, one for his birthday and one for New Year's Day. These two odes are sung, in a large concert-hall, in the presence of the king and of all the court. Cibber has had little success with his odes, and Mr. Pope has successfully mocked him, chiefly in his famous mock-epic poem called *The Dunciad*, that is to say "la Sottisade". He has had great quarrels with Mr. Pope. *Cibber* is the author of several famous comedies, especially one called *The Careless Husband, Le Mari sans souci*. He has also given us his life history, written in the form of an *Apology*, a work which has greatly delighted the public. It must be admitted that Cibber has much vitality, that he is a good story-teller, and that his sense of humour is refined and tasteful. But he is a bad Poet, particularly in the lyric. You know, and I have had the honour to tell you in the past, that all our comedies are in prose, and never in verse. We do not imitate the French, who put measure and rhyme in the mouth of Thalia and make her recite Alexandrines; something which seems strange to us. The verse of Plautus and of Terence little deserves the name of verse, and we believe we imitate them by an elegant and somewhat rhythmic prose, like the prose of Molière.

Parson Adams is an extremely poor vicar, as are most of them, being in the pay of the rector or the curate who, drawing sometimes ten thousand livres of revenue from his benefice, gives hardly fifty or sixty pistols each year to his vicar, who is frequently a married man with nine or ten children, while the curate who is sometimes un-married, is overflowing with wealth. This is truly a problem for us which our late Queen Anne tried unsuccessfully to solve.

If, prejudiced by your noble French ideas, you find in this book some descriptions that you feel are trifling, I beg you to recall that we scorn nothing which represents nature. The works of the spirit form pictures for us. Every picture which paints nature faithfully is always beautiful, whatever it may show. We banish only the filthy and the disgusting from our works, as from our painting. Does not one esteem the paint-ings of Heemskerk, and other Dutch painters, however base the sub-ject matter may be? According to the prejudices of your country, there is baseness in *Don Quixote*, in your *Roman comique*, in *Guzman* d'*Alfarache*, in *Lazarillo de Tormes*, in your *Gil-Blas de Santillane*. According to our own prejudices, we find stiffness, metaphysic, coldness, and flatness in the majority of your fashionable Parisian novels.

The *Chroniques de Baker*, mentioned at the beginning of the Book, is a *History of England* by the Knight [Sir Richard] Baker. You will be surprised to see a minister such as Adams travelling and drinking in every inn along the way, with two of his young parishioners who are in love with each other. The simplicity and justice of his character excuse this conduct. Besides, what scandalizes you does not scandalize us as much. Scandal is quite an arbitrary thing. For example, in Paris I saw clergymen at the *Comédie* and at the Opera. This would be considered shocking in London, where clergymen never appear at the theatre.

In the original version, Mrs. Slipslop speaks in a ridiculous jargon, distorting many words, especially the scholarly vocabulary which she affects to use without understanding it, and from time to time a lofty speech which in the mouth of a soubrette is very comic. I had to search for correspondences in your language to approximate her saucy speech.

Where we live, lackeys enter the opera and take their places in the upper gallery. This is an unfortunate practice. They often make a horrible racket, and I have often seen them interrupt the performance, even in the presence of the king. Would to God the theatre guard were as good in London as in Paris, where it is excellent. Of course there are always some soldiers of the king's guard in our theatres; but they never impose silence, and they are more afraid of the people than the people are of them. We have greater respect for civil authority than for military force.

Parson Barnabas, who drinks beer in a cabaret of his parish, will scandalize you unless I inform you that we permit clergymen to go to the cabaret and to drink beer and 'ponche' there as long as they do not get drunk. Nevertheless, when they go to the cabaret, they customarily wear a grey overcoat underneath their robe or cassock, which they roll up. For about twenty years, they have not mixed with the crowd very much while wearing their cassocks; they are also less stared at than in earlier times.

The English lord who drives his own carriage, in Chapter XVI of Book I, will acquaint you with the fact that there are many in England who have this hobby, and who most often drive them recklessly. There was a Peer of the Realm who, having had a carriage built after the fashion of public conveyances, drove it himself, his lackeys being inside in the capacity of travelers. The peer was dressed like a coachman, with a handkerchief around his neck, small boots, and a large whip in his hand, He enjoyed the company of professional coachmen. He believed himself as skilled in his own talent as one of his ancestors, who had guided the helm of state; and he found no other difference than that between the physical and the moral. His horses, his vehicle and those who rode in it, seemed to him a state, of which he was the minister. The dialogue between milord the coachman and his friends on board is a criticism of the ordinary conversation of young lords, who have no inward culture, no firm foundation, and who only amuse themselves with trifles, with bad jokes, with hunting dogs, horses, etc.

Whitefield and Wesley, of whom Chapter XVIII [XVII][1] speaks, are two Anglican Preachers who are not permitted to preach in the churches, which are forbidden to them, and who for this reason preach in the streets and crossroads of London and of our provinces. They preach in open air and in the fields. The usual subject of their discourse is the question of Predestination and Grace, and they cry out against the excesses of the century. Whitefield has just been preaching in America. Some consider them to be saints, others judge them to be madmen, and some believe they are scoundrels. In my opinion, their doctrine is equally opposed to common-sense and to the Gospel. In this chapter, I have omitted many features which would have little interest in France regarding the famous Doctor Benjamin Hoadley, today the Bishop of Winchester. This prelate made a lot of noise during the reign of George I, and his sermons were strongly censured. There was a faction in the high church who claimed that he was a heretic. He had some serious quarrels with Dr. Francis Atterbury, Bishop of Rochester, who died in Paris about ten years ago. One certain thing is that Bishop Hoadley was a learned prelate, an honest and very charitable man. Woolston, who is mentioned here again, wrote several quite audacious tracts against the miracles of Jesus Christ, which caused him to be considered a mad scholar and to be locked up in prison.

In the same chapter, the word that Mrs. Tow-wouse uses against her servant, is one of the most abusive in English, and one doesn't dare write it out in the original. However it is nothing in French, since it only means dog, a quite ordinary word in your language. The connotation which the English attach to this word will cause you to understand the cries of Nanon [Betty] when it was applied to her, and the

[1] For explanatory notes relating to *Joseph Andrews*, see Martin C. Battestin's edition (1967).

meaning of her reply. In the text it says 'I have done nothing unnatural.' I have replaced that with 'I have only done what is human,' which seems to me better and more intelligible to Frenchmen.

BOOK TWO

In Chapter I, there is a joke concerning a certain way of publishing books, which had been practiced in earlier times and which is just as disgusting today, although pleasant and easy for the booksellers; this is the publishing successively of portions or segments of a book, in fascicles of four or six leaves in folio or in quarto. Eight leaves sell for a shilling or twenty-four 'sols' in your currency. The *Traduction du Dictionnaire de Bayle* and the *Histoire d'Angleterre par Mr. de Rapin* were sold in this manner. The result is that sometimes a large Work, of which part is published every eight days, does not appear in its entirety for ten years. Usually, one begins well and ends badly.

To have the right to hunt in England, it is necessary only to have a certain revenue from land in the country.

Our twelve London judges travel in pairs through the provinces of the realm, twice each year, conducting criminal and civil actions. When they pass through a locality, all of high society and the masses assemble. The lawsuits are pled and judged during the day, and in the evening there are balls and other diversions. This mixture of joy and sorrow, of comedy and tragedy, of business and pleasure, lasts four or five days, after which the judges go elsewhere.

You know that we have two political parties; one dedicated to the interests of the court, and the other to the interests of the 'country'. You can imagine what that means. This last party is always opposed to the government and for this reason it is never given responsibilities. A job, a responsibility, a pension often means abandoning the country party.

Funeral orations are very common in England. The panegyrist suits his flattery to the remuneration which he expects. Poets are lesser liars than these makers of funeral orations, who are neither Bossuets nor Fléchiers.[1]

Do not be surprised at the zeal of that gang described in this same book. By an Act of Parliament a reward of eight pounds sterling is offered to whoever arrests a highwayman. When he is taken by several persons, they all share the reward.

[1] Jacques-Bénigne Bossuet, Bishop of Meaux, and Valentin-Esprit Fléchier were well known for their elegant funeral orations.

When a woman is condemned to death where we live, she is examined by matrons to see if she is pregnant, in which case one waives punishment until after the lying-in; but one ordinarily shows mercy until after the confinement. Also wives and young girls awaiting the death sentence try to become pregnant. That is to be expected. This child, to which they give life, saves its mother's.

Some centuries ago, in order to interest the English in their studies, they showed mercy to a criminal who knew how to read and write. That was called the Benefit of the Clergy, the *Bénéfice de la Cléricature*.

We are assured that he who is presented here under the name of Trulliber, once taught Latin to the author of this book. If that is so, it is scarcely recognizable, or else the master did not cause himself to be admired and loved by his student. An infinity of vicars or ministers in our provinces perform the trade of Trulliber, being in charge of children, and their fee being insufficient for their upkeep; many even run taverns where they play the violin to amuse their customers. What indecency!

On Sundays and holidays, our peasants amuse themselves mightily by beating each other with sticks the length of an ell. Whichever of the two champions first has his head cracked is considered the loser. The whole village gathers to watch the show which these fights present. This seems senseless, but it serves to support the courageous and warlike humour of the nation.

It is a miserable and extravagant custom in England, that when one eats at the home of a person of distinction, one passes through a row of valets posted to wait on the guest, who is obliged to pay for his meal as one pays for cards in French gambling houses; which also has an indecent flavour. The least that one gives to each one is a shilling, that is to say twenty-four 'sols' in your currency. The most remarkable thing is that persons of a certain rank pay nothing. However, there are a good many people who forbid their servants to receive anything from those who eat at their homes.

What we call a drawing room is a large assembly hall in the royal palace, where high society gathers twice a week between 9:30 p.m. and midnight. There one can see the king and queen, the princes and princesses, who play there. One talks of all kinds of things there, and for this reason this drawing room is like a large 'Caffé du Royaume'.

In London, dramatic poets receive for their new plays all the theatre's profits on the third, sixth, and ninth performances, after costs are deducted. If the play is only performed once or twice, they get nothing:

it does not always run until the sixth or ninth, after which there is no more to claim. The Poet lays hold of tickets for these days, which he brings and presents to persons of distinction, and which he sends to his friends, who do not fail to pay for them in advance: something which is quite low, but it is the practice. You have equally repulsive practices in France, which custom can justify with regard to each particular to which one basely submits. Such is the practice of cringing in order to raise oneself to certain literary and cultural honours, making use for this end of solicitations, intrigues, servilities, which tarnish these honors and render ridiculous, at least in our eyes, those who succeed by these unworthy paths, more open to fools than to men of merit.

We call a sergeant who arrests people for their debts a bailiff. Sometimes these bailiffs, after having arrested debtors, free them for seven or eight days on their word of honour, in return for guineas given to the sergeant. Those who are arrested for debt, and who have some money, are led to the home of the arresting sergeant; they can live there eight or nine days, in order to see if they will be able to pay before being led to prison. The sergeants charge a high price for this stay in their homes. This dishonesty grew to such an extent a few years ago, that an Act of Parliament was necessary to restrain the greed of these men.

THIRD BOOK

In my translation, I omitted an allusion to Mr. Henley, who would never have been understood in France, if I had left him in the text. This Mr. Henley is an Anglican minister. After leaving Cambridge University, he became known through his writings. His hopes for promotion in the Church having been thwarted, he opened a small, separate church. There, he made public prayers and preached every Sunday. He set up and had printed a formulary of prayers, which he caused to be read in his church. On other days of the week he gave secular discourses on literature and morality, in which he sounded like the *Encyclopédie*. He wished to make the room in which he preached on Sundays into a kind of academy, which each would pay a shilling to enter. Finally he struck a sort of silver medallion which would be a perpetual entrance ticket for all those who had bought it. He was usually called Orator Henley, and his speeches contained comic and burlesque features after the fashion of your Scarron. His Sunday sermons continue to this day, but he is not discussed as much as he used to be. He always gives his speeches, however ludicrous they may be, in the dress of a minister: a laughable contrast. He has had some serious arguments with our Bishop of London, who wanted to stop him from putting on such comedies; but he has been supported and has at last borne away the victory, by virtue of an Act of Parliament which permits people of all manner of religion to hold religious meetings and to preach. All that must seem very strange to you.

Mr. Mallet, who is discussed in this book, is a good poet and the author of tragedies which have been well received. He published the *Life of Chancellor Bacon*, at the beginning of the edition of the complete works of this great man, which appeared in 1740 in 4 volumes in folio. This Life is very well written, and I shall send it to you at once, translated into French. As letters here lead sometimes to employment and to success, he is actually administrative secretary of the Prince of Wales.

The *Life of Cicero*, brought up here, is the Work of Dr. Middleton, Librarian of Cambridge. Much has been written for and against this Book, which is not universally admired. It is said that the author has made many mistakes.

Shakespeare and Otway are the two most famous English tragic poets. The noble tragedy by Otway is *Venice Preserv'd, or The Conspiracy Discovered*. Otway lacked prudence: after having been highly favored by the great, he died miserably in a beer-hall. Lee is another famous tragedian. He wrote one or two plays, in collaboration with our illustrious Dryden. Lee's tragedies have many fine qualities, but he is too bombastic. He went mad, was placed in a hospital, and died in the streets of London one night when he had escaped.

In England, when those who dwell in homes in a town, in a borough, or in a village, die penniless, the parish in which this house is situated is obligated to feed the father, mother and children of the deceased, and to take care of the latter until they can be made apprentice to some trade or profession.

Our ladies of quality often dress like peasant women and appear thus publicly in their carriages and on their excursions. That will seem as strange to you as it does to us that your ladies cover their faces with rouge; something which is unheard of in England, and would seem extremely ridiculous.

These various remarks, Madame, will give you the key to several parts of the book which I am honored to send you. I have made many changes in my translation, because my long stays at St. Germain, in Paris, and then at Montpellier have given me a knowledge of French taste. Just as I have omitted certain things that would not have been well-received in France, I have also dared to make some additions which I believed suitable. Since the French like neat, precise, unified thought, I have also taken the liberty to make certain corrections in the Preface which, translated literally, would perhaps have made difficult reading in France. I hope that the manner and the tongue in which I have rendered Mr. Fielding's work will be to the taste of Frenchmen, who received so favorably, in spite of the negligence of the style and the length of the narration. This present work is of a truly different flavour, and is in an entirely opposite genre.

I beg you to pay my compliments to . . . I am etc.

50. Unsigned review of Desfontaines' French translation of *Joseph Andrews*

1744

Third edition (Amsterdam, 1744) In *Bibliothèque Françoise, ou Histoire Littéraire de la France* (1744), xxxix. 201–15. (Translated.)

To compose a novel in the manner of *The Adventures of Don Quixote* is not an undertaking without its difficulties. It will be for the public to decide whether Mr. Fielding has succeeded; we shall limit ourselves to giving some idea of his work. And first, in order to grasp exactly what it is necessary to understand here by 'writ in the manner of the *Adventures of Don Quixote*,' we must look at a passage from the Letter of the English Lady who has translated this novel into our language (her Letter follows immediately after the author's 'Preface'). [Quotes No. 49 above, p. 129, last paragraph.]

From these words one would almost believe that the English are to the French as all the other nations formerly were to the Chinese, who imagined other men to be dwarfs and little monsters, and whose ancient maps are full of such figures. In France one is far from being gulled by the account of the English. I suspect also that Fielding fails to consider the novel of *Don Quixote* as more than, generally speaking, a portrayal of Spanish customs; I would sooner believe, as I have read somewhere, that this work is a satiric allegory of the life of the Duke of Medina-Sidonia, a very illustrious figure in Spain of the time when the book was written. At any rate, if this is the portrayal of English customs, we must acknowledge that, from the chaos we find there, it does little honour to that nation. For the rest, it is certain that this novel is full of paltry things, and the English Lady who has taken the trouble to translate it has herself well foreseen that a reader will not be overly pleased to find in *The Adventures of Joseph Andrews and his Friend* certain images that could hardly be put into a work with much success. She has thought to anticipate the bad effect that this impression would cause by defining what is meant in England by a work of genius. [Quotes p. 130, last paragraph.][1]

In short, the author of the letter in question, supposedly an English Lady, or some other person, would appear to be clearly biased in favour of English wit and discontented with French taste in novels, above all with the novels of this century, as well as of earlier times, which are fairly despised (she says) by English connoisseurs. Of Mr. Fielding, the author of these adventures, the English Lady speaks in these terms. [Quotes p. 128, ll. 17–26.]

What then is the subject and what the wisdom with which it is treated? The explanation of this point will put the reader in full possession of the whole novel, of both its content and form, and it is once more the English Lady who will supply this in continuing to speak of her Mr. Fielding. [Quotes p. 128, l. 26–p. 129, l. 4.]

Were we to speak seriously, we might well ask our female translator where she got that idea, and if she believes that what is quite excellent in an infinitely respectable Book could not become, by application, or otherwise, very bad and profane in a novel of the sort written by Mr.

[1] In this quotation, after 'I beg you to recall that we scorn nothing which represents nature', the reviewer adds a footnote: 'Apparently the author follows the definition given here of an English *Bel-Esprit*, when he makes the following picture to portray an amorous woman'; and he quotes the simile in Bk. I, Chap. 6, that compares Slipslop to a hungry tigress or a voracious pike.

Fielding? But rather let us make known the other characters of this marvelous epic poem. [Quotes p. 129, ll. 17-26.][1]

At the end of the 'Letter of an English Lady,' one finds some explanations for certain passages of that work. I am going to transcribe some of these, and as we have just spoken of Parson Adams, I shall begin by the revelation that treats him. [Quotes p. 130, l. 23-29, p. 131, ll. 5-11.]

This is true, but the example alleged is not altogether just. 'In Paris,' we are told, 'I saw clergymen at the *Comédie* and at the Opera. This would be considered shocking in London where clergymen never appear at the theatre.' It would be necessary to know what our translator means by clergymen; for those who have taken orders do not dare appear in such places as the theatres of Paris. I would not insist on that, however, not having precise information on the matter. But as to the scandal a clergyman gives who travels and drinks in a tavern on the road, I do not know in what it could consist. I believe that is the way it is practised in all of Paris. However it may by, the author gives in general a very scanty idea in his book of curates or of English country parsons; 'their fee being insufficient for their upkeep, many . . . run taverns where they play the violin to amuse their customers. What indecency!' Here the scandal would be better in its proper place.

The English Lady claims, moreover, that she has suppressed a passage that alludes to Mr. Henley in her translation, and which would never be understood in France if it remained in the text. The explanation we are given on that matter seems to me curious, and perhaps will appear such to our readers. To make doubly sure, here it is. [Quotes p. 135, l. 23-p. 136, l. 6.]

I have not spoken yet of the author's 'Preface', and I hope I will be excused this small confusion. The author there gives an idea of his novel and presents a dissertation on this kind of writing, 'which has never been tried in our language', as Mr. Fielding says.[2] He takes the thing from far back, going back as far as the epic poem, divided into two

---

[1] In a footnote to 'there is no one in England who would not recognize him', the reviewer notes the inconsistency between Fielding's remark that he describes not an individual but a species (Bk. III, Chap. 1) and the Lady's reference to copies of particular people (p. 129).

[2] Fielding's English has been *re*translated from the French, since the French translation quoted is a very free one indeed.

kinds: the tragic and the comic. According to Mr. Fielding, epic poetry is arbitrary in its form, 'and the author of a poem of that kind can write in prose or in verse'; thus the *Telemachus* of M. de Fénelon appears to our author to merit the name of epic as much as the *Odyssey* of Homer. The Lady who has translated these adventures is of the same opinion. 'Wholly English as I am,' she says, 'I have no fear to assert that France has in the *Telemachus* a poem well above that of our Milton, who is no more than a monster.'[1] However this may be, our author is of the opinion that a novel such as 'the novels of Cervantes, of Scarron, or this one, is an epic poem, a poem in the comic genre, which is written in prose'.[2]

To admit the burlesque is a privilege of this kind of writing——a privilege of which the author has availed himself, as he informs us himself, to describe more than one adventure which he could only spin out by this means; but although he thinks of burlesque almost as did Lord Shaftesbury, who maintained that one cannot find it in the writings of the ancients, he nevertheless does not abhor it quite so much .'My indulgence in that regard,' he adds, 'is less due to the success my works of that kind have had on the stage, than to the conviction of its utility for contributing to mirth and purging the spleen, by the laughter it can excite; that which renders a remedy more specific against all the symptoms of hypochrondria, than any we can imagine.'

As ridicule also enters into the author's plan, he explains what he intends by the word; and according to the remarks he has been able to make on this subject, he has concluded that the source of ridicule is none other than affectation, and this can be divided into an infinite number of branches. He admits two kinds of affectation, of which the one draws its origin from vanity, and the other from hypocrisy. For it is the discovery of affectation that gives birth to ridicule, and this discovery strikes, astonishes, amuses the reader more when hypocrisy is at bottom than when it is only vanity. To 'unmask a man who has appeared to be the reverse of himself, surprises more, and appears infinitely more ridiculous than to find him only a little different from what he had appeared before, that is to say less replete with the good

---

[1] The quotation is from Desfontaines's note to Fielding's preface, p. v.

[2] At this point the reviewer adds a footnote: 'We will willingly pardon Mr. F. for having such a good opinion of his work, when we know that according to his taste the histories of Lord Clarendon, Whitlock, Eachard, and Rapin de Thoyras are "no other than a Romance, in which the Writer hath indulged a happy and fertile Invention." (Bk. III, Chap. 1) I had at first thought that the author intended a joke, and I acknowledge that I have not yet altogether abandoned that idea.'

qualities that he has pretended to than one had thought'. It follows from this that the evils and calamities of life, no less than the imperfections of men, become ridiculous only by affectation. Finally, the author holds that great faults must be the object of our aversion, lesser ones of our compassion. Therefore affectation alone appears to Mr. Fielding worthy of ridicule. 'Perhaps it may be objected to me,' he says, 'that against my own rules I have introduced vices, and heinous vices into the body of my work. To which I answer: 1. That it is very difficult to pursue the actions of men for some time without unavoidably running into them. 2. The vices to be found in my book are rather the accidental consequences of the frailty of nature than habits brought about by the corruption of the mind. 3. They are set forth as the objects of detestation and never of ridicule. 4. They are never the principal figures who occupy the scene. 5. Finally, they are never allowed to triumph.' This is how Mr. Fielding saves himself from the objection that he has made. He adds some words touching the characters of his actors, protesting strongly that he has no design against the reputation and honor of actual contemporaries.

I have thought it not unfair to enter into a little detail concerning the two pieces that precede *The Adventures of Joseph Andrews and his Friend, &c.*, the author's 'Preface' and the 'Letter of an English Lady,' presuming that by doing so I have given some idea of this new 'epic poem.' I feel strongly however that one has the right to expect of me something more precise, which will demonstrate the ability of Mr. Fielding and his talent at producing such delicate compositions in which 'affectation,' however little it may be in evidence, would cast over the author and his poem a more than moderate 'ridicule'. But when it is a matter of choosing the suitable passages in a work of this order, the choice becomes embarrassing. We will do well then, I think, to borrow from what the Lady, who has taken the pains to translate this work, has informed us in her account of the author; to know that he shines above all by the 'dialogues, the art of which he possesses in the highest degree.' Here is an attempt.

I have already spoken of the amorous inclination of Lady Booby for Joseph, her servant, and the hero of the novel. After the death of this lady's husband, the author represents her for us in her bed at ten in the morning, and alone when Joseph enters by her order [Bk. I, Chap. 5]. 'She had him approach her and had him sit down, and letting her hand fall on his with a distracted air, she asked him if he had never been in love. Joseph answered blushing that he was young and there remained time enough for him to think of that. "Despite your youth," she replied, "I am persuaded that you have already experienced the effects of that natural passion. Go, Joseph, admit to me the truth, name for me the happy girl who has made a conquest of you." "All women are equally indifferent to me," replied Joseph. "How?" said Lady Booby, "are you then already a libertine? But no, you are like beautiful women who are often long and difficult in fixing. But you will never persuade me that you are so free as you would appear. I rather impute your reserve to your secrecy, and I can only praise you: there is nothing more unworthy in a young man than to betray any intimacies with the ladies." "Ladies!" cried Joseph interrupting, "Madame, be assured that I never had the impudence to think of any that deserve that name," ' &c. The rest of the dialogue is in the same vein, for example Lady Booby losing patience, says to Joseph angrily: ' "You are a fool, or pretend to be so. I find I was mistaken in you, so get you out of my chamber." "I beg you, Madame," says Joseph, "do not think any evil of me. I have always served you, Madame, with all the fidelity and affection possible, and my late master also." "Leave villain!" cried the Lady, weeping, "Why have you named the dear departed? Is it to increase my regrets by recalling this sad memory? Be gone, I can endure you no more." '

After this beautiful dialogue, we will dispense, perhaps without regret, with transcribing another. In any case, the novel of Mr. Fielding is full enough of such scenes, and the reader can return if he is curious to see other examples of the marvelous art attributed to Mr. Fielding for his dialogue.

Let us not forget to say that it happily chances that the hero of this piece, the incomparable Joseph Andrews, is brother of the modest and wise Pamela, whose famous adventures have been universally admired. It would, in truth, be too bad if there were to be only two members of that famous family, or that it would be misunderstood for lack of historians. It is evident that such would be a loss for the public.

51. [John Mottley (?)], 'Fielding'

1747

From entry on Fielding in 'A Compleat List of all the *English* Dramatic Poets, and of All the Plays ever printed in the *English* Language, to the Present Year M,DCC,XLVII', appended to Thomas Whincop, *Scanderbeg: or, Love and Liberty* (1747), p. 232.

* * *

[Fielding] is supposed to be the Author of *The Adventures of* Joseph Andrews, &c. a diverting Romance, wrote in Imitation of *Cervantes* . . .

---

52. Thomas Birch, letter

19 January 1747–8

From a letter to the Earl of Orrery, *The Orrery Papers*, ed. the Countess of Cork and Orrery (1903), ii. 14.

---

*   *   *

Mr. Fielding is printing three volumes of Adventures under the title of *The Foundling*. Mr. Littelton, who has read the manuscript, commends the performance to me as an excellent one,[1] and abounding with strong and lively painting of characters, and a very copious and happy invention in the conduct of the story.

1 For a similar statement see Birch's letter of 30 September 1748, ii. 43.

---

53. From 'Trott Plaid Excused'
The London Evening Post
28–30 July 1748

A personal attack on the Fielding of *The Jacobite's Journal*, this poem at one point turns to his non-political work.

$\star$ $\star$ $\star$

> *Low Humour,* like *his own,* he once exprest,
> In *Footman, Country Wench,* and *Country Priest:*
> But all who read, must pity, or must snore,
> When TROTT-PLAID's *humble Genius* aims at *more.*

$\star$ $\star$ $\star$

54. 'Epitaph', *Old England*

20 November 1748

Reprinted in the *Gentleman's Magazine*, December 1748, xviii. 515
The epitaph celebrates the discontinuance of *The Jacobite's Journal*
in November 1748 with some general remarks on its author.

Beneath this stone,
Lies *Trotplaid John*,
His length of chin and nose;
His crazy brain,
Unhum'rous vein
In verse and eke in prose
Some plays he wrote,
Sans wit or plot,
Adventures of inferiors!
Which, with his lives
Of *rogues* and *thieves*,
Supply the town's posteriors.
But ah, alack! He broke his back,
When politics he tried:
For like a ——
He play'd his part,
Crack'd loudly, stunk, and died.

55. Lady Frances Hertford, Duchess of Somerset, letter

20 November 1748

From a letter to Lady Henrietta Luxborough, printed in Helen S. Hughes, *The Gentle Hertford* (1940), p. 388.

*   *   *

I have been very well entertained lately with the two first volumes of *The Foundling*, which is written by Mr. Fielding, but not to be published till the 22nd of January; and if the same spirit runs through the whole work, I think it will be much preferable to *Joseph Andrews*.

*   *   *

56. Thomas Birch, letter

20 December 1748

From a letter to the Earl of Orrery, *The Orrery Papers*, ii. 49.

*   *   *

Mr. Fielding's novel, called the *Foundling*, in 6 volumes, was expected before this time, but will not be published before the middle, or perhaps end, of next month. Humour is the chief characteristic of it, though I am told by my friends, who have seen it, that it is not destitute of the instructive and pathetic.

*   *   *

57. Unsigned 'Plan of a late celebrated Novel'

The London Magazine

February 1748-9, xviii. 51-55

A Book having been lately published, which has given great Amusement, and, we hope, Instruction to the polite Part of the Town, we think ourselves obliged to give our Readers some Account of it.

It is intitled, *The History of* TOM JONES, *a Foundling, by* Henry Fielding, *Esq*; being a novel, or prose epick composition, and calculated to recommend religion and virtue, to shew the bad consequences of indiscretion, and set several kinds of vice in their most deformed and shocking light. This piece, like all such good compositions, consists of a principal history, and a great many episodes or incidents; all which arise naturally from the subject, and contribute towards carrying on the chief plot or design. Through the whole, the reader's attention is always kept awake by some new surprizing accident, and his curiosity upon the stretch, to discover the effects of that accident; so that after one has begun to read, it is difficult to leave off before having read the whole.

The principal history is that of *Tom Jones* the foundling, who is the hero, and of Miss *Sophia Western*, who is the heroine of the piece; which is as follows.

Thomas Allworthy, Esq; of *Somersetshire*, was a man of an agreeable person, a sound constitution, a solid understanding, a benevolent heart, and of one of the largest estates in the country. He was a widower without any children, and therefore his sister, Miss *Bridget*, lived with him as his house-keeper, being then a maiden lady of no great beauty, about 30. This gentleman returning home, after having been three months at *London*, and stepping into bed, found in it an infant wrapt up in some coarse linen, on which he called his sister's maid, and ordered her to take care of the child; but next morning, at the desire of his sister and her maid, an enquiry was made in the neighbourhood after the mother, when one *Jenny Jones* confessed, upon the first challenge, that she was the mother. This *Jenny* had lived some years as servant-maid in the family of a schoolmaster in the parish, named *Partridge*, by whom she had been taught not only to read *English*, but understand *Latin*, and being a girl of quick parts, soon got so much learning as to make her the envy of the neighbourhood; which was increased by her appearing lately at church in a new silk gown and lac'd cap, from whence, and from her being turned out of her place by the jealousy of her mistress, a suspicion arose, that she was the mother of the child. When she was brought before Mr. *Allworthy*, as a justice of the peace, she confessed her being the mother, but said she was bound by the most solemn oaths not to discover the father, for that time at least, which oaths no punishment should force her to break; and he, in consideration of her firmness, as well as frankness, and to prevent her utter ruin, sent her to a remote part of the country, where she was not known, instead of sending her to the house of correction; resolving, at the same time, to take care of the child, to whom he gave the name of *Thomas Jones*.

Tho' this proceeded entirely from his benevolent disposition, yet it raised a suspicion, that he himself was the father of the child; which he long neglected. In the mean time, as he was a man of great hospitality, he had always in his house some gentlemen, whose fortunes consisted only in their learning or wit, which in most countries is a sort of coin not current at any common market. Among the rest was one Dr. *Blifil*, who soon discovered, that Miss *Bridget*, notwithstanding her age, longed much for what few women can easily live without; but as he had himself a wife, he could make no addresses; therefore he introduced his brother Capt. *Blifil* into the family, who soon prevailed with miss to marry him privately, and the doctor got him reconciled to the 'squire; so that from that time till his death he lived in the family, from which he very soon most ungratefully banished his brother; and having, soon after the marriage, a son by his wife, he was at the same pains, but not with the same success, to get the foundling, *Tom Jones*, banished, by directly accusing the schoolmaster, *Partridge*, with being the father, which obliged Mr. *Allworthy* to make an enquiry into the fact; and tho' *Partridge* stoutly denied it, yet upon the evidence of his wife, he was found guilty; which brought so many misfortunes upon him, that he was forced to fly the country.

However, Mr. *Allworthy* continued to provide for the foundling, and had him brought up and educated in his own house, with young Mr. *Blifil* his nephew. Tho' these two were brought up together, they soon appeared to be of a very different character: *Jones* was a lad of quick parts, high metal, a benevolent disposition, and a free open temper;

by which he made himself very agreeable, but was often led into little rash indiscretions. On the other hand, *Blifil* was of slow parts, a phlegmatick, reserved temper, and an artful, cunning disposition; but as he was the presumptive heir of 'Squire *Allworthy*, he was the favourite of parson *Thwackum* and Mr. *Square*; the former a zealous churchman their tutor, and the latter a moral philosopher and freethinker, entertained at the 'Squire's house.

As *Jones* soon became an excellent sportsman, he recommended himself highly to the favour of 'Squire *Western*, a neighbouring gentleman of a great estate, and father of Miss *Sophia Western*, a man of a boisterous stupid, obstinate nature, who neither loved nor knew any thing but hunting and drinking, yet had a great love, in his way, for Miss *Sophia* who was his only child, and a young lady of exquisite beauty, great sense, nice honour, and a most amiable temper.

Jones, by being her father's companion, was of course often in her company, and being most agreeable in his person, as well as conversation, without any design in either, they became, by degrees, deeply enamoured with each other; so deeply, that neither could ever banish the tyrant love from the heart, tho' both endeavoured it, because they could never expect her father's consent to a match.

In the mean time, Mr. *Allworthy* was taken dangerously ill of a fever, upon which he called his family about him, when he told *Blifil*, whose father had died some years before, and his mother was absent on a visit, that he had left him his whole estate, except the following legacies, *viz.* 500*l.* a year to his mother during her life, 500*l.* a year, with 1000*l.* in money, to Mr. *Jones*, 1000*l.* to *Thwackum*, the like sum to *Square*, small legacies to his servants, and some charities. Whilst he was giving this account, with some good advices, to his family, a footman came and told him, that an attorney from *Salisbury* was come with a message, which, he said, he must deliver to himself. As he was not in a condition to receive it, he desired Mr. *Blifil* to go and receive the gentleman's message; which he did, and they all retired to leave the sick gentleman to compose himself to rest.

Upon Mr. *Blifil's* return to them, he told them, with a melancholy countenance, that the attorney, whose name was *Dowling*, had brought an account of his mother's dying suddenly at *Salisbury*; on which it was debated, whether this should be communicated to Mr. *Allworthy*. The physician opposed it, but Mr. *Blifil* insisted it should, and upon hearing the news, he directed Mr. *Blifil* to take care of the funeral.

Mr. *Allworthy*, however, recovered; but before he could come out of his room, a quarrel happened between *Jones* and *Blifil*, which not only increased the hatred of the latter, but was the cause of Mr. *Western's* sister's discovering, that his daughter *Sophia* was in love, either with *Jones* or *Blifil*, though as yet not certain which. Upon her communicating this suspicion to her brother, he presently resolved to propose to Mr. *Allworthy* a match between his daughter and Mr. *Blifil*, which the other agreed to, on condition, that the young people liked each other; but Mr. *Western*, who had not half his sense, nor any of his humanity, resolved within himself to force his daughter to say she liked the match, whether she did so or not.

In the mean time, the aunt discovered, that *Sophy's* love was for *Jones*; and upon communicating this to her brother, they both resolved, that *Sophy* should, as soon as possible, be married to *Blifil*, and poor *Jones* was banished the house. But this was not the only misfortune that befel him. Mr. *Western* flew in a rage to acquaint Mr. *Allworthy* with what had been discovered. The latter fell into a passion at *Jones*, who was absent; and *Blifil* being present, took that opportunity to tell all the bad stories he could think of relating to *Jones*; all which he got *Thwackum* and *Square* to confirm, and upon this *Jones* was banished that house also, and ordered never to see Mr. *Allworthy's* face any more.

Jones's first design was to go to sea, and for that purpose he took the road to *Bristol*; but in the way, meeting with a party of soldiers going to join the army under the duke, then marching against the rebels, he resolved to go and serve as a volunteer in the army. In his way thither he, by accident, met with *Partridge*, who begg'd and obtained leave to accompany him as a servant. After passing *Gloucester*, they lost their way in the night and came into a wood, where *Jones* rescued a lady, by knocking down a fellow who had tore all the cloaths off of her back, and was going to murder her. This lady he conducted to *Upton*, where he discovered, by some soldiers, that the lady's name was *Waters*, the wife or mistress of a captain in their regiment; and the lady was so grateful, when they were alone together, as to make broad signs, that he might, after the people were gone to bed, slip into her room and have a share of hers, if he pleased, which offer he had too much gallantry not to embrace.

After their arrival, a coach and four came in with two ladies from *Ireland*, who intended to refresh there, and set out again to *Bath*; but the coachman got so drunk, that he could not set forward, and consequently the two ladies were forced to take up their lodging there, which made them very uneasy. However, to bed they went, and Mr. *Jones* and Mrs.

Waters went likewise to the chambers provided for them; but Mr. *Jones* soon left his own, and slipt into that of Mrs. *Waters*. Whilst they were in bed together, one Mr. *Fitzpatrick* arrived from *Ireland* in pursuit of his wife, who was a cousin and intimate acquaintance of Miss *Sophia Western*'s and had run away with and married Mr. *Fitzpatrick*, but was so ill used by him, that she was obliged to elope. This gentleman, upon hearing a description of Mrs. *Waters*, presently imagined her to be his wife, and being shewed her room, he broke open the door, and rushed in; on which Mr. *Jones* leaped out of bed, and a skuffle ensued, in which Mr. *Fitzpatrick* got some hearty knocks which he could not forget; but upon the maid's coming in with a candle, he found he was mistaken, so begged pardon and retired. Upon his return to the kitchen, the coachman, who was now a little sober, told him he had two empty places in his coach, which he and another *Irish* gentleman in the inn might have, to which they agreed; so that, if it had not been for the noise of the above fray, he might next morning have seen his wife in the coach; but as she was awaked by the noise, and knew her husband's voice as soon as she heard he was gone to bed, she got up, and together with her maid went off on horseback towards *London*.

Soon after this fray was over, arrived at the same inn Miss *Sophia Western* and her chamber maid, she having made her escape from her father's house, by the help of her maid, to prevent her being forced to marry *Blifil*. Upon her arrival she heard that Mr. *Jones* was in the house, and by bribing the maid, she learned that he was in bed with a lady; on which, fired with disdain, she presently set out again from thence, but left her muff with a bit of paper in it, on which she wrote *Sophia Western*, which she desired the maid to lay in his way, and by which he found, as soon as he got up in the morning, that she had been in the house, and that she had made her escape from her father. This made him instantly resolve to go in pursuit of her, and tho' he had no knowledge of the road she was to take, by several accidents he found that Miss *Sophia* and her maid, together with another lady and her maid, (Mrs. *Fitzpatrick* and she having fallen in company together upon the road from *Upton*) had met, at an inn upon the road, with an *Irish* peer of the other lady's acquaintance, who took them into his coach and six, and that they were all gone together for *London*.

Upon this, *Jones*, with his man *Partridge*, took post for *London*, where he arrived soon after his beloved *Sophy*, but was some days before he could find out where she was, and much longer before he could see her; and he had but once, by great accident, got an opportunity to speak with her; when her father having been informed where she was, came to town, seized her, and carried her with him to his own lodgings. Upon which Mr. *Allworthy* and *Blifil* being sent for, they came both to town, so that poor *Sophy* was again in danger of being forced to marry the man she hated, or to live a prisoner in her father's house upon bread and water, as he often threatened.

When Mr. *Jones* came first to town, he took lodgings at the house of Mrs. *Miller*, a clergyman's widow, who had been long supported by the charity of Mr. *Allworthy*, and with whom he always lodged; so that upon his coming to town, Mr. *Jones* was obliged to quit his lodging; but while he was there, he had done a signal service to Mrs. *Miller*, and had so far recommended himself to her favour, that she became a great instrument in reconciling him to Mr. *Allworthy*.

Mr. *Jones* being now in the greatest distress about the danger to which his *Sophy* was exposed, a revengeful project of Mrs. *Fitzpatrick*'s carried him to her lodgings, and as he came out from thence, he met Mr. *Fitzpatrick* in the street, who directly attacked him. They both drew, and he ran *Fitzpatrick* thro' the body, on which he was committed to the *Gatehouse*. While he was there, Mrs. *Waters*, who had come to town, and lived with Mr. *Fitzpatrick*, came to see him. Here *Partridge*, had time to look at her, which he never had while at *Upton*; and therefore, as soon as she was gone, upon having heard, by their discourse, that this was the same woman, Mr. *Jones* had been in bed with at *Upton*, he came trembling in to his master, and told him, that she was his mother.

Whilst *Jones* was in this agony, *Allworthy* received a letter from *Square*, upon his death-bed at *Bath*, confessing the villanies that had been set on foot against *Jones*, and the false evidence he had given against him; and upon the back of this he found, that *Blifil* had been endeavouring to suborn witnesses against *Jones*, in case *Fitzpatrick* had died of his wound. In this *Blifil* had employed *Dowling*, whom Mr. *Allworthy* then employed as his steward, and had brought to town with him. As Mr. *Allworthy* was upon this enquiry, Mrs. *Waters* got access to him, and informed him, that she was not the real mother of *Jones*, but that Miss *Bridget*, his sister, was, and had hired her not only to drop the child where she did, but to acknowledge her being the mother, and that his sister often said, she would communicate the secret to him before she died. Upon this, *Dowling* happened to come in; and Mr. *Allworthy*, after making him confess, that he was employed by Mr. *Blifil* against *Jones*, said, he believed, that he would not have accepted of any such employment, had he known that *Jones* was his nephew. I am sure, answer'd *Dowling*, it did not become me to take any notice of what I thought you desired to conceal.—How, cries *Allworthy*, and did you know then? Upon this he declared, that Mrs. *Blifil's* last words were, to tell him, that *Jones* was her son and his nephew, when she delivered him her letter which he brought from *Salisbury*. What letter, cries *Allworthy*? The letter to you, Sir, answered *Dowling*, which I delivered with the message to Mr. *Blifil*, when you was ill in bed; to which he added, that *Blifil* afterwards told him, he had delivered both letter and message to his worship, but that out of regard to his sister his worship intended to conceal it from the world.

This brought to light the whole truth relating to *Jones*, and the whole villany of *Blifil*; on which the latter was discarded the lodging, and would have been absolutely abandoned by *Allworthy*, had it not been for the intercession of *Jones*, who was now declared sole heir to his uncle's estate; and as *Fitzpatrick* was out of all danger, he was bailed out of prison, and soon after married to Miss *Sophia Western*.

Thus ends this pretty novel, with a most just distribution of rewards and punishments, according to the merits of all the persons that had any considerable spare in it; but this short abstract can only serve as an incitement to those, that have not yet had the pleasure of reading it; for we had not room for many of the surprising incidents, or for giving any of them in their beautiful dress.

58. From *The Fan*

1749

From *The Fan: A Heroi-Comical Poem, in Three Cantos*, pp. iii–iv ('The Design'), 5–9 (Canto I); printed in Alan D. McKillop, 'An Iconographic Poem on *Tom Jones*', *Philological Quarterly* (1938) xvii, 403–5.

The Loss of a Lady's FAN, at a late Assembly, gave Rise to the following Poem. Every thing else, that is built on that, is fictitious; and *Lydia* no more comes up to the Original, than *Belinda* did to Miss *Isabella Fermor*. The painting of her Fan, is as imaginary, as the Person that stole it; and tho' not real, shews what a rich Fund, for the Pencil, there is in the Scenes of *Tom Jones*: No weak Argument for their Beauty, when they still please, though stript of Words. I hope this will prove a Hint to some ingenious Artist.

*   *   *

A favourite Fan fair *Lydia* possess'd,
Preferred by her to the unnumber'd rest,
For Ladies take a Liking to a Fan,
They know not why, just as they do to Man.
Yet why so favour'd let me not conceal,
She lov'd the Toy, because she lov'd the Tale.
Within the Painter had employ'd his Art
To move the Passions, and to please the Heart;
He guides the Pencil, draws the living Line,
She gives the Fancy and the bright Design:
The Foundling's Story touch'd the tender Dame,
The Foundling's Story then was all her Theme.

*There first in lively Colours was exprest,
The early Workings of a generous Breast;

---

* In Imitation of ARCHILLES *Shield*, so nobly describ'd by HOMER.

Tommy high-mounted on a Branch appear'd,
His Hand just stretch'd to catch *Sophia's* Bird;
The Branch gives Way, you'd think you hear the Sound;
While underneath in lighter Shades is found
The deep Canal, whose unrelenting Wave
Threatens poor *Tommy* with a wat'ry Grave.
Blifill displays the unnat'ral Heart in Paint,
And *Sophy* even in Colours seems to faint.

The Artist next employ'd his utmost Skill,
And Passions rose obedient to his Will.
Tòm, kneeling, owns it was a Fault indeed,
But then that Fault procur'd the Needy Bread;
What Scenes of Misery, what deep Distress,
O! had you seen it, you'd have done no less.
Alworthy melts, the Tears start in his Eyes,
And pleas'd, admires his Virtues with Surprize.

Not far the Painter drew a tender Scene,
Such as nor Verse can paint, nor Words explain;
'Twas when *Sophia*, Thunder-struck, espy'd
Jones broken Arm hang dangling by his Side;
There Looks of Tenderness and Pity strove
To show Regard just ripening into Love.
He smiles to see *Sophia* free from Harm,
And wrapt in Extasy forgets his Arm.

Jones in the next Design was well repay'd,
The Muff in Danger now alarm'd the Maid,
She flies to save it from th' unpitying Flame,
And shows a Something more than Muff could claim.
Love first displays his Power in *Jones's* Face,
While *Western* in a Laugh compleats the Piece.

The Comick and the Tragick next combin'd,
To please the Fancy, and divert the Mind.
Moll Seagrim's Bed-Chamber the Painter drew,
Here hung a greasy Cap, there lay a Shoe;
One Hole admitted both the Light and Rain,
One Wisp of Straw excluded both again;
A Fragment of a Looking-Glass stood near,
What Time *Moll* had to spend, she spent it there.
The Rugg falls down, *Square Shakes* abash'd with Shame,
Moll seems to shriek my Honour! and my Name!

Jones from Surprize recover'd laughing stood,
Forgives and owns the Force of Flesh and Blood.

The Painter next a mournful Tale had wrought
Where Colours labour'd with expressive Thought.
An awful Foe to Vice *Alworthy* stands,
Jones pale and trembling hears his fixt Commands,
Acquits his Judge, himself accuses most,
Grieves at his Fate, but more *Sophia* lost.

The Robber suppliant next demands his Life,
And pleads a starving Family and Wife;
Jones melts at this, you'd see his Pity rise,
His Purse he gives him, and his Wants supplies;
A pale-fac'd comick Figure lies hard by,
And *Partridge* trembling dies, or seems to die.

The Pencil next display'd its utmost Art,
To draw a generous Deed and godlike Part;
The vary'd Group the varying Passions move,
Repentance *Nightingale,* but *Nancy* love;
A laughing Face shows *Betsy's* little Soul,
While *Jones* in calmer Transports feels the Whole;
Repay him, Heav'n! the Mother seems to say,
For Heav'n such Goodness only can repay.

A Piece came next which horribly alarms,
Where *Fellamour* attacks *Sophia's* Charms;
You dread th' Event, till thro' the half-op'd Door,
Western gives Ease, who never did before.

That Piece came last, where urg'd by sweet Command
Sophia with her Heart resigns her Hand;
Such winning Beauties, such excelling Grace,
The Painter, trust me, drew *Maria's* Face,
Her Heav'n-touch'd Looks, her gentle winning Air,
And from a real rais'd th' imagin'd Fair.
Her Hand *Jones* presses to his eager Lip,
Alworthy smiles, and *Western* seems to skip.

Along the circling Edge he drew the Skies,
In shining Colours and in varying Dyes;
The vernal Clouds tipt round with lucid Hue,
Hang o'er the Whole, and terminate the View.

157

Say, happy *Fielding,* can thy laurell'd Brow
Give half that Joy, as *Lydia* gives thee now?
Say, could you hope thy Scenes would leave behind
Such deep Impression, and so touch the Mind?
When Female Sense and Female Softness meet
To praise thy Work, thy Work is sure compleat.

TOM JONES AND
JOSEPH ANDREWS

59. William Shenstone, letter

22 March 1748–9

From a letter to Lady Henrietta Luxborough, *Letters of William Shenstone*, ed. Mallam, p. 138.

. . . I return your two first volumes of Tom Jones which I have read with some Pleasure, tho' I see no Character yet y^t is near so striking as Mr Abraham Adams. *That* was an *original*, I think; unattempted before, & yet so natural y^t most people seem'd to know y^e ¦Man. As you have been so kind to give me ye reading of ye first volumes, I believe I must beg Leave to borrow ye remaining volumes before ye first Part of ye Story slips out of my Memory. . . .

60. Lady Henrietta Luxborough, letter

23 March 1748–9

From a letter to William Shenstone, *Letters Written by the Late Honourable Lady Luxborough to William Shenstone, Esq.* (1775), pp. 88–89.

My solitude is commonly more strict when I wish it to be varied, by the arrival of some merry companion or other to entertain me and my friends: yet I might live at least five hundred years in this place before one quarter of the incidents happened which are related in any one of the six volumes of Tom Jones. I have not yet read the two last: but I think as you do, that no one character yet is near so striking as Adams's in the author's other composition, and the plan seems far-fetched; but in the adventures that happen, I think he produces personages but too like those one meets with in the world; and even among those people to whom he gives good characters, he shews them as in a concave glass, which discovers blemishes that would not have appeared to the common eye, and may make every modest reader fear to look in such a glass, as some do who have been beauties, and would choose to fancy themselves so still. The Beauty herself might shun it equally; for that sort of glass would not flatter, and defects would appear, as there is no perfection in us mortals.—If Mr. Fielding and Mr. Hogarth could abate the vanity of the world by shewing its faults so plainly, they would do more than the greatest divines have yet been capable of: But human nature will still be the same, and would, I am afraid, furnish them, if they lived till the world ended, with such imperfect objects to represent.

★   ★   ★

61. *The Gentleman's Magazine*

March 1749, xix. 126

From a footnote to 'A Extract from a famed Sermon . . . by Edw. Cobden, D. D. Archdeacon of London, and Chaplain ordinary to his Majesty'.

The *Gentleman*'s editor (Samuel Johnson?) adds a footnote to Cobden's sermon, 'A Persuasive to Chastity', at the point where it is describing the miseries resultant upon fornication.

Of this wretched state, a most lively and striking picture is exhibited in *Roderick Random*, which we have copied here as a warning to one sex, and a remonstrance against t'other.

[excerpt from Random follows]

Some strokes of this kind appear also in *Tom Jones*, and in Mrs. Philips's *Apology*.[1]—Indeed as this subject is capable of very high colouring, almost every writer has exercised upon it his skill in painting. However, the loose images in these pieces perhaps invite to vice more than the contrast figures alarm us into virtue.

---

[1] The scandalous *Apology for the Conduct of Mrs. Teresia Constantia Philips* had been published in 1748. As Blanchard adds, 'One can imagine the smile of Mr. Urban's editor, as he put Fielding's great work in the same category as the *Apology* of the notorious Mrs. Phillips' (p. 37).

62. Captain Lewis Thomas, letter

3 April [1749]

From a letter to Welbore Ellis, written in Carlisle, in the Mendip Papers, University of Chicago Libraries. All but the last paragraph is quoted by J. P. Feil, 'Fielding's Character of Mrs. Whitefield', *Philological Quarterly* (1960), xxxix. 509–10. Mr. Feil has kindly supplied us with the last paragraph from his transcript of the letter.

I am just got up from a very Amazing entertainment; to use a Metaphor in the Foundling, I have been these four or five days last past a fellow traveller of Harry Fieldings, & a very agreeable Journey I have had. Character, Painting, Reflexion, Humour, excellent each in its Kind, in short I found every thing there, You said I should find, when you gave me an Account of the Writing. If my design had been to propagate virtue by appearing publickly in its defence, I should rather have been ye Author of Tom Jones than of five Folio Volumes of sermons.—so much for my opinion of the Book, on which, I could write a great deal of Common Place, if I was not writing to You, & had not indeed myself some better employment.

I read it in company with a Brother officer who came to Carlisle on purpose to live with me, & is a sort of eleve of mine. When we came to ye conversation piece of the officers, he was reading to me, & stopt suddenly when he came to my Name, to ask if I was acquainted with Fielding, 'for here is your Picture with yr Name Under it, & the Greek Book in yr. Pocket.'[1] It was really Whimsical he should have Pitch'd on my name when he mention'd a circumstance that agreed with the character I bore in the Regiment. My Army Friends, (such of 'em as can read,) will think I was the Person design'd; but I assur'd him I had not the honour to be in the least known to Mr. Fielding. And tho' there

---

[1] The passage referred to is Ensign Northerton's comment on Homer: 'Damn Homo with all my heart,' says Northerton; 'I have the marks of him on my a— yet. There's Thomas, of our regiment, always carries a homo in his pocket; d—n me, if I ever come at it, if I don't burn it' (Bk. VII, Chap. 12).

were as many Figures in it as an old Gothick Cathedral, I was not considerable enough to have ye least Nich there. He has drawn a Portrait of my Friend Mrs. Whitfield at ye Bell in Gloucester such as Painters commonly draw; (I remember I was once at Ramsay's & saw a Picture that pleased me extreamly, it was a Young Lady that would have justified a mans falling in Love at ye first sight; upon my praising it, Ramsay told me if I would walk into ye Next Room I might see ye Original; I saw her indeed, but tho' there was some resemblance in the features, hardly a grace appear'd that had so much charm'd me in the Copy—) I breakfasted two or three times with Mrs. Whitfield, we talk'd of nothing but gayety & Assemblies; she let me into a Short History of her Lovers, & told me ye conquests she had made when Younger, & if I might put any faith in her own Commentaries, she had had as many occasions of triumph as Julius Caesar; in short I went away extremely disgusted with the Folly & behaviour of my Coquet Landlady. How ye Devil came it into Fielding's head to praise this Woman so exuberantly? If I was Master of the Bell Inn, I vow I should be absolutely Jealous.

★　　★　　★

While you are talking of Nothing but Peace, we here have had Nothing but battles & Bloodshed; ah! had I the tongue of Homer or Rather of Harry Fielding, how would I celebrate the courage of the Muffs, the Grays & the Ginger-Reds, the weapons they us'd, & the Wounds they gave and receiv'd. sed non haec mihi vis[1]—Pray has not this cock-fighting something wantonly cruel in it? I unhappily think so & have Incurr'd by it the high contempt of all the Squire Westerns about the country. . . .

1 'But this power is not vouchsafed me.'

63. William Shenstone, letter

7 April 1749

From a letter to Lady Henrietta Luxborough, *Letters of William Shenstone*, ed. Mallam, p. 140.

. . . I think as you do y^t that ye Plan [i.e. of *Tom Jones*] is by no means easy, but must own at the same time y^t several *Parts* have afforded me much Amusement. There is a good deal of wit dispers'd thro'out, or rather ty'd up in Bundles at ye beginning of every *Book*. You will conclude my Taste to be not extremely *delicate*, when I say I am cheifly pleas'd with ye striking Lines of Mr *Western's* Character. It is I fancy a natural Picture of thousands of his majesty's rural subjects; at least it has been *my* Fortune to see ye original pretty frequently. Tis perhaps a Likeness y^t is easily taken, & moreover he seems to apply it too indiscriminately to Country-gentlemen in general. But it is ye only Character y^t made me *laugh*; & y^t is a great Point gain'd, when one is in danger of losing y^t *Faculty* thro' Disuse. Tis moreover a Character better worth exposing than his Landlords & Landladys wth which he seems so delighted—his Serjeants & his Abigails &c . . .

64. Joseph Spence, letter

15 April 1749

From a letter to Burrell Massingberd, in Austen Wright, *Joseph Spence* (1950), p. 232, note 29 (letter in possession of Austen Wright).

* * *

Tom Jones is my old acquaintance, now; for I read it, before it was publisht: & read it with such rapidity, that I began & ended within the compass of four days; tho' I took a Journey to St Albans, in ye same time. He is to me extreamly entertaining; & will be so, I believe, to you. A set of 2500 Copies was sold, before it was publisht; which is perhaps an unheard-of case. That I may not seem to write Riddles, you must know that the way here generally is, to send in their number of Books to each of the Booksellers they deal with, four or five days before the Publication; that they may oblige people, who are eager for a new thing. In y^s case, the 10th of Febr^y was fixt for ye Publication; & by the 10th, all the books were disposed of. The author sold ye Copy for 100^L each Volume; & might probably have got 5 times as much by it, had he kept the right in his own hands; but authors at first dont know, whether their works are good or bad; much less, whether they will sell or not.

* * *

65. Catherine Talbot, letter

22 May 1749

From a letter to Elizabeth Carter, in *A Series of Letters* . . . i. 206.

*   *   *

The more I read Tom Jones, the more I detest him, and admire Clarissa
Harlowe—yet there are in it things that must touch and please every
good heart, and probe to the quick many a bad one, and humour that
it is impossible not to laugh at.

*   *   *

66. 'Aretine'
Old England

27 May 1749

From a letter signed 'Aretine' to 'Selim Slim' (George Lyttelton).
Except for the following excerpt, the letter is made up of strictly
personal abuse of Fielding and his patron.

*   *   *

Who undertakes to write ought to be well versed in such Arts and
Sciences as may be requisite to conduct him thro' the Subject he is
engaged in. History requires a good Knowledge, as well in Geography,
the Situation of Countries, the Interest and Connexion of Nations, as

in the Manners, Characters and Dispositions of People. The *Justice* [i.e. Fielding] affects to call his aforesaid *Labours of some Years of his Life*, an History. But whether we consider him as an Historiographer or Biographer of *Tom Jones*'s particular Life, I doubt we shall find him deficient in either Case. The Performance is beneath the Dignity of regular Criticism; so, leaving many a Slip and many a Blunder to the Observation of every attentive Reader, it shall suffice us at present to point out one single Specimen only of his great Skill in *Chorography* to public View, which can in no wise be imputed to a Lapse; for, on the contrary, it carries along with it indisputable Marks of Ignorance. Our Author says, that 'Mr. *Allworthy*'s Gothic Seat stood on the *South-East* Side of a Hill, sheltered from the *North-East* by a Grove of Oaks; and from a Lake at the Foot of the Hill, issued a River that for several Miles *was seen* to meander thro' Meadows and Woods, 'till it emptied itself into *the Sea*, with a large Arm of which, and an *Island* beyond it, the *Prospect* was closed.'[1] To reconcile this Description with Probability will be the Difficulty; for, unlucky for our Author, the Counties of *Devon* and *Dorset* stretch out between *Somersetshire* and the Sea; and, if we place this Seat in the *North-West* part of that Shire, the Hills of *Devon* will intercept the View to the Sea: And if we should imagine the Scite to be in the *South East* Part of that County, then *Dorsetshire* interferes, with an Extent of Ground of no less than 30 Miles across to *Portland*, which, if the Author means any thing, must be the Island that terminates the Prospect. A most extensive Ken indeed! and shews the accurate Author endued with more than a *second-sighted* Mind.

The *Justice* asserts, there is 'nothing in his History prejudicial to the Cause of Religion, or inconsistent with the Rules of Decency, or that can offend the chastest Eye'.[2] In Answer to the two last Parts of this modest Assertion, I would only recommend to you the Contemplation [of] the Figure which Mrs. *Waters* made in her Dishabille at the Inn, and the Manner she revelled away the Night in the Embraces of her Gallant. Add to this the ludicrous Attitude of the naked Philosopher *Square*, in the Hall beside *Moll Seagrim*'s Bed. And if these two Instances are not sufficient to convince, I will present you with a third, in *Moll*'s own dainty Appearance, when she presented herself in her sweetly-larded Smock, with a Pitchfork in her Hand, before the Hero of the History; and how these two innocent Lovers employed themselves among the Fern. Chaste Ideas these! in no wise inconsistent with our Author's

[1] I. iv.
[2] Dedication.

Rules of Decency! But why the Pitchfork? I doubt it is as little conducive, in her Hand, to the History, as *Toby*'s nameless Dog was at
Toby's Heel.

That this motely [*sic*] History of Bastardism, Fornication and Adultery, is highly prejudicial to the Cause of Religion, in several Parts of it,
is apparent in the gross Ridicule and Abuse which are wantonly thrown
on religious Characters. Who reviles the Clergy may be well said to be
upon the very Threshold of Immorality and Irreligion. A Contempt
inculcated of the first brings on the last of Course. The Character of
Thwackum is drawn out in the most odious Colours that can possibly
raise Detestation in the Mind of the Reader; and *Supple* is painted in the
contemptible Light of an insignificant formal Fool. Is this, Sir, 'the
sincere Endeavours of your Author in recommending Goodness and
Innocence?' Or, is the marrying of a Reverend Clergyman to a common
Harlot his Way of *rewarding* Virtue? It is amazing, Sir, [i.e. Lyttelton]
you should venture on commending a Book so truly profligate, of such
evil Tendency, and offensive to every chaste Reader, so discouraging to
Virtue and detrimental to Religion!

*   *   *

67. Elizabeth Carter, letter

20 June 1749

From a letter to Catherine Talbot, in *A Series of Letters* . . ., i. 207.

I am sorry to find you so outrageous about poor Tom Jones; he is no doubt an imperfect, but not a detestable character, with all that honesty, goodnature, and generosity of temper. Though nobody can admire Clarissa more than I do, yet with all our partiality, I am afraid, it must be confessed, that Fielding's book is the most natural representation of what passes in the world, and of the bizarreries which arise from the mixture of good and bad, which makes up the composition of most folks. Richardson has no doubt a very good hand at painting excellence, but there is a strange awkwardness and extravagance in his vicious characters.

★   ★   ★

68. Duchess of Bedford, letter

26 June 1749

From a letter to her mother in *A Duke and His Friends: The Life and Letters of the Second Duke of Richmond*, ed. the Earl of March (1911), ii. 665.

The Duchess, wife of Fielding's patron, remarks in passing:

Lady Kildare reads mighty well. Have you finished Tom Jones? She likes it vastly.

★   ★   ★

69. From an unsigned letter

30 June 1749

From Dalkeith House to Samuel Richardson, Forster MS. XV. 2,
f. 22 (Victoria and Albert Museum, London.)

* * *

I am vastly diverted with a book of Fieldings that is come out lately,
Tom Jones by Title. He has I believe a Fund of humour which will
never be exausted and I suppose his new profession of Justice of the
Quorum will furnish him with fresh Supplys of Matter to set in an
entertaining Light, if he has a mind to it.

* * *

70. Solomon Lowe, letter

10 July 1749

From a letter to Samuel Richardson, Forster MSS., XV. f. 50.
    When Richardson had read the following letter from his friend
and neighbour, Solomon Lowe, he folded it and wrote on the back
'Cracker, T. Jones'.

* * *

The more critically your performance is considered, the more unexceptionable it appears, nay the brighter it shines. The fame of it (I

find by Cave's magazine) is got into Holland;[1] and I do not doubt but all Europe will ring of it: when a Cracker, that was some thous^d hours a-composing,[2] will no longer be heard, or talkt of.

71. Samuel Richardson, letter

12 July 1749

From a letter to Aaron Hill, Forster MSS., XIII. iii, f. 112; reprinted, *Selected Letters of Samuel Richardson*, ed. John Carroll (1964), p. 126.

. . . While the Taste of the Age can be gratified by a Tom Jones (Dear Sir, have you read Tom Jones?) I am not to expect that the World will bestow Two Readings, or One indeed, attentive one, on such a grave Story as Clarissa,[3] which is designed to make those think of Death, who endeavour all they can to banish it from their Thoughts. I have found neither Leisure nor Inclination yet to read that Piece; and the less Inclination, as several good Judges of my Acquaintance condemn it, and the general Taste together. I could wish to know the Sentiments of your Ladies upon it. If favourable, they would induce me to open the Six Volumes; the rather, as they will be so soon read.

. . . Their Opinions of Tom Jones I will accept as Payment for the Honour they had intended for Clarissa.

★   ★   ★

[1] A 'character of Clarissa, from a book lately published at Amsterdam,' *Gentleman's Magazine* (June 1749), xix. 245–6.

[2] *Tom Jones*, Bk. XI, Chap. 1.

[3] The first two volumes of *Clarissa* had been published in December 1747, the next two in April 1748, and the last three in December 1748.

72. Astraea and Minerva Hill, letter

27 July 1749

From a letter to Samuel Richardson, Forster MSS., XV. ii. ff. 74–7. In a letter of 20 July, Hill explained to Richardson that if his daughters had not been serving as his nurses at present, 'they wou'd have obey'd you instantly, about *Tom Jones*: and they will certainly have sauciness enough to do it, being of late, grown borrowing Customers to an Itinerant Bookseller's Shop, that rumbles, once a week, through Plaistow in a wheel-barrow: with Chaff enough, of Conscience! and sometimes a weightier Grain, that now and then turns up among the Heap, and looks like a Temptation' (Forster MSS., Vol. XIII). Astraea and Minerva sent their report to Richardson on the 27th:

*   *   *

But the Commission you, at present, charge us with tends no farther than *Tom Jones*: and Tom Jones is not a *Clarissa*. . . . my sister and myself, laying our two wise heads together, have agreed to hazard this Discovery of their Emptiness; and send you our impertinence, by way of our opinion.

Having with much ado got over some Reluctance, that was bred by a familiar coarseness in the *Title*, we went through the whole six volumes; and found much (masqu'd) merit, in 'em All: a double merit, both of Head, and *Heart*. Had there been only That of the last sort, you love it I am sure, too much, to leave a Doubt of your resolving to examine it —However, if you do, it shoud be when you can best spare it your attention—Else, the Author introduces all his Sections, (and too often interweaves the *serious* Body of his meanings) with long Runs of bantering Levity, which his good sense may suffer the Effect of. It is true, he seems to wear this Lightness, as a grave Head sometimes wears a *Feather*; which tho' He and Fashion may consider as an ornament, Reflection will condemn, as a Disguise, and *covering*.

Girls, perhaps, of an untittering Disposition, are improper Judges of what merit there may be in Lightness, when (as seems here intended) It endeavors rather at ironic satire, than Encouragement of Folly.— But, tell us Dear Sir, are we in the right, or no, when we presume to own it as our Notion, that however well-meant such a Motive may have been, the Execution of it must be found distasteful?

For we can't help thinking that a mind fram'd right for Virtue courts and serves her with too much Respect, to join in throwing a Fool's Coat upon her—One of us two forward Prattlers dares be bold enough to add, that sometimes weighing *Hudibras*, himself, with all his high Encomiums, in the Scale of Her, whose name she ought to blush to carry,[1] if she did not dare to think impartially, she has been forc'd to own his *wit* extraordinary; but compassionated Every where his want of Delicacy.—Indeed 'twas happy for that Writer's Character, that Charles the Second cou'd stop short at mirth, and never try'd it by the measures of Decorum. Had I been the Heir of an ill-fated Prince, whose Crown, and Head, had fallen in sacrifice to a Rebellion then, so recent, and so widely overfill'd with serious miseries, I cou'd never have digested Pleasantry, and Ridicule, where *Horrors* had *unfarc'd* the Story.— One is naturally apt to treat as Banters the best meant advices of a Friend, who gives 'em with a laughing Countenance. And if, in Truth, we are condemn'd to live in such a trifling Age that, to make wisdom look'd upon as worth regarding, we must shew her with a Monkey's Grin, methinks the Expectation that she shou'd have any Influence, above an apish one, is but a bottomless Presumption.

Meanwhile, it is an honest pleasure, which we take in adding, that (exclusive of one wild, detach'd and independent Story of a *Man of the Hill*, that neither brings on Anything, nor rose from Anything that went before it) All the changefull windings of the Author's Fancy carry on a course of regular Design; and end in an extremely moving Close, where Lines that seem'd to wander and run different ways, meet, All, in an instructive Center.

The whole Piece consists of an inventive race of Disappointments and Recoveries. It excites Curiosity, and holds it watchful. It has just and pointed Satire; but it is a partial Satire, and confin'd too narrowly: It sacrifices to Authority, and Interest.——Its *Events* reward Sincerity, and punish and expose Hypocrisy; shew Pity and Benevolence in amiable Lights, and Avarice and Brutality in very despicable ones. In every Part it has Humanity for its Intention; in too many, it *seems* wantoner than It was meant to be: It has bold shocking Pictures; and

[1] i.e. Minerva.

(I fear) not unresembling ones, in high Life and in low.——And (to conclude this too adventurous guess-work from a Pair of forward Baggages) woud, everywhere, (we think) *deserve* to please.——if stript of what the Author thought himself most sure to *please by*.

73. Samuel Richardson, letter

4 August 1749

From a letter to Astraea and Minerva Hill, Forster MSS., XV. ii. ff. 78–9; Carroll, pp. 127–8.

*　　*　　*

I must confess, that I have been prejudiced by the Opinion of Several judicious Friends against the truly coarse-titled Tom Jones; and so have been discouraged from reading it.—I was told, that it was a rambling Collection of Waking Dreams, in which Probability was not observed: And that it had a very bad Tendency. And I had Reason to think that the Author intended for his Second View (His *first,* to fill his Pocket, by accommodating it to the reigning Taste) in writing it, to whiten a vicious Character, and to make Morality bend to his Practices. What Reason has he to make his Tom illegitimate, in an Age where Keeping is become a Fashion? Why did he make him a common—What shall I call it?— And a Kept Fellow, the Lowest of all Fellows, yet in Love with a Young Creature who was trapsing after him, a Fugitive from her Father's House?—Why did he draw his Heroine so fond, so foolish, and so insipid?—Indeed he has one Excuse—He knows not how to draw a delicate Woman—He has not been accustomed to such Company— And is too prescribing, too impetuous, too immoral, I will venture to say, to take any other Byass than that a perverse and crooked Nature has given him; or Evil Habits, at least, have confirm'd in him. Do Men expect Grapes of Thorns, or Figs of Thistles? But, perhaps, I think the worse of the Piece because I know the Writer, and dislike his Principles, both Public and Private, tho' I wish well to the *Man*, and Love Four worthy Sisters of his, with whom I am well acquainted. And indeed should admire him, did he make the Use of his Talents which I wish him to make; For the Vein of Humour, and Ridicule, which he is Master of, might, if properly turned, do great Service to ye Cause of Virtue.

But no more of this Gentleman's Work, after I have said, That the favourable Things, you say of the Piece, will tempt me, if I can find Leisure, to give it a Perusal.

I greatly admire what you say of Hudibras: And yet, dear Ladies, I cannot but think that Butler had a better Excuse for his Fools Coat, than the Author of the Foundling: Since from the Puritanical Pretences of ye Leaders among the Round-Heads, as they were called, arose principally all the serious Mischiefs which you, dear Ladies, so judiciously observe upon. And which Spirit of Fanaticism was far from being quell'd, till the Spirit of Dissoluteness encouraged in the newly-restored Court introduced the contrary Extreme, and overspread the Face of the Nation. I say not this, however, to excuse that want of Decorum, which ye so justly censure, and for which no Wit can atone. But in an Age so dissolute as the present what can be said for the Morality (for the Morality shall I say?) propagated in Tom Jones?

But his Judges, by whom I have been govern'd, are perhaps too severe. I am sure I am disinterested enough, if I do read it, to give it (to the best of my Judgment) its due Praises, as well as Censure. But I thought to have said no more of it till I had run it over. . . .

74. Samuel Richardson, letter

18 August 1749

From a letter to Aaron Hill, Forster MSS., XIII. iii. f. 126; Carroll, pp. 128–30.
In a letter of 11 August 1749, Hill told Richardson that his daughters were distressed by Richardson's letter to them of 4 August. 'They, Both, fairly cry'd,' he said, 'that you shou'd think it possible they could approve of Any thing, in Any work, that had an Evil Tendency, in any Part or Purpose of it' (Carroll, p. 128n.). Richardson quickly replied with reassurances.

*   *   *

How much am I afflicted, that I was capable of giving, by what I wrote, a Moment's Uneasiness to Ladies, to whom it would be the Pride of my Life to give Pleasure! But how, dear and good Sir, was it possible for them to take what was written in the Sense they took it? 'I imagined, I said, that the Censurers of Tom Jones were too severe: And why? Because Ladies superior Delicacy were so good as to overlook the Passages unworthy of their Regard, and find a good Intention in the rest,' I said, that, knowing the Man, I had the more Suspicion; for he is a very indelicate, a very impetuous, an unyielding-spirited Man, and is capable of forming a Morality to his Practices. But I undertook to bestow a Reading upon it. *Bestow*, I say—having so much upon me that I have hardly time for Reading of any kind, that I could dispense with. Let me add, that I spoke the freer of my Friend's Censure, from the delicate Dispraise of your good Ladies. Did they not say, 'that it was not without Reluctance, that they read a Piece, the familiar Coarseness of whose Title was forbidding?' That 'tho' there was Merit in the Piece, it was masqued Merit?'—That 'it should not be read, but when the Attention could best be spared?' That 'the Author's good Sense might suffer by his long Runs of bantering Levity, which Reflection would condemn?' That, 'however well-meant this Levity might be, it was *their* Notion, that the Execution must be found distasteful!' And why? 'Because,' as they as wisely as nobly say, 'that a mind rightly formed, courts and serves Virtue with too much Respect, to join in throwing a Fool's Coat upon her,' Again, I read with Pleasure this fine Reflection: 'One is naturally apt to treat as Banters the best-meant Advices of a Friend, who gives them with a laughing Countenance: And if, in Truth, we are condemned to live in such a trifling Age, that to make Wisdom looked upon as worth regarding, we must shew her with a Monkey's Grin, methinks the Expectation that she should have any Influence above an Apish one, is but a bottomless Presumption.'— Again—'The story has just and pointed Satire in it; but it is a partial Satire. It sacrifices to Authority and Interest—In too many Places, it *seems* wantoner than it was meant to be. It has bold shocking Pictures.' Could I have imagined, Sir, that I, in following this Clue, and in writing freely what those Censurers have said, who were disgusted with these Faults, and looked upon them in a Light too strong, without considering the rest with that Candour which your Ladies have laudably manifested, for what must *therefore* be praiseworthy in it, or even for expressing my own Disgust on several of the Passages that I had read, should have written so, as to have affected the dear Ladies?—I cannot forgive myself. And pray, Sir, obtain for me their Pardon. . . .

JOSEPH ANDREWS AND TOM JONES

75. 'T.P.'

The Gentleman's Magazine

June 1749, xix. 252

From a letter signed 'T.P.' to 'Mr. Urban'. The writer is referring to the fact that Warburton's edition of Shakespeare has not sold well:

. . . Granting what is here insinuated to be true, that is, granting that the greatest treasure of critical learning that ever was offer'd to the world is, at present, thrown by as rubbish; will it be any great wonder to a man, that considers how the world is run a madding after that fool parson *Adams*, and that rake *Tom Jones*? But the time will shortly come, when these trifles shall vanish in smoak, and the best edition of *Shakespeare* shall shine forth in all its glory. . . .

76. Thomas Cawthorn

The Gentleman's Magazine

August 1749, xix. 371

'To Henry Fielding Esq; On reading his inimitable history of Tom Jones.'

Edward Cave, the editor of the *Gentleman's Magazine*, evidently assumed when he printed this poem that its author was James Cawthorn, the master of the Tunbridge Grammar School and well known for his occasional poems. In the September issue (xix. 464) Cave inserted a notice explaining that 'the verses to Henry Fielding, Esq;' were not written by this poet, but by someone else of the same surname.

To HENRY FIELDING *Esq*;

On reading his inimitable history of Tom Jones:

————*neque*

Si chartæ sileant, quod bene feceris,

Mercedem tuleris.————

HOR. LIB. IV. ODE VIII.[1]

Long, thro' the mimic scenes of motly life,
Neglected *Nature* lost th' unequal strife;
Studious to show, in mad, fantastic shape,
Each grinning gesture of his kindred ape,
Man lost the name: while each, in artful dress,
Appear'd still something more of something less:

---

[1] 'If future pages are silent about the good you have done, you will not have had your reward.'

Virtue and vice, unmix'd, in fancy stood,
And all were vilely bad, or greatly good;
Eternal distance ever made to keep,
Exciting horrour, or promoting sleep:
　Sick of her fools, great *Nature* broke the jest,
And *Truth* held out each character to test,
When *Genius* spoke: Let *Fielding* take the pen!
Life dropt her mask, and all mankind were men.

THO. CAWTHORN.

JOSEPH ANDREWS AND
TOM JONES

77. Lady Mary Wortley Montagu, letter

1 October [1749]

From a letter to the Countess of Bute, *The Complete Letters of Lady Mary Wortley Montagu*, ed. Robert Halsband (1966), ii. 443.

*   *   *

I have at length receiv'd the Box with the Books enclos'd, for which I give you many thanks, as they amus'd me very much. I gave a very ridiculous proofe of it, fitter indeed for my Grand daughter than my selfe. I return'd from a party on Horseback and after have [*sic*] rode 20 mile, part of it by moon shine, it was ten at night when I found the Box arriv'd. I could not deny my selfe the pleasure of opening it, and falling upon Fielding's Works was fool enough to sit up all night reading. I think Joseph Andrews better than his Foundling. I beleive I was the more struck with it, having at present a Fanny in my own House, not only by the Name, which happens to be the same, but the extrodinary Beauty, joyn'd with an understanding yet more extrodinary at her age, which is but few months past sixteen. She is in the post of my Chambermaid. . . .

78. Tobias Smollett, letter

1 October 1749

From a letter to Alexander Carlyle, in National Library of Scotland, Edinburgh, MS. 3464, f. 131; see Henry W. Meikle, 'New Smollett Letters', *Times Literary Supplement*, 31 July 1943, p. 372.

Unfortunately Carlyle's letter of adverse criticism of *Tom Jones*, to which Smollett is replying, has not survived. The tone of this letter, however, should be compared with the abusive personal animus of *Habbakkuk Hilding* (1752), which is often attributed to Smollett; the latter accuses Fielding of stealing his Partridge and Miss Matthews (in *Amelia*) from, respectively, Smollett's Strap and Miss Williams in *Roderick Random*.

★   ★   ★

If I should pretend to set up in defence of Tom Jones, in these particulars where he is affected by your Censure, you would easily discover my affectation and he justly offended at my feigned Candour: I will therefore own that the same observations occurred to me which you have communicated and are indeed obvious to every reader of discernment, even the Authors most sanguine adherents confess that there is an evident difference between that part of his Book which he wrote for the Town and that which was composed for the benifit [*sic*] of his Bookseller.

★   ★   ★

79. [Lady Dorothy Bradshaigh], letter

[November 1749]

From a letter to Samuel Richardson, signed 'Mrs. Belfour', *The Correspondence of Samuel Richardson*, ed. Anna L. Barbauld (1804), iv. 280–1.
Cf. Richardson's letter to Lady Bradshaigh ([1751], Carroll, p. 178), in which he compares the character of Clarissa and Sophia: 'Why, I attempted to draw a good woman; and the poor phantom has set half her own sex against her. The men more generally admire her, indeed, because bad men, as I have quoted . . . from Lovelace, admire good women. But with some of the sex she is a prude; with others a coquet; with more a saucy creature, whose life, manners, and maxims, are affronts to them. Mr. Fielding's Sophia is a much more eligible character.'

*   *   *

As to Tom Jones, I am fatigued with the name, having lately fallen into the company of several young ladies, who had each a Tom Jones in some part of the world, for so they call their favourites; and ladies, you know, are for ever talking of their favourites. Last post I received a letter from a lady, who laments the loss of her Tom Jones; and from another, who was happy in the company of her Tom Jones. In like manner, the gentlemen have their Sophias. A few days ago, in a circle of gentlemen and ladies, who had their Tom Jones's and their Sophias, a friend of mine told me he must shew me his Sophia, the sweetest creature in the world, and immediately produced a Dutch mastiff puppy.

*   *   *

80. 'The Preface', *The History of Tom Jones, the Foundling, in his Married State*

1750 [November 1749]

In its preface, this Fielding imitation, which appeared in November 1749, criticizes Fielding's dedication to *Tom Jones* and goes on to give its statement of the Fielding novel. The novel itself fulfils the prophecy at the end of *Tom Jones* and shows Tom fighting off threats like Lady Bellaston to become a good husband and prudent country squire. The review in the *Monthly* (1749, i. 25–26) says it bears no marks of Fielding's 'spirit, style, or invention'.

The Author should scarce think it necessary to trouble the Reader with a Preface, was it not his Intention that the World should be satisfied that HENRY FIELDING, *Esq; is not the* Author *of this Book, nor in any Manner concerned in its Composition or Publication.*

FOR, as to the Work itself; though it cannot boast of being warmly recommended *by an honourable* Lord of the Treasury, *BEFORE it appears in Public, the Author's Station of Life, setting him at too great a Distance from Court, where such a Patronage is to be sought; yet he hopes the Subjects contained therein will be found so interesting, in the most useful Parts of Life, among all Degrees, as to engage* the warm Recommendation, *not only of That Gentleman, but of All serious and well-meaning Readers.*

IF he has stepped out of the common Road of Historians, *it was with an Intention to draw Nature more to the Life; and to gather proper Antidotes against the many and common Vices of the Age. And where he has been obliged to descend to Particulars, he has neither used a luscious nor ambiguous Diction: It being as necessary to guard the Reader from the Poison of Words, as from the Vice they seem to conceal; a Caution too seldom regarded by those who pretend to write to please the* Taste *of the Times. Which cannot, by any Means, be accounted a Compliment to their Readers.—*

HE has only introduced such Characters as Young and Old frequently meet with, or may observe at a Distance; so that they may not only amuse, but conduct the Reader thro' many otherwise difficult Cases. In fine, these Sheets may be justly stiled an Admonition to the unthinking Part of both Sexes; and a Guide to preserve the most Virtuous, against the Delusions and false Appearances, which mix so frequently in the Transactions of Life.

81. Samuel Richardson, letter
[November–December 1749]

From a letter to Lady Dorothy Bradshaigh, Carroll, pp. 133–4.

. . . But for what should I set about the work I had once in view?[1] To draw a good man—a man who needs not repentance, as the world would think! How tame a character? Has not the world shewn me, that it is much better pleased to receive and applaud the character that shews us what we are (little of novelty as one would think there is in that) than what we ought to be? Are there not who think Clarissa's an unnatural character?

I will only say, that when the world is ready to receive writings of a different cast, I hope writers will never be wanting to amuse, as well as instruct. Nor perhaps may the time be very far off. So long as the world will receive, Mr. Fielding will write. Have you ever seen a list of his performances? Nothing but a shorter life than I wish him, can hinder him from writing himself out of date. The Pamela, which he abused in his Shamela,[2] taught him how to write to please, tho' his manners are so different. Before his Joseph Andrews (hints and names taken from that story, with a lewd and ungenerous engraftment) the poor man wrote without being read, except when his Pasquins, &c. roused party attention and the legislature at the same time, according to that of Juvenal, which may be thus translated:

> Would'st thou be read, or would'st thou bread ensure,
> Dare something worthy *Newgate* or the *Tower*.[3]

In the former of which (removed from inns and alehouses) will some of his next scenes be laid;[4] and perhaps not unusefully; I hope not. But to have done, for the present, with this fashionable author. . . .

[1] i.e. *Sir Charles Grandison* (1754).
[2] *Pamela* had been published in November 1740; *Shamela* in April 1741.
[3] *Satires*, I. 73–4.   [4] i.e. in *Amelia*.

82. 'Orbilius', from *An Examen of the History of Tom Jones, a Foundling*

1750 [December 1749]

. . . In *Two Letters to a Friend, Proper to be bound with the Foundling*
Although dated 1750, the *Examen* was advertised as published on
9 December 1749 (*Old England*). On the 16th *Old England* commented that Fielding 'is under a most sensible Mortification from
an *Examen* into his *Foundling*'. 'Orbilius' (a Roman grammarian,
noted as a flogger) has not been identified. Unfortunately lack of
space prevents reprinting the pamphlet in full.

TO THE

MAN-MOUNTAIN.

Most Sublime SIR,
AMONG all the personages I have been so long acquainted with, I
could not think of any one so proper for a Patron of the following
laborious *Examen,* as yourself: For are you not the worthy Progenitor
of *the Man of the Hill*? And can you be supposed to be interested in the
Event of the Story of an insignificant *Foundling*, any more than your
Son, who has been so impertinently made to interrupt the Thread of it?
It is true, Mr. *F.* has *murdered* you, as he has done the rest of his Characters. But, this notwithstanding, all the World knows you are still alive,
and will live as long as the immortal *Gulliver*. Let this therefore be
added, by way of Appendix to the rest of Mr. *F.'s* Incredibilities; and
believe me to be the common Friend of you, and of *the Man in the
Moon*, where the modern Philosophy has discovered an *illustrious* Group
of your Brethren, as far surpassing our sublunary ones, as you surpass

them all in Size, and equal them in Duration. I am, Sir, in *profound* Admiration of your *extensive* Abilities,

> *Your most* HUMBLE *Servant,*
> (*and never was the diminutive Epithet*
> > *more properly applied*)

ORBILIUS

LETTER I.

The Task of examining Mr. *F.*'s late celebrated Performance, called *The History of a Foundling,* chiefly with a View to Morals, at your Request, I willingly undertake. But as, in attending my Author in every Stage, and through every Inn he drives to (where I shall at least be sure of good Chear), I foresee that I shall be obliged to run to some Length, I will not take up your Time by a longer Introduction.

In prosecuting my Design, I shall not be deterred by any thing that looks like (or is) Prolixity in my Author; but give to every Chapter its full Weight of Censure (if Censure it deserves); agreeably to the Practice of the great *Bentleius,*[1] of formidable Memory to all bad Writers, whether on Subjects of Religion, Learning, or Humour.

And first we alight at the Portal, which will give us a specious Plan of the whole Fabric.

The DEDICATION.

Does Mr. *F.* really owe the *Existence* he mentions to the worthy Gentleman, to whom he dedicates this Monument of his Labours? This seems not to be so agreeable as might be wished to his Patron's *Dislike of public Praise,* of which Mr. *F.* thinks it convenient to assure us, especially as the Author declares at the End of this Epistle (as he calls it), that what he hath said in it, *is not only without, but absolutely against* his Patron's *Consent.* If this were true, with regard to the *First Edition,* methinks it was very disobliging in Mr. *F.* to continue this excessive and disgustful Incense throughout the future Editions: For it cannot be doubted, but that Mr. *L.* made use of all his Interest with Mr. *F.* to get him to omit what was so offensive to his Modesty, after he had seen it in Print.

There are other Persons praised, as well as Mr. *L.* in this Dedication; who, no doubt, will take very great Pride in the Merit they have with the Public, in contributing to the Existence of this renowned Author.

The present Work, it seems, is the *Labour of some Years.* Can that be?

---

[1] i.e. Richard Bentley.

Some Years about such a Performance as *Tom Jones*!—We all took Mr. *F.* to be endowed with quicker Parts than this *Labour of his Brain* warrants our ascribing to him; since, instead of a *Minerva,* he has only been delivered of her Owl. If a Man presents his Readers with his *Dreams,* need he take up *Years* in telling them? *John Bunyan* perform'd, as it seems, a Work infinitely superior and more useful, with much greater Ease. And *John Bunyan's* Performance was a Work of Genius: But *John Bunyan was a* Genius, though a grave one. Mr. *F.* on the contrary, is so volatile, that I dare say he never pursued any one thing for a Year together; much less such a *skipping* Work as this before us; which, though it comprehends an unmeasurable Length of Time, need not have cost much in writing, if we may guess by the Correctness of the Style. *John Dryden,* otherwise an incomparable Writer, boasted of his having produced a bad Play in a Fortnight:[1] Mr. *F.* more inconsistently, of having spent *some Years* (which others may interpret *many*) in corrupting Youth, *i.e.* in writing *Tom Jones.* Yet *the Reader,* Mr. *F.* tells us, will find *nothing in the whole Course* of his Performance, *prejudicial to the Cause of* RELIGION *and* VIRTUE: *Nothing inconsistent with the* STRICTEST RULES *of* DECENCY; that is, according to Mr. *F.'s* Notions of Decency, we may presume; *nor which can offend even the* CHASTEST *Eye in the Perusal.*—TO RECOMMEND GOODNESS AND INNOCENCE, HATH BEEN the Author's SINCERE ENDEAVOUR IN THIS HISTORY. How unhappy, if he should fail in an Endeavour *so sincere!* Could one imagine, that after this solemn Declaration, the Author cannot, in the same Paragraph, forbear giving a loose Picture of VIRTUE itself, by *his Idea of that Loveliness which* Plato *asserts there is in her* NAKED *Charms?* Whether this Gentleman hath not wronged *Plato* by this Epithet, which was only inserted for the sake of the Pleasure he takes in such Images, will be seen by the Passage itself referred to, as it stands in *Cic. de Fin.* Lib. II. *Oculorum, inquit* Plato, *est in nobis sensus acerrimus: quibus* SAPIENTIAM *non cernimus. Quam illa ardentes amores excitaret sui, si videretur!*[2] I have put on my Spectacles; but cannot see here any Word answering to the Adjective NAKED;— not to take Notice, that what *Plato* says of Philosophy, Mr. *F.* makes him say of Virtue: But this comes of citing without Book; or producing AUTHORITIES without AUTHORS, in a Work too that took up so

---

[1] In the Dedication to *Amboyna* (1673) Dryden says that he wrote the play in a month.
[2] ' "Sight," says Plato, "is our acutest sense; yet we do not see wisdom by means of it. What violent passions would it excite if it could be seen in itself!" ' *De Finibus Bonorum et Malorum,* II. xvi.

much Time, and cost him so much Labour. But more of this, when we come to Book XVIII. Chap. III. Our Author *hath* (for I shall use his own elegant Termination of *th* instead of *s* in the third Person Singular, as often as the auxiliary Verbs *do* and *have* shall occur) been very fair, in presenting so early to the Eye of the Reader a Criterion, by which to judge of his whole Work: And I will not anticipate, but proceed to try him by this Criterion, through all his following Scenes. A worthy Design he *hath* had: Pray Heaven it be found as well executed as formed! He *hath shewn,* he says, *that no Acquisition of Guilt can compensate the Loss of that solid inward Comfort of Mind, which is the sure Companion of Innocence and Virtue.* More he says to prove the Goodness of his Moral. And as ALL HIS WIT AND HUMOUR (*p.* 14.) have been employed in the Piece before us, this will furnish us with a further Criterion how far this *Wit and Humour* of his really extend: Which, by the Majority of Readers, have been thought inexhaustible.

But before we proceed, it may be proper (in order to elucidate several Points which I shall but just touch upon, and to save you the Trouble of referring to the Book for any Matters that may be doubtful) briefly to give you a Sketch of this *delectable* History, so far as the Hero and Heroine are concerned.

Tom Jones, then, the spurious or misbegotten Issue of Miss *Bridget Allworthy,* and dropt by that Lady in her Brother Mr. *Allworthy*'s Bed, is by this Gentleman, in order, I suppose, to illustrate his Prudence, as well as Morality, educated in so *genteel,* or rather loose a Manner, between the contrary Disciplines of the rigid Churchman Mr. *Thwackum,* and the Moral Philosopher Mr. *Square,* as gives an unhappy Prognostic of his future Follies and Vices; since a Man, who in his Youth has not had the Advantage of some settled Principles of Religion, rarely settles himself afterwards in right Principles or Practices (who better than our Author should have known that?) This being the Case, it is no Wonder that *Tom* scarce finds himself released from the too slack Government under which he had been educated, but he plunges into every Debauchery. Add to this, That *Allworthy,* though a Man of Virtue himself, had not the Prudence to instil into his vicious Foster-Son a Remembrance of his disadvantageous Birth, which might have restrained him from many Enormities; nor even to give him any Employment, which might teach him, that he was not born merely to gratify his natural Propensity, which led him headlong into an early Commerce with Women. The first whom he attempted, and successfully, was *Moll Seagrim,* the (*fair,* shall I say? or) sooty Daughter of *Black*-guard *George* (Two exemplary Characters of our Author; whose *sincere Endeavour hath been to recommend* GOOD- NESS *and* INNOCENCE). The Effects of this Commerce discovering itself, and some of *Tom*'s other Actions being *misrepresented*, as Mr. *F.* will have it, to *Allworthy*, he is, with as much Improbability, as there was Folly and Weakness in his first Adoption by that Gentleman, dis- missed with Money, and a Bill for 500l. in his Pocket; the latter (he being a *near Relation* of our Author's *Parson Adams*, it may be presumed) he soon carelesly lost: And, as I before hinted, had no Talents to recom- mend himself to any reputable Livelihood: The too natural Con- sequence of which was, his returning to his former evil Courses; which he did as soon as they offered themselves; first, by the Means of Mrs. *Waters* (the Paramour of Captain *Waters*, who is only introduced as one of Mr. *Bayes*'s Lumber-Troop,[1] to *fill up*, not to *further*, our Author's wonderful Plot); who inveigles the Hero on the Road, after he had rescued her from being robbed and murdered; and, next, by his Amours with Lady *Bellaston*, to whom he goes to inquire News of *Sophia*, under the *plausible* Pretence of restoring to the latter the 100l. Bill, which, as an Instance of the Author's Invention, she had as heedlesly dropped as the Hero had his 500l. To Lady *Bellaston*, suitably to his infamous Birth, he performed the Offices of a *Maskwell*,[2] for which she becomes his Tributary. In this scandalous and despicable manner does he live with that Quality-Strumpet, till, having danger- ously wounded one *Fitz-Patrick*, who had married a Cousin of *Sophia*, he is thrown into Prison, and is in imminent Peril of his Neck: Whence at last he is rescued by the *seasonable* Recovery of *Fitz-Patrick*, and as *seasonable* Arrival of *Allworthy*; to whom the whole History of his *honourable* Birth is revealed by that very Mrs. *Waters*, who had per- sonated his Mother, and debauched (if we may use the Word of one before debauched) her supposed Son. This Discovery restores her Credit with *Allworthy*, who had banished her the Country on her false Confession, that she was the Mother of *Tom*; and at the same time ingratiates the latter with his Uncle *Allworthy*. Nothing therefore re- mains but the rewarding Mr. *Jones* for his former Rogueries, with as fine and as virtuous a Woman as our Author and his honourable Coadjutor are capable of painting: Which leads me to say something of

Sophia: Who was the Daughter of 'Squire *Western*, an ignorant, clownish, obstinate, Jacobite Country Justice. A Whig, or ministerial

---

[1] In *The Rehearsal* (1671).
[2] In Congreve's *The Double Dealer* (1694).

Justice, no doubt, he had been, with a small Change in his Qualities, had our Author been so *many Years* about this Work, as to have drawn this Character, when he thought himself a* *Champion,* and capable of wielding the Club of *Hercules*; which was indeed *Herculis cothurnos optare infanti.*[1] *Sophia* herself is with great Pomp introduced to the Veneration of the Reader for her Modesty, and other good Qualities; but as it is certain, that Mr. *F.* is utterly unable (as we see in all his Pieces, but most flagrantly in this) to draw a Woman of true Virtue and Modesty; so in nothing is she so illustrious as in her Partiality to the well-known Debaucheries of *Jones*, and in her Elopement from her Father's House, on Pretence of avoiding a disgustful Match with *Blifil*, the legitimate Son of *Allworthy*'s Sister, which nevertheless she had no just Ground to fear, as we shall hereafter shew†: However, out she sets, partly padding it, partly riding; arrives at her Relation's, the worthy Lady *Bellaston*; who, being acquainted with her strong Attachment to *Jones*, baffles her for some time, in order to keep the Hero to herself: At last, forms a Plot to have her ravished by Lord *Fellamar:* A strangely unnecessary Scheme! (but not the less likely to be Mr. *F.*'s for *that*) since that Nobleman was afterwards to patch up a Marriage with her for her Fortune's sake, as well as for the real Affection he seems to have borne her, when he would have courted her honourably: But Lady *Bellaston*, being disappointed in her admirable Project, lays a Scheme to have *Jones* pressed; in which also failing by his being arrested, an open Way seems to be made for *Sophia* to run into his Arms, after a few sham Reluctances on her Part, and some few Sparks of Displeasure at *Jones*'s supposed publishing her Story in Inns, *&c.* not in the least reproaching him with his repeated Failures in Point of Fidelity.

And now arrives the Time, when our Author, being at a Loss to contrive Ways and Means to raise the Character of his Hero, since he could not in Merit, and would not at *Tyburn*, reconciles him to *Allworthy* by the Means before mentioned; *Allworthy* reconciles him to *Sophia*; and the Fiddles strike up (not without the Melody of Marrow-bones and Cleavers, we presume) to the Joy of every Fortune-hunter and rathe-ripe[2] Virgin in the Kingdom.

I mention not our Author's Under-characters, nor his useless Con-

---

* The Author of the *Champion* takes the Name of *Hercules Vinegar:* A *Vinegar* no doubt! he knew his own Excellence; and rightly assumed the Character of a Bear-garden Hero.

[1] 'Trying to put the boots of Hercules on a baby.' Quintilian, *Institutio Oratoria*, VI. i. 36.

† See our Remarks on Book VII. Chap. VII.

[2] i.e. precocious.

clusion, after all that could engage the Reader's Attention, was over (most of which will be considered in the Course of our Remarks): Only thus much I thought fit to premise for your clearer Conception, before we proceed to

BOOK I. CHAP. I.

Mr. *F.*'s *Ordinary*, unless we should unhappily choose *another*, or a *better*, if such there *can* be; and if we must be forced to *d—n our French and Italian Hashes and Ragoûts*; which our Author inconsistently dignifies by saying, that they are *no other than* HUMAN NATURE. But what then is Nature? It is indeed the *Nature* of a HOG to wallow in the Mire, and to lick up all the Filth he can any-where meet with: And perhaps this is also the *Nature of some Authors*. But, for the Honour of the Creator, as well as of the Creature, let us not suppose this to be HUMAN NATURE in the Abstract. Mr. *F.* indeed acknowleges, that *true Nature is as difficult to be met with in Authors, as the Bayonne-Ham, or Bologna Sausage* [by which Similes he seems to be a Person of most exquisite Relish] *is to be found in the Shops*; and of this we shall see that he has given almost as many Instances as Chapters. The *Cookery of an Author* is a *Metaphor* in which Mr. *F.* delights to *continue*: But it is un-happily applied in the *Beginning* of this Work; since hereby his Reader may be probably reminded rather to recur to the Dishes of a *Pontac*,[1] or, to use his own Example, an *Heliogabalus,* than to the more lean Diet to be purchased at this Author's Stall.

CHAP. II.

Having sketched out the Character of Miss *Bridget Allworthy*, a Character, which, from its Insignificancy, he could not surely be *many Years* in drawing, the Author *desires the Critics to mind their own Business:* Whereby he seems to shew some Fear of the Lash.—He may justly fear it; but his Time is not yet come. Nor will his *Plea to the Jurisdiction* of the Court of Criticism (erected by himself in a former periodical Per-formance*) at all avail him; since before that impartial Court must his Fate be decided, as he himself, when seated on that usurped Bench, decided the Fate of others.

1 Or Pontack (1638?–1720?), a well-known London tavern-keeper.
* The *Jacobite* Journal. *Requiescat in Pace*. [Fielding's periodical had come to an end on 5 November 1748.]

CHAP. III.

Mrs. *Deborah Wilkins* is introduced, doing the first Offices to our filthy Author's stinking Hero: *Faugh! how it stinks!* faith *she* here, as I doubt the Reader will say hereafter. *It doth not smell like a Christian*, adds *Deborah*. But if this fetid Foundling *maketh* no worse a Figure in the rest of the Book, than he *now* doth, bad, however, as that is, he may, for aught I know, prove a very innocent Person. If he *doth* not now *smell like a Christian*, how will he smell hereafter?

CHAP. IV.

The Author would do well to answer the Objections made to his Chorography, by a Gentleman who signs *Aretine*, in *Old England* of *May* 27, 1749.[1] *Mr.* Allworthy's *Gothic Seat*, says Mr. *F. stood on the* South-East *Side of a Hill, sheltered from the* North-East *by a Grove of* Oaks; *and from a Lake at the Foot of a Hill, issued a River that for several Miles* was seen *to meander thro' Meadows and Woods, till it emptied itself into* the Sea, *with a large Arm of which, and an* Island *beyond it, the* Prospect *was closed.* 'To reconcile this Description with Probability, will be the Difficulty; for, unluckily for our Author, the Counties of *Devon* and *Dorset* stretch out between *Somersetshire* and the Sea; and, if we place this Seat in the *North-West* Part of that Shire, the Hills of *Devon* will intercept the View to the Sea: And if we should imagine the Seat to be in the *South-East* Part of that County, then *Dorsetshire* interferes, with an Extent of Ground of no less than thirty Miles across to *Portland*, which, if the Author means any thing, must be the Island that terminates the Prospect. A most extensive Ken indeed! and shews the accurate Author endued with more than a *second-sighted* Mind.'

But, alas! my *Neck* (as well as our Author's) was in *Danger* before I was aware,—by looking down from the Precipice to which Mr. *F.* had conducted me from his *Gothic Building*; tho' I was not apprehensive of a Fall from the HILL of Mr. *Allworthy*'s Perfections, which I do not conceive extraordinary, any more than the mean Metaphor used to express them. A *Gothic Building* indeed is an ill Presage of want of Symmetry in the Pile, which our Author has raised to eternize his and *Allworthy*'s Memory, in the present Work. Nor do I perceive the Use of so particular a Description of this rude Structure, with *Hills, Groves, Lawns, Springs, Lakes, Plains, Rivers, Woods, Seas, Abbeys,—Hills,*

[1] See No. 66.

Lawns, Wood, and *Water* again, *in infinitum;* unless it be to introduce Mr. *Allworthy* as a Spectacle on the Terrace, whose Benevolence, *well* described, would have afforded a *more glorious Object,* than all the inanimate Scenes of Nature put together. But what does this truly *Gothic* Description explain? or who can explain *it*? Whoever does, *Erit mihi magnus Apollo.*[1]

Great was Miss *Bridget's Surprize* at seeing her Brother's *Present* of the Infant Hero; she *imagining,* our Author supposes (with as much Affectation as herself), *it had been a Gown, or some Ornament for her Person;* when in Truth it was the Image of her Person itself. *Great* also must be the Reader's *Surprize,* if he casts his Eye forward upon some future Pages; particularly Book XVIII. Chap. VII. by comparing which with these, that Lady's Conduct will appear altogether unaccountable (*Sed nunc non est his locus*); where he will see, with what Propriety *the Tongue of Virtue* (of Miss *Bridget's* Virtue) *lashes those who bring a Disgrace on the Sex.*

CHAP. V.

The Grimace of *Deborah* and *Bridget,* in their alternate Displeasure at, and Fondness for, this Brat (who, by-the-bye, was *found,* tho' never *lost*), seems to be carried to an extravagant Pitch. To make a Prude condescend, tho' she does it grumblingly, to take care of a Bastard, and this recommended to her by her good-natur'd Brother, who had *twenty Ways* of disposing of the Infant for its Education, and to the advantageous Display of his own Humanity, carries a Face of Improbability, that even its being her own Child cannot reconcile. A Prude would rather have found Means (and Means she *had*) to remove it to a proper Distance. A fine Instance of the Pregnancy of Mr. *F.*'s Invention!

CHAP. VI.

The like Inconsistency and Improbability, which I charged, under Chap. IV. upon Miss *Bridget,* I must now charge on *Jenny Jones,* for Reasons which may be seen by comparing Book XVIII. Chap. VII. where her Motion for *murdering* the Child will be found to be only a pecuniary Reward for murdering her own Reputation by *acknowleging* it: A Motive how unequal! An *Acknowlegment* how untrue! Besides, the Author's Design of exposing the Method of giving young Women a Taste for Learning would bear controverting; since, if the probable Consequence of a learned Education were to be, that Pride should take

[1] 'He will be great Apollo to me.'

the Place of Humility, and Dissoluteness of Chastity, (a fine Compliment to the Sex!) then would all Parents in middle and low Life, as well as *Jenny*'s Neighbours, have Reason to *felicitate themselves* (as Mr. *F.* gravely phrases it) *that their* Daughters *had* neither Learning, nor Silk Gowns. But if, on the contrary, Learning teaches both Modesty and Humility, with an Elevation of Mind above all Kinds of Vice, which fixes a deeper Stain and Dishonour on Persons eminent for Parts and Education; then this Character is equally faulty and unnatural. However, in Charity to the Ladies, we will suppose, that Mr. *F.*'s *Jenny* had only Learning enough to make her proud, but not enough to make her humble.

CHAP. VII.

In this Chapter there is something which shews the Inattention of Mr. *Allworthy*, or rather of his Author: It is this; That among the dehortatory Monitions that worthy, tho' weak Magistrate gives to *Jenny* on her imputed Slip, he mentions *one, which, if attentively consider'd, must deter all,* OF HER SEX, AT LEAST, *from the Commission of the Crime.* Now I would fain know, how this Crime can be forborne by the *one* Sex, and yet committed by the *other*? This Figure of Rhetoric the *Greeks* would probably express by the Words τὸ ἀναχόλδθου, and the *English* by the Monosyllable BULL.[1] 'Tis the more extraordinary, that the Magistrate should be made so inattentive, just as the Words *if attentively consider'd* were in his Mouth. Nor can I see how a Woman's *pleading the Passon of Love would be owning herself the Tool and Bubble of the Man,* any more than *vice versa. Love,* says he, *can never be* VIOLENT, *but when reciprocal.* I should think the direct contrary. What Occasion for *Violence* in reciprocal Affection, when Opposition is ceased, and total Consent takes place? By this way of Reasoning the House of Commons would always be most *violent,* when most *unanimous.* For *violent* therefore let us read *complete*; and then see whether the Reasoning will not hold good. And yet I am not sure, that Mr. *F.* who has *peculiar* Notions of *Delicacy,* may not have *peculiar* Notions of *Love.* If so, his *Love* may be *Rage*: And he may call that *Gentleness,* which others would call *Worrying.*

Omne adeo genus in terris HOMINUMQUE FERARUMQUE
In FURIAS *ignemque ruunt.* AMOR *omnibus idem,* &c.

VIR. GEORG. III. 242, &c.[2]

---

[1] i.e. anacoluthon. 'Bull' is slang for 'self-contradictory statement' or simply 'blunder'.

[2] 'Man and beast, every race on earth rushes into fire and passion. In all of them love is the same.'

Mr. *F.* and *Virgil* therefore mean the same thing by the Word *Love*, to which the graver Folks would give a Name less pleasing to the tender Ears of the modern Gentry, but perhaps not less proper for all that.

The Insincerity and Shuffling of *Jenny*'s Answer to *Allworthy*'s generous Speech must be referred to the Place cited above, which will fully explain it. Whether *she disdained to* EXCUSE *herself by a Lye*, as the Author affirms she did, can admit of no Dispute, but must be given in the Negative, since by her *Acknowlegement*, as Mr. *F.* stiles her false Confession, and whereby the ACCUSED herself, she was certainly guilty of a Falshood.

CHAP. VIII.

Miss *Bridget*'s and Dame *Wilkin*'s Listening, and the Event of it, when Miss *Bridget*, like Death, *grinn'd horrible a ghastly Smile* of Resentment against Mrs. *Deborah*, for her Impertinence in resolving to search into a Secret, which it was not *Bridget*'s Interest to be known, may be endured: But the School-Maxim, *De non apparentibus, & non existentibus, eadem est ratio*,[1] implies that the Author, like Miss *Bridget*, being never *seen to blush, did never* really *blush at all*; or it smells strongly of the Days of *gude* King *James*, when Pedantry passed for Wit and Humour. Let not Mr. *F.* be angry, if I glean after him those Passages which he seems either to have mistaken or overlook'd in the Course of this Work. For,

> ——*Sunt & mihi carmina: me quoque dicunt*
> *Vatem pastores:* sed non ego credulus illis.
>
> VIRG.[2]

CHAP. IX.

The ill-natur'd Reflections are such as become the *Mob:* Which is very properly defined by an Author, who must be allowed to understand them perfectly in all the Senses which he affixes to the Word. And here likewise, by an indirect Reflection, he takes care to ridicule a learned Education in Women, perhaps invidiously, as conscious how much he is excelled by one of his own Name among that Sex.[3]

CHAP. X.

Dr. *Blifil*'s Education in the Study of Physic, contrary to the Bent of his

---

[1] 'What is not apparent must be treated as if it did not exist.'

[2] 'I, too, have poems; the shepherds call me a poet, too. But I do not believe them.' *Eclogues*, IX. 33–4.

[3] i.e. Fielding's sister Sarah.

Genius, must have had a lamentable Effect upon his Mind as well as Fortune. But when the Author adds, in summing up his Character, that he will *not presume to say, whether his Religion was real or* hypocritical; and that he hath *no Touchstone to distinguish the true from the false*; I am sorry for him; since the Test of true Religion is to be found in *Jam. i.* ult. *Pure Religion and undefiled—is this, To visit the Fatherless and Widows in their Affliction, and to keep himself unspotted from the World*. In the preceding Verse the Apostle had said, *If any Man among you seem to be religious, and bridleth not his Tongue, but deceiveth his own Heart, this Man's Religion is vain*. Behold here the most perfect Definition ever given both of true and false Religion. After reading which (for we may presume one of his Function is no Stranger to the Scripture) how can the Author say he has no *Touchstone* to distinguish the one from the other, unless he *deceiveth his own Heart*? The *Purity of the Dr.'s Passion* for Money, would alone induce one to doubt the *Purity* of *his* Religion. And moreover, did not the Author know what he designed him to be? As to the Dr.'s Brother, the Captain, when he *chose the Church Militant, and preferred the King's Commission to the Bishop's,* I understand not what Mr. *F.* means by the *Church Militant*. That Church I had always thought to be the whole Body of Christians fighting in this Life against the Temptations of the World, the Flesh, and the Devil. But, according to Mr. *F.* they must be only the Gentlemen of the Army, some of whom, I am afraid, know as little of the Church as an Academical Doctor does of the Drawing-Room. This Epithet *militant* is the more unhappy, as the Author hath inserted it in his List of *Errata;* when the Word *military,* the supposed *Erratum,* would have better answered the Character of the Church to which the Captain belonged: But then indeed it would not have so well answered the Author's Talent of ridiculing a religious Term: And why ridiculing it?—Because, as is plain in this Instance, as well as in almost every other, in which Religion is concerned, he hath not given himself the Pains to inquire into the Meaning of the very Terms he makes use of.

CHAP. XI.

Miss *Bridget's* Motives for choosing the Captain were gross, and given in the true *F—ding* Taste. The *Limbs of a Ploughman,* the *Shoulders beyond all Size,* and the *Calves of a Chairman,* are Ideas that rise in our Author's Mind from that *sincere Endeavour,* which he avows, to *recommend* in his History nothing but GOODNESS and INNOCENCE.

CHAP. XII.

Allworthy's Speech upon the opening of the Marriage to him, when he alleges, as an Argument for his Acquiescence in it, *that a Woman upwards of thirty must* CERTAINLY *be supposed to know what will make her most happy*, gives me as mean an Opinion of his Understanding, as of his Concern for the Honour of his Family: For the whole Force of this Observation is, that since a Woman of Miss *Bridget*'s Years *ought to have* Discretion, therefore she *certainly had it:* Like the absurd Proposition of the *Roman* Church in the Article of Transubstantiation, *Crede quod habes, & habes*. This convinces me, that the Author intended to make the benevolent Mr. *Allworthy* a Fool, and perhaps to ridicule that *Charity, which thinketh no Evil*, as he had in a former Performance killed *Joseph* the Patriarch, and his own *Joseph Andrews*, with the same Stone. *Allworthy*'s Speech is fitly called a *Sermon:* And a most extraneous one it is to the Matter in Hand. To hear a worthy Man talk of Prudence, yet neglect it in a most essential Article, by suffering his Sister, without the least Admonition, to fling herself away upon a penyless and infamous Fellow, may be *Nature* in Mr. *F.*'s Way; but it is not *Example*.

CHAP. XIII.

As a Proof of Mr. *F.*'s Proficiency in the Royal Science of Demonology, he gives us a *late Maxim* of *the Devil's; When once you are got up, to kick the Stool from under you.* I will not absolutely deny the Author's Acquaintance with his sulphurean Majesty; but he seems to be as little read in the infernal Law-books as he is in those of his Country; since Ingratitude is *Very near as old as the Creation*: Witness the stale Deception of *Satan*, when he persuaded *Eve*, who persuaded her Husband, to disobey their Creator in eating the prohibited Fruit. Dr. *Blifil*, however, resenting his Brother the Captain's Ingratitude, *could not bring himself to submit to a Confession* of his own Guilt by accusing his Brother of the Part he bore in the Plot they had mutually laid to marry Miss *Bridget* to the Captain.—Very likely!—That *the worse his Brother was, the greater would his own Offence appear to be*, is certain: But then this is the same thing which had been just observed in the Clause immediately preceding this Sentence, *viz*. That he *must take to his* own *Share so great a Portion of Guilt*; and need not have been distinguished as a new Argument, by the Adverb *besides*: So that the latter Clause in the

Paragraph was plainly added merely to fill it up, and not to augment its Sense.

*   *   *

BOOK V. CHAP. I.

The Author asks, 'Who ever demanded the Reasons of that nice Unity of Time or Place, which is now established to be so essential to Dramatic Poetry?' It is likely some one had demanded these Reasons, or *Rapin* (after *Aristotle*) had not given them in the following Words: 'Unless there be the Unity of Place, of Time, and of Action, in great Poems, there can be no Verisimility. Indeed it is by these Rules that every thing becomes just, proportionate, and natural; for they are founded upon GOOD SENSE, and SOUND REASON, rather than on AUTHORITY and EXAMPLE'.[1] He again questions, 'What Critic hath been EVER ASKED, why a Play may not contain two Days as well as one, or why the Audience—may not be wafted fifty Miles, as well as five?' This being the first Time of Asking, I shall forbid the Banes of the Author's Conclusion, and give this short Answer; That the Reason why a Play may not contain two Days as well as one, arises from the Improbability, that the Audience should pass two Days without eating or drinking, or travel fifty Miles without one hospitable Inn of Mr. *F.*'s providing, to entertain themselves by the Way. The next Question, which is, 'Hath any Commentator well accounted for the Limitation which an antient Critic hath set to the Drama, which he will have contain neither more nor less than five Acts?' hath been answered, whether well or not, is under the Decision of the Public, by the Rev. Mr. *Francis*, on the Verse of *Horace*, which establishes this Rule;[2] to which I refer our Author. Whose last Question is, 'Hath any one living attempted to explain what the modern Judges of our Theatres mean by the Word *low?*' Mr. *F.* can best explain it, and seems to be conscious how fitly it has been applied to his Works. But his Question may be further answer'd by informing him, that *low* Characters are those in which Nature is degraded beneath the Standard at which it of right ought to be placed, by making them too much, or too little, what they should be; some Examples of which we have given, and are afraid, in the Course of this our laborious Criticism, of being able to give many more. Only we must observe on this Occasion, that Mr. *F.*

---

[1] 'Reflections on Aristotle's Treatise of Poesie', I. xii, in *The Whole Critical Works of Monsieur Rapin* (London, 1706), ii. 146.

[2] *The Art of Poetry*, l. 189.

has happily evaded the following Difficulty mentioned by the immortal *Swift:*

> Remains a *Difficulty* still;
> To purchase Fame by writing ill:
> From *Flecnoe* down to* *F—d—g*'s time,
> How few have reach'd the *low Sublime!*
>
> RHAPSODY.[1]

The Critics have in this Chapter incurred our Author's heavy Displeasure: And natural it is, that they should: For does not the Culprit
hate the Sight of a Judge? The Questions put by him I, as *Clerk* to the
Court of Criticism, have answered: And tho' the Author should *unfortunately not be able to see* the Validity of the Reasons given, this ought
not to avail in Arrest of Judgment; since, if the Court is satisfied, the
Prisoner may be as blind as Mr. *F.*'s Blind Man *in likening* Bombast *and
Fustian to the Sound of a Trumpet;* and yet Sentence be given agreeable
to Justice.

*   *   *

CHAP. IV.

The *little Incident* of the Muff, on which Mrs. *Honour*, or the Author, so
profusely wantons, is at the same time a *great* one against *Sophia*'s
Delicacy, who could value it the more for Mr. *Jones*'s egregious fooling
with it; and conveys to young Gentlemen and Ladies admirable Instructions in the Art of Toying. But whether these Instructions contain
nothing inconsistent with the strictest Rules of Decency, according to the
Author's early Declaration, must be left to the *chaste Eye* of the Reader,
and need not be further dwelt upon here.

*   *   *

BOOK VI. CHAP. IV.

This calm Villain *Blifil* may have had all the ill Qualities ascribed to
him: But how is it, that one more Vice was not added to the rest, I
mean that, which Mr. *F.* had called *Hungering after Women*, Chap. I. of
this Book? to which he had such Excitements in the Beauty of *Sophia*.
The Author paints him as without Desires of this Sort; which how he
will make agreeable to Nature, I know not. He seems indeed to have
this cold Temper allotted to him, to detract from the Value of the

---

* Some Copies have *Howard's:* But this Reading is obsolete; as it cannot be proved by
ocular Testimony, that any such Author ever lived. [The actual reading, of course, is
'Howard's'.]

[1] *On Poetry: A Rapsody* (1733), ll. 367–70.

Virtue of Chastity, by representing it only as constitutional; which is the Character of an Eunuch; and the contrary Vice to be so largely distributed to *Jones*, to advance in like manner the Credit of Incontinence, which few, besides our Author, will think at too low an Ebb in this Age and Nation.

★ ★ ★

BOOK IX. CHAP. II.

Mr. *F.* in summing up the Qualifications which make a Man look like an Angel, has unhappily forgot that only Ingredient which constitutes the Effence of an Angel, as far as the Nature of those glorious Beings can be made known to us: This is, VIRTUE. As to *Person, Features, Youth, Health, Strength, Freshness, Spirit,* and *Good-nature* in the popular Sense, some of these are ridiculous, when applied to Angels; and they were all possessed perhaps in as eminent a Degree by Captain *Macheath,* as by our Hero. Yet Captain *Macheath*'s Author was not so conceited as to imagine his infamous Hero resembled one of that beatified Order, who *Are happier than Mankind, because they're better*—But, with the strictest Poetical Justice, dooms him to Death for his Villainies, tho' the Royal Mercy interposes to save the Criminal, and prevent the Damnation of Mr. *Gay*'s Comic Opera. And whoever compares that Opera (bad as it is) with Mr. *F.*'s Production, will find the former infinitely surpass the latter in Morality, as well as in *all* that *Wit and Humour*, with which our Author supposes he hath cloathed his dirty Characters, purely with a Design to conceal their Turpitude from the Eye of the less discerning Reader.

★ ★ ★

BOOK XI. CHAP. IV. V. VI. VII.

I Shall, as before, with regard to the *Man of the Hill,* throw Mrs. *Fitzpatrick*'s History into one View: Weak she was by her own Acknowlegement: But she had little Reason to be angry with her Husband for preferring his own Seat to *dirty Lodgings at* Bath: Less, to *despise* him for living in an hospitable manner with the neighbouring Gentlemen. If he was *surly,* she ought to have ascribed this to her own discontented Temper; and not to have arraigned him for *maintaining a constant Lye* in his Actions abroad, when compared to his Behaviour at home. On the contrary, that Temper, in which a Man spends most of his Hours, ought to denominate his Character, not *vice versa*; especially since so good a Reason might be given for the Change. But Mrs. *Fitzpatrick,* had she known her Cousin's Story, might easily have retorted upon her, instead of her Question, 'Why, why, would you marry an *Irishman*?' in the last of these Chapters, the following just Reproof, 'Why, why would you marry a Whoremaster, and a Vagabond?'

★   ★   ★

BOOK XIII. CHAP. VIII.

Fifty Pounds given to *Jones* for his Gallantry is a most excellent Instance of *Christian Charity*! *Jones's* indeed to *Anderson* is praise-worthy. But this impudent Quality-Whore's is beneath Censure. Can any thing be more odious, than for a Woman of Figure to divest herself of her Dignity for a vile Satisfaction, and heap on her Partner in Guilt so ample a Reward of his Baseness? Where is Female Decency, that seeks to be courted, even when its own Inclination forwards the Courtship? Can any *English* Lady of Quality be so gross a Sensualist?—Perhaps she may: But is this corrupted Scene to be called Nature? And shall an Author glory is describing the Jakes of an human Mind, and say that he drew his Character from the *original Book of Nature*, as he expresses himself Book VII. Chap. XII? Ought he not rather to conclude with *Thwackum*, Book III. Chap. III. *that the human Mind, since the Fall, is nothing but a Sink of Iniquity*? Now then is the Time that the worthy Mr. *Jones* is *Right Honourably* taken into Keeping: In which he will makes as illustrious a Figure as any-where else in this Work.

★   ★   ★

CHAP. X.

That so great a Voluptuary as Mr. *Jones* should be alternately committing Acts of Debauchery, and tasting, by conferring, the Pleasures of Beneficence (which he does in this Chapter by leaving his Beneficiary, to attend the Call of the infamous Lady *Bellaston*), is an Inconsistency in Character never before heard of. To *earn the Wages of Iniquity*, in order with those Wages to merit Heaven by Acts of disinterested Beneficence, may qualify him indeed for a Place in the *Roman* Calendar of Saints, but in no other Chair of Beatification, I doubt. And Mr. *F.* must certainly have searched the Breviary to find so mixt a Character, where Instances of Oddity are easily to be met with, which, in any less grave Book, might perhaps pass for Instances of Humour also.

CHAP. XI.

The apropos Distinction of the *Heart* being absent from the rest of the Body in that prompt Apology of *Jones* for his unfaithful Behaviour at

Upton ('My *Heart* was never unfaithful to you: *That* had no Share in the Folly I was guilty of') is an Apology which might be made with equal Justice by the most abandoned Libertine that ever haunted the Purlieus of *Drury-Lane* or *Covent-Garden*. They must all therefore be excused alike: And a Lady of Honour, who has once assured herself of her Lover's *Heart*, never need be concerned for what becomes of the rest of his Body. This is Doctrine fit to be preached to the *Grand Turk*'s favourite Sultana: But dismal will be the Condition of this Island, and its dazling Beauties, who might rival any of the Gems of the Orient, when it comes to be endured here. But why say I, *endured*? Is it not more than this already? Is it not liked, applauded, devoured? *O Tempora! O Mores!* If this is admired, then may also *Sophia*'s yielding and foolishly fond Behaviour in this Scene (not resenting *Jones*'s Infidelity, but only her being made a Talk in Inns) be applauded too.

    Qui Bavium non odit, amet tua carmina, Mævi.[1]

★   ★   ★

BOOK XIV. CHAP. IV.

'I Have been guilty with Women,' says *Jones*; 'but am not conscious, that I have ever *injured* any.' What Sophistry is this! Is it not the greatest Injury Men can do to their Fellow-creatures, either to incite or consent to Acts of Wickedness? Is not the Soul (If there is a Futurity!) equally endangered by both? And can the Soul be at all endangered, where there is no sort of Injury committed? Let. Mr. *F.* solve these Theses, *in Foro Conscientiæ*, and then I will acknowlege, that Mr. *Jones* may be *guilty with* a Woman, without doing an *Injury to* her.

★   ★   ★

BOOK XVII. CHAP. I.

That the Author is not *of a tragic Complexion*, he has sufficiently shewn in *the most tragical Matter in* his *whole History*, Book XV. Chap. IV. where the intended Rape of *Sophia* affords excellent Farce: But as he compares himself to *the Devil* in tormenting poor *Jones*, in this he agrees with the Rev. Mr. *Whitefield*,[2] whom I have formerly heard with great Vociferation contend, that Man was a Composition half Brute, half Devil; in which Composition he ingenuously made himself one Ingredient, and in which Point none of his Friends or Adversaries

---

[1] 'May whoever does not hate Bavius love your poems, Maevius.' Virgil, *Eclogues*, III. 90.

[2] George Whitefield (1714-70), Methodist evangelist and missionary.

disagreed with him. But why should Mr. *F.* so far deride his Reader, as to advise him *not to lose any Time in taking a first Row at* Tyburn to see *Jones's* Execution, when he knew in his own Heart, that he never intended to bring the Hero thither? Is not this to affront his Reader, by intimating, that he cannot see further than his Nose?

CHAP. II.

Plutarch hath the Honour of being copied by Mr. *F.* who, he says, *is the best of our* BROTHER-*Historians.* But here the Honour is Mr. *F.*'s own, not *Plutarch's*; since, if I remember right, that great Philosopher and Historian wrote of Persons who really existed, and of Matters which were really brought to pass. Fiction was not his Talent; but Experience. Mr. *F.*'s lies another way. But the Vanity of ranking so loose a Novelist with an Historian (as the Eastern Emperors arrogantly styled themselves BROTHERS *of the Sun and Moon*; and who is to him as a regular Physician to an Empiric) may be set in a clearer Light by the following Verses:

> Thus *Lamb*, renown'd for cutting Corns,
> An offer'd Fee from *Radcliff* scorns:
> *Not for the World!*—WE *Doctors*, BROTHER,
> *Must take no Fees of one another.*
> Thus to a Dean some Curate Sloven
> Subscribes, *Dear Sir, Your* BROTHER *loving.*
>
> SWIFT.[1]

But, after all, we ought here to admit a various Reading; and, for *Plutarch*, substitute *Lucian*, who was as great a Scoffer, and as *true* an *Historian*, as Mr. *F.* himself.

CHAP. III.

'Affectation of Wisdom in a young Woman is as absurd as any of the Affectations of an Ape.' It is more absurd: For what Mr. *F.* calls, a little improperly, *the Affectations of an Ape*, are Parts of that Animal's Nature; and an *ignorant Satirist* (See Book XIV. Chap. I.) might perhaps say the same thing of those of the Fair Sex. *I* am not so severe; but construe Affectation to be a *Deviation* from the Simplicity of Nature: Which must be therefore *more* absurd in a young Woman than in an Ape. As to *Sophia*'s declining to give her Decision in a Point debated between *Thwackum* and *Square,* it was perhaps out of her Power, or any

---

[1] 'On the Words—Brother Protestants, and Fellow Christians . . .' (1733), ll. 15-20.

Mortal's. For which of the two can be right, when, as far as we have hitherto seen, both those Gentlemen confound their own Arguments? It was not therefore *the Modesty of a Learner,* but the Ignorance of one perplexed and confounded, which disabled her from entering into the Dispute. A *Deference* indeed *to the Understandings of Men* ought always to be *shewed,* as *Allworthy* says, by young Women. But this need not make them absolutely dumb, when appealed to; but should only keep them at a proper Distance from dictating and dogmatizing, when their Sentiments are asked, with a View only to examine the Depth of their Heads, and not to take Oracles from their uninformed Lips.

CHAP. IV.

Upon my Soul, swears *Sophia, it is true:* And it *was* true. Which is too singular to be passed over. But we hasten to

CHAP. V.

Where the Hero appears

> Confin'd and conjur'd into narrow
> Inchanted Mansion, to know Sorrow.
>
> HUD. Part I. Canto III.

And where we are unnecessarily informed, that *Jones* lived with *Nightingale,* of which we had heard Book XV. Chap. X. 'Tho' I have been hurried into Vices,' says *Jones,* 'I do not approve a vicious Character.' Hardly any wicked Man does. It is this which constitutes his Wickedness, that, knowing the Error of his own Conduct, he disapproves of the like Conduct in another; yet allows it in himself. This is therefore no great Palliative. But as Mr. *Jones* seems to have left his Vices, we will not at present dwell longer upon them.

CHAP. VI. VII. VIII.

Mrs. *Miller's* Embassy, the Opera, and the Drum, compose the first of these Chapters; the same Gentlewoman's apologetic Oration to *Allworthy,* the next; and Lord *Fellamar's* fruitless Courtship, the Third; rendered remarkable by the double Oath of the meek *Sophia; Upon my Honour*; and, as if this might be suspected, she immediately adds, *Upon my Soul.*

CHAP. IX.

If the *superior Throne, on which,* Mr. *Jones* says, *he hath some Reliance, affords him* not more *Protection* than *he* MERITS, I doubt, desperate would be his Case. His *Merit* here can bear no larger a Sense, than his Innocence in the Matter of *Fitzpatrick:* But every one knows the proper Sense of Merit has a much more spacious Scope, than to bear relation to a particular Circumstance only.

BOOK XVIII. CHAP. I.

Good Mr. *F.* since you are at last come to be *plain and serious,* and to lay aside your *Jokes and Raillery,* let me ask you one *plain and serious* Question: Which is, Pray, what *obliged* you to *cram into this Book* so great a *Variety of Matter?* Were you not at Liberty to omit any of your Episodes, that of the *Man of the Hill,* that of Mrs. *Fitzpatrick's* History, or that of *Partridge* at *Hamlet,* which ever you thought least entertaining, that so you might have found room to move, and that nevertheless your Readers might not have been disappointed in paying for an even Six? If thus you play, you are always sure of the Game, and your Competitors can only throw Deux-Ace. I therefore admire your *Policy* in choosing a perfect Number, as an Omen of your Success: Which your Bookseller can tell hath been well answered. You teach us also to admire you for your *Brevity,* when you say, that the Reader will *think the Number of Pages contained in* this Book *scarce sufficient to tell the Story.* But you forget, that you ought before this time so to have conducted your Story, as not to have been in Danger of *cramming.* If you take your Readers indeed for so many Chickens, you are extremely right in *cramming* them, before you eat your Dinner on them. If you have been treated with *Scurrility,* I condole with you on the Occasion: But hath not your Pen well revenged you? If you wrote once against the Court, and your Brother-Writers have hit you in the Teeth with your temporizing, do you not enjoy the Sweets of such a Conversion, and laugh, in a whole Skin, at those who only bark at you, because you outran them?

> ——Hic murus aëneus esto,
> Nil conscire *tibi,* nulla pallescere culpa.[1]

---

[1] 'This should be a bronze wall around *you*: to be conscious of no guilt, to turn pale at no sin.' Horace, *Epistles,* I. i. 60–61.

CHAP. II.

Shews Mr. *Jones* in a *very tragical* Light indeed, in the Character of an *Oedipus:* The Tragedy concerning whom, as written by *Sophocles,* is proposed by *Aristotle* as a perfect Model for all Tragedies; not so much from the Circumstances of Horror contained in it, as from the admirable Command over the Passions, which that Author hath demonstrated in it. Far otherwise Mr. *F.* who, being of the comic Class, only sets before us *Jones* and *Partridge* standing speechless and motionless; in which dumb and inactive Posture he leaves them, referring the Reader *to the Pencil, not the Pen, to describe the Horrors, which appeared in their Countenances.* For my part, as I prefer the durable Traces of the Pen to the fading Colours of the Pencil, I own I should have been pleased, if the Tragic Muse would have condescended, in this Place only, to have tied on Mr. *F.*'s Feet and Legs the *Sophoclean* Buskin, *which Mr.* Locke's *Blind Man would not have grosly erred in likening to the Sound of a Trumpet,* for which see Book IV. Chap. I. and in which tho' Mr. *F.*'s Supporters might have *made a good gouty Appearance,* they would nevertheless have gained the Point of astonishing the Reader with the very Apprehension of so terrible a Crime as Incest.

CHAP. III. IV.

The ungraceful Chiming in the Words *the* AUTHORITY *of* AUTHORS is increased by Mr. *F.*'s *insisting upon as much* AUTHORITY *as any* AUTHOR. But, as *Thwackum* says in his most barbarous and uncharitable Letter, these are *as trifling Matters as the small Tythes—compared to the weighty Matters of the Law.* One of these weighty Matters, in my Judgment, is the plain Inconsistency between the Character of *Thwackum,* as laid down by himself in his Letter, with that given of him by the Author a few Lines after. By the Letter itself it appears, that he was, to the highest Degree, uncharitable, proud, and self-interested: All which we conclude by his destining *Jones* to *the Place of Wailing and Gnashing of Teeth*; by his undeservedly rough Treatment of *Allworthy* himself; and by his eager Grasping as well at the Living of *Westerton,* in which he was disappointed, as at that of *Aldergrove,* which was not vacant: A Pluralist therefore he was, if not guilty of Simony. After all these Deviations from Honesty and Religion, how can the Author consistently celebrate him for *an unimpeached Honesty, and a most devout Attachment to Religion*?

CHAP. V. VI.

Mrs. *Miller*'s Interposition, who is one of the most innocent Characters in this History, and *Allworthy*'s Examination of *Blifil* and *Partridge*, are the Subjects of the former Chapter; and a farther Examination of *Partridge*, of the next. But Oh! that *Partridge*'s *Pig, which broke out, and did a Trespass,* had been driven with the rest of the Herd into the Sea, and perished with his other tedious Circumlocutions! What a Jockey would Mr. *F.* make, if he thus stopped his Horse in the middle of the Course! Surely this is not the Way to win the Plate!

CHAP. VII.

Here at length is Miss *Bridget*'s Virtue detected, whose Tongue had severely *lashed those who bring a Disgrace on the Sex,* so early as Book I. Chap. IV. The Propriety of her so doing is likewise seen, as I hinted on that Passage. Her Surprize and Virtue were equally affected. But the former Objection remains in full Force against the Propriety of her retaining the supposititious Child, instead of removing it out of *Allworthy*'s Sight or Knowlege. See our Remarks on Book I. Chap. V.

CHAP. VIII.

No'orow a Father is Mr. *Western*'s Dialect here: Formerly, as in Book XVII. Chap. III. we find, used by the same Gentleman, NARRO' *Woman upon Earth would ha' me.* Whence this Difference in the *Zummerzetshire* Alphabet? Let Mr. *Western* be constant to his Errors at least.—I urge not against the Author the Absurdity of Mrs. *Waters*'s Encomiums on *Jones* (with whom she had been guilty) for his Virtue, where she says, 'No young Gentleman of his Age is, I believe, freer from Vice; and few have the twentieth Part of his Virtues;' since it may be supposed, that Women of her Stamp lay no Stress on the single Virtue of Chastity. But I hope the Author does not put such a Sentiment into her Mouth, to avoid the Odium which might arise in the Hearts of his uniformly virtuous Readers against himself, for entertaining so base an one, as to conclude the Depravity of Mankind in general from one Instance; which would be the same as to judge of the Whole from a single Part.

CHAP. IX.

Allworthy seems to glory in his Sister's Shame—'Nor am I ashamed of owning him,' says he. 'I am MUCH MORE ashamed of my past

Behaviour to him' [How could he be *much more* ashamed of this, when he was not at all ashamed of the other?] 'But I was as ignorant of his Merit, as of his Birth.' His Birth therefore is the Thing which helps to reconcile *Jones* to his Uncle: Which is strange. For, tho' no Disgrace could attend poor *Jones* on this score singly, neither could any Honour. His Merit therefore should have been the only Reason for *Allworthy*'s Esteem. But Merit is a costly Drug: And we will charitably suppose, that the Author, being very rich in it himself, is, like other rich Men, who know the Value of their Acquisitions, unwilling to lavish it among his Characters. *Upon* her *Honour*, exclaims *Sophia*, notwithstanding *Jones*'s great Merit, she *will never receive* him *as* her *Husband.* Sincerity, I have before hinted, is not to be numbered among that young Lady's Accomplishments. But tho', under *Jones*'s present Disgrace, her *Honour* would not permit her to favour him, we are not without Hopes, that she, who hath so long, thro' so many Perils, been seeking an Husband, will not at last lose him, for the sake of a foolish Adherence to Honour. All, which she says about her *fixed Principle never to have married without* her Father's *Consent*, being compared with her *Hudibrastic* Elopement from his House, is mere *Ipsa dicit*, and ought to weigh just as much as Words, when compared with, and confuted by, Facts.

CHAP. X.

We know not whether we ought to regret the Loss of a Conversation, *which,* our Author assures us, *was pleasant enough.* He indeed lays the Loss to its *not happening earlier in* the *History:* But, as this is his old Excuse for *cramming* (See Chap. I. of this Book), we are of Opinion, that he only intends to run upon Tick[1] for *future Praise*, on which he, *feeds* (See Book XIII. Chap. I.); and that, in Truth, the Conversation omitted was neither pleasant nor pertinent.

CHAP. XI. XII.

The former is filled with the Raptures of *Jones*, Mrs. *Miller*, and the *Zani Partridge.* In the next, *Western* cannot restrain his Obscenity in the very first Words he utters; the bare mentioning of which is a sufficient Condemnation. When *Sophia* consents, before her Father and *Allworthy*, to marry *Jones*, this is her affected Speech: 'Such are your Commands, Sir; *and I dare not be guilty of Disobedience.*' Who ever suspected her Dis-

[1] i.e. to run into debt.

obedience, when her Inclination was complied with? Of *Jones* she was as fond, as our Author of *future Praise*; and when she knew there was no Obstruction to her Desires, then, gentle Reader! (Sure you will not be so unpolite as to contradict a Lady!) she *dares not be guilty of Disobedience*.

CHAP. *the Last.*

What Rhetoric *Allworthy* had used with old *Nightingale*, which could be more prevalent with him, than his adored Gold, to reconcile him to his Son's Marriage with a moneyless Girl, so as to *receive him much more kindly than he expected*, is uncertain: But some Rhetoric must have been used: And, the History drawing so near to a Conclusion, our Author hath been forced to omit it. Mere *Necessity* could not be an Inducement to such a Father to rest satisfied with his Son's disadvantageous Marriage, because no Miser would ever admit that as a Plea, which is a Term he hates: Nor will the Reasons our Author assigns for this unexpected Behaviour have much more Weight. A Principle of Avarice was still predominant in his Breast; or he would never, with Uneasiness, have considered *the Contents of* Western's *Coffers*, and regretted that his own Son had missed so rich a Prize. And who ever knew a Miser sit down contented with the Loss of a considerable Sum, because another had lost as much or more? So that, tho' the two Brothers lived in perpetual *Contention about the Government of their Children*, their mutual Disappointment would rather increase their Rage, than alleviate it: For nothing but Virtue can establish a sufficient Basis for Contentment. At last, every body being settled according to their Wish, except *Black George*, who, for aught we can tell, hath been sent to t'other Gentleman in Black (but to whom the Author might have been more favourable for *Jones*'s and *Molly*'s sakes, and in regard to the Plea which Mr. *Jones* makes for him to *Allworthy* Chap. XI. of the present Book), *this History is concluded*.

And now, Sir, upon the Whole, I must acknowlege, that, were it not for the bad Morals, which, especially in the earlier Parts of this Work, are insinuated, I should hardly have troubled you or myself with so long a Course of Criticism: An Office, from which, as it is principally conversant in finding Faults, I am extremely averse. Had not these Faults been so glaring, the Author's *counterfeit* Wit might have pass'd for *true*, and dazled the Eyes of our Beaux and Belles with its tinsel Lustre, for any thing I should have done to prevent it. But so much Notice has been taken of this Performance, as an* *inimitable* one, that, when I was opposing the Author's Scheme of Morality, I could not avoid lifting up the censorial Rod against the other also. Yet have I no personal Pique against this Gentleman; but admire some irregular Touches of Wit and Morality, which, like the few fertile Spots to be seen among the most barren Parts of the *Alps*, may be found in travelling thro' his Volumes. But these are so over-balanced by their Contraries, and by what we have Reason to fear (from comparing our Author's former Works with his latter) of his future Degeneracy from the *Milk of human Kindness* to the Pap of infantile Inspidity, that we cannot help exclaiming with *Horace*,

> Ætas parentum, pejor avis, tulit
> Nos nequiores, mox daturos
> Progeniem vitiosiorem.

Carm. III. vi. 46, 47, 48.[1]

I am, SIR,
Your most humble Servant,

Orbilius.

---

* See certain Verses to *Henry Fielding*, Esq; *on reading his* INIMITABLE *History of* Tom Jones, published in the *Gentleman's* Magazine for *August*, 1749, which have been wisely disowned by a Gentleman of the same Name with their Author by a public Advertisement. [See No. 76].

[1] 'Our fathers, a worse generation than their fathers, have sired a still more corrupt race in us, who will soon bring forth an even more vicious progeny.'

83. Unsigned review of *An Examen of the History of Tom Jones*, *The Monthly Review*

December 1749, ii. 93–94

The anonymous author of this critical work, is quite dissatisfied with the whole of Mr. *Fielding*'s celebrated performance, which he takes all to pieces from beginning to end; finds, or makes, faults in every chapter; and damns every character in the history. He appears continually angry, ill-natur'd, and malicious; and seems to have every quality of the late redoubted Mr. *Dennis*, except his real talents for criticism. He should have entitled his pamphlet an *Invective*, instead of an *Examen*. A true critic is candid, and tempers his censures with generosity, good nature, and good manners; but this author has not the least air of any of these. He has nothing of the gentleman about him; scurrility seems to be his talent.

'Tis true, indeed, that he has pointed out some real faults in the *Foundling*; but then they are most of them beneath the notice of one who would rather choose to give himself pleasure by the perusal of a work chiefly calculated for entertainment, than to put himself out of humour at every little slip of a pen, from which, at the same time, so many beauties are continually flowing. In truth, this pretended critic seems to be one of POPE's *Word-catchers*, that live upon *Syllables*. And he who treats with an air of the highest contempt, so considerable a writer as Mr. *Fielding*, does not, himself, appear to be able, if one may judge from his *Examen*, to produce any thing with half the merit in it, that may be found in the worst performances of the author of *Tom Jones:* indifferent as some of them, we mean his *theatrical pieces*, may be deemed.————After what we have said of this work, it would certainly be thought impertinence, and absurdity in us, to take up any more room in these sheets, by an extract of it, especially as we have a greater number of articles this month, than will be easily contracted within the narrow limits of our *Review*.

84. [Lady Dorothy Bradshaigh], letter

16 December 1749

From a letter signed 'Mrs. Belfour', to Samuel Richardson, Barbauld, iv. 309–11.

*   *   *

I shall not say a word more toward persuading you to read Tom Jones, and beg pardon for having done it; but I meant not to compel; how could you insinuate such a thing? You really seem not only grave, but angry with me. Had you gone thro' it, your censure or praises would have had agreeable weight with me, as some things I approve, but disapprove many more. I should have been glad to have known how far my opinion corresponded with yours. It was your repeated persuasions that prevailed upon me to read the three last volumes of Clarissa; but I did not look upon myself as compelled.

I do assure you, Sir, Mr. Fielding's private character makes him to me appear disagreeable; so I am no ways prejudiced in his favour, I only impartially speak my opinion.

As to my pointing out the moralities which I think may be found in this work, I must beg to be excused; for as you think the piece not worth your perusal, I must think that a research is not worth my trouble, tho' I persist in thinking there are many good things in it.

I believe I may have been more unforgiving to the female than the male delinquents; and it is because I love them better, and their crimes touch me nearer; and that I wish to behave up to the honour, modesty, and virtue, so becoming, and necessary to render them valuable.

Whatever I may have said, it is not that I think better of the men— worse, worse, a thousand times! I assure you, Sir. . . .

85. Samuel Richardson, letter

22 January 1749–50

From a letter to Frances Grainger, Carroll, pp. 143–4.

---

*　　*　　*

I cannot but be pleased at your Hint that if the Modern Ladies were to allow to the Character of Clarissa its due Merit, they would 'own themselves very weak'—to use your own Words—'and her very Wise.' 'And what Lady,' say you, 'would chuse to do that?'—This is the very Reason by which I have taken the Liberty to account, elsewhere, for the good Reception the Character of the weak, the inspidid, the Run-away, the Inn-frequenting Sophia has met with. In that, as in the Character of her illegitimate Tom, there is nothing that very Common Persons may not attain to; Nothing that will reproach the Conduct or Actions of very ordinary Capacities, and very free Livers: while Clarissa's Character, as it might appear unattainable by them, might be supposed Prudish, too delicate, and a silent Reproach to themselves. Had I been at Leisure to examine *The History of Tom Jones*, But I might have been at Leisure indeed to set about such a Task! And yet I am sure I should have been able to do the Author Impartial Justice. But I should have known whom by the Examination to have called Sophias and whom Clarissas.

I join in your wish that Ladies would remember 'that even Lovelace,' the Favourite of some of those whom he would have despised as un-worthy of his Attempts, and perhaps as too easy preys, 'would not have thought Clarissa worthy of the Pains he took in endeavouring to seduce her had she not been thus admirable in herself.' And indeed he every-where declares that a Conquest of her would be a Triumph over the whole Sex. This must be inferr'd, without incurring ye Censure of Uncharitablesness, that those Ladies who are fond of Lovelace, are not those who would have prov'd Exceptions to his haughty Triumph over the whole Sex, had he rated them in his *Attempts* as highly as he did the *too delicate* Clarissa.—Have you, Madam, well considered his letters to

Belford, No. xv., xvi., xvii., in Vol. iii? If you have not, I wish you would, and inforce them upon the Young Ladies who may have the Benefit of your Acquaintance. You cannot imagine, Madam, how much the Characters of Clarissa, of Miss Howe, of Lovelace, of Mr. Hickman, have let me into the Hearts and Souls of my Acquaintance of both Sexes, some of which those of Sophia and Tom Jones have greatly confirmed.

★　　★　　★

86. From *The Student, or, The Oxford and Cambridge Monthly Miscellany*

20 January 1750

In collected edition (1751), ii. 178.

> *If knowledge of the world makes men perfidious*
> *May* JUBA *ever live in ignorance.*
>
> ADDISON's Cato.

Our language scarcely affords a more common phrase than that of *knowing the world*, nor is there, I believe, any, that from the mouth of a preceptor can possibly have a more evil tendency; and yet no sooner are our youth capable of comprehension, than the first thing they are taught to comprehend is, that seemingly necessary and important doctrine, how to *know the world*.

I wou'd not so far discourage all *knowledge* of the world, as to have young men be so little acquainted with the ways of it, as to be impos'd upon by every one: but this phrase includes more in it than this; (if it did not where were the fault?) it designs not only to keep us from being impos'd upon ourselves, but spurs us to impose upon others, or in better words, *makes men perfidious*.

I have heard the character of Mr. ADAMS the clergyman, in an ingenious work of FIELDING's, highly condemn'd, because, it seems, he *knew not the world*; and I am sorry to find that many of our divines are of the same opinion, and for the same reason.——But how much more laudable and agreeable figure does he now make, than he wou'd have done, had he been represented as ready to impose, as he is now liable to be impos'd upon? I know not what may be the opinion of others, but to me, his innocent ignorance of this world and its ways, demonstrates him not to have been a child of it, and if so, what they, his brothers of the cloth, who are so thoroughly knowing in this point, are, who is not able to guess?

★ ★ ★

JOSEPH ANDREWS AND TOM JONES

87. From *The History of Charlotte Summers, the Fortunate Parish Girl*

1750

i. 1–11 (Introduction); i. 28–34 (Bk. I, Chap. ii); i. 220–2 (Bk. II, Chap. i.)

★ ★ ★

You must know then, I am the first Begotten, of the poetical Issue, of the much celebrated Biographer of *Joseph Andrews*, and *Tom Jones*; I dare not pretend to be legitimately begotten; I believe I must content myself with the Honour of being only a natural Brat of that facetious Gentleman; for I dare swear he does not remember when he became my Father, and has had scarce any Conversation with my Mother, either before or since that happy Encounter, which gave Being to your humble Servant; therefore I am afraid, I should scarce be able to fix a Marriage upon the Squire, especially as the Ceremony of poetical Espousals is so much controverted by the Priests of *Parnassus*, that its next to impossible to settle the Ritual, that would convey the Privilege of Legitimacy to the Offspring of the Poets.

However, whether he owns me as a lawful Son, or a bye Blow, or disclaims all Kindred to me, I find so much of his Blood in my Veins, that I have found myself, ever since I was a Boy, under the strongest Impulse to mimic every Action of that Gentleman, whom my Mother declared on her Death Bed, in the most solemn Manner, to be the only Person on Earth to whom I owed my poetical Being; of Course its no Wonder, now, that I am obliged to look about for a Settlement in the World, that I should chuse a Profession nearly of Kin to that, in which he has lately made such a glaring Figure.

My worshipful poetical Sire having with so much Satisfaction to the Public, so much Honour to himself, and with so much Profit to his industrious Drawer, Mr. M——r,[1] discharged the Station of Master of an Ordinary, I could not think of any Branch of Business so likely for me to thrive in as that of a Publican. My Countrymen, I know, love good Eating as well as any Nation on Earth, which was certainly the Reason, that induced the facetious Mr. F——g to assume the Character of an Ordinary-Keeper, being persuaded that nothing puts a Man in better Humour than a full Stomach, but if he has entertained you with the plain, but mighty roast Beef of *Old England*. . . .

But I must remember I am not at present writing my own History, and however unwilling I may be to quit the dear Subject, I must return to my Sign-Post, and acquaint my Reader with the Nature of it, that he may know it again when he meets it in his Travels. I was a long Time before I could fix a Resolution in the important Point. A Number of curious Devices were suggested to me by the Connoisseurs in that mysterious Art of Signography. I was for a whole Week in the Mind to have charged my Board with the Figures of an Ass and an Owl, the true Emblems of superlative Dulness, intending it by way of Contrast to the facetious Entertainment within Doors; which is one of the Secrets of the Art of Pleasing I learned from my worshipful Father, who tells us in his droll Way, that he often dipped his Pen in Dulness, meerly for a Relaxation to his Readers, and to whet their Appetite for a new Course of Wit and Pleasantry; but I at last considered that some few of my Readers might mistake the Conceit, and take these two grave Creatures for the Prototype of myself and my Work, and that others might be a little superstitious, and unwilling to live under such dull Planets; I laid aside therefore the Thought, and was for a considerable Time full of the Design of assuming my worshipful Father's Head for my armorial Bearing; but on consulting an able Artist, I was let to understand, that however witty my Father's Countenance might appear, when situated near the Eye, yet the facetious Features were too weak to be discernable in so elevated an Attitude, and besides that, it would be making too free with magisterial Dignity, to make his Phiz the Signal of a mere Punch-House; at last, after labouring with many Conceits for near two Months, I resolved to charge my Board with the true Effigy of my Parish Girl, where though she appears a most charming Woman, yet I can assure the Reader, the Painter has not flattered her, for she has some natural Graces it's impossible for any Pencil to

[1] i.e. Andrew Millar, Fielding's publisher.

imitate, or even the sublime Pen of a *F——g*, when warmed with the dear Idea of his lovely *Sophia*, to describe.

★　　★　　★

CHAP. II.

On the Use of Chapters, and the Advantage of natural Stupidity.

As the worshipful Mr. *F——g*, whom I have chosen as my Pattern in compiling of this true History, has been very full in displaying the Convenience of these Kind of Divisions, commonly called Chapters, both to the Authors and his Readers, I hope the Public are so fully convinced of their great Utility, and so perfectly satisfied with the Weight of his Authority, that I need not offer at any Apology for following so worthy an Example. However as he has establish'd it as an infallible Doctrine, that an Author, in spite of all critical Authority, has an absolute Right to digress when and where he pleases, and to amuse himself and his Readers with any thing that comes uppermost in his Head, whether it has any Connection with the Subject in Hand or not; I here, once for all, put in my Claim to that extensive Privilege, and declare my Intention of using it in the Course of this History with as much Freedom as I think proper; and for this Reason I am now determined to say something of the Convenience of Books and Chapters, no matter whether the Reader has ever had any such Thoughts or not. I look upon these sort of Divisions in this Species of Writing to be like the Acts and Scenes in a Play; the main Design of which must be to give Time for shifting of the Scenes and conveying the Audience without hurry or apparent Absurdity to and from the several Places and Apartments, where the Poet has laid his Action; . . .

. . . The Truth is, my worshipful Father is naturally a Man of good Humour himself, and resolved to be pleased as easily as he can; he has so little Bile in his Constitution, and so large a Quantity of Mercury, he is seldom or never sad himself, and in writing his *Tom Jones*, he wrote nothing but what tickled his own Fancy, and never put Pen to Paper but when he was perfectly pleased with himself and all about him; by this Means nothing flowed from him but what was facetious and witty. On the other Hand, the Historian of *Clarissa* is possessed of an infinite deal of Good-nature, but has such a peculiar melancholy Cast in his Temper, that it is very rare that he can be prevailed on so much as to smile, but he is pleased with the most tender and pathetic Scenes of Life, and never can see Distress but he feels it, and never wrote till he had wrought up his Imagination into a real Belief of the Reality of the Misfortune of his Heroine. His Sighs, his Tears, and Groans guided his Pen, and every Accent appears but the Picture of his own sad Heart, that beats with tender Sympathy for the imaginary Distress of his favourite Fair. Thus both these great Men, while they were writing for the Entertainment of the Public, were pleasing themselves in their different Tastes; *Tom Jones* was pleased when he laughed, and *Clarissa* when she cried; and as both presented their natural Countenance, we could not help joining in Concert, for Laughing and Crying, as well as Yawning are both catching, that is, when they are both natural and not forced.

* * *

88. Lady Dorothy Bradshaigh, letter

27 March 1750

From a letter to Samuel Richardson, Barbauld, vi. 7–8.

When I saw you last, I forgot to tell you I had read Charlotte Summers; but did not find any thing relating to you, like what you told me. I doubt I do not well remember what he says; but I think it is, that we are taught the art of *laughing* and *crying*, from your *melancholy* disposition, and Mr. Fielding's *gay* one; and I think passes a compliment upon each, though perhaps he might design to sneer.[1]

There are very different kinds of laughter: you make me laugh with pleasure; but I often laugh, and am angry at the same time with the facetious Mr. Fielding.

* * *

[1] See No. 87.

TOM JONES IN FRANCE

March 1750

89. Pierre Antoine de la Place, letter

1750

From the Preface to his translation of *Tom Jones, Histoire de Tom Jones, ou L'Enfant Trouvé* (1750), i. vi–xii. Translated from the French.

TRANSLATION
of a Letter written to MR. FIELDING
Author of this Work

I have never seen you, Sir, but I am fond of you; I have never known you, but I admire you: what better reasons for winning the favour of the Author of *Joseph Andrews*,* and of *The Foundling*? This last product of your pen has captivated me to the point that I have not been able to resist the temptation to translate it into my native tongue: my satisfaction would be incomplete if I did not share with my compatriots the pleasure that you have given me, and if they could never join with me in applauding the glory of the worthy author of a history as agreeable and as useful to mankind as is that of *Tom Jones*. I hope to send you soon a copy printed satisfactorily, in four volumes, and embellished with engravings according to the designs of Mr. Gravelot. I shall certainly be pleased, if the respectable father of the beloved of Jones deigns to recognize a cherished daughter, in French clothing! never fear, Sir, she is unchanged: she is always the same Sophia, deserving object of your goodness and of our tenderness.

But your most amiable Englishmen, whose intention is not to travel

* This short Novel, of which a French Translation was hardly possible, has made a great fortune in England.

223

across France like meteors, those in a word who intend to live among us for a while, do they not make a French adaptation? do they not join to their own native charms all the graces and ornaments, in style, of a nation in which everyone (whatever they may say about it) is secretly flattered by pleasing in many different ways. And now this reflection; if Mr. Fielding, I have said, had written for the French, he probably would have suppressed a large number of passages which are very excellent in themselves, but which would have seemed out of place to them. Once heated with the interest that comes from a moving and skilfully-woven plot, they endure impatiently all manner of digressions, of essays,* or of moral treatises, and they consider these ornaments, however fine they may be, as just so many obstacles to the pleasure which they are eager to enjoy. I have done what the Author himself would have done.

Such is, Sir, my full apology, for having dared, not to change, but to adapt certain parts of your work to the taste of a people in whose eyes a selection of English dramatic works, and the tragedy of *Venice Preserv'd*[1] adapted to our theatre, have had the good fortune to be pleasing.

My remaining fear, if you will please excuse me, arises from the small amount of time which I have been able to devote to such a work. It was absolutely unknown to me before last June 13; and rumour was already spreading that the booksellers of Holland, always looking out for their interests, were rushing out a translation. The work of Mr. *Fielding* had made me too much the author's friend: this news alarmed me. I took pen in hand, firmly resolving not to let up until I had completed my enterprise. I wish, even more than I dare hope, to see my efforts worthy of your approval. I would continue to feel, in any case, the most sincere esteem and respect, etc.

DE LA PLACE

P.S. Please have the goodness to excuse the style of a Frenchman, who since his childhood has never written in your language. It is never my pen which speaks to you, it is my heart.

---

* The History of *Tom Jones* is in 6 volumes, containing 18 books, each one of which is preceded by a Preliminary discourse, in the form of a Dissertation, on some literary or moral question, often unrelated to the subject. I felt that I should omit these otherwise excellent pieces which, in the sequel, we can make into a small, separate volume that is as instructive as it is amusing.

[1] By Thomas Otway (1682).

90. Unsigned review of *Histoire de Tom Jones*, *The Gentleman's Magazine*

March 1750, xx. 117–18

A literary Article from Paris.

Histoire de Tom Jones, *ou* L'Enfant trouvé; the History of *T. Jones*, or the *Foundling*, translated into *French* by M. *de la Place*, and adorned with cuts designed by M. *Gravelot*.

If we believe the epistle dedicatory, addressed to a commissioner of the *British* treasury (*George Lyttelton, Esq*;) 'The strictest regard to religion and virtue has been observed throughout the whole course of his history, and the reader will find nothing in it contrary to the severest rules of decency, or offensive to the most tender imagination.'* We must here suppose that, by *virtue*, M. *Fielding* would not have us understand a rigorous observation of all the precepts in the christian system of morality, but only the practice of the principal offices of justice and humanity; otherwise the loose manners of his heroe might give occasion to upbraid the author with neglecting to fulfil exactly the first of his promises. And that we may have room to discharge him from the breach of the last, it is necessary to imagine yourself transported to the country where the scene is laid. In *France* the ladies would be shock'd at the repeated breaches of faith in *Tom Jones* to his mistress, and fathers and mothers would exclaim against that resolute boldness with which Miss *Western* abandons her father's house to preserve herself inviolate to her lover. In *England* they are not so rigorous; every father and mother indeed, in *London* as well as *Paris*, would be glad to have their children perfectly obedient to their will; but the love of liberty in the *English*, renders them generally more disposed to forgive the disobedience of a daughter, when her obedience might make her miserable. Inconstancy

---

* The *English* editor says,—'*From the name of my patron*, I hope my reader will be convinced, at his very entrance on this work, that he will find in the whole source of it nothing prejudical to the cause of religion and virtue, nothing inconsistent with the strictest rules of decency, nor which can offend even the chastest eye in the perusal. On the contrary, I declare, that to recommend goodness and innocence hath been my sincere endeavour in this history.'

in a lover, will no more be pardon'd by an *English* than a *French* woman, but the first will sooner pass by a slight neglect; in general, the *English* ladies are more jealous of a man's sentiments, the *French* of his actions. M. *de la Place,* the translator of this piece, would have done well perhaps to have inserted these remarks, which we have ventur'd to make, in his *preliminary discourse,* in order to prevent those objections which some cavillers might make against M. *Fielding.*

A synopsis of so long a series of events as the history of *Tom Jones,* would take up too much room in this collection; we shall therefore only endeavour to shew the merit of this ingenious work of imagination. The public has not for a long time been entertain'd with a piece where the principal persons are more engaging or more interesting, the episodes better connected with the principal action, the characters more equally sustained, the incidents more artfully prepared, or more naturally arising one out of another. Miss *Western* is a truly admirable character; *Tom Jones,* as much a libertine as he is, engages all sensible hearts by his candor, generosity, humanity, his gratitude to his benefactors, his tender compassion, and readiness to assist the distressed. The name of *Alworthy,* which in *English* signifies *supereminently good,* could never be more justly bestow'd than on the respectable uncle of *Jones.* The character of *Blifil,* in opposition to that of the *Foundling,* presents us with an admirable contrast, and is dress'd up with singular art. The author has employ'd no less skill about his other characters, in assigning to every one his station and business, so that, among so great a number, they all, except one, appear necessary to the action. *Sancho Pancho* was the original by which M. *Fielding* drew his *Partridge,* who indeed is not so entertaining as the 'Squire of Don *Quixote,* but however cannot fail of pleasing an *English* taste.

Whether the author's imitating the manner of *Cervantes, Scarron,* and *le Sage,* in the titles of his chapters, is approved by his countrymen, we cannot say; but if we may give our opinion, how proper soever it seems in works of fancy designed for delight and amusement, it is altogether as improper in a piece whose principal design is interesting and instructive.

M. *de la Place* has considerably abridged this *romance,* which in the original makes 6 volumes. We would advise him to make some more retrenchments when he comes to give * a second edition of his trans-

---

* Since the writing of this article, the edition, to which was *artfully* put *printed for* Mr. Nourse *in* London, has been suppressed by an arrêt of the council of state.

lation. In a letter which is addressed to Mr *Fielding* he justifies his abridgment after the following manner.

'Do not the most agreeable *English* women, who make the tour of *France*, and traverse not the country like meteors, but chuse to stay there some time, strike into the air and manner of the *French* women? Are they not ambitious of adding to their natural charms, all the graces, with all the modish ornaments of a nation, in whose eyes, every one of them, whatever she may pretend, secretly flatters herself with appearing amiable? On this consideration, if Mr *Fielding* had written for the *French,* he would probably have suppressed a multitude of passages, excellent indeed in themselves, but which would appear to a *Frenchman,* unseasonable or misplaced. When he has once warmed his imagination with the interesting result of an intrigue highly pathetic, and artfully laid, he becomes impatient under all sorts of digressions, dissertations, or moral touches, and regards all such ornaments, however fine, as obstacles to the pleasure which he is in haste to enjoy. I have done no more than what the author himself would have done.'

It is very seldom that a work of wit and entertainment does not suffer by a translation; for instance, the person introduced by Mr *Fielding,* under the name of *Fitz Patrick,* is continually talking in a mixture of *Irish* and *English,* which tickles the ears of an *Englishman,* but has no effect on the *French. M. de la Place* has however in his translation, preserved most of the graces of the original. He is not indeed absolutely correct, but so far from deserving censure for some negligence of style, that it is surprising to see so few faults of that kind, since he spent but about five months on so long and diffuse a work.

The designs of M. *Gravelot* for the cuts which adorn this edition well deserved to be executed by the best of our engravers.

91. Friedrich Melchior, Baron Grimm

Spring 1750

From *Correspondance Littéraire, Philosophique et Critique* (Paris, 1877), i. 410. (Translation.)

Grimm's *Correspondance Littéraire* was a miscellaneous information sheet sent to a small group of subscribers that included Catherine the Great of Russia, the Queen of Sweden, the King of Poland, and a number of German princes and princesses. In general, Grimm was a disciple of Diderot and repeated his ideas; he admired both Fielding and Richardson, but distrusted Marivaux and other French novelists.

Cf. also Grimm's very high opinion of Richardson: *Correspondance Littéraire,* iii. 161, iv. 24–5, v. 23.

Twelve or fifteen months ago a novel entitled *The Foundling* was published in London. This work of Mr. Fielding had the most prodigious success. M. de la Place, author of *Théâtre anglais*, has just translated it into French.[1] Here is the gist of it: Mr. Allworthy, going to bed, finds there a newborn infant, and raises him under the name of Tom Jones with as much care as if he were his own son. Jones falls in love with Sophia Western, daughter of a gentleman neighbour of Allworthy. He has for rival one Blifield [*sic*], nephew of his protector. This treacherous youth exerts all his influence on his uncle until he makes Jones appear a monster and has him expelled. Sophia, who is subsequently being forced to marry Blifield, runs away, and it is only after many adventures that she marries Jones, who is finally recognized as Allworthy's nephew, and as innocent of all the crimes of which he has been accused.

However much the translator has condensed the work, it is still too long. The characters are well enough drawn and various enough, but

---

[1] La Place's translation (see No. 89).

the multitude of dramatis personae produces a kind of confusion. The interest a reader must take in the two heroes of the novel is weakened by the attention he must devote to all the subordinate characters. Jones' infidelities to Sophia are another mistake. The low details of the work may please the English, but they are overridingly displeasing to our ladies. I do not know whether the original, which I have never seen, is well written, but the translation is often enough *gothique*. It is rather slow going.

92. Samuel Johnson, *The Rambler No. 4*

31 March 1750

Although Fielding's name is not mentioned, he is clearly the
writer Johnson has in mind when he refers to those who 'mingle
good and bad Qualities in their principal Personages' and 'confound the Colours of Right and Wrong'. Chalmers stated that
this *Rambler* was 'occasioned by the popularity of *Roderick
Random*, and *Tom Jones*' (*The Works of Samuel Johnson*, 1816, iv.
24).

Simul et jucunda et idonea dicere Vitæ. HOR.[1]

The Works of Fiction, with which the present Generation seems more
particularly delighted, are such as exhibit Life in its true State, diversified
only by the Accidents that daily happen in the World, and influenced by
those Passions and Qualities which are really to be found in conversing
with Mankind.

THIS Kind of Writing may be termed not improperly the Comedy
of Romance, and is to be conducted nearly by the Rules of Comic
Poetry. Its Province is to bring about natural Events by easy Means,
and to keep up Curiosity without the Help of Wonder; it is therefore
precluded from the Machines and Expedients of the Heroic Romance,
and can neither employ Giants to snatch away a Lady from the nuptial
Rites, nor Knights to bring her back from Captivity; it can neither
bewilder its Personages in Desarts, nor lodge them in imaginary Castles.

I REMEMBER a Remark made by *Scaliger* upon *Pontanus*, that all his
Writings are filled with Images, and that if you take from him his
Lillies and his Roses, his Satyrs and his Dryads, he will have nothing

[1] For the second edition Johnson supplied 'And join both profit and delight in one
—Creech'.

left that can be called Poetry.[1] In like Manner, almost all the Fictions of the last Age will vanish, if you deprive them of a Hermit and a Wood, a Battle and a Shipwreck.

WHY this wild Strain of Imagination found Reception so long, in polite and learned Ages, it is not easy to conceive; but we cannot wonder, that, while Readers could be procured, the Authors were willing to continue it: For when a Man had, by Practice, gained some Fluency of Language, he had no further Care than to retire to his Closet, to let loose his Invention, and heat his Mind with Incredibilities; and a Book was produced without Fear of Criticism, without the Toil of Study, without Knowledge of Nature, or Acquaintance with Life.

THE Task of our present Writers is very different; it requires, together with that Learning which is to be gained from Books, that Experience which can never be attained by solitary Diligence, but must arise from general Converse, and accurate Observation of the living World. Their Performances have, as *Horace* expresses it, *plus oneris quantum veniæ minus*,[2] little Indulgence, and therefore more Difficulty. They are engaged in Portraits of which every one knows the Original, and can therefore detect any Deviation from Exactness of Resemblance. Other Writings are safe, except from the Malice of Learning; but these are in danger from every common Reader; as the Slipper ill executed was censured by a Shoemaker who happened to stop in his Way at the *Venus* of *Apelles*.

BUT the Danger of not being approved as just Copyers of human Manners, is not the most important Apprehension that an Author of this Sort ought to have before him. These Books are written chiefly to the Young, the Ignorant, and the Idle, to whom they serve as Lectures of Conduct, and Introductions into Life. They are the Entertainment of Minds unfurnished with Ideas, and therefore easily susceptible of Impressions; not fixed by Principles, and therefore easily following the Current of Fancy; not informed by Experience, and consequently open to every false Suggestion and partial Account.

THAT the highest Degree of Reverence should be paid to Youth, and that nothing indecent or unseemly should be suffered to approach their Eyes or Ears, are Precepts extorted by Sense and Virtue from an ancient Writer by no Means eminent for Chastity of Thought.[3] The same Kind, tho' not the same Degree of Caution, is required in every thing which is laid before them, to secure them from unjust Prejudices, perverse Opinions, and improper Combinations of Images.

[1] Scaliger, *Poetics,* V. iv.   [2] *Epistles,* II. i. 170.   [3] Juvenal, in *Satires,* XIV.

In the Romances formerly written every Transaction and Sentiment was so remote from all that passes among Men, that the Reader was in very little danger of making any Applications to himself; the Virtues and Crimes were equally beyond his Sphere of Activity; and he amused himself with Heroes and with Traitors, Deliverers and Persecutors, as with Beings of another Species, whose Actions were regulated upon Motives of their own, and who had neither Faults nor Excellencies in common with himself.

But when an Adventurer is levelled with the rest of the World, and acts in such Scenes of the universal Drama, as may be the Lot of any other Man, young Spectators fix their Eyes upon him with closer Attention, and hope by observing his Behaviour and Success to regulate their own Practices, when they shall be engaged in the like Part.

For this Reason these familiar Histories may perhaps be made of greater Use than the Solemnities of professed Morality, and convey the Knowledge of Vice and Virtue with more Efficacy than Axioms and Definitions. But if the Power of Example is so great, as to take Possession of the Memory by a kind of Violence, and produce Effects almost without the Intervention of the Will, Care ought to be taken that, when the Choice is unrestrained, the best Examples only should be exhibited; and that which is likely to operate so strongly, should not be mischievous or uncertain in its Effects.

The chief Advantages which these Fictions have over real Life is, that their Authors are at liberty, tho' not to invent, yet to select Objects, and to cull from the Mass of Mankind, those Individuals upon which the Attention ought most to be employ'd; as a Diamond, though it cannot be made, may be polished by Art, and placed in such a Situation, as to display that Lustre which before was buried among common Stones.

It is justly considered as the greatest Excellency of Art, to imitate Nature; but it is necessary to distinguish those Parts of Nature, which are most proper for Imitation: Greater Care is still required in representing Life, which is so often discoloured by Passion, or deformed by Wickedness. If the World be promiscuously described, I cannot see of what Use it can be to read the Account; or why it may not be as safe to turn the Eye immediately upon Mankind, as upon a Mirrour which shows all that presents itself without Discrimination.

It is therefore not a sufficient Vindication of a Character, that it is drawn as it appears; for many Characters ought never to be drawn; nor of a Narrative, that the Train of Events is agreeable to Observation and Experience; for that Observation which is called Knowledge of the World, will be found much more frequently to make Men cunning than good. The Purpose of these Writings is surely not only to show Mankind, but to provide that they may be seen hereafter with less Hazard; to teach the Means of avoiding the Snares which are laid by TREACHERY for INNOCENCE, without infusing any Wish for that Superiority with which the Betrayer flatters his Vanity; to give the Power of counteracting Fraud without the Temptation to practice it; to initiate Youth by mock Encounters in the Art of necessary Defence, and to increase Prudence without impairing Virtue.

MANY Writers for the sake of following Nature, so mingle good and bad Qualities in their principal Personages, that they are both equally conspicuous; and as we accompany them through their Adventures with Delight, and are led by Degrees to interest ourselves in their Favour, we lose the Abhorrence of their Faults, because they do not hinder our Pleasure, or, perhaps, regard them with some Kindness for being united with so much Merit.

THERE have been Men indeed splendidly wicked, whose Endowments throw a Brightness on their Crimes, and whom scarce any Villainy made perfectly detestable, because they never could be wholly divested of their Excellencies; but such have been in all Ages the great Corrupters of the World, and their Resemblance ought no more to be preserved, than the Art of murdering without Pain.

SOME have advanced, without due Attention to the Consequences of this Notion, that certain Virtues have their correspondent Faults, and therefore to exhibit either apart is to deviate from Probability. Thus Men are observed by *Swift* to be grateful in the same Degree as they are resentful.[1] This Principle, with others of the same Kind, supposes Man to act from a brute Impulse, and pursue a certain Degree of Inclination, without any Choice of the Object; for, otherwise, though it should be allow'd that Gratitude and Resentment arise from the same Constitution of the Passions, it follows not that they will be equally indulged when Reason is consulted; and unless that Consequence be admitted, this sagacious Maxim becomes an empty Sound, without any relation to Practice or to Life.

NOR is it evident, that even the first Motions to these Effects are always in the same Proportion. For Pride, which produces Quickness of Resentment, will frequently obstruct Gratitude, by an Unwillingness to admit that Inferiority which Obligation necessarily implies; and it is

[1] *Thoughts on Various Subjects.*

surely very unlikely, that he who cannot think he receives a Favour will ever acknowledge it.

IT is of the utmost Importance to Mankind, that Positions of this Tendency should be laid open and confuted; for while Men consider Good and Evil as springing from the same Root, they will spare the one for the sake of the other, and in judging, if not of others at least of themselves, will be apt to estimate their Virtues by their Vices. To this fatal Error all those will contribute, who confound the Colours of Right and Wrong, and instead of helping to settle their Boundaries, mix them with so much Art, that no common Mind is able to disunite them.

IN Narratives, where historical Veracity has no Place, I cannot discover why there should not be exhibited the most perfect Idea of Virtue; of Virtue not angelical, nor above Probability; for what we cannot credit we shall never imitate; but of the highest and purest Kind that Humanity can reach, which, when exercised in such Trials as the various Revolutions of Things shall bring upon it, may, by conquering some Calamities, and enduring others, teach us what we may hope, and what we can perform. Vice, for Vice is necessary to be shewn, should always disgust; nor should the Graces of Gaiety, or the Dignity of Courage, be so united with it, as to reconcile it to the Mind. Wherever it appears, it should raise Hatred by the Malignity of its Practices; and Contempt, by the Meanness of its Stratagems; for while it is supported by either Parts or Spirit, it will be seldom heartily abhorred. The *Roman* Tyrant was content to be hated, if he was but feared; and there are Thousands of the Readers of Romances willing to be thought wicked, if they may be allowed to be Wits. It is therefore to be always inculcated, that Virtue is the highest Proof of a superior Understanding, and the only solid Basis of Greatness; and that Vice is the natural Consequence of narrow Thoughts, that begins in Mistake, and ends in Ignominy.[1]

---

[1] An article on romances in *The Royal Female Magazine* (Jan. 1760), i. 9–10, follows Johnson's *Rambler* in showing great concern at the power of Fielding's work to seduce, and commends Richardson's chaste novels. Dedicated to the instruction of women, the author rules out Fielding's work, especially for female readers.

93. 'Eubulus', *Old England*

7 April 1750

From a letter signed 'Eubulus'.

On 8 February and 8 March London had experienced earth-quake tremors, and a third was prophesied for April. Exploiting the general alarm, Thomas Sherlock, Bishop of London, issued in March a Pastoral Letter denouncing vice and admonishing Londoners to repent, mentioning among other depravities of the age the publication of obscene books. *Old England*'s 'Eubulus' quotes from the Bishop: 'Have not Histories or Romances of the vilest Prostitutes . . . been published, merely to display the most execrable Scenes of Lewdness?'[1]—which he interprets to mean 'such as *Tom Jones*, who is a Male-Prostitute'. He translates a news item from the French periodical *A-la-Main* of 16 March:

An Arrêt of the Council of State is issued for suppressing a certain immoral Work, entitled The History of TOM JONES, translated from the *English*.[2]

From the banning of *Tom Jones* by the French, he launches into praise of the newly published *Examen of Tom Jones* (No. 81), which he liberally quotes.

★   ★   ★

Permit me to add some Passages from the *Examen* hinted at, which will evince this Point.

[1] *A Letter from the Lord Bishop of London, to the Clergy and People of London and West-minster, On Occasion of the Late Earthquakes* (1750), p. 9; an abstract was published in *The Gentleman's Magazine* (March 1750), xx. 123–4.

[2] See E. P. Shaw, 'A Note on the Temporary Suppression of Tom Jones in France', *Modern Language Notes* (1957), lxxii. 41: 'A bookseller of Paris, named Jacques Rollin, had taken it upon himself to print the *Histoire de Tom Jones* under a foreign title-page and to sell copies of it before he had received a privilege or permission from an official censor. Later, evidently desirous of augmenting his profits by legitimate means, he was either bold or stupid enough to request permission to print the same work which he had already illegally distributed. Detected by the police, Rollin's plan did not succeed; it was con-sidered that he had flagrantly disregarded the regulations of the *librairie*; he was fined 500 livres; his edition of *Tom Jones* was banned and those who owned copies were ordered to relinquish them immediately at the *greffe de la police*.' (Bibliothèque Nationale, Fr. 22092, pp. 151, 152 (52), 24 February 1750.)

Whoever would know the true Design of this vitious Book, may find it delineated to his Hand in the *Examen*, p. 5–8 [No. 81, pp. 191–3]. Nay, the Author himself seems to give up all Pretensions to a Regard for Religion, as will appear by the following Extract from his Examiner, p. 15— . . . [pp. 197–8].

Indeed, that Author's gross Ignorance of the *Scriptures* is as remarkable as his Ignorance of *Religion*, which he owns; and of *Nature*, in which he conceits himself perfectly skilled. See a flagrant Instance of this, *Examen*, p. 44, 45.

I cannot but wish, that the Examiner would have applied to Mr. *F.* in censuring him for the latter Defect, the following Passage of *Mr.* Collier's *Defence of his short View of the Stage*, p. 10. of the first Edition; where that Gentleman rightly observes, that 'the Pretence of *Nature* and *Imitation* is a lamentable Plea. Without doubt there's a great deal of *Nature* in the most brutal Practices. The infamous *Stews* 'tis likely talk in their own Way, and keep up to their Character: But what Person of Probity would visit them for their Propriety; or take Poison, because 'tis true of its kind.'

The Examiner indeed observes something like this, where he is exploding what Mr. *F.* calls HUMAN NATURE . . . *Examen* p. 8 [p. 193.]

Mr. *Collier* further remarks, p. 11. that 'To do an ill Thing *well*, doubles the Fault: The Mischief rises with the Art; and the Man ought to smart in Proportion to his Excellency.' But in this latter, I believe, Mr. *F.* will be found *Not Guilty*.

Of the grand Hero *Tom Jones*, may be also said what the just-mentioned Mr. *Collier* applies to another scandalous Character: 'He would gladly blanch this foul Character: But, alas! 'tis to no Purpose to wash and rub: The Spots are not *Dirt* but *Complexion*,' p. 81. Which will be found equally true of the infamous *Jones*, whose Character is laid down by Mr. *F.* in such Terms, as *are sufficient*, as the Examiner observes, p. 29 *to nip him in the Bud*.

'There is not (says Mr. *F.* Book XIV. Chap. I) a greater Error, than that which universally prevails among the VULGAR (a most shameless Assertion!); who, borrowing their Opinion from some *ignorant Satirists*, have affixed the Character of *Lewdness* to these times.' On this the Examiner observed, that 'Were not the prevailing Character of this Age *Lewdness*, Mr. *F.* would never have found readers enough in High Life to take off his numerous Editions of the present Work; in which if Lewdness doth not prevail, neither does it in this Age and Nation.— Nor are they only *ignorant Satirists*, but learned Divines and Philosophers, who have laid the same Charge of Lewdness against some of the highest Rank in the Kingdom.' Of this we have seen a very late Testimony (besides those which the Examiner cites) in the Lord Bishop of *London*'s Letter, and in the very Paragraph from thence, which I have produced above. So that either his Lordship is ranked by Mr. *F.* among the *Vulgar*, or Mr. *F.* himself must be content to take his Place in that *low* Class of Men, for his ill-manner'd and ill-founded Assertion.

Upon the whole, I hope that the P——t of *England* will take Example from their late Enemies, and discourage Books of Immorality and Profaneness, as the Bane of the Youth of this Nation; that *London* may be no longer esteemed *the Mart for Infidelity,* as his Lordship excellently observes; and that a Protestant King and free People will shew at least as much Concern for the Integrity of their Morals, as a Popish Government, defended by arbitrary Power, have demonstrated they have had for the Security of theirs.

I conclude this Epistle with another Extract from Mr. *Collier,* p. 122. 'He who makes it his Business to exterminate Virtue and Conscience, and debauch both Practice and Principle, must needs be a Misfortune to the Age.'

SIR,

Your humble Servant,

and constant Reader,

EUBULUS.

94. From 'The Antisatyrist; a Dialogue'
The Gentleman's Magazine
May 1750, xx. 229

In this poem 'Mitio' and 'Demea' argue the question of whether
satire can be justified. Mitio, who claims it cannot, says at one point
that instead of ridiculing corrupt public officials he would 'draw
a *Patriot* . . . ennobled, less by blood, than real worth'. When
Demea interrupts with the suggestion that he 'Make honest
[Tom] *Jones* a minister of state', the author adds this note, which
probably alludes to La Place's mutilations in his French translation.
See the *Gentleman's* earlier comments, No. 90 above.

An *ill-natured* Sarcasm, from peevish Demea: *for none, but an ignorant
and pretending* Sign *dawber, would presume to make alterations in a most
celebrated and complete* original.

95. Samuel Richardson, letter
21 January 1750-1

From a letter to J. B. de Freval, Carroll, p. 175.

★   ★   ★

Tom Jones is a dissolute book. Its run is over, even with us. Is it true,
that France had virtue enough to refuse a licence for such a profligate
performance.

★   ★   ★

AN ENQUIRY INTO THE CAUSES
OF THE LATE INCREASE OF
ROBBERS

January 1750–1

---

96. Unsigned Review, *The Monthly Review*

January 1750-1, iv. 229–39

The *Gentleman's Magazine*'s unsigned notice said only, 'This excellent pamphlet being but just published, we had not room left to do it justice, by a proper specimen' (Jan. 1751, xxi. 4). Looking back, many years later, Horace Walpole wrote: 'A committee had been appointed to consider on amending the laws enacted against the vices of the lower people, which were increased to a degree of robbery and murder beyond example. Fielding, a favourite author of the age, had published an admirable treatise on the laws in question, and agreed with what was observed on this occasion, that these outrages proceeded from gin' (*Memoirs of the Reign of King George the Second,* ed. Lord Holland, 1846, i. 44). The long quotations from the *Enquiry,* most of which are omitted, are generally garbled.

An Inquiry into the Causes of the late Increase of Robbers, &c. with some proposals for remedying this growing evil. By Henry Fielding, *Esq; Barrister at Law, and one of his Majesty's Justices of the Peace for the County of* Middlesex, *and for the City and Liberty of* Westminster, *Octavo Pamphlet, Price 2s. 6d. Printed for* A. Millar.

The public hath been hitherto not a little obliged to Mr. *Fielding* for the entertainment his gayer performances have afforded it; but now this gentleman hath a different claim to our thanks, for services of a more substantial nature. If he has been heretofore admired for his wit and humour, he now merits equal applause as a good magistrate, a useful and active member, and a true friend to his country. As few writers have shown so just and extensive a knowledge of mankind in general, so none ever had better opportunities for being perfectly acquainted with that class which is the main subject of this performance: a class of all others the most necessary and useful to all, yet the most neglected and despised; we mean the labouring part of the people.

In this treatise our author professes impartially to expose the present reigning vices, and largely and freely to examine the laws relating to the provision for the poor, and to the punishment of felons: and this he has done with much spirit, judgment, and learning. In his preface he sets out with an explanation of the nature and fundamentals of our political *constitution*; which, as he justly observes, is a word in the mouth of every man, and yet there is no subject on which our ideas are more confused and perplexed. 'Some, continues he, when they speak of the constitution, confine their notions to the law; others to the legislature; others again to the governing or executive part; and many there are who jumble all these together in one idea. One error, however, is common to them all: for all seem to have the conception of something uniform and permanent, as if the constitution of *England* partook rather of the nature of the soil than of the climate, and was as fixed and constant as the former, not as changeing and variable as the latter.——Now in this word, the *constitution*, are included the original and fundamental law of the kingdom, from whence all powers are derived, and by which they are circumscrib'd; all legislative and executive authority; all those municipal provisions which are commonly called *the laws*; and *lastly*, the customs, manners, and habits of the people. These joined together, do, I apprehend, form the political, as the several members of the body the animal œconomy, with the humours and habit, compose that which is called the natural constitution.' In short, Mr. *Fielding* further explains this, by a comparison with the *Greek* philosophy concerning the foul, which some of them held to result from the harmonious composition of the several parts of the body, as music from the several parts of a well tun'd instrument: in the same manner, says he, from the disposition of the several parts in a state, arises that which we call the constitution.

'If the constitution, as I have above asserted, be the result of the disposition of the several parts, it follows that this disposition can never be alter'd, without producing a proportional change in the constitution.

'Our known division, says Mr. *Fielding*, of the people of this nation, is into the nobility, the gentry, and the commonalty. What alterations have happen'd among the two former of these I shall not at present enquire; but that the last, in their customs, manners, and habits, are greatly changed from what they were, I think to make appear.'—And this our author does by a view of the antient vassalage of the common people, who were all servilely subject to the superior ranks, by slavish tenures the very names of which are now almost as little known to them as their nature. He then remarks on the vast alteration that trade has produced in the condition of the commonalty, and their present almost unbounded liberty, or rather licentiousness; and infers, that while the lower class hath acquir'd an immense addition of power, the civil power having not increased, but decreased in the same proportion, is not able to govern them.—Thus far our abstract of the preface; which is follow'd by a short introduction, from which we shall give a passage or two, to explain our author's idea of the importance of his design.

[Quotes as follows: 'The great increase of robberies . . . faults in the constitution'; 'For my own part . . . false witnesses ready to support it' (Henley, xiii. 19–21).]

Mr. *Fielding* adds, that having seen the most convincing proofs of all this, he cannot help thinking it high time to put some stop to the further progress of such impudent and audacious insults, not only on the properties of the subject, but on the national justice, and on the laws themselves. The best means of accomplishing this, that he can think of, he submits to the publick consideration, after having first inquired into the causes of the present growth of this evil.

In section the first he considers the too frequent and expensive diversions among the lower kind of people; which he looks upon as the cause of many thefts and robberies, to which tradesmen are too frequently tempted by the wants and necessities their taste this way often brings upon them.

Section 2d treats of drunkenness, as a second consequence of luxury among the vulgar. This vice, as our author justly remarks, ought by no means to be considered as a spiritual offence only, since so many temporal mischiefs arise from it, among which are very frequently robbery and murder itself. I do not know, says he, a more excellent institution than that of *Pittacus*, mentioned by *Aristotle* in his *politics*; by which a blow given by a drunken man, was more severely punished than if it had been given by one that was sober; 'for *Pittacus*, says *Aristotle*, consider'd the utility of the public, (as drunken men are more apt to strike) and not the excuse, which might otherwise be allow'd to their drunkenness.' And so far both the civil law and our own have follow'd this institution, that neither have admitted drunkenness to be any excuse for any crime.

After a cursory view of our laws for the suppression of this vice, the author observes, that the legislature have been abundantly careful on this head; and that the only blame lies on the remissness with which these wholsome provisions have been executed.

[Quotes as follows: 'But though I will not undertake to defend . . . and to smell too'; 'Now, besides the moral ill consequences . . . and desperate enterprise'; 'But beyond all this . . . with stench and diseases' (Henley, xiii. 33-4).]

The subject of the third section, is *gaming*, among the vulgar, a third consequence of their luxury. This vice our author considers as the school in which most of our eminent highwaymen have been bred. He has several lively and affecting observations on the folly and infamy of this fashionable and deceitful diversion. Gamester and sharper have indeed long and universally been synonimous terms; and when a man is reduced to the last necessities, how easy, as our author justly remarks, is the transition from fraud to force; from a gamester to a rogue? Perhaps, indeed, says he, it is civil to suppose it any transition at all.

Mr. *Fielding* concludes on this head, with a sketch of our several laws against this vice; and this he does partly for the use and encouragement of informers, and partly to insinuate the question to certain persons, with what decency they can openly offend against such plain, such solemn laws, the severest of which many of themselves have, perhaps, been the makers of?

The 4th section is much larger than any of the foregoing. It consists of 37 pages; and contains a view of the laws relating to the provision for the poor. This is a very important chapter, which we could wish every master of a family in the kingdom would read, and attentively regard. Having before run thro' the several immediate consequences of a general luxury among the lower people, all which, as they tend to promote their distresses, may be reasonably supposed to put many of them of the bolder kind upon unlawful and violent means of relieving the mischief which such vices have brought upon them; he comes now to a second cause of the evil, in the improper regulation of what is called the poor in this kingdom, arising, as he thinks, partly from the abuse of some laws, and partly from the total neglect of others; and somewhat perhaps from a defect in the laws themselves: All which he examines with the learning of a good lawyer, and the judgment of an able magistrate. We could with pleasure give some extracts of this useful chapter, but cannot dwell too minutely upon every part of this work. For we entirely think with our author, 'that it must be matter of astonishment to any man to reflect, that in a country where the poor are, beyond all comparison, more liberally provided for than in any other part of the habitable globe, there should be found more beggars, more distrest and miserable objects than are to be seen throughout all the states of *Europe*'.

In section the 5th, the author treats of the punishment of receivers of stolen goods. He examines the laws made for this purpose, and finds them greatly defective; and in order effectually to suppress this set of most infamous miscreants, he likewise thinks, and certainly with great reason, that it would be very proper to put an effectual stop to the present scandalous method of compounding felony, by public advertisements in news papers. 'Might not, says he, the inserting such advertisements be rendered highly criminal in the authors of them, and in the printers themselves, unless they discover such authors'.

In fine, he hopes that some methods will be found out, to put a stop to the present practice of receiving stollen goods, knowing them to be such: 'of which, says he, I daily see the most pernicious consequences; many of the younger thieves appearing plainly to be taught, encouraged, and employed by the receivers'.

The laws relating to vagabonds, are the subject of Section VI. in which he considers what remedy our laws have applied to the public grievances arising from the great number of wandering vagabonds, beggars and thieves, with which both town and country are so intolerably pester'd; and wherein, these remedies appear defective. He observes that another great encouragement to robbery, besides the certain means of finding a market for the booty, is the probability of escaping punishment.

[Quotes as follows: 'First, then, the robber . . . deserts of *Africa* or *Arabia*' (Henley, xiii. 82–3).]

After a recital of all our laws, from *Alfred* to the present time, for the apprehending, regulating, and punishing of vagabonds, with observations on them, our author shews wherein they are still defective, and suggests a method for improving them: but for this we refer the reader to the book itself.

The 7th section relates to the difficulties attending the apprehending of felons, which he considers as another encouragement that the thief flatters himself with. Those who are unacquainted with the laws for empowering both officers of justice and private persons to serve their country in this respect, are much obliged to Mr. *Fielding* for the full information he has here given concerning such laws: To which he has added proper answers to all those arguments which weak persons, carried away by popular prejudices, usually bring in excuse for any occasional remissness in the bringing of villains to justice: such as the vulgar and absurd odium commonly affix'd to the name of an informer, a thief catcher, or a hangman.

The eighth section has for its subject, the difficulties which attend prosecutions; which he ranks as the fourth encouragement of robbers; whose spirits are greatly held up by the remissness of prosecutors, who, says our author, are often,

1. Fearful, and to be intimidated by the threats of a gang; or,

2. Delicate, and cannot appear in a court; or,

3. Indolent, and will not give themselves the trouble of a prosecution; or,

4. Avaricious, and will not undergo the expence of it; nay, perhaps find their account in compounding the matter; or,

5. Tender-hearted, and cannot take away the life of a man; or,

Lastly, Necessitous, and cannot really afford the cost, however small, together with the loss of time which attends it.

The first and second of these he justly looks upon as too absurd, and the third and fourth as too infamous to be reason'd with; but on the two last he bestows more particular notice, as the fifth is an error springing originally out of a good principle in the mind, and the sixth is a fault in the constitution very easy to be remedied.

The ninth section treats of the trial and conviction of felons. Here he enumerates the advantages which criminals frequently have, either from the caution of the prosecutor's evidence, or the hardiness of their own; the difficulty of convicting street-robbers, from the circumstances of their generally committing their robberies in the dark, and when the persons robb'd are in coaches or chairs, or, if on foot, being first knock'd down, and for the time depriv'd of their senses; and from the various arts which the rogues make use of to prevent their being seen, or known.——In a matter of so much concern to the public, Mr. *Fielding* offers his sentiments with great force of reasoning, and proposes that greater latitude should be allowed to the force of impeachments by accomplices, than hitherto the law hath thought fit to allow.

Section the tenth is employed on the encouragement given to robbers by frequent pardons. Here he directs himself only to those persons who are within the reach of his majesty's ear. Such will, he hopes, weigh well what he has said (in another part of his book) on the subject of false compassion. He also hopes too much good-nature will never transport any of them so far as it once did a clergyman in *Scotland*, who, in the fervor of his benevolence pray'd to God that he would graciously be pleased to pardon the poor Devil.

After doing ample justice and honour to that amiable virtue *mercy*, he concludes, that if the terror of example is the grand thing proposed by the execution of a criminal, when one man is sacrificed to the preservation of thousands;

[Quotes as follows: 'If there the terror of this example . . . the unbounded exercise of pity' (Henley, xiii. 121).]

Section XI. and last treats of the manner of execution. And here we entirely agree with our author, whose observations on this head are drawn from uncontrovertable experience. As to the more practised, and spirited, and most dangerous rogues, the day appointed by law for the execution of such a one, Mr. *Fielding* says is the day of glory in the opinion of the criminal himself. His procession to *Tyburn*, and his last moments there, are all triumphant; attended with the compassion of the meek and tender-hearted, and with the applause, admiration, and envy★ of all the bold and hardened. His behaviour in his present condition, not the crimes, how atrocious soever, which brought him to it, are the subject of contemplation; and if he hath sense enough to temper his boldness with any degree of decency, his death is spoke of by many with honour, by most with pity, and by all with approbation.

[Quotes as follows: 'How far . . . they see to day'; 'The design of those . . . with any sensation' (Henley, xiii. 122-3).]

[Quotes as follows: 'To effect this . . . entertain the mob'; 'if executions were . . . flatter his ambition'; 'the execution should be . . . impression on the mind'; 'In *Holland* . . . on the minds of every one' (Henley, xiii. 123-6).]

The author's conclusion follows this last quotation, and is well worth a reader's attention; but it is now time for us to put a period to this article.

★ Our author's painting upon the whole, is here very just except that his colouring is a little too high; the word *envy* might as well have been omitted.

97. Lady Henrietta Luxborough, letter

13 February 1750–1

From a letter to William Shenstone, *Letters Written by . . . Lady Luxborough to William Shenstone*, p. 237.

★　　★　　★

Her Grace [the Duchess of Somerset] says there is an inundation of new books. She commends Mr. Fielding's Enquiry into the Cause of the Increase of Street-Robberies.

★　　★　　★

98. From 'To the Worshipful Justice Fielding', *An Apology for the Life of Mr. Bampfylde Moore Carew, Commonly call'd the King of the Beggars*
n.d. [1751?], pp. iii–xxix

Robert Goadby first published the *Apology*, based on Carew's *Life and Adventures* (Exeter, 1745), in 1749. A second edition, with additions, appeared early in 1750, and a subsequent edition (called fifth by the British Museum cataloguer) appeared in 1750 or 1751 with the satiric dedication 'To the Worshipful Justice Fielding'. This was inspired by Tom's encounter with the gypsies in Book XII, Chapter 12.

For the bibliography of these volumes, see C. H. Wilkinson, ed., *The King of the Beggars: Bampfylde-Moore Carew* (1931), pp. vii–ix; Martin C. Battestin, 'Tom Jones and "His Egyptian Majesty": Fielding's Parable of Government', *PMLA* (1967), lxxxii, 68–9. Battestin dates this edition November 1751, but it had to have appeared before February 1750–1, when the *Essay on Mr. Fielding's New Species of Writing* was published, which mentions the criticism of Fielding in its preface (No. 99).

Also included in the fifth edition of the *Apology* was an appendix, 'The full and true History of Tom Jones, a Foundling; without Pattering', a four-page distorted summary of Fielding's story—a 'Parallel drawn after the Manner of Plutarch, between Mr. Bampfylde-Moore Carew and Mr. Thomas Jones'. At best the pretended parallels between Carew and Tom suggest something of Tom's picaresque origins, but do not qualify as criticism. The dedication itself is less criticism than exploitation, but does make some shrewd points and demonstrates a general dependence on the *Examen*. Redundant footnotes have been omitted.

To the WORSHIPFUL
JUSTICE FIELDING.

Sir,

'Notwithstanding your constant Refusal, when I have ask'd Leave to prefix your Name to this Dedication, I must still insist upon the Propriety of desiring your Protection of this Work.'[1]

IT may well be thought that amongst the many noble Families my Hero is allied to, I might have found a more proper Patron for this true History of his Life; but as through our strict regard to Truth, there will appear in it some of those '*little Blemishes*, quas humanana parum cavit Natura,' [x.i] we were afraid many that we might otherwise have applied to, would have disdainfully refused their Protection of such a Character: But you, Sir, '*who are admitted behind the Scenes of the* Great *Theatre of Nature, know that it is often the same Person who represents the* Villain *and the* Hero [VII. i.]*; that we ought not to condemn a Character as a bad one, because it is not perfectly a good one; and that there is no good Purpose serv'd by brining to Light Characters of such Angelick Perfection; and nothing of more moral Use, than a few Imperfections in the best of Characters* [X. i]*; for though it is* Villainy, *it is* Nature *for all that.'* [VII. i] I am the more embolden'd to beg your Protection of my *Hero,* as I can assure your Worship, upon the strictest Enquiry it appears he was never once concern'd in his Youth in demolishing any Brothel whatsoever; for to be sure, Sir, to you who are so great a Connoisseur of *Human Nature,* it must appear strangely unnatural for a young Fellow in the Heat of Blood, who must have often Occasion for such Houses, to lay violent Hands upon them: I should therefore never have thought of offering my Hero to your Protection, had I not found him entirely innocent of this great Offence.*

AND now, Sir, tho' I must confess, you have sufficiently shown, in sundry Instances, your Dislike of *Publick Praise*; yet I cannot help bedaubing you a little with it, for though it may not be quite so decent to accept of it, yet who can be displeas'd, when it is forced upon them, whether they will or no; besides, Sir, at the same Time I am praising you, I may find an Occasion of saying a few Things of my own great Merit, and that of my Work, by acquainting the World with the high

---

[1] *Tom Jones,* Dedication. Many of the quotations from the novel are joined out of sequence, garbled, or otherwise distorted. Book and chapter references for them appear in brackets in the text.

* Alluding to Mr. *Fielding's* Case of [Bosavern] *Penlez,* executed for assisting in pulling down Bawdy-Houses.

Encomiums you have bestow'd upon it;* *'for, indeed, what are your Objections to the Allowance of the* Honour *which I have solicited? Why, you have commended the* Book *so warmly, that you should be asham'd of reading your* Name *before the* Dedication.' Now, Sir, though I don't imagine any of my Readers will understand this Sentence, it being the true *Burtonic Sublime*, most admirable when least understood; yet, Sir, as this *Dedication* is only intended for you and myself, it is no Matter whether it is understood or not by any one else.

EVERY one must acknowledge, Sir, it is a most presumptuous Absurdity for a little Reptile of a Reader *'to find Fault with any Part of your* great Creation *of the History of* Tom Jones, *before he comes to the final Catastrophe;'* and it is still the greater Absurdity, as you are an *'Author of the first Rate;'* [X. i] and your Readers (excepting *Right Honourables*) all of them the *lowest* [XI. i]: But I dare say you will not be offended, if one of these Readers should espie out any striking *Beauties* in your *great Work*, though they should happen to appear in the first Page of it: Permit me, therefore, to say (though it may perhaps have escaped the Notice of many of my Fellow Reptiles, your Readers) that your wonderful *Sagacity* and *Ingenuity* in the Opening of your *Work*, exceeds every Thing of the Kind; for in my Opinion, that well adapted Compliment of *Virgil* to his Patron, *Tu Marcellus-eris,* &c. which the Criticks have made so much ado about ever since, is not fit to be compar'd with your more *delicate one*, in the Proem to your *Work*.

IT is well known, Sir, that one of those *golden Images* which *Nebuchadnezzar* the King set up, and which you, Sir, have thought it Wisdom not only to bow the Knee to, but to worship with the Understanding, has, like the famous one of *Bell,* consum'd whole Provinces *'in the very Quintessence of* Sauce *and* Spices;' [I. i] or, to bring the Comparison nearer Home, *like the famous* Dragon *of* Wantley

> HOUSES *and* CHURCHES,
> *To him have been* GEESE *and* TURKIES.

How then could you better engage the gracious Ear, or pay a more refin'd Compliment in the Proem to your *Work*, than by transforming yourself into a *Cook*, offering a Bill of Fare, comparing *Human Nature* to a *Tortoise* and *Bologna Sausage*, acquainting us it was a Dish of great Variety, and might be peper'd and salted, boil'd or roasted; broil'd, stew'd, hash'd, or ragoo'd, to please every Taste by a good *Cook* of an *Author*.

* Mr. *Fielding*'s Dedication of his History of *Tom Jones*.

BUT, Sir, as you seem greatly pleas'd with informing us in sundry Places of your *Work,* that you are the *Founder* of this Kind of *Writing* or *Cooking,* for it seems they are synonimous Terms, what Occasion had you to share the *Honour* of this wonderful *Metaphor* with Mr. *Pope?* for I dare say, notwithstanding your Quotation, he never once thought of either hashing or ragooing *Human Nature*; nor do I remember, among all his Similies, that he has ever once been so happy as to compare it to a *Tortoise* or a *Sausage.*

At the same Time I take Notice of your too great *Modesty* in sharing that *Honour,* which you might with very great Justice have taken all to yourself, I must be so free to vindicate the poor Animals, whom I think you have as needlessly aspersed; for though I have been conversant many Years with the Animal Part of the Creation, and know as much of their Language and Sentiments as any Man living, yet I never could find they had any Notion of the '*Honour of having their Flesh eaten at the Table of a* Duke; *nor any Sense of the Degradation they suffer, by being serv'd up at a* Porter's *Table:*' [I. i] And though I cannot assert any Thing positive on this Head, not having ever heard them express their Sentiments upon it, (for, as Mr. *Pope* Observes, *Providence* has kindly hid the *Book* of *Fate* from them) yet, if we may be allow'd to argue *a Priori,* and to judge of what we don't from what we do know, I will venture to affirm, from a nice Observation of the *Goodness* of their *Natures,* that did they know one of the two to be unavoidable, they would think it a much greater *Honour* to refresh the *Spirits,* and renew the *Strength* of a *Porter* or poor *Mechanick,* exhausted by useful *Labour,* than to be hash'd and ragoo'd to please the *pamper'd* Appetite of any *idle Duke* whatsoever.

In short, Sir, I suspect, from the vast Knowledge you have shewn in *Cooking,* that you entertain some Hopes, when your Writings, '*which all tend to recommend* Innocence *and* Virtue,' have so far amended Mankind, that the *Emoluments* of your present *Office* may not be sufficient to reward your *great Abilities,* that you shall be then advanc'd to be chief *Cook* to the *Idol* we have just now mentioned. The Publick, Sir, after the strange Metamorphoses you have already undergone, will not be surpriz'd to see you poring over the *Compleat Housewife,* or Mons. *La Chapelle*'s Cookery Book, instead of the *Statutes*; or instead of a Pen twirling a Sausepan to make Ragoos, Hashes, or forc'd Meat Balls; since you have so delicately ragoo'd, hash'd, and forc'd *Human Nature.* There may be sundry great Advantages arise to the Publick, as well as to yourself, Sir, from this Advancement; which I shall not at present enumerate, but only pray that it may speedily take Place.

NEXT to this fine Compliment in the Proem of your *Work*, which I think cannot be outdone; you have shown the highest *Wisdom* and *Treatment* of your *Readers*; first, by stunning them, and putting out their Eyes with the Splendour of the extraordinary *Praises* your princely and noble Friends have bestow'd on your *great Work*; and then by informing them in sundry Parts of it, that you are a much better *Judge* of what is proper and fit for them to read, than they are themselves. That such pitiful Wretches as Readers (saving *Right Honourable* ones) have no Business to judge of right or wrong; 'that they are your Subjects, and are bound to believe in and obey whatever you are pleas'd to dictate, [II. i] even though yourself are able to assign no Reason for it;' [V. i] and that all who will not do so, are ignorant *Wretches, Slanderers,* and *Hangmen.*

BUT at the same Time I commend your proper Aplication of these Doctrines, I cannot flatter you with being the *Founder* of them; *for in short, Sir, I suspect,* that you have borrow'd them from one of the two Sets of People you have lately much convers'd with; for you must needs acknowledge, Sir, that it has been the Doctrine and Language, of all Courts, ever since Courts existed, that the Reptiles, the Worms, the Dolts, alias the People, are no Judges of what is right or wrong; that *They* best know what is for the Reptiles Good; and that such Creatures have no Business to concern themselves about what *They* do, as they are accountable to none; and if any of the Reptiles will be meddling, they are presently honoured with the Titles of *Fools, Slanderers, Disaffected, Seditious,* and in some Countries with that of *Jacobites.*

BUT there are another Set of People that you, Sir, have had much to do with, from whom you may have probably borrow'd the Art you have made so happy an Use of: These in their own Language (which I make no Doubt you are a great Proficient in) are stiled AMUSERS; who, as I find them describ'd in an ingenious Author who has wrote of these People*, are such as throw Dust in the Eyes of those they intend to trick: Now, Sir, as you tell us yourself *'you don't disdain to borrow* Wit *or* Wisdom *from any Man,'* [I. i]† it seems to me very likely that you borrow'd the Thought of blinding your Reader's Judgment from these People; and it was with the highest *Prudence* and *Sagacity* you did so,

---

* See the Canting Dictionary, describing the Language and Tricks of Sharpers.

† This you have given several Instances of, in particular the wise and witty Speeches of Mr. *Fitzpatrick*, in your 3d Volume, borrowed from the *Cambridge* Jest Book, printed in 1746, page 196.

for had you not, how would your Readers, in a Work, that they were told, in the Dedication of it to a *Champion* of *Christianity*, '*contained in the whole Course of it nothing prejudicial to the Cause of* Religion *and* Virtue; *nothing inconsistent with the strictest Rules of* Decency, *nor which can offend even the chastest Eye in the Perusal; that to recommend* Goodness *and* Innocence *was the sole Intent of the History: that* Example *is a Kind of* Picture, *in which* Virtue *becomes as it were an Object of* Sense, *and strikes us with its* Loveliness:' After so pompous an Introduction, how would your Readers, I say, Sir, (if you had not first taken Care, with a great deal of Art, to fling Dust into their Eyes, I mean the Eye of the Mind) have been astonish'd to find the principal Hero of it vicious and ungovernable in his Childhood, debauching a poor Girl almost as soon as he had entered Youth, (for in his own Mind he really did so) soon after resolving to leave her for another of greater Fortune, before he knew she had given him the least Occasion to do so, and at a Time when he imagined her whole Happiness depended upon him, and that he was under the greatest Obligations to her: How would the Reader's Astonishment have encreas'd, to find him in his Manhood, when he had engag'd his Affections to the *most adorable of Women* and had met with a reciprocal Affection, forgetting her Love without the least Repugnance, to lie in the Arms of the wanton Mrs. *Waters*, who he had Reason to think a married Woman; and after this becoming a hir'd Stallion to a lascivious old Woman, though the mean while very deeply enamour'd of the most adorable Miss *Sophia Western*; and all this without any Sign of the least Compunction, Regret or Repentance: How, Sir, could your Readers have possibly imagin'd, had you suffer'd them to have made Use of their Eyes, this was the Example in which 'Virtue *was to become an Object of Sight, and strike us with its* Loveliness;' It was by the same Method too that you prevented '*the chastest Eye of your Readers from being offended with the Perusal of your Work*,' otherwise the wanton Fancy of your Hero in the Grove, in meditating on Miss *Sophia*, his retiring into the thickest Part of it with *Molly Seagrim*, after a short Parley, the Description of his being in Bed with Mrs. *Waters*, and the Introduction of two or three Heroes in their Shirts, the lascivious Wantonness of Lady *Bellaston*, your Rutting Simile, &c. might have offended the chastest Eye; unless you are of Opinion Sir, that there can be nothing inconsistent with *Decency*, nor the chastest Eye offended, nor the warmest Imagination fir'd, unless by the grossest Terms.

I am of Opinion too, Sir, that you owe the favourable Reception of your benevolent Character[1] to the abovemention'd happy Expedient; otherwise, how would your Readers, after having been told there was *'a stronger Picture of a truly benevolent Mind to be found in your* Work, *than any other*, (not excepting even the Scriptures) *who was a more glorious Object than the Sun in the full Blaze of his Majesty:'* [I. iv]. How would, I say, your Readers have been shock'd to have seen this benevolent Character, more glorious than the Sun itself (though that is the Image of the Divine Goodness) devoting a Fellow Creature to Misery, Want, and all the ill Consequences which might flow from thence, only for *springing of* HARES: Besides, your fine Comparison (for the Sake of which, by your own Confession, you endanger'd the Necks of your Readers) falls here all to Pieces; for you should have remembered the Sun bestows its Beneficence upon the *Unworthy* as well as the *Worthy*; and if, Sir, you had ever read a certain Book,[2] in which are several Pictures of a truly benevolent Mind, as much stronger and excellent than Your's notwithstanding all that your *great Friends* may say, as the fine Pictures of a *Reubens* or *Titian* are than those, with which the Walls of *Moorfields*, and some other publick Places, are often adorn'd; and which are valued at the Sum of one Halfpenny Sterling each: Had you perus'd, Sir, the Book I am speaking of, (which I believe you must have seen) you would have found that your great Pattern of Benevolence is but a half finish'd Draught; for to be kind and beneficent to those only who really deserve it, though it is commendable, yet it is but little more than paying a just Debt; but Benevolence is that Quality which inclines us to do *Good* to those who have highly offended us, and who have no Claim to it, but what arises from inward Benevolence, which desires to see every Creature *happy*.

YOUR Readers, Sir, might likewise have been surpriz'd to find, that in a Book, in which they were told *'there was nothing prejudical to* Religion', to find all the Characters in it, who borrow their *Principles* from that *Fount*, to be worthless Wretches: Thus *Thwackum* is made a most *impious* Man. *Supple* a *weak* and *foolish* one; and if these might be passed over as Men who had formed wrong Notions of *Religion*, yet what religious Mind would not have been shock'd at your Character of the Man of the *Hill*; who, after he has utter'd a *Discourse* which might do *Honour* to the most *pious Christian*, and profess'd, *'that he had made the* Scriptures *his chiefest* Study,' [VIII. xiii] is artfully describ'd immediately after, as void of *Honour, Gratitude, Courage, Hospitality* and *Humanity*;

---

[1] i.e. Allworthy.
[2] i.e. the New Testament.

for though you are not pleas'd to tell your Readers so much of him in direct Words, yet, had you allow'd them the Use of their Eyes, they would easily have seen that you intended to express so much, when you describe your Hero (who you know borrows none of his *Actions* from the Principle of *Religion*) running into the midst of a Wood to the Cries of the distressed Mrs. *Waters*, with only an Oaken Cudgel, while the *good Man* of the *Hill* very contentedly lets him go alone; '*and though he had a Gun in his Hand, sat down on the Brow of the Hill with great Patience and Unconcern, attending the Issue,*' [XI. ii] altho he had but just before owed his Life to Mr. *Jones*, and consequently one would have thought should have been in some Concern about his Safety; and when Mr. *Jones* returns, and acquaints him with the Distress of Mrs. *Waters*, this *good Man*, who borrow'd his *Principles* from the *Scriptures*, has neither *Hospitality* nor *Humanity* enough to assist a distressed Woman with the Shelter or Refreshment his Cottage might afford; but without Ceremony, sends her naked as she was to a Town at some Distance.

YOUR Readers would undoubtedly have thought it a very odd Way of being serviceable to *Religion*, to insinuate under all your Characters, that nothing *noble*, nothing *great*, nothing *generous*, nothing *worthy*, was to be expected to spring from that Root; but the happy Thought you borrowed from your *good Friends* the AMUSERS, prevented all these and many other Observations, such as, several of your Characters, (*mutato Nomine*, the Name only chang'd) being exactly the same you had before exhibited; your false affected *Wit*; the infinite Prejudice you must do to your younger Readers, by throwing down that strong Security of *Innocence* and *Virtue*, the FEAR and SHAME of first entering upon *Vice*; by insinuating into their Minds, that it is nothing more than NATURAL; that there is no *struggling* with our *Inclinations*, and that we may be great and good Men, though we indulge them in whatever they prompt us to.

I have often, Sir, heard it affirm'd by the Searchers into *Nature*, that all Animals have implanted in them a natural *Antipathy* to such particular *Things* as may be most *hurtful* to them; but I was never thoroughly convinced of the *Certainty* of this *Observation*, till I observ'd the strong *Instance* which has lately appeared in *yourself* Sir, in Regard to the little Word LOW; this poor Word is very offensive in itself, expresses *Humility* in its Signification, and contains but three Letters, and those none of the harshest, being two *soft* Vowels to one Consonant; but notwithstanding its great *Humility* and *Softness*, the Sight of it seems to fill you with Indignation and Terror, and you seem more to *dread* the *Sound* of it, than a 24 Pounder discharg'd close to your Ear; I, therefore cannot but admire your *Prudence* and *Sagacity* in endeavouring to extirpate the common *Use* of this Word, by telling us in some Part of your *great Work*, that it has no Meaning at all; and '*that no Man alive has ever attempted to explain it*;' [V. i] and in another Place, '*that it does not become any Mouth but a* Right Honourable *one*;' [XI. i] which, by the bye, I am afraid your *great Friends* will think no Compliment, as it seems to imply, that Words without Meaning are all that are expected from their Mouths. Many other Degradations have you applied to this Word, which lowly as it was, never expected to be attack'd by an Author of the first Rate.

BUT, Sir, at the same Time I applaud your *Wisdom* in the useful Attempt of *demolishing* this Word, I must be so free as to say, I could have wish'd you had made Use of some fitter Means to have done it; for to be sure, Sir, you must needs be sensible, if you have made any Observations at all, that there is not a *Basket Woman* or *Porter* in the City of *London*, who is ignorant of the Signification of the Word L o w; indeed some learned Men have thought that every Man brings the *Idea* of this *Word* into the World with him: Thus, Sir, if you had gone but a few Steps out of your Chair, you might have observ'd and heard, that when any one of the Sisterhood of Basket Women makes Use of, in the Chit Chats they hold together, while they are waiting for Employment, the *Language* and *Sentiments* of a *Cinder Wench*, whom they look upon as infinitely below their Order, the whole Society immediately gives the *Offender*, who talks so much below their *Dignity*, the Title of a Low Wretch, and soon discard her from their publick Conversations: In like Manner, when any of the Society of Porters adopts the *Language* and *Sentiments* of a *Shoe Black*, the whole Brotherhood immediately think him a Low Fellow, and banish him their Clubs, and even the Conversations they hold together in the Streets.

EVERY one knows too, Sir, that when this Word is made Use of in the *Theatre*, or with Regard to an Author, it means that the *Action, Language*, or *Sentiments*, are beneath the *Dignity* of the *Auditors* or *Readers*. Thus, if Mr. *Garrick* thought proper to exhibit upon the Stage a Couple of Clowns eating hot Hasty Pudding, would not the Audience have Reason to think it beneath their Dignity, and to consider it as an Affront to their good Sense and Judgment; and how could they better express their Contempt of it, than by the little Word Low; or if Mr. *Garrick* thought proper to put into the Mouths of any of his Characters *Language* and *Sentiments*, for which a Basket Woman would be *hooted* out of the Sisterhood of them; what more expressive Term can the Audience make Use of to express their Dislike, than LOW Stuff; the same may be most emphatically apply'd to any Author who fills the greatest Part of his Work with *Language* and *Sentiments* that would be a *Disgrace* to the *lowest Order* of Men; and has not the Reader great Reason to think his Dignity affronted, and to groan out LOW, very LOW, when he finds he has paid his Money to read fictitious Characters, uttering such *Language* and *Sentiments*, which if he had ever been so unhappy to have heard in real Life, he should have either kick'd the Utterers of them out of his Company, or if necessitated to have heard them, cry'd out in a sweating Agony, with *Horace*,

—————————*O te* Bollane *cerebri*
Felicem,
               O happy Bollanus, *who hast a dull Brain.*[1]

BUT this perhaps may be better illustrated with an Example, as follows,

[Quotes from IV. x as follows: 'The squire gave him a good curse . . . many's the good time and often'; 'I should be sorry that he should do himself any injury . . . Allworthy at college'; 'and many a wench . . . the women will like un the better for't'.]

I am afraid Sir, what I have now said too plainly proves that every Body knows what the Word LOW means, and that it is likewise very *expressive* in its Signification, I am therefore doubtful that the Publick will not think, what you have assign'd Sir, a sufficient Reason for the *Disuse* of it: I cannot flatter you neither that they will fall in with your Sentiments of confining the Use of this Word to *Right Honourables*, and putting a Gag in the Mouths of all under that Rank, for tho' you, Sir, are in too great a Station now, to suppose the PEOPLE know any thing, yet there happens to be two small Objections to this Opinion of your's; the first is, that the wisest and most learned Men, of all Ages have thought directly contrary; the second is, that Experience has shewn that the PEOPLE, that is, what you with so just Contempt denominate Gentlemen of the Law, Apprentices, Clerks, *&c.* and if you had added Shoemakers and Taylors, it would have made no Difference; have always been right in their Judgment, unless biass'd and led astray by superior Examples . . . [Digresses at length on this idea, citing various ancient and modern authorities.] . . . So that I must needs say, Sir,

[1] Satires, I. ix. 11—12.

the *Sentiments* of the most *learned Men, common Experience* and *Philo-sophical Experiment* are all different from you on this Head.

HOWEVER, Sir, this need give you little Concern; for notwith-standing all, you are an *Author* of *Authors* still; for you draw Characters after *Nature*, while others draw them after their own wicked *Imagina-tions*: For it seems, Sir, *Homer, Virgil, Horace*, and the other *little* Authors of Antiquity, were stupid enough to think there were many Characters in ev'ry Station of Life, unfit to be drawn at full Length, as being un-worthy of the Dignity of their Pen, or the Sight of their Readers; they therefore either intirely pass'd them by, or, if oblig'd to introduce them, put them into as tolerable a Dress as they could, lent them a few decent Words to appear with, and presently pack'd them off the Stage again. They were likewise foolish enough, in drawing fictitious Characters after *Nature*, to imagine they ought to carry them to the highest Pitch of Perfection, the *Station* the Character bore in Life, might possibly attain to; thus, if they introduc'd a *Shepherd* or *Cowherd*, though they did not make him talk like a Man of Letters, yet they made him make Use of some of the best Words he had pick'd up in the City, when he went there upon any Occasion, or from his Landlord in the Country; and if his Stock was not copious enough they lent him a few Words of their own; so *Virgil* makes *Melbœus* fay

> *Tityre tu patulæ; recubans sub tegmine fagi,*
> *Silvestrem tenui Musam meditaris avena.*[1]

Now, Sir, if *Virgil* had but understood the Art of Writing after *Nature* half as well as you, he would to be sure have wrote it thus,

> *Titeroous too patoole, reckqubance cub tagmanne faggy,*
> *Cylvassterm tenooi Moozam meddytearis aveena.*

I likewise find that he makes all such like People as wise and knowing as they could ever arrive to, under the most favourable Circumstances in their Station: thus, tho' they are not Scholars, yet they are Men of plain good Sense, are honest and skilful in their own Spheres, and have borrow'd some useful Knowledge from their Observations of *Nature*, whereby the Reader is oftimes agreeably improv'd: In like Manner he has drawn all his Characters to the highest Pitch of their several Stations; if he describes a *Gentleman*, he has all the Learning and Qualities of a compleat *Gentleman*; if a *King*, he has all the more Majestick *ones* of the best of *Kings*; it is pretty evident too, that *Virgil* copied *Homer* in all this Stuff, for *Horace* tells us of *Homer*,

[1] *Eclogues,* I. 1–2.

that————————*Nil molitur inepte,*
and that——————————————*quæ*
Desperat tractata nitescere posse, relinquit.[1]

HORACE himself too was so ignorant, as to tell us, that even in *Satire*, when he intended to make any Person or Vice ridiculous, he lov'd to do it in good Language.

Non ego inornata, & dominantia nomina solum,
Verbaque, Pisones, Satyrorum scriptor amabo.[2]

OUR own *Shakespear* has likewise followed these bad Examples, and made his lowest Characters talk Sense and *English*; and that other foolish Fellow *Cervantes* has made *Sancho Pancha*, an illiterate Country Clown, convey many sensible Hints to the Reader.

O then *happy, thrice and four Times happy*, you, Sir, who are the sole *Founder* of a new *Kind* of *Writing*, where none of these unnatural Rules are observ'd.

To you, Sir, the Honour belongs of presenting Characters to the Reader's Sight, that they would otherwise never have seen; for it is without all Dispute, a noble Thought of your *own*, that *ignorant, stupid, low, vicious* Characters are as worthy the Reader's Attention, as *wiser* and more *virtuous* ones, and make full as good *Pictures*, and therefore ought to be drawn at full Length.

ANOTHER Thing which you have succeeded in beyond all Example, is the putting proper Language into the Mouths of these Characters: Thus how just! how congruous! how beautiful! how instructive! is the Language of your 'Squire *Western*, 'I wull have Satisfaction of thee, so doff thy Cloaths; at unt half a Man, and I'll lick thee as well as wast ever licked in thy Life:' [VI. ix] And again, [Quotes from VI. x as follows: 'O, matter enow . . . meat for his master'; 'if she will ha un . . . zinking fund'; 'I little thought . . . and zu may tell un.']

AGAIN, Sir, what intelligent Person would have been willing to have lost one single Line out of the forty five of that curious instructive Letter of Mrs. *Honour Blackmore*'s, which begins thus,
'I shud sartenly haf kaled on you a cordin too my Prommiss haddunt itt bin that her Lashipp prevent mee for too bee sur, Sir, you nose very well that every Person must luk furst at Ome, &c.' [XV. x]

---

[1] 'He undertakes nothing foolishly . . . he leaves out whatever he despairs of making shine.' *The Art of Poetry*, ll. 140, 149–50.
[2] 'If I were to write satiric plays, Pisos, I would not use plain language only.' *The Art of Poetry*, ll. 234–5.

How beautifully expressive is this Letter of Mrs. *Honour's* Abilities and Character, and how much *Wit* and *Instruction* does it convey to the Reader! Innumerable are the Instances of this Sort, which your Genius has brought forth in your Works; and of which *Kind* of Writing you are without all Dispute the *Founder*.

BUT notwithstanding so many beautiful Pictures of *Nature*, so great is the Malice and Envy which attends great Authors, that I have heard several affirm, that your Worship (so far from drawing your Characters after *Nature*) does not know what the Word *Nature* means; *Nature*, say these Gentlemen, is the highest Degree of Perfection, with which that Order of Beings we are speaking of, is generally indued with; or, as the ingenious Mr. *Martin* defines it in his Dictionary,[1] the *Inclinations, Faculties, Properties, Qualities,* or *Affections* which any Thing has ORIGINALLY: Now, say these Criticks, it is absurd, because there may chance to be some single Characters in Life, who by bad Example, Idleness, or Drunkenness, have lost all their *original* Properties, to draw these at full Length, and tell us it is *Nature*, as if a Painter was to draw any of his principal Figures with scald Heads and blear Eyes, and tell us it was NATURE, because he had sometimes happened to have seen such; or would not an Anatomist, say they, be laugh'd at, who shall call a Child born with two Heads and five Legs, or any other monstrous Birth, NATURE, because there has now and then happen'd to be such brought into the World.

OTHERS are so envious to say, they don't believe there is so stupid and ignorant a Character in Life (at least not above the Station of a Kennel-Raker) as your 'Squire *Western*; and I must confess, tho' I have made very diligent Enquiry, yet I have not met with any Body who has ever seen such a one, and indeed most are of Opinion it never existed in Life, but was taken from a Copy rummag'd for in the *nastiest* of all Places.

BUT, Sir, you have no Need to regard any of these Cavils or Objections, for as you rightly observe Page 60 of the 3d Vol. of your excellent Work, [XI. i] it is all *Slander*, and dev'lish *Slander* too; and I am of Opinion, if they won't hold their slanderous Tongues, you may bring an Action of *Scandalum Magnatum* against them, for you know you are a very great Man, and *Slander* and *Scandal* may easily be made the same *Thing*.

I will detain you Sir, no longer, but with recommending my Hero to

---

[1] Benjamin Martin, *An English Dictionary* (1749).

your Protection, hoping you will not find him of too '*angelick a Perfection*' for your Esteem and Approbation.

> *I am Sir,*
> > *Your most humble Servant,*
> > The HISTORIOGRAPHER
> > > *To Mr.* BAMPFYLDE-MOORE CAREW,
> > *King of the* BEGGARS.

99. [Francis Coventry], from *An Essay on the New Species of Writing* . . .

1751

An Essay on the New Species of Writing founded by Mr. Fielding: with a Word or Two upon the Modern State of Criticism. Francis Coventry was the author of *Pompey the Little* (see No. 134). For a useful introduction and notes (on which we have based our notes), see Alan D. McKillop's facsimile edition of the *Essay* (Augustan Reprint Society, Publication No. 95, 1962).

The Essay was reviewed unfavourably by the *Gentleman's Magazine* (March 1751), xxi. 143: 'Contains a parallel between *Charlotte Summers* and *Tom Jones*, some trite remarks on novel writing, and is in general an encomium on Mr. Fielding and his writings.'

> *Qui, quid sit pulchrum, quid turpe, quid utile, quid non,*
> *Pleniùs ac meliùs Chrysippo et Crantore dicit.*
> *Cur ita crediderim, nisi quid te detinet, audi.*
>
> HOR.[1]

PREFACE

GENTLE READER,

The *new Sect of Biographers (founded by Mr. Fielding) is already grown so very numerous from the Success of the Original, that an Attempt of this Kind is in some Measure necessary, to put a Stop to the unbounded Liberties the*

---

[1] 'He who says more fully and sweetly than Chrysippus or Crantor what is beautiful, what is base, what is useful, what is not. Unless I am detaining you, listen to why I think so.' *Epistles*, I. ii. 3–5.

Historians of this comic Stamp might otherwise indulge themselves: and, if possible, to prevent any from undertaking the Labours of Mr. Fielding, without an adequate Genius. Should the following Sheets be of Force enough to hinder the weak, sickly Birth of a Joe Thompson, Charlotte Summers, *or* Peregrine Pickle, *in Embrio;*[1] *the Town would undoubtedly be glad to exchange the heavy Work of a voluminous Scribler for the more easy Burden of a loose Pamphlet.*

The first Critics drew their Rules from the first Professors of the Art they made their Observations on; which were afterwards the settled Standards by which the Worth of their Successors was to be determin'd. In Imitation of so great an Example are the Rules for the future Historians of this kind drawn from the Works of their Original Mr. Fielding. But I have even ventur'd to exceed these Limits, which I propos'd to myself on first setting out, and have dar'd to censure very freely some Parts of the Works of their great Original; which had I pursu'd, in remarking on the long Series of his Imitators, my Pamphlet would have insensibly swell'd into an enormous Volume. This Part of my Task may, without Vanity, be said to be perform'd in a more Gentleman-like Manner than our Author has yet been us'd by any of his Critics. If the Examiner of Tom Jones, *and the Author of* Bampfylde-Moore Carew *may deserve that Name. Think not, Gentle Reader, that the Objection made to those Writers are meant to intimate the pre-eminent Worth of this Performance; which, should it meet with Success in the World might entice the Author to expose himself by some future Pieces. If otherwise, will (more perhaps to his Credit) warn him to take an everlasting Farewell of Authorism.*

★   ★   ★

I shall now begin to take a critical Review of these Histories in general, in performing which, if even Mr. *Fielding* himself does not confess that my Proceeding is impartial, I'll be content to send him my Name, that he may punish me *propriâ personâ* in the next humorous Piece he publishes.

Sometime before this new Species of Writing appear'd, the World had been pester'd with Volumes, commonly known by the Name of Romances, or Novels, Tales, *&c.* fill'd with any thing which the wildest Imagination could suggest. In all these Works, Probability was not required: The more extravagant the Thought, the more exquisite the Entertainment. Diamond Palaces, flying Horses, brazen Towers, &c. were here look'd upon as proper, and in Taste. In short, the most

---

[1] Edward Kimber, *The Life and Adventures of Joe Thompson* (1750), claimed he was writing biography rather than fiction, while in fact imitating Fielding and Smollett. *Peregrine Pickle* was published early in 1751; for *Charlotte Summers,* see No. 87.

finish'd Piece of this kind, was nothing but Chaos and Incoherency. *France* first gave Birth to this strange Monster, and *England* was proud to import it among the rest of her Neighbour's Follies. A Deluge of Impossibility overflow'd the Press. Nothing was receiv'd with any kind of Applause, that did not appear under the Title of a Romance, or Novel; and Common Sense was kick'd out of Doors to make Room for marvellous Dullness. The Stile in all these Performances was to be equal to the Subject—amazing: And may be call'd with great Propriety, 'Prose run mad.' This obtain'd a long Time. Every Beau was an *Orondates*, and all the Belles were *Stariras*. Not a *Billet-doux* but run in Heroics, or the most common Message deliver'd but in the Sublime. The disease became epidemical, but there were no Hopes of a Cure, 'till Mr. *Fielding* endeavour'd to show the World, that pure Nature could furnish out as agreeable Entertainment, as those airy non-entical Forms they had long ador'd, and persuaded the Ladies to leave this Extravagance to their *Abigails* with their cast Cloaths. Amongst which Order of People, it has ever since been observ'd to be peculiarly predominant.

His Design of Reformation was noble and public-spirited, but the Task was not quite so easy to perform, since it requir'd an uncommon Genius. For to tread the old beaten Track would be to no Purpose. Lecture would lose it's Force; and Ridicule would strive in vain to remove it. For tho' it was a Folly, it was a pleasing one: And if Sense could not yield the pretty Creatures greater Pleasure, Dear Nonsense must be ador'd.

Mr. *Fielding* therefore, who sees all the little Movements by which human Nature is actuated, found it necessary to open a new Vein of Humour, and thought the only way to make them lay down *Cassandra*, would be to compile Characters which really existed, equally entertaining with those Chimaeras which were beyond Conception. This Thought produced *Joseph Andrews*, which soon became a formidable Rival to the *amazing* Class of Writers; since it was not a mere dry Narrative, but a lively Representative of real Life. For crystal Palaces and winged Horses, we find homely Cots and ambling Nags; and instead of Impossibility, what we experience every Day.

But as Mr. *Fielding* first introduc'd this new kind of Biography, he restrain'd it with Laws which should ever after be deem'd sacred by all that attempted his Manner; which I here propose to give a brief Account of. The first and grand one of all, (without which, in however regular a Manner the rest is conducted, the whole Performance must be dead and languid) is, that thro' the whole Humour must diffuse itself. But this can by no Means be perform'd without a great Genius, nay, even a particular Sort of one: for tho' Mr. *Bayes* informs us, any Man may commence Poet by his infallible Rules,[1] yet in this Kind of Writing he must be at a Stand without this grand Requisite. But to proceed.

The next Thing to be consider'd, is the Choice of Characters, which tho' striking and particular must be exactly copied from Nature. And who can doubt, when they see the Features of an *Abraham Adams*, or Madam *Slipslop*, faithfully delineated, but that Field will afford an agreeable Variety? Every Word they speak must be entirely consonant to the Notion the Author would have his Readers to entertain of them: And here it may not be amiss to remark the great Analogy there is between these Histories and Dramatic Performances, which Similitude I shall enlarge upon occasionally in the Progress of this Review. In regard to Character, after what I have mention'd as necessary, it would be the greatest Affront on the Reader's Understanding to point out the Comparison.

As this Sort of Writing was intended as a Contrast to those in which the Reader was even to suppose all the Characters ideal, and every Circumstance quite imaginary, 'twas thought necessary, to give it a greater Air of Truth, to entitle it *an History*; and the *Dramatis Personæ* (if I may venture to use the Expression) were christened not with fantastic high-sounding Names, but such as, tho' they sometimes bore some Reference to the Character, had a more modern Termination.

At the same Time Mr. *Fielding* ordain'd, that these Histories should be divided into Books, and these subdivided into Chapters; and also that the first Chapter of every Book was not to continue the Narration, but should consist of any Thing the Author chose to entertain his Readers with. These if I don't forget, Mr. *Fielding* himself has nominated, the several Stages of his History, which he metaphorically calls a Journey, in which he and his Readers are Fellow-Travellers. His particular Success in these preliminary Essays demonstrates (notwithstanding what the Author of *Charlotte Summers* hints on that Head) that these are not the easiest Part of his Task: Which I believe, Mr. *Fielding* somewhere says himself.[2]

---

[1] *The Rehearsal*, I. i, where Mr. Bayes says, 'And I do here averr, That no man yet the Sun e'er shone upon, has parts sufficient to furnish out a Stage, except it be with the help of these my Rules.'

[2] *Tom Jones*, V. i.

The Story should be probable, and the Characters taken from common Life, the Stile should be easy and familiar, but at the same Time sprightly and entertaining; and to enliven it the more, it is sometimes heightened to the Mock-heroic, to ridicule the Bombast and Fustian, which obtain'd so much in the Romances. Of this Kind are his various Descriptions of the Morning, and his diverting Similes occasionally dispers'd thro' the Body of his Work. *Horace* tells us, *dulce est desipere*, but Mr. *Fielding* remember'd he added *in loco*.[1] For which Reason, he always takes care to indulge himself in these Liberties of Stile where the Story is least interesting. The last Book of *Tom Jones* is a convincing Proof, that he can comprize a great Variety of Circumstances in as small a Compass as any Author whatsoever. Besides these Descriptions, Similes, &c. there are other Licenses of Stile which it would be too tedious to be so minute as to enlarge upon. One Circumstance however, as it is a particular one, I cannot entirely pass over in Silence. Take it then as follows.——An Author of true Humour will consider, that his Book should be entertaining in the smallest Particulars, and afford Amusement

ab ovo
Usque ad mala.

For which Reason Mr. *Addison* prefix'd Mottos to his Spectators, and at the Corner of each Paper added some particular Letter, which he himself imagin'd to be not the least entertaining Part of his Speculations. And nearly for the same End, Mr. *Fielding* thought proper to be facetious in the Titles to the several Chapters of his Histories, to shew the Reader he would not permit the least Occasion to slip which offer'd an Opportunity of amusing him.

As I am fallen on the Subject of the Titles to his Chapters, it will not be improper to consider them more largely, since it will only be mentioning now some Remarks I should be obliged to make by-and-by, which, for the Sake of the Connection, I rather chuse to insert here. And perhaps I may convince the Reader, these little Scraps, if rightly manag'd, conduce more to his Entertainment than he is at first aware of. 'Tis quite opposite to the Custom of the very best Writers in this Way, to give too full an Account of the Contents: it should be just hinted to the Reader something extraordinary is to happen in the seven or eight subsequent Pages, but what that is should be left for them to discover. Monsieur *Le Sage*, in his *Gil Blas*, (one of the best Books of the

---

[1] 'It's nice to be foolish—sometimes.' *Odes,* IV. xii. 28.

Kind extant) has always pursu'd this Method: He tells us *Gil Blas* is going to such or such a Place, but does not discover the least of his Adventures there; but he is more particularly cautious when any unexpected Event is to happen. The Title to one of his Chapters of that Kind is—*A Warning not to rely too much upon Prosperity.*—To another—*Chapter the fifth, being just as long as the preceding:* With many others which it is needless to enumerate. Note, 'Tis to be wish'd this Custom had been observ'd by the Author of *Roderick Random*, who tells us in his Preface, his Book is wrote in Imitation of the *Gil Blas* of Monsieur *Le Sage*. But with very little Success in my humble Opinion. As to the Titles of his Chapters, he is particularly tedious in them. This judicious Method of detaining the Reader in an agreeable Suspence, though it is right at all Times, is more particularly necessary when the History is near ended. No Writer has so strictly kept up to this as Mr. *Fielding*, in his *Tom Jones*. We are too well assured of *Gil Blas's* Prosperity a long Time beforehand, to be surpriz'd at it. But at the Beginning of the last Book of *Tom Jones*, the Reader is apt to think it an equal Chance whether he is to be hanged or married; nor does he undeceive him but by gradual Narration of Facts: And lest the Reader's Curiosity should pry too far into the Truth, what admirable Titles has he invented for his Chapters in order to keep him the longer in the Dark! such as——*In which the History draws near to a Conclusion: In which the History draws nearer to a Conclusion,* &c. &c. which every Body will own conduces greatly to their Entertainment, and a Reader of the least Discernment will perceive how much more Consequence the clever Management of these Scraps prefix'd to each Chapter is of than he at first imagin'd. With how little Judgment has the Author of *Charlotte Summers* conducted this Particular! whose great Fault is Anticipation: That is, forestalling, by too explanatory a Title, the most remarkable Occurrences in his History. This appears even in the Title to his Book, which is, *The History of* Charlotte Summers: *or The* FORTUNATE *Parish Girl*. What Mr. *Addison* says of the Tragedies that conclude happily, may with equal Justice be apply'd here. 'We see without Concern (says he) illustrious People in Distress, when we are sure they will at last be deliver'd from their Misfortunes.'[1] Other Writers content themselves with entitling their Pieces, *The History of a Foundling, of Joseph Andrews, of Gil Blas, Roderick Random*, &c. without informing us as to the Event. As I find myself drawn into an unforeseen Length, I shall only subjoin one Instance from his Chapters, but at the same Time such an one, as

---

[1] *Spectator* No. 40, 16 April 1711 (misquoted).

will convince the Reader of Mr. *Fielding's* Excellence in this Particular. The Eighth Chapter of the last Book is perhaps one of the most interesting in the whole History, and I dare say drew Tears from many Readers. For my own Part, I am not asham'd to own I have so much of the 'Milk of human Nature' in me, that I should have been in the greatest Concerns for the Misfortunes of the unhappy Miss *Summers*, if unluckily the Author had not assur'd me before I enter'd on these distressful Scenes, she would certainly be deliver'd from her momentary Afflictions before I had read three Leaves further. To confess the Truth I was fastly angry with him for depriving me of such entertaining Sadness. We hope this Instance will convince all future Writers, that the Pleasure of the Reader is much more exquisite from the Reserve in the Title. These Thoughts upon the Inscriptions to the Chapters were thrown together to shew, that Mr. *Fielding* had another Intention besides making the World laugh in the Lines prefix'd to each Portion of his History. Permit me therefore, gentle Reader, upon the Authority of a Critic, to banish from all Histories above the Rank of those printed in *Black-fryars*, and sold at the small Price of one Penny, to tell us— *As how* Thomas Hickathrift *carried a Stack of Corn*. Or—Thomas Thumb *was swallow'd by a Cow*, in a Title longer than the Chapter itself. After this Exertion of my Power, as a Critic, and dispersing these my Presents to all whom they may concern; let us return whence we digress'd.

*   *   *

These Remarks could hardly make a just Claim to that Impartiality, I have all along been so great a Stickler for, was I entirely to pass over in Silence the few Mistakes our Author has been guilty of in the Conduct of his several Performances. But I shall be very little inclin'd to enlarge on so disagreeable a Part of the Critic's Office. First then for *Joseph Andrews*.—We are told, that the chief End of these Pieces is the Extirpation of Vice, and the Promotion of Virtue; to say the Truth, which the general Bent of them always tends to. But we fear this grand Rule has in some Places been too much disregarded. As the Works of Mr. *Fielding* are in every Body's Hands, there ought not to be a Line in them which should cause the modestest Lady a single Blush in the Perusal. This Delicacy of Stile and Sentiment has been quite neglected in some Dialogues between the wanton Lady *Booby* and most innocent *Joseph Andrews*; and more particularly so in one Chapter, which must occur to the Remembrance of every Reader conversant with these Works. We may venture to say this one Chapter has been prejudicial to the young

People of both Sexes, and that more Readers have look'd upon the Innocence of *Joseph Andrews* as Stupidity, than theWantonness of Lady *Booby* as Guilt. Lewdness is too mean a Branch of Humour (if indeed it is a Branch of Humour) for a Man of Mr. *Fielding*'s Sense to have Recourse to: and we hope that he will henceforth leave it to those barren Writers of Comedy who have no other Way of pleasing, but a scandalous Coincidence with the deprav'd Taste of a vicious Audience. The next Objection we shall make to *Joseph Andrews* is a general one, which includes the whole Performance. My Reader will start perhaps at the Thoughts of so extensive an Objection, but I must beg leave to say, that tho' the Narration is conducted with great Spirit, and there are innumerable Strokes of Wit and Nature throughout, it is no small Derogation to the Merit of this Work, that the Story on which it is founded is not sufficiently interesting. The Characters indeed are equally natural and entertaining with those of *Tom Jones*, but the Parts they are allotted engage much less of our Attention. In Dramatic Pieces, where the Story must be stretch'd into Five Acts, there is some Excuse for this Inaction, and Want of Incidents, but in these Performances, where the Length of the Work is left entirely to the Discretion of the Writer, little can be alledg'd in his Defence.

We will here take our Leave of *Joseph Andrews*, and briefly observe what deserves Reproof in Mr. *Fielding*'s last Piece, *viz. Tom Jones*; a Performance which on the whole perhaps is the most lively Book ever publish'd, but our Author has here and there put in his Claim to that Privilege of being dull, which the Critics have indulg'd to the Writers of Books of any Length.

——-Opere in longo fas est obrepere somnum.

HOR.[1]

——Sleep
O'er Works of Length allowably may creep.

FRANCIS.

The most glaring Instance of this kind in all this Author's Works is the long unenliven'd Story of *the Man of the Hill*; which makes up so great a Part of a Volume. A Narration which neither interests or entertains the Reader, and is of no more Service than in filling up so many Pages. The Substance of the Story is such as (to make use of Mr. *Shirley*'s Phrase)

'almost staggers Credibility.'[2]

[1] *The Art of Poetry*, l. 360. [2] *Edward the Black Prince*, p. 1.

For though I have heard it affirmed, that there is such a Character as the *Man of the Hill*; yet I believe the Generality of Readers concurr'd with me in thinking it chimerical and unnaturally singular. I am very sorry Mr. *Fielding* should have introduc'd so improbable a Story, because there is no kind of Writing where the Rule of *Horace*, concerning Probability, should so strictly be observed, as in these Works.

> *Ficta voluptatis causâ sint proxima veris;*
> *Nec quodcunque volet, poscat sibi fabula credi.*[1]

Of which be pleas'd, my courteous *English* Reader, to accept the following free Translation.

> The Life-wrought Tale should ne'er advance
> A Line that favours of Romance.

I am now most heartily tired of cavilling, for which Reason I shall take no Notice of the other few Blemishes in the Works of this Author, which may have arose from Heedlessness; or the Frailty of human Nature may have given Birth to. And which are more conspicuous in Writings so lively in general, as Freckles are more remarkable in those of Fair Complexions. Praise is Insolence where the Man that praises dares not discommend: on which Account I trust that our *English Cervantes* will not be offended at the Freedom I have taken in censuring some Parts of his Works. I have all along endeavour'd to act according to the laudable Resolution I took at my first setting out; that is, to proceed without Prejudice, or Partiality, like a candid, honest Critic, who will, (according to *Shakespear* in his *Othello*)

> Nothing extenuate,
> Nor set down aught in Malice.

---

[1] *The Art of Poetry*, ll. 338–9.

THE ENQUIRY, TOM JONES, ETC.

100. From *The Magazine of Magazines*
April 1751, i. 286–9.

Dear POLITIAN,

As our magazine has frequently been published a day or two after the expected time: to shew our readiness in obliging our subscribers, we now publish it a day before, notwithstanding we have not had a receipt of you for the last number, but imagining our correspondent's stock was then low, or that he had not an opportunity of making the usual remittances, we give in our numbers as usual. Thus far by way of advertisement, which may very properly lead us to consider advertisements in general, as it is an art of science, well worth the consideration of the learned world, and therefore we shall regard it meerly, in the literary way, or as it relates to the works of the learned; that this is not a trifling speculation will appear, if we reflect that it requires more wit and sagacity to draw up an advertisement, to give a plausible title to a book, and to chose a proper motto, than to write the book itself. The world is pestered with so many clamorous petitioners with, 'hear me, hear me, read me,' &c. that it is necessary to be a master of a great deal of art and circumspection to draw in charitable folks, or to speak more intelligibly, to draw money out of their pockets. Authors therefore may be compared to common mendicants and I will venture to say, that in the space of one week, 'tis difficult to determine, whether if one walks from *Ludgate* to *Charing-Cross*, one shall meet with more beggars in the streets, or in booksellers shop windows—I have sometimes amused myself with this thought in my progress through *Fleet-street*, and could not help comparing the several low arts of beggars, with the equally low arts of authors,—a beggar at one corner of the street shall make a long miserable harangue, and at the opposite shop, you shall see an author in as ragged a coat in a window, with as long a title page; both equally endeavour to excite your curiosity, to stay your attention, and to gain the poor author a dinner; step a little farther and you shall see a beggar with a most lamentable countenance, fixed up against a wall, and not opening his mouth; He regards you not, gentle passenger, but 'tis only in hopes that you will regard him, and moved with dumb eloquence imagine the worst. Go on, and the next beggar you shall meet is an author, who scarce says a word—'Tis only,——*The history of a foundling* ——*The Adventures of Peregrine Pickle*——*The Scribleriad*——[1] He says no more; he thinks he has occasion to say no more; his appearance must move you, you must take home the *Foundling*—You must be civil to the stranger—and sure you must have a regard for the grandson of the *Dunciad*——The beggars in the streets, honest traveller, you will observe, carry passes and petitions in their hands some-times, and at the bottom too there are some considerable names; so too in the petitions of some of those beggars that hang in the windows, peeping out like the *Ludgate* debtors, shalt thou observe at the bottom the great names of *Knapton, Millar, Dodsley*[2]——Well, my honest friend, let us no more regard the poor eager supplicants both within and without doors; come, let us go into the next coffee-house, and instead of beggars read of robbers; but here too you will find, that while the street-beggar is committed to *Newgate*, in the very next side the shop-beggar is picking your pocket: observe what a gang of thieves there are upon this paper, who are suffered to impose on the unthink-ing world, and to rob with impunity—Let us hear one of them, 'Gentlemen I can only stay to inform you, that there will come out next week, an enquiry ushered into the world by the great *Millar*.—— Here comes an arch fellow, he is very sensible how much the public loves secret history:——Gentlemen I have got the secret history of lady—— ——; I am much afraid it will be smuggled or pirated, there-fore depend on't this only is genuine, take it in time, whilst you may ——here come a troop of thieves, who observing that *novelle* taste is in high vogue; have drest up a —— parcel of dirty ——, given them all their allurements in their out-side; tacked them in a blue gown, with a little red and white in their faces, and now they swarm all over the *Strand*, and bullies without number attend them. Many an honest country gentleman, and many a raw university boy falls a prey to them; they pick his pocket and debauch him from morning to night.—The most noted of these——are *Harriot Stuart, Fanny Hill, Charlotte Summers,*

---

[1] Richard Owen Cambridge, *The Scribleriad* (1751).
[2] John Knapton, Andrew Millar, and Robert Dodsley were London booksellers, publishers of the above-mentioned books (Millar was Fielding's publisher).

lady *Frail*, &c. &c.[1] But here comes an excrable crew, marching along and bidding defiance to every body, and with such *Magazines* as must quickly over-run the nation. There is *Jonathan Wild* alias *Urban*,[2] with his brother *B—*, have robbed for these twenty years; next advances one who aims at *universal* monarchy,—him follows one who is content with *British* empire; him another that lodges travellers for three pence——here's a lady for threepence more—a poetical entertainment for three pence more, and an old woman to put you to bed for the other three pence.—— Here's an *university rogue* too, who robs once a month, (sophistry is come to a fine pass in our universities) here's another, like the ordinary of *Newgate*, gives you a review of the lives of all the robbers for the last month. Next comes a very honest gentleman call'd the *robber* of *robbers*, or a general receiver of stolen goods—Such is the gang—*Jonathan Wild* restores several lost goods, but how he came by them the Devil knows. The universal monarch is a rogue of modern date, and chiefly pilfers amongst country people; the *British* emperor (for ev'ry rogue assumes some grand name) is the most honest of any of them: the travellers lodgings are very sorry, the lady cursedly foundered, and the old woman crazy, prattling nonsensical beldame. The last fort of literary highwaymen go under the name of subscriptionists, or who raise a purse in the most genteel manner imaginable.——Other highwaymen will run the risk of their lives for the meer hopes of getting a few pence, but these gentlemen have the happy art of borrowing money on receipts, which generally are of no sort of estimation: the public, however, think that they do a great kindness to a man by lending him half a crown to buy him a dinner, are pleased to see their names enrolled amongst a list of charitable disposed persons, and do not altogether despair of having their pennyworth for their penny.

Such is the gang of literary beggars, rogues and highwaymen that swarm both in town and country.—The causes seem to be very nearly allied to those that justice *Fielding* recounts in his excellent enquiry, 'The prevailing fondness for novelty, diversion, entertainment, the want of a proper employment for the poor, &c.'

When people cannot employ their hands, they will set their heads, at work to do mischief; and while the taste of the nation is degenerated into such a longing appetite for amusements, it is but varnishing over

---

[1] Charlotte Lennox, *The Life of Harriot Stuart* (1751); John Cleland, *Fanny Hill, The Memoirs of a Woman of Pleasure* (1747); anon., *The History of Charlotte Summers* (1750); Dr. John Hill, *Lady Frail, the History of a Woman of Quality* (1751).

[2] i.e. the *Gentleman's Magazine*, by 'Sylvanus Urbanus'.

the pills, and they are greedily caught at. There seems at first sight, perhaps, very little connection, or rather quite a distinction and contrariety
between drunkenness and reading; but if we consider the thing duly, we
shall find that drunkenness, if it be not the cause, will be the certain
effect of this prodigious encrease of pamphlets, for such a variety of
books, like a variety of different liquors, must make people very besotted; or else 'tis the being besotted by ale or gin, that must make
people vomit out such crude undigested stuff upon the populace.

In time, if the progress of magazines continues, I shall expect to see
written on every country sign,

> *Harkee my friend if you come here,*
> *You may be trimm'd for a mug of beer,*
> *And read each magazine throughout the year.*

Heretofore honest countrymen were content with hearing a sermon
(which if you consider it in a *collective* sense is as good as a *magazine of
magazine*) once a week; sometimes seeing the market-town journal, and
debating on the politicks of the nation on a Sunday in the church-yard.
But in this improved age, sermons are the most awkward thing imaginable, and a bible the most unfashionable book in the world. Magazines
will presently make a man a politician, a free-thinker; a moralist, a
farmer, a physician, a poet and a philosopher.

The squire's daughter will talk to the parson of nothing else but the
last new songs at *Vauxhall*, the plays that were acted at both houses, and
the novels that were published last month; on the whole, it would not
be unworthy the genius of a *Fielding* to draw up, *An enquiry into the
causes of the late great encrease of magazines and other pamphlets, occasional
and periodical, with some proposals for remedying the growing evils.* In this
capacity Mr. *Fielding* may act as an enquirer, as a justice, as a law-giver,
and an executioner; for whoever is acquainted with his writings must
confess, that there is no body so well acquainted with human nature, so
capable of representing virtue in its own amiable dress, or vice in its
native deformity, that has such a thorough insight into the causes and
effects of things, is such a master of character, and so able to draw the
picture of an author, and a reader of every kind.

★　　★　　★

101. 'On the incomparable History of Tom Jones', *The Ladies Magazine*

20 April—4 May 1751, ii. 202

Hail! happy Fielding, who with glorious ease,
Can'st Nature paint, and paint her still to please.

Each humorous incident is finely hit,
With justness, symmetry of parts, and wit.

Nature throughout the drama plays her part,
Behind the curtain lurks assisting art.

102. [Élie C. Fréron], review

6 July 1751

A review of La Place's French translation of *Tom Jones*, Lettre I,
6 July 1751, *Lettres sur quelques écrits de ce tems* (1751), v. 3–22.
(Translation.)

It should not astonish you, Sir, that on those happy shores where taste
holds sway, there are some minds unamenable to their lessons: among
the most civilized people one meets some barbarians. But that an entire
nation, that has for long cultivated literature, that sees itself enriched
with the treasures of Athens, Rome, and Paris, has not yet reached the
point of producing a work deserving to be acknowledged by its
masters: how do you explain such a phenomenon? Do the English, so
jealous of their independence, wish to extend it to their manner of
writing? Do they regard the Aristotles, the Horaces, the Quintilians
and Boileaus, these wise legislators, as tyrants who enslave them? The
form of their books (excuse the parallel) resembles that of their government, and recalls, so to speak, the three powers that unite in Westminster. The royal majesty is, in a sense, represented by the truly
sublime strokes that sometimes escape them; the House of Lords, by
the noble sentiments they express; and the House of Commons (the
most numerous) by the small objects they amuse themselves by painting, by the trivial ideas they do not know how to avoid, by the lowness
of the 'characters' they present to us. In short, their Mount Parnassus is
another Mount Etna, that vomits fire, ashes, and smoke.

I do not believe that one can pass a more favourable judgment after
having read *The History of Tom Jones, or the Foundling*. In English that
novel consists of eighteen books, in six volumes. Each book is preceded
by an introductory discourse, in the form of an essay, on some literary
or moral point, usually extraneous. This pedantic taste rules also in the
body of the work, and often cuts short the action at the most exciting
moments. M. de la Place, who has enriched us with this new English

production, has prudently reduced it to four volumes. He has sensed how many kinds of prefaces, digressions, and treatises spoil the beauty of a work of this kind, where, as in a well-made play, far from letting the interest cool that results from a pathetic intrigue, one should proceed as rapidly as possible to the end. Another interpreter might have pushed his severity further than M. de la Place. He has suppressed all the low comic scenes spread in profusion through this history; he has spared us, for example, the barber Partridge, a detestable joker and dull pedagogue, who at the least excuse emits scraps of Latin. He has changed especially the chapter titles, which degenerate sometimes into insipid buffooneries. Here are examples: Book I, Chapter 5[7]. 'Containing such grave matter, that the reader cannot laugh once through the whole chapter, unless peradventure he should laugh at the author.' That's the truth. Book III, Chapter 3[4]. 'Containing a necessary apology for the author; and a childish incident, which perhaps requires an apology likewise.' Book IV, Chapter 7. 'It is very well done, someone will say'(?). [Chap. 7 is 'Being the shortest chapter in this book.'] Book V, Chapter 1[3]. 'Food for those who have a heart' [in Fielding's English, 'Which all who have no heart will think to contain much ado about nothing']. Chapter 2. 'Second service for the same people'(?). Book VII, Chapter 5[10]. 'Containing several matters, natural enough perhaps, but low.' Almost all the chapters of this work are announced under this agreeable tone, for which some French novelists have produced the model. What I find good is that the English author has rendered them justice.

Some reasonable readers may also wish that M. de la Place had corrected the lack of vraisemblance one notices in this story.[1] Mr. Allworthy, the richest gentleman, the most just and generous in the country, lived in his house with Miss Bridget Allworthy his sister, whom he loved tenderly. He has given shelter to a young man named Summer, who has completed his studies. This Summer was the son of one of Allworthy's dearest friends. He did not long profit from the bounty of his benefactor; a premature death carried him away. Miss Bridget loved him, and secretly married him some days before he died: she was left pregnant. What do you suppose she did? Another in her place would have revealed all to her brother. Her fault was repaired by her marriage; the good Allworthy, who had never had a child, would have been enchanted to see himself reborn in an heir. The dis-

---

[1] We have not pointed out all the factual errors in the French retelling of Fielding's plot, which are sometimes due to the translation and sometimes to the critic himself.

creet Bridget is far from following this line of conduct. She prefers to confide her secret to a certain Jenny Jones, who has served many years in the house of Partridge, the schoolmaster of the parish, of whom I have spoken. This girl is willing to take the risks of the venture. Miss Bridget profits, for her lying in, from a trip her brother takes to London. The mother of Jenny Jones takes away the fruit of love and guards it in her house. But the prudent Bridget, who, to judge by the interest she evinced in concealing the mystery, had wished the child to be raised far from the manor, now orders her confidante to put him in her brother's own bed the night he returns from London. Imagine the surprise of this gentleman, when lifting the cover of his bed he finds a baby wrapped in swaddling clothes sound asleep. He is overcome by compassion for this tiny innocent. He calls a servant, and orders her to find a nurse. The next day there is a great deal of noise and gossiping in the parish. Suspicions fall on Jenny Jones, who does not defend herself. She implores the mercy of Mr. Allworthy, who pardons her and even, to screen her from the looks and malignant talk of the gossips of the district, enables her to look elsewhere for shelter. She has refused to name the baby's father; but she has promised to tell Mr. Allworthy someday. Miss Bridget is indifferent during all this uproar. She even pretends to look with favour upon the child only out of respect for her brother. But at bottom she is pleased that he will be brought up in the manor. However, this tender mother shortly after falls head over heels in love with Capt. Blifil, whom she marries. How does a girl, whom an accident like hers has befallen, dare to marry, above all a captain who ought to be very knowledgeable about such things? One hardly recognizes in this act the delicate Bridget. It was moreover to sacrifice her son's estate—the son whom she loved so—and declare him a bastard for all his life. It is very difficult to reconcile her actions with her sentiments.

She has another son by her second marriage. He is brought up with the earlier one; their characters are well contrasted. The young Blifil is very promising; he is docile, contemplative, sober, sedate, pious, discreet, attentive to the lessons of his teachers; underneath he is a base soul, a false spirit, a Tartuffe without honour or faith. Tom Jones is quick, improvident, dissipated, and regarded as a very bad one. His penchant for libertinage was manifested ever since his infancy. 'He was convicted,' says the author, 'of having stolen fruit from a neighbor's orchard, a duck from a farmer, and a ball from Blifil's pocket' [Book III, Chap. 2]. But gradually he grew up and gave proofs of his good heart, of that generous frankness and probity that unhappily were not sufficient for success in the world. These beautiful qualities are more detrimental than advantageous, if not accompanied by prudence and circumspection. Tom Jones put them to the test. Thoughtlessness was the source of his misfortunes. I will not give you, Sir, the details of his adventures. Suffice it to know that he fell completely in love with Sophia, only daughter of Squire Western, a neighbor of Allworthy. The portrait of this gentleman is taken from nature. He is one of those frank countrymen, obstinate of their rank, who divide their time between the chase and the table. After his horses and his dogs, Sophia was his greatest love. She was not insensible to the passion of Jones. But how to be joined to so base a lover? Blifil, whom she detests, is intended for her husband. Her father, irritated by her refusal, detects the cause. A bastard daring to love his daughter! It did not take much to provoke the testy gentleman. He carries his complaints to Allworthy, who, already unhappy with Jones for some small escapades that Blifil has exaggerated, sends him away, giving him a considerable sum in bank notes.

Thus our hero has departed, thinking of his dear Sophia, who for her part, in order to escape the object of her aversion, and doubtless to find her lover, flees one beautiful night from her father's house, and seeks refuge in London with a relative, Lady Bellaston. The first thing Tom Jones does is to lose the notes Allworthy had given him, so that nothing remains but the little ready money he has on himself. He is only halfway bothered by this loss. The image of his Sophia alone fills his mind and heart. Nocturnal combats, meetings with thieves and bohemians, quarrels in the inns, the episode of the Man of the Hill who had stolen forty guineas from a comrade at school, and the deliverance of a young lady who was being hanged in a wood by a scoundrel, and who to show her gratitude submits her physical charms to her savior: it is through these pleasures and dangers that our knight-errant arrives in London with his faithful squire Partridge.

The author begins his thirteenth book with an invocation which he concludes thus: He speaks to Genius: 'Strip off the thin disguise of wisdom from self-conceit, of plenty from avarice, and of glory from ambition. Come, thou that hast inspired thy Aristophanes, thy Lucian, thy Cervantes, thy Rabelais, thy Molière, thy Shakespeare, thy Swift, thy Marivaux, fill my pages with humour.' I did not know that there was in England a famous author named Marivaux, worthy to be compared with Aristophanes, Lucian, Molière, &c.

Tom Jones takes a room in London in Mrs. Miller's house, where Allworthy himself was accustomed to stay when he went to the capital. This Mrs. Miller had two daughters, of which the elder named Nancy was loved by a young man who for proximity to his love occupied an apartment in the same house. Nightingale was his name. His father wanted him to marry a rich heiress. Obliged to obey, he abandoned his dear Nancy, without noticing the cruel position in which he had put her. She bore the sensible marks of her attachment to a perjurer. All the family is in tears; Jones hastens to their cries. Informed of the trouble, he flies to Nightingale's room. He makes him see all the horror of his action. The discourse he delivers appears to me of the greatest beauty, and the most sublime eloquence. It is in vain that Nightingale argues that he dares not acknowledge Nancy for his wife, nor show himself in the world. [Quotes Bk. XIV, Chap. 7, Jones' speech to Nightingale.]

Nightingale surrenders to such strong and touching reasons. It is now only a question of his father; Jones undertakes to go and find the obstinate old man. He works so skilfully that at length he has the happiness to see Nancy marry her lover.

This passage must give you, Sir, a clear idea of Tom Jones. In effect he is portrayed as the greatest honour to humanity. Probity, candour, good faith, charity are the soul of all his actions. One can only reproach him with the infidelities to his mistress. He is a modern Celadon. Despite his passion for Sophia, friend Jones, as the author calls him, is hardly severe to other ladies. While living with Allworthy, he had a successful liaison with a certain Molly Seagrim, daughter of the game keeper. You have seen that on his way he surrendered himself willingly to the gratitude of the unknown lady whom he saved from the hands of a madman. Finally, when he is in London, he lets himself be kept by Lady Bellaston, at whose house Sophia is staying, without knowing anything about it.

If I were to follow the author in all his digressions, we would never reach the end. After many more very romantic incidents, the birth of Jones is revealed. A long time ago Blifil's father had died; Miss Bridget, his wife, had died in Salisbury. In her last hour she had declared that she was the mother of our hero. She even wrote to her son. An attorney was charged to carry the letter, but as Allworthy was sick, it was the young Blifil who received it, broke it open, and saw the secret fatal to his fortune and to his hatred of his rival. He decided not to show the letter to his uncle, who continued to regard Jones as a foundling.

Allworthy came to London. Jones was in prison for a duel with Mr. Fitzpatrick, who lived with Mrs. Waters, the same woman whose life Jones had saved in the woods. This woman was in fact Jenny Jones, who had given her name to Miss Bridget's child. The squire Partridge recognizes her when she goes to visit Jones in prison. When she has left, Partridge makes haste to tell his master that she is his mother. What a shock for the virtuous Jones, who believes he has committed incest! He is shortly disabused of this notion. Mrs. Waters reveals all to Allworthy; her account is confirmed by the attorney who had seen Miss Bridget die and became Allworthy's steward. This man had never dared say a word of what he knew, deceived by the treacherous Blifil, who had convinced him that it would displease his uncle to be told of his sister and Tom Jones. He was even associated in Blifil's dark projects; he had bribed the witnesses to undo Jones, under the pretext that he had murdered Fitzpatrick. But the latter declared that he was himself the aggressor. Jones leaves prison in trimph. Allworthy takes him in his arms and acknowledges him as his nephew. Western, who had come to London to carry away Sophia, whose retreat he had discovered, hears with transports the happy discovery that renders Jones worthy of his daughter. He consents to their union, and the marriage takes place with equal satisfaction for both families. The wretched Blifil is expelled in his turn from his uncle's house and is given enough to enable him to live honestly.

Despite the vices of this novel, I am forced to admit that I have read it twice with great pleasure. There are passages so touching and so pathetic; the sentiments are expressed with such force and truth; the moral is so beautiful; the characters so true and well sustained, that one cannot deny the author great genius and the ability to portray men. Moreover, the aim he has proposed is so noble and in general so happily fulfilled, that one must pardon his errors, attributing them more to his country than to his own genius. His design, in the whole course of this work, is to render innocence and charity equally lovable, and above all to make evident, by the portraits of Jones and Blifil, that the difference is great between the faults that too much candour makes degenerate into imprudences, and those that proceed solely from a false and tainted heart.

The author of this book is Mr. Fielding, long known in England for various writings. He first worked in the theatre without remarkable success; which he attributes, I am told, to the manoeuvres and cabals of a celebrated rival in certain respects. This is the famous Colley Cibber, son [*sic*] of the comedian, actor himself, and very good at comedy.[1] But he has not acted since he was decorated by the court with the glorious title of Poet Laureate. This title, or this charge, obliges him to compose two odes a year in praise of the king, one for his birthday, the other for New Year's Day. These two odes are sung in a concert before the king and his whole court. Cibber fails miserably in the lyric, and Pope has made fun of him, especially in his famous mock-epic poem *The Dunciad*, as we would say *La Sottisade* or *L'Hebetiade*. Cibber is the author of some estimable comedies, especially one called *The Careless Husband*, or *Le Mari sans souci*. He has also written the story of his life, which has greatly amused the public, at his expense. In all Mr. Fielding's works there is more than a little criticism, direct or indirect, aimed at this poet laureate.

Mr. Fielding, after having left the theatre, threw himself into periodical writing. His *Champion*, among others, where he did signal service against the ministry and notably against the celebrated Robert Walpole, drew upon him, so it is claimed, singular sorrows and consolations from the minister. *The Adventures of Joseph Andrews and Parson Adams*, a novel of his making in two volumes, published in 1742, had the greatest success in England for the same reasons that prevented its success in France. The ridiculous local characters, the indirect passages aimed at different known persons, the naïve portraiture of the behaviour of the low, and the delicate views of the author had nothing in it that appealed to our taste or interest. The late M. Abbé Desfontaines, who praised this work so often and prodigiously in his journals (he translated it), wished to attribute to that sole cause the coolness with which his version was received. *The Foundling* has crowned the glory of Mr. Fielding. An Englishman told me that the first edition was sold with the leaves still wet, and was followed by three others that enriched both author and bookseller. The latter was seen to purchase an equipage. How different is one country from another! In France the better novel barely gives its author enough to live on for a year. The work of Mr. Fielding, repaid by the public, was also repaid by the court which has named him justice of the peace for the county of Westminster, that is, of the court itself.[2]

---

[1] The remainder of this paragraph is adapted without acknowledgement from Desfontaines's introduction to his translation of *Joseph Andrews*; see above, No. 49, p. 130.

[2] Lettre II (p. 24), which follows this one, suggests a brief comparison between *Tom Jones* and *Charlotte Summers*, which had also been recently translated into French.

FIELDING'S 'NEW SPECIES OF WRITING'

103. William Warburton, a note

1751

From a note in his edition of *The Works of Alexander Pope* (1751), iv. 169. In this footnote on the history of romance Warburton says that the French were responsible for developing the modern novel.

* * *

At length this great People (to whom, it must be owned every branch of Science has been infinitely indebted) hit upon the true secret, by which alone a deviation from strict fact, in the commerce of *Man*, could be really amusing to an improved mind, or useful to promote that improvement. And this was by a faithful and chaste copy of real LIFE AND MANNERS.

In this species of writing, Mr. De Marivaux in France, and Mr. FIELDING in England stand the foremost. And by enriching it with the best part of the *Comic* art, may be said to have brought it to its perfection—

* * *

104. [Dr. John Hill], from *The History of a Woman of Quality: A Parallel between the Characters of Lady Frail, and the Lady of Quality in 'Peregrine Pickle'*

1751, pp. 3–5

Hill, in this pamphlet of self-praise, opens with a handsome tribute to Fielding.

Mr. *Fielding*, one of the greatest Genius's in his Way, that this, or perhaps any Age or Nation have produced, was happy enough, some Years ago, to strike out a new Road of Entertainment in the Relation of Occurrences, like those of real Life;[1] introduced by the Means of Characters full of Singularity, but not out of Nature. Every Man's Heart told him the Descriptions were just, while he was reading them, and every Incident had its peculiar Moral or Instruction couch'd under it, inspiring to something laudable, or cautioning against some Foible, which all Characters of a like Turn must have a Propensity to.

In the Course of these Histories our Hearts were mended, while the Imagination seemed even to ourselves all that was concerned in the

---

[1] Cf. Hill's introduction to *The Adventures of Mr. Loveill* (1750), p. 3: 'It does not appear', he remarks, that 'every writer' of novels 'can be the father of a *foundling*'. Before his violent attacks on Fielding in the 'paper war' between 'The Inspector' in *The London Daily Advertiser and Literary Gazette* and *The Covent-Garden Journal*, Hill had on other occasions called his works 'inestimable' (15 March 1750–1) and remarked: 'A chapter in the Bible, 'tis too certain, will be, to the generality of modern readers, as much a novelty as one in *Tom Jones* could be, when new fallen from the almost creative pen of its author; and I have so good an opinion, or, to use a juster phrase, so much knowledge of the present taste of the polite world, that, in spite of all their flights and wildnesses, I am persuaded a man who could give a good account of the one, would be at least as well received by the company, as he who could exert himself in comments on the other' (No. 94, collected ed., 1753, ii. 74). Hill had himself imitated *Tom Jones* in *The Adventures of Mr. Loveill*.

Attention we paid them; and we were instructed while we thought we were only entertained.

The Reception an Age like this could not but give to Works of such a Turn, is obvious: Their Success happily encouraged the Author to pursue the Plan; but as every Thing that has its good Consequences is chequered with its bad ones too, the Approbation his Pieces met with spirited up a Multitude of other People to attempt writing in the same Way, without giving themselves Leisure to enquire whether they had the requisite Qualifications; or even going so far as to inform themselves in what it was that the Merit of the original Author's Works peculiarly consisted. They perceived that Stories were told, and that People were pleased while they read them; and they seem to have concluded from this, that nothing was necessary to please, but to tell a Story.

On this judicious Plan we have had Histories, Lives, and Memoirs of Whores, of Parish-Girls, and of Lap Dogs, from Time to Time transmitted to us, almost without Number, more than almost without one Spark of the Promethean Fire of the Original.

Imitation seems of all Things in the Author's Province the most easy; but like many other Effects that appear extremely familiar, it is one of the most difficult in the Execution. An Author must be understood before he can be imitated; something like his own Genius must be found in the Man who would have his Productions carry but the faintest Resemblance of his; and Judgment must be called in to assist in determining what are the peculiar Parts most worthy to be set up as Models: For want of this we see continually Imitators strictly like their Originals in every trifling Irregularity, or little Foible, but with no one Resemblance to any of their Perfections.

★   ★   ★

105. Eliza Haywood, from *The History of Miss Betsy Thoughtless*

1751, i. 76–7

Writing of the mid-1730s:

* * *

There were no plays, no operas, no masquerades, no balls, no public shews, except at the little theatre in the Hay-market, then known by the name of F——g's scandal-shop; because he frequently exhibited there certain drolls, or, more properly, invectives against the ministry: in doing which it appears extremely probable, that he had two views; the one to get money, which he very much wanted, from such as delighted in low humour, and could not distinguish true satire from scurrility; and the other, in the hope of having some post given him by those whom he had abused, in order to silence his dramatic talent. But it is not my business to point out either the merit of that gentleman's performances, or the motives he had for writing them, as the town is perfectly acquainted both with his abilities and success; and has since seen him, with astonishment, wriggle himself into favour, by pretending to cajole those he had not the power to intimidate.

* * *

AMELIA

18 December 1751

---

106. From *Old England*

21 December 1751

A leader discusses the decline of learning in England, and especially in the novel (meaning Fielding's *Amelia*):

---

*   *   *

I shall not at present be more particular, or triumph too cruelly over the almost lifeless Corpse of poor, wretched, departing *Novel*. While She yet lives, she may avail herself of the Rights of Hospitality: but (according to laudable Custom) as soon as the Breath is out of her Body, the Public may expect the Memoirs of the deceased Lady, with a true and faithful Account of her debauched Life, Amours, &c. in the *Covent-Garden* Journal, usher'd into the World by *Goody Trotplaid*, *Justice Quidd*, and several other good Wives and eminent Gossips.

Thus will the Quill be still busy: Tho' *Romance* subside; tho' *Bedlam* & The *Mint* shall sleep; tho' the *Grubstreet Lyre* shall twang no more: yet will the *Garden Humstrum, her Worship*'s twice weekly-strung *Hurdi-gurdy,* hum out the Noise of all:—Romance & Bedlam, *Mint* & *Grubstreet,* venerable Names! will all write in the sole and pre-eminent

COVENT-GARDEN JOURNAL!

Here the Debauched, the Diseased, the Rotting and the Rotten, may be instructed and amused, if not cured and reformed: Here will be seen the quaint Device; the old *Badger* preaching Continence (in the *Aesopian* Stile) to the young *Wolf,*—The Type of *Impotence* correcting *Vice*!

*   *   *

107. Thomas Edwards, letter

23 December 1751

From a letter to Samuel Richardson, Forster MS. XII, i. f. 35. Richardson had sent off a copy of *Amelia* to Edwards, and on this fragment he has written 'On Reading Mr. F's Amelia.'

See A. D. McKillop, *Samuel Richardson, Printer and Novelist* (1936), p. 174. Thomas Edwards also expressed his disapproval to Philip Yorke, 8 January, 1752, Bodley MS. 1011, pp. 311–12: 'Just before I came out of Town I saw part of the first Volume of Amelia, and I have since read the Covent-garden Journal; from both which specimens I conclude that the Justice has spoiled the Author, and should imagine that the best way to recover his reputation would be to take away his present office and income; since it is probable that he would find his Wit when he was obliged to live by it.' For other vituperative remarks on 'Justice Dingo' (as he called Fielding), see his letters to Yorke, 19 January 1748–9 (Bodley MS. 1011, pp. 98, 101); to the Rev. Lewis Crusius, 20 January 1748–9 and 3 May 1749 (ibid., pp. 102, 130–1); and No. 116 below.

Dead small-beer . . . [Ch]ampagne. [In]deed it will never do, my dear Mr. Richardson. I thank you however for [y]our kindness, but I shall have no very great longing to see the sequel of so extraordinary a beginning. Go on my good Friend to shew these [P]eople how they ought to write. Though [y]our prescriptions may perhaps work slowly, I do not doubt but that they will mend the Age.

108. Unsigned review, *The London Magazine*

December 1751 and Appendix for 1751, xx. 531–5, 592–6

This review was reprinted in the *Ladies Magazine* (1752), iii. 83–4, 99–100, 115–16, 131–2, 147–8.

An Account of a NOVEL *lately published, intitled,* AMELIA. *By* Henry Fielding, *Esq; To which are added some general Remarks.*

VOL. I.

THE two chief persons in this novel are Mr. Booth, a young half-pay officer, and his wife Amelia, a lady of good family in the West of England, and the scene opens with Mr. Booth's being unjustly committed to prison for beating a watchman, by an ignorant and mercenary justice of peace, where Booth had his coat stript off of his back by the prisoners, because he had no money to pay garnish. Soon after his commitment a beautiful young lady, finely dressed, and full of money, was brought in, having been committed for murder, by the name of Vincent, and as she had money to pay for it, she had a room in the prison by herself; but as she passed through, Booth thought he had seen her before, and asked the keeper if her name was not Mathews.

As Mr. Booth had no money, nor any friend in town to whom he could apply, either for bail or money, he continued the first day without any thing to eat or drink, as well as without his coat; but next morning he received a packet, from whence he did not know, with a guinea enclosed; and suspecting it had been delivered to him by mistake, he made proclamation in the prison to see if any could lay claim to the packet, which several did, but none could make out their title by declaring the contents; so he applied it to his own use, by redeeming his coat, recovering his snuff-box which had been picked out of his pocket by a pretended methodist, and purchasing a dinner, to a share of which he invited a fellow prisoner, called Robinson, who had shewn him some civilities, and who in the afternoon won all the rest of his money at cards, but next day would not lend him a shilling to purchase a breakfast; so that he found himself in danger of starving in jail.

Whilst poor Booth was ruminating upon his melancholy situation, the same person that had brought him the packet, came and told him, a lady in the house (as he called the prison) desired the favour of his company. He immediately obeyed, and was conducted to the room, where he was soon convinced, that Mrs. Vincent was really his old acquaintance Miss Mathews, who upon hearing that he had asked if that was her name, took a view of him from her window, and presently recollected who he was.

Having thus met in a place where neither of them could have ever expected to have seen the other, they give each other the history of their lives, from the time of their having last seen one another.

Miss Mathews began by informing him, that he was himself the first man she was ever in love with, which he could not have missed observing, if he had not been then engaged with her neighbouring young lady, whom he soon after married, and who was then his wife. She then gave him an account how she had been inveigled and debauched by a cornet of dragoons quartered in the neighbourhood, whom her father grew so fond of, as to invite him to live in his house, and how by him she had been persuaded to elope from her father, and live with him in London as his mistress, on a promise that he would marry her as soon as it was in his power; but instead thereof, he had just married a young widow of her acquaintance who had a great jointure; and that upon her being assured of this by a letter from himself, she went directly to his house, where she had stabbed him to the heart, with a penknife which she had prepared on purpose, for which she was immediately seized, and committed to that place.

As to Mr. Booth's history he relates it thus: That, after many crosses and disappointments, he had, by means of Dr. Harrison, parson of the parish, been married to his Amelia, with whom he had fallen desperately in love, not only on account of her beauty, but on account of the patience and magnanimity with which she bore the misfortune of having her nose beat to pieces by the overturning of a chaise; and that by the doctor's means he was reconciled to her mother, Mrs. Harris, who had resolved to settle the greatest part of her estate, which was very considerable, upon Amelia and her children, and to furnish him with money to purchase a commission in the horseguards; but before this could be done, he was obliged to go with his regiment to Gibraltar, which was then besieged, leaving his Amelia big with child, and taking with him Joe Atkinson, her foster-brother, as his servant. During the siege he was twice wounded, and was the last time in such a dangerous way, that Amelia hearing of it, left her mother, and son lately born, and repaired to him at Gibraltar, where by her care he recovered; but she was taken ill, and the siege being over, he was advised to carry her to Montpelier, and got leave of absence for himself from the governor, for that purpose. Upon this Amelia wrote to her mother for a remittance, his lieutenant's pay not being sufficient for such a journey; but instead of a remittance, she received a most insolent letter from her only sister Betty, as she said, by her mother's order. Upon this Mr. Booth was obliged to apply to his friends at Gibraltar to borrow some money, which Atkinson, whom he had got made a serjeant, hearing of, he came and offered him 12l. which he had saved or got by plundering the enemy; but as Mr. Booth thought it might ruin the young fellow, he would not accept of it. At last he was furnished with what money he wanted by Capt. James, an officer in the same regiment, and with Amelia presently set out for Montpelier, where they became acquainted with major Bath and his sister, and Amelia was there brought to bed of a daughter. Amelia being perfectly recovered, as also Miss Bath, after a dangerous illness she had at Montpelier, and Capt. James being arrived there from a tour he had made to Italy, and having again equipt Mr. Booth with money, they all set out together for Paris, in which journey Capt. James fell so much in love with Miss Bath, that he soon after married her.

As Amelia, while at Montpelier, had wrote several times both to her mother and sister, without any answer, Mr. Booth at last wrote to their friend Dr. Harrison, an account of their distress for want of money, and desired him to direct his answer to Paris, which they received a few days after their arrival, with the fatal news that their mother Mrs. Harris was dead, and that she had left her whole fortune to her daughter Betty, but that their son was well, and should be taken care of, and concluding his letter with an order for 100l. upon a banker at Paris. This recruit brought them to London, from whence they set out presently for their mother's seat in Wiltshire, now inhabited by sister Betty, from whom they met with nothing but hypocrisy and insolence, but with the utmost kindness and hospitality from Dr. Harrison with whom they lodged.

Soon after their arrival here, Mr. Booth had an account, that the company in which he was lieutenant, being an additional one, was broke, and he thereby reduced to half-pay, on which it was not possible for him and his family to subsist; therefore by the doctor's advice he resolved to turn farmer, and the doctor not only let him his parsonage farm at an easy rent, but as the stocking it did not require much money, he furnished him with what was wanted. Here his wife brought forth another son, and he lived a most tranquil and agreeable life, until the doctor was called upon to attend his patron's eldest son in his travels, by which means he was deprived of the advice of that excellent friend; and being willing to increase his gains, in order to provide for his family, he took a lease of a neighbouring farm; but soon found that he had a very hard bargain, by which, and by some other mistakes, he was ruined, and forced to fly to London for fear of being arrested, where he had but just taken a lodging in the verge, and wrote to his Amelia, when a fray happened at night in the street, and as he endeavoured to assist the injured party, he was seized by the watch, carried to the Round-house, and in the morning committed to that prison.

In the interim of this mutual relation, dinner had been served up, and Miss Mathews having furnished Mr. Booth with money, they both dined with the master of the prison and his company, which consisted of the chief of the prisoners, and one Murphy, an attorney, whom the master recommended strongly to Miss Mathews for her lawyer, but he insisted upon having more money in hand than she could furnish him with. However, in a little time after, the master came to her, and told her, that the gentleman she thought she had killed, was not dead, nor in danger, so that if she took proper measures she might be bailed the next day; but she waved the discourse, being more fond to hear Mr. Booth's story, who now found that he was known, for the master called him Capt. Booth, supposed him to have been a highwayman, and told him, that Murphy and Robinson were plotting something against him.

VOL. II.

As it began to be late before Mr. Booth finished his history, the master came soon after he had done to tell them it was locking up time, on which Miss Mathews asked, after having called for a bowl of rack punch, if the captain and she might not sit up all night in her room, which the master agreed to on being paid half a guinea for the indulgence, and presently locked them up together, where they passed the night in a manner not very consistent with the rules either of chastity or constancy; and in this way they continued for a whole week, but Booth was all the time so checked by his conscience, that he began to grow melancholy, whereupon she expressed some resentment, and then shewed him a letter she had just received signed Damon, which told her, that the writer felt inexpressible horrors at hearing of her confinement, upon his arrival in town that morning; that as the man she had hurt was out of all danger, she might expect his attorney with two of his tradesmen to bail her out, and his chariot to carry her wherever she pleased.

Mr. Booth thought he knew the hand, but she did not give him time to recollect, for taking the letter she immediately shewed him what was contained in it, which was [a] 100l. bank-bill, and presently after the chariot with the attorney arrived, who brought her discharge from confinement. She returned her thanks to the gentleman, but would not make use of the chariot, pretending that she would not leave such a place in a triumphant manner; but the truth was, she would not leave it till she had procured Mr. Booth his discharge, and offered him the bank-bill, which he would by no means accept of; but at her desire, and with her money the master brought him a discharge, for she intended to have taken him along with her; in which, however, she was disappointed; for at that instant Amelia arrived, and Miss Mathews was obliged to go off in a hackney coach by herself.

Mr. Booth, with his Amelia, went away in the hackney coach that brought her, and upon his inquiring how she came to know where he was, she told him, that she heard it in the country, the news of his imprisonment having been spread thro' the whole neighbourhood by her sister. Tho' Miss Mathews had got a new lover, who not only could, but would furnish her with every thing she could reasonably desire; yet, as she was in love with Mr. Booth, and was violent in all her passions, it was but three days before she wrote to him, to let him know where she lodged, and desiring to see him; and upon his not obeying, he had, in three days more, another from her, with very strong expressions of love, but equally strong of resentment, which made him very uneasy, lest her revenge should prompt her to communicate to his wife their criminal correspondence, which he was resolved not to renew. Before his receiving this second letter, he had met with his old friend captain, now colonel James; for by the death of an uncle he had come to the possession of a large estate, and the command of a borough, for which he had got himself and his brother-in-law, major Bath, chosen members, and by that means had obtained a regiment, of which he had made his brother-in-law lieutenant colonel. Col. James shewed, that neither his friendship nor generosity was altered by his good fortune; for he not only offered Mr. Booth his interest towards obtaining a company in his regiment, but gave him a 20l. Bank bill, and said he would give him 30l. more the next time he saw him. In the perplexity Mr. Booth was under, upon receiving the second letter from Miss

Mathews, he thought he could not do better than ask the advice of his friend col. James, to whom he opened the whole affair, and shewed him the letter; whereupon the colonel told him, that if he would give him the letter, and promise upon honour never to see the lady again, he would pay her what money she had given, or advanced for him in prison, and take care that she should never trouble him any more; which he readily agreed to; but the colonel took no notice of the 30l. he had promised him, nor any notice of him the next time he saw him in the Park, at both which he was surprized, but soon found out the cause; for by a letter from Miss Mathews, full of upbraidings, he was informed, that col. James was his rival, and the very man who sent her the letter signed Damon, when she was in prison; tho' with all the expence he had been at, he had never yet obtained that favour, which she had in a manner forced Mr. Booth to accept. Having thus found out the cause of the colonel's coldness, they came to an explanation at their next meeting, and they were not only reconciled, but the colonel presented him with the 30l. he had promised, and declared, he would take the first opportunity to sollicit his preferment; soon after which, as Mr. Booth and his Amelia were walking in the Park, they met with Joe Atkinson, who was now a serjeant in the guards.

By the means of Mrs. Ellison, the landlady of the house where they lodged, they were acquainted with one Mrs. Bennet, the widow of a young clergyman, and also with a noble lord, who visited Mrs. Ellison as a relation, and who pretended to be vastly fond of Mr. Booth, protesting, that he would do him all the service in his power, which Booth was the better pleased with, as he had found himself in some measure deserted by his friend col. James; which brought on a quarrel and a duel between him and col. Bath, whom he ran thro' the body, but the wound proved not to be mortal; and this occasioned a new reconciliation with col. James, and a detection that the last breach had been occasioned by the revengeful suggestions of Miss Mathews against Booth.

From the noble lord we have mentioned, Booth received many promises, his children many presents, and Mrs. Ellison many visits, at all which she took care to have Amelia present, and sometimes Mrs. Bennet, who had now privately married serjeant Atkinson, happened to be there. At last his lordship sent Mrs. Ellison two tickets for the masquerade at Ranelagh, and she invited Amelia to go along with her, which Mr. Booth at first violently opposed, having heard something of my lord's character from col. James; but as Mrs. Ellison had said, that the present was designed chiefly on his lady's account, they were both afraid, lest her refusal might affront his lordship, and prevent his doing any thing for him; so he at last consented, and her going was resolved on, in the presence of Mrs. Bennet, who happened by chance to be there at the time. But next morning early the maid brought him a sealed note she had received from a chairman, in which were written these lines:

> Beware, beware, beware!
> For I apprehend a dreadful snare
> Is laid for virtuous innocence,
> Under a friend's false pretence.

This alarmed them both: They at first supposed, that somebody had laid a plot to betray him to the bailiffs, who, as he had been informed by Mr. Atkinson, were upon the watch for him, having been employed by the attorney Murphy; but this could no way relate to virtuous innocence, which made Amelia peruse the note a second time, and then she recollected that it was Mrs. Bennet's hand writing, which she knew by having seen a letter of hers to Mrs. Ellison, wrote at the time of her husband's death; upon which she went immediately to Mrs. Bennet's lodging to have the note explained.

VOL. III.

Mrs. Bennet gave Amelia an account of her melancholy history, from which it appeared, that Mrs. Ellison was not a relation of my lord's, but a bawd employed by him to tempt and betray the innocent; that she had been betrayed by her, which she feared had been the death of her husband, tho' the physicians imputed it to another cause, and that she was convinced, there was some such plot laid against her, which was the cause of that note. After this she confessed her being married to Mr. Atkinson, which she had scarce done, when he came in, and told Amelia of her husband's being arrested at the suit of Dr. Harrison. Mr. Booth had some time before received a very angry letter from the Doctor, then at Paris, which shewed, that some malicious tales had been wrote to the Doctor concerning him, but he thought that as soon as he saw him, he could easily convince him of their falsehood, for which he had no opportunity, as he had not heard of the Doctor's being returned to England; and he was trapanned into this arrest, while his Amelia was at Mrs. Bennet's, by a fellow in the dress of a footman, who came running, and told him, that she was taken violently ill, and carried in to Mrs. Chenevix's toy-shop, on which, without reflecting, he ran to see her, and as soon as he got out of the verge, was surrounded by the bailiffs, who carried him to their spunging-house in Gray's-Inn Lane, where he was presently attended by serjeant Atkinson, who had been told of his being arrested by a soldier that saw it, and heard the directions given to the coachman. As Mr. Booth had not yet been informed what sort of woman Mrs. Ellison was, he sent for her to join with the serjeant in bailing him; but by this time he was charged with above 400l. which was more than they could swear themselves worth; and upon Mrs. Ellison's return, she whispered to Amelia, that if she would keep her promise, and go with her to Ranelagh that evening, she would meet with one who had both the power and the will to serve her upon that occasion, notwithstanding the large sum her husband was charged with. This confirmed all that Mrs. Bennet, now Mrs. Atkinson, had said; and upon this they both came to an open breach with Mrs. Ellison, who now found herself detected.

In the afternoon Amelia was visited by col. James, who protested, that he would do all in his power for her husband's relief, obliged her to accept of a 50l. Bank bill, said a great many civil things to her, and at her desire went that very evening to see her husband, and promised to return next morning to be his bail; after which the colonel paid another visit to Amelia, and sat with Mrs. Atkinson, and her, till it had struck one. After he was gone, Mrs. Atkinson observed to Amelia, that the colonel was certainly in love with some body, and that she suspected it was with her. In the morning the colonel was attended by the faithful serjeant Atkinson, who told him, that he had procured an unexceptionable house-keeper to join with him in a bail-bond for the discharge of Mr. Booth; but instead of an answer, the colonel began to extol the beauty of Amelia, to bewail her misfortune in being married to such an imprudent man, and at last said, he could not go that day to Mr. Booth, but desired the sergeant to return to him at seven. The reason of this sudden change was, his having formed a scheme to keep Booth in prison till he could get him a commission some where abroad, and then to employ the sergeant, as his pimp, for debauching Amelia. And presently after the sergeant was gone, he sent his own wife to see Amelia, and to invite her, in the most pressing manner, to come with her children to live with her during her husband's confinement, which she had like to have consented to, but being put upon her guard by Mrs. Atkinson, she afterwards peremptorily refused.

Before the sergeant returned with the bad news to Mr. Booth, he was informed of it by the bailiff, who had been that morning with the colonel, and upon the colonel's refusing, he began to treat his prisoner with insolence, on which Mr. Booth collar'd him, and gave him such a shove, as frightened him. On this he presently called up two or three of his followers, and was just going to carry him to Newgate, when the sergeant entered; and soon after, Dr. Harrison himself, with an attorney, and the house-keeper procured by the sergeant, who joined with the doctor in a bail bond, and Mr. Booth was discharged; and the sergeant having met Dr. Harrison in the street, he carried him to see Amelia, from whom he soon learnt the falsehood of all he had heard, and upon that he not only got her husband discharged, but afterwards paid all the debts he then owed.

Presently after Mr. Booth returned, and while Dr. Harrison was with him at his lodgings, col. James entered, and tho' the colonel's visit was designed to Amelia, without knowing any thing of her husband's return before he entered the house, yet he with much gaiety went directly up to Booth, embraced him, and expressed great satisfaction at finding him there, then made an apology for not attending him in the morning, and declared he intended it in the afternoon; and the doctor and he being made acquainted, he invited him and Mr. Booth, and his lady, to dine with him the next day, which both the doctor and Booth promised; but as Amelia was now convinced of the colonel's villainous design, she seemed a little displeased with the promise her husband had made, tho' she durst not refuse going, or tell him the reason of her being displeased, for fear of its producing a duel. Accordingly they all dined there that day, and next morning Mr. Booth, at the colonel's desire, went to wait on him, when the colonel told him, that there was a company then vacant in America, which he would not only procure for him, but would lend him money to pay all his debts, on a bond not to be paid till he was colonel of a regiment; but all this on condition, that he should leave his wife and children behind him, and if he pleased, they should be welcome to stay with his wife till his return, which should be as soon as he could get him provided for at home.

This proposal Mr. Booth with great uneasiness communicated to Amelia for her approbation; but she insisted upon going with him wherever he went; and Dr. Harrison coming in, he joined with Mr. Booth in solliciting her consent, so that at last she found herself obliged to make a confident of the doctor, and having sent for him, communicated her secret reason to him, by informing him of col. James's criminal plot against her virtue, whereupon she desired his advice; but the doctor, after highly commending her conduct, said he would take time to think of it. Next day Mrs. James paid a morning visit to Amelia, and carried her and Mr. Booth to lady Betty Castleton's morning rout, where Booth met with his old acquaintance capt. Trent, and Amelia was addressed by her former lover, the noble lord, with as much freedom, as if he thought that she knew nothing to his advantage; but as he found her very much upon the reserve, he soon left her, and she prevailed on her husband to return home, after he had lost five guineas at cards.

VOL. IV.

Col. James having presented two masquerade tickets to Mr. Booth, and made a party for himself and Mrs. James, Mr. Booth and Mrs. Booth to go together, Mr. Booth insisted upon his Amelia's going; and accordingly, as Mr. Booth thought, they all went together from his lodgings. At the masquerade they soon separated, and a domino accosted the supposed Amelia, and carried her to the further end, and they sat down together, whom she soon discovered to be her old lover the peer, who presently began to make vehement love, but applied more to her avarice and ambition than to any other passion. In a little time col. James came up, and pretended to know her, but she positively insisted she knew nothing of him, which made him think he was mistaken; so that he went about for a long time in search of Amelia without finding her. As to Mr. Booth, he was soon picked up by a lady in the dress of a shepherdess, who at last discovered herself to be Miss Mathews; and he had no way to prevent her exposing both him and herself but by promising to make her a visit. The colonel soon after came up to him, and shewed him the lady he had taken for Amelia, at the same time informing him, that the domino along with her was the noble peer, her lover, and that they had been sitting there together the whole night. Whilst he was looking stedfastly at her, she beckon'd to him with her fan, on which he went directly to her, and she asked him to go home, which he readily agreed to, and they went in two chairs to his lodgings. The lady getting first out of the chair ran hastily up into the nursery, as was Amelia's custom, and he went into the dining-room, where Amelia soon came to him, in her usual dress, and found him very peevish, which surprised her. At last he asked her, who that gentleman or nobleman was with whom she had sat so long at the masquerade? And she not being able to satisfy him, she was at last obliged to tell him, that she was not there, but had privately whipt her domino upon Mrs. Atkinson who went along with them in her stead; and she being called down in her masquerade dress, confirmed what Amelia had said, which satisfied Mr. Booth, and made him, if possible, more in love with his wife than he had ever been before.

At this masquerade col. James dropt by accident out of his pocket a very serious and religious letter, without any name to it, which had been wrote to him by Dr. Harrison, against the crime of adultery; and this letter coming to the hands of Mr. Booth, who knew the doctor's hand-writing; as soon as he found it had been sent to the colonel, he began to suspect the treachery of his friend, and resolved to take the first opportunity to get him to read it in his presence, in order to discover from his countenance, whether he was guilty or no; but in the mean time, having gone to the tavern with capt. Trent, and some other officers, where they engaged at cards, Mr. Booth lost by betting not only all the money he had in his pocket, but 50l. he had borrowed from Trent. Next day Trent told him, he did not want his money, and should never ask for it, if he was never able to pay; and as Mrs. Trent had been to visit Mrs. Booth, Mr. Trent invited Mr. Booth and his lady to sup with him the next evening; and that night he and Trent went to the tavern by themselves, where Trent began to insinuate, that he might make his fortune by sacrificing his wife to the noble lord before-mentioned, or at least by getting her to play the jilt towards his lordship, which Booth said he disdained, and from thence began to conceive no very good opinion of his friend.

Whilst they were together, Amelia received a most passionate love-letter from the noble lord, in which he talked of their having been together, and of her having sollicited him for a commission to her friend, which was inclosed. This surprised Amelia, as she knew nothing of the matter; but Mrs. Atkinson, upon seeing that the commission was for her husband, began to rejoice, and said, Madam, as I was accosted by the peer, as soon as I went into the masquerade, and found that he took me for you, I encouraged a little his addresses, which were very warm and full of promises of what he would do; and as a testimony of the sincerity of his promises, I sollicited him for a commission for Atkinson, which he promised, and which you now see he has performed. Amelia thought her character might suffer by this means, and therefore began to find fault with what Mrs. Atkinson had done; on which the latter, now proud of being an officer's wife, flew into a passion, and was scolding at Amelia when Atkinson came in and Booth returned from the tavern; upon this Atkinson carried his wife out of the room, and pacified her a little; but Booth declared he would stay no longer in that house, and accordingly left it next morning.

After Mr. Booth had settled his family in their new lodging, he in his walks met a brave old lieutenant, then retired on half-pay, who had never got higher in the army, because he had nothing but his merit to recommend him; and from this lieutenant he learned the whole history of capt. Trent, which was, that he had sacrificed his own wife to the noble lord, that she was now a sort of procuress for his lordship, and that she at his expence kept an assembly for that very purpose.

Mr. Booth having sent his excuse for not supping with capt. Trent that evening, the captain, notwithstanding his promise, sent him a dunning letter next morning, which laid him under a necessity of opening the whole secret of his misfortune to his dear Amelia, who, without the least hesitation, and with alacrity, offered to pawn all the little trinkets she had left, and even her wearing apparel, to raise the money, which she accordingly did, while he was gone to an appointment with one belonging to the war-office, who pretended he could get him a commission, and upon his return, she brought him the money he wanted, with which he joyfully went to pay Trent, but found him not at home; and in his return, meeting the old lieutenant before-mentioned, was over-persuaded by him, to give the money to his friend at the war-office, who, he assured him, could do much, but would do nothing without the money in hand. This Mr. Booth complied with, and the lieutenant was to go to Mr. Trent, to make an excuse, and to obtain forbearance; but Trent was no-where to be found.

Whilst Mr. Booth was gone in search of their servant wench, who had marched off that morning, and carried most of the things her mistress had left along with her, Mrs. Atkinson came in, looking like a woman distracted, and told her, that Mr. Atkinson's concern at their quarrel had thrown him into a fever, which was so violent, that the physicians had given him over, and that he begged to speak with her before he died. At the same time she told her, that she had been with the noble lord, and had explained to him the whole affair of the masquerade; so that her character was not now in any danger on that account. Amelia went directly with her, and Mr. Atkinson, after every one was withdrawn, told her, that it was he that had stolen her little picture, which she had missed before her husband went to Gibraltar: That it was not on account of the value of it, but that he might have her lovely image always in view; and as he could not die in peace while he had it in his possession, he then restored it to her.

Mr. Booth, by chance, met with the damsel he went in search of, and got all of his wife's things restored; but as he was returning home, he met with Miss Mathews in her chair, who as soon as she saw him, bolted out, and would part with him upon no condition, but that of his promising to sup with her that night; for, says she, tho' I have failed in my first attempt, if you do not, I will take care not to fail in my second, to communicate your usage of me to your wife. Upon this Mr. Booth desired her to explain herself, and she freely told him, she had wrote to his wife a full account of their affair, but was now glad it had miscarried. As he was afraid of nothing so much as of his wife's hearing of this affair, he was obliged to promise to sup with her, and resolved to keep his promise; but with a determined purpose, not to answer the fair lady's expectations, whatever might be the event.

Before his return to his lodgings, Amelia having recovered her picture, which was set in gold with some small diamonds round it, and raised nine guineas upon it, she had provided a supper for him, which he little expected, as he had left her without so much as one shilling; but with grief he told her, that he could not sup with her, being engaged about business of the utmost importance, which she readily excused, and gave him as much of the money as he would take, which was but one guinea; he then went to keep his appointment, after a promise to return as soon as possible; and at eleven o'clock, upon a knock at the street door, and she going to open it, expecting it was her husband, she received a letter addressed to him, which she opened and read, according to his direction, as he hourly expected one from his friend at the war-office; but how was she surprised, when she found it was a letter from col. James, upbraiding him upon being that night alone with Miss Mathews at supper, and challenging him to meet him next morning at six o'clock in Hyde-park, with a severe reproach upon his breach of faith to the most inestimable jewel of a wife! But this was not all; for this was immediately followed by a letter from her husband, dated at the bailiff's house, where he had been before, and acquainting her, that he was there a prisoner at the suit of capt. Trent.

Altho' this was a misfortune, yet in her present circumstances, it was a comfort, as it shewed her, that he neither was with Miss Mathews, nor could keep any appointment with col. James the next morning. But our readers will now be curious to know how Mr. Booth came to be arrested; therefore we shall tell them, that all the kindness he had received at first from capt. Trent, proceeded from the latter's being employed as a pimp by the noble lord so often before mentioned (we wish the author had given him a name, for there are so many of the same character that it could not have been identified.) For this purpose his lordship had given the captain a bank bill of 100l. to invite Mr. Booth and his lady to his house; but upon Booth's sending his excuse, and Mrs. Atkinson's unfolding the secret of the masquerade, it was found, that nothing would do but bringing the husband into the utmost distress; upon which capt. Trent took out a writ, and employed bailiffs. At the same time col. James having heard that Miss Mathews spoke to Booth at the masquerade, he grew jealous, and ordered one of his setters to watch her lodgings, to see if Booth ever went there: This setter was likewise employed by Trent, and knew the bailiffs he had employed; so upon seeing Booth go in, he ran to the bailiffs, and had them waiting for him against he came out.

Thus he was arrested, and the good-natured forgiving Amelia went to see him the next morning, when he opened to her the whole affair between him and Miss Mathews, that they had the night before come to an open breach, and that he would never see her more. Amelia answered, that she believed all he said, but she could not then forgive him, because she had forgiven him long ago; and then shewed him the letter she had some time before received from Miss Mathews, which the latter thought had miscarried. This flung him into raptures with his Amelia; and after conjuring him not to apply to, or see col. James, she departed to go in search of Dr. Harrison, who was every moment expected in town, and whom she found at her lodgings upon her return. To him she related the whole affair of the debt for which her husband had been arrested, and of the challenge from col. James, and with some difficulty prevailed on him to go and bail Mr. Booth, which the doctor, out of compassion to their children, at last agreed to, but went first to col. James, and got him to promise upon honour, in the presence of col. Bath, not to pursue any further his resentment against Booth, which he the more readily agreed to, as he could not tell either of them the true cause of the quarrel.

Having so far succeeded, the doctor went next to Mr. Booth, and while he was waiting for another person, whom his attorney Murphy was to bring, in order to stand bail with him, the bailiff came in and told him, that a prisoner above stairs, who had been dangerously wounded that morning, by resisting arrest, desired to speak with him, and, he believed, it was to pray by him: As the doctor never refused such a call, let the person be never so poor, he went presently up to see the sick man, who began with informing him that his name was Robinson, that he formerly lived in the same town with the doctor; and lived with Murphy, who was then a practicing attorney in that town, and that he had been accessary to Mrs. Booth's undoing, for which he would now make the utmost reparation in his power. Mrs. Booth's undoing! How, by what means, cries the doctor? The other then told him, that Mrs. Harris, some time before she died, having taken a dislike to her daughter Betty, made her will, by which she gave Betty but 1000l. and left all the rest of her great fortune to Mrs. Booth, to which Murphy, himself, and another person now dead, were witnesses; but that after the old gentlewoman was dead, Murphy, at Betty's desire, secreted this will and forged a new will, by which all was given to Betty except a legacy of 10l. to Mrs. Booth, and that Murphy, himself, and that other person subscribed this new will as witnesses; and that, he believed, the real will was still in Murphy's possession, together with other writings belonging to the family, and a silver cup which he stole out of the house. By this time Murphy had returned, the doctor presently seized him, and a search warrant being obtained, the things above related were found in his chambers, together with some letters from Miss Harris, which cleared up the whole affair, whereupon he was sent to Newgate. Mr. Booth was bailed by the doctor and the justice of the peace they had employed, who invited them to dine at his house, where Amelia came to them; but they did not think proper to communicate the good news to her that night, lest she should be overpowered with joy; and next morning she received a letter from Mrs. Atkinson, with the news of her husband's being almost recovered, offering his service, weak as he was, and 20l. in money if she wanted it; which Mr. Booth now proposed to accept, but she opposed it, saying, we can never repay it, and these poor people cannot spare to lose so much money; but Mr. Booth insisted, that she should send for Mrs. Atkinson to breakfast. Accordingly she came with the 20l. along with her, after which the doctor arrived, and at breakfast the news was by degrees communicated to Amelia, whose first care was to warn her sister that she might make her escape, and to assure her, that she would never suffer her to know any distress. Miss Harris having likewise had full information from the attorney, took care to make her escape in time; and in a few days after, Mr. Booth with his Amelia and children, the doctor, capt. Atkinson, and Mrs. Atkinson, all set out for Amelia's house in the country, where they arrived amidst the acclamations of all their neighbours, and every publick demonstration of joy.

In this history, we have been obliged, for brevity's sake, to omit several episodes, and many incidents which point out the characters of the several persons introduced; but upon the whole, the story is amusing, the characters kept up, and many reflections which are useful, if the reader will but take notice of them, which in this unthinking age it is to be feared, very few will. However, there are some imperfections, as there are in all human productions. A novel, like an epick poem, should at least have the appearance of truth; and for this reason notorious anachronisms ought to be carefully avoided. In this novel, there is a glaring one; for Gibraltar has not been beseiged since the year 1727, consequently, if Mr. Booth was wounded at that seige, and married to his Amelia before it, he could neither be a young man, nor his wife a young handsome lady, when the masquerades began at Ranelagh, which is not above three or four years since. Another imperfection, in our opinion, is, that the author should have taken care to have had Amelia's nose so compleatly cured, and set to rights, after its being *beat all to pieces*, by the help of some eminent surgeon, that not so much as a scar remained, and that she shone forth in all her beauty as much after that accident as before, to the unspeakable sorrow of all her envious rivals.

Both these were owing, we suppose, to the author's hurry of business in administering impartial justice to his majesty's good people; but there is another, and a most unpardonable one, because it seems to be designed, which is his ridicule upon *Liberty*, in the second chapter of his eighth book; and since his catchpole could not tell him what *Liberty* is, we will tell him what it is not, by boldly affirming, that there can be no liberty in a country where there is not a free and independent senate or parliament, chosen by the general and uncorrupted voice of the people. There may be a shadow of *Liberty*, there may be a senate or parliament, there may be annual popular elections, nay, there may be a mild and gentle administration of government: All this they had at Rome under Augustus Cæsar; but in the reign of Augustus Cæsar, the Romans had no more *Liberty*, than they had in the reign of Tiberius, or of Nero.

This the author, as well as every honest man in the kingdom, ought seriously to consider; and as he has in this piece very justly exposed some of the private vices and follies of the present age, we hope, that in his next he will direct his satire against those who have been tempted by their ambition, vanity or avarice, to oppose every new law that could be thought of for preventing bribery and corruption; for if he does not, people will be apt to say, that he and his patrons now do, as the enthusiasts did in the days of Hudibras,

> *Compound for sins they are inclin'd to,*
> *By damning those they have no mind to.*[1]

[1] Pt. I, Canto I, ll. 215-16.

109. [John Cleland], review, *The Monthly Review*

December 1751, v. 510–15

AMELIA. *By* HENRY FIELDING, *Esq.*

12mo: 4 vols. 12s. Millar

The ingenious author of this piece is already so well known to the public for his talents in novel-writing, and especially that original turn which he gives to all his works in that way, that it would be superfluous to say any thing more of his literary character.

To give a just idea of this his last production, which, from the choice of his subject, appears to be the boldest stroke that has yet been attempted in this species of writing, will be sufficient.

The author takes up his heroine at the very point at which all his predecessors have dropped their capital personages. It has been heretofore a general practice to conduct the lover and his mistress to the doors of matrimony, and there leave them, as if after that ceremony the whole interest in them was at end, and nothing could remain beyond it worthy of exciting or keeping up the curiosity of the reader. Instead of which, Mr. *Fielding*, in defiance of this established custom, has ventured to give the history of two persons already married, but whole adventures, hardships, and distressful situations form a chain of events, in which he has had the art of keeping up the spirit of his narration from falling into that languor and flatness which might be expected from the nature of the subject; for, virtuous and laudable as the tenderness and constancy of a wife to her husband must for ever be considered, these affections are, however, too often esteemed as merely matter of pure duty, and intirely in course; so that he who does not peruse this work, will hardly imagine how the relish of such conjugal endearments, as compose the basis of it, could be quickened enough to become palatable to the reader. The author, however, has interwove such natural situations, such scenes of trial, taken from nature, that the attention is for ever kept on the stretch, and one is led on by the attraction of a curiosity artfully provoked, to pursue the *heroine* through all her adventures, and an impatience to know how the married pair will be extricated out of the successive plunges in which they are represented, and in which the writer often successfully presses vice into the service of virtue.

There have been amongst the *French* authors, and even amongst the ladies of that nation, novel-writers, who have given themselves the false air of turning conjugal love into ridicule. One of the most celebrated of them, madam *Villidieu* says expressly, '*that husbands are the last persons on earth one should love*,' and in another place, '*That regrets and tears last but a short time when a lady has only the loss of a husband to be grieved for, and that a gallant easily comforts one, upon such an occurrence.*'[1] Sentiments so loose, and libertine, as these are, might justly indispose the virtuous, and well-minded, to writings which generally speaking, ran in this vein. But be it said, to the honour of the *English*, and to this writer in particular, that he never thought so ill of the public, as to make his court to it at the expence of the sacred duties of morality. Wherever the obligation of painting the corruptions of mankind, and the world, *not as it should be, but as it really exists*, forces him into descriptions in which his actors depart from the paths of virtue and prudence, he is sure to make examples of them, perhaps more salutary, than if he had made them too rigidly adhere to their duty. Their follies and vices are turned so as to become instructions in the issue of them, and which make a far more forcible impression than merely speculative maxims and dry sentences. *Longum iter est per præcepta, breve et efficax per exempla.* Sen. Epist. 6.[2]

By this means too the author imitates nature in inforcing its capital laws; by the attractions of pleasure he puts Morality into action; it is alive, and insinuates its greatest truths into the mind, under the colours of amusement and fiction. Readers are, by the magic of this association, made to retain what has at once instructed and diverted them, when they would be apt to forget what has perhaps no more than wearied, or *dulled* them. The chief and capital purport of this work is to inculcate the superiority of virtuous conjugal love to all other joys; to prove that virtue chastens our pleasures, only to augment them; and to exemplify, that the paths of vice, are always those of misery, and that virtue even in distress, is still a happier bargain to its votaries, than vice, attended with all the splendor of fortune. So just, so refined a morality, would alone, with a candid and ingenuous reader, compensate for almost any imperfections in the execution of this work, some parts whereof will

---

[1] Catherine des Jardins, 'Madam de Villedieu'. The quotation probably comes from her *Memoires de la vie de Henriette-Sylvie de Molière* (1672; tr. 1672, 1677).

[2] 'The way is long through precepts, short and effective through examples.'

doubtless appear, admidst its beauties, to stand in need of an apology: *for example*, where the characters are, however exact copies of nature, chosen in too low, and disgustful a range of it, and rather too often repeated, and too long dwelt upon. The humours of an inn-keeper, an inn-keeper's wife, a gaoler, a highwayman, a bailiff, a street-walker, may, no doubt, with great propriety find their place in these novels, of which the matter is taken out of common life; it would even be an absurd affectation to omit them, in compliance to a false delicacy, which calls every thing *low*, that does not relate to a high sphere of life, especially when they present themselves so naturally as in many places of this author's works. But when they occur too often, when the ingredients are not sparingly mixed, they will disgust even those, who, from their distance in rank or circumstances from these subjects, may be curious to have some idea of them, and can only come at it in such descriptions.

To proceed then to a sketch of this work, the following will, it is hoped, be sufficient to give all the pre-notion of it, which is required from us.

In the first volume, the author sets out with committing his hero Mr. *Booth* to gaol, for a riot in which he was unfortunately and innocently involved; upon which occasion, the character of an ignorant, rash, mercenary, trading justice is humorously exposed. Then follow the prison scenes, which cannot please the more for being a just picture of their nature. Here he meets with a young lady who had been sent there for the murder of her lover who had slighted her, and married another, and whom upon that account she had stabbed, but as it afterwards proved, not mortally. Mr. *Booth* and Miss *Mathews* were old acquaintances, and upon their re-meeting here, the narrative of his courtship, and marriage with *Amelia*, the heroine of the piece, naturally finds its place. After which, (Volume the 2d) Miss *Mathews*, whose passions were violent, and whose heart had felt its first alarms of love, for Mr. *Booth*, which, however, had hitherto wanted the opportunity of coming to any effect, makes the forwardest advances to him, and procures herself to be *locked up* with him; so that, it appears plain enough in his excuse, that he is forced to drop the husband, and assume the gallant. This fault appears so severely punished in the consequences, not only in his own remorse for the injury done to his amiable, virtuous wife, but in the loss of a serviceable friend, and in other numerous inconveniences, all tending to establish the danger of giving way to one guilty step, in the vain hopes of impunity; that this weakness of Mr.

Booth's, becames a moral warning, and fulfills its part, in the province assigned by *Livy* to history. *Inde tibi quod imitari cupias, inde foedum inceptu, foedum exitu, quod vites.*[1] Mr. *Booth*, however, as soon as he is released from his dismal confinement, returns to *Amelia*, with redoubled fondness, and much inward remorse for his failure towards her, which his pride, and fear of too much offending her makes him keep a secret: though, when it came afterwards to be discovered, *Amelia* behaved upon it like one who knew how much fitter mildness than rage is to reclaim, or even shame, the delinquent out of the repetition of his fault.

Chapter the 6th of the 2d volume, *Amelia* is visited by one of her old acquaintance, Mrs. *James*, whose character is finely touched, and indeed excused by examples, if the number of them at least may pass for an excuse. 'What was her present behaviour more than that of a fine lady, who considered form, and show, as essential ingredients of human happiness, and imagined all friendship to consist in ceremony, curt'sies, messages, and visits? In which opinion she hath the honour of the concurrence of much the larger part of one sex and no small number of the other.'—If this is not true painting of life, as life really is, what is there can be called true painting? To strengthen these touches, the following extract will not be unwelcome, being applied to the same character. (Page 130. vol. 2.) '*Amelia* soon after took her leave, without the least anger, but with some little unavoidable contempt for a lady (Mrs. *James*) in whose opinion, as we have hinted before, outward form and ceremony, constituted the whole essence of friendship, who valued all her acquaintance alike, as each individual served equally to fill up a place in her visiting roll, and who, in reality, had not the least concern for the good qualities, or well-being of any of them.'

Here there is no taking leave of this common character in life, without inserting one fine stroke of the author's, which shows that knowledge of the human heart, by which he generally keeps up his characters to truth and nature: it is on the occasion of Mrs. *James*'s learning that her husband, Colonel *James*, was gone to fight a duel.

Vol. II. p. 166. '*Talk not to me of comfort, replied the lady; it is a loss I cannot survive; but why do I sit here lamenting myself? I will go this instant and know the worst of my fate, if my trembling limbs will carry me to my coach.—Good-morrow, dear brother, whatever becomes of me, I am glad to find you out of danger.*' The colonel paid here his proper compliments,

---

[1] 'From these examples you may choose what to imitate, while from these others, foul from beginning to end, you may know what to avoid.' Livy, *Ab urbe condita*, Praef. 10 (misquoted).

and she then left the room, but returned instantly: *Brother, I must beg the favour of you to let your footman step to my mantua-maker, I am sure it is a miracle, in my present distracted condition, how it came into my head.* The footman was presently summoned, and Mrs. *James* delivered him his message, which was to countermand the orders which she had given that very morning to make up a new suit of brocade. *Heaven knows,* says she, *now, when I can wear brocade, or whether ever I shall wear it.* And now having repeated her message with great exactness, she again lamented her wretched situation, and then departed, leaving the colonel in full expectation of hearing speedy news of the fatal issue of the battle.

   Book the IId. p. 65. Mr. *Booth* and his *Amelia*, meet by chance with Mr. *Atkinson*, a serjeant, and foster-brother to *Amelia*. This character, though taken in so low a rank, the author has raised so much into the reader's notice, and even concern, by the good qualities he bestows upon him, that he probably cannot, without pain, see him no better rewarded than by marrying a woman, debauched by a nobleman, through a cruel stratagem; in which, indeed, her innocence appears; but where the ideas of her husband dying through the consequences of it, also of herself having received the foul disease from her rather ravisher than seducer; of her taking to drinking; of her pedantry, and insulting this her second husband with the superiority of her acquisitions in *Latin* and *Greek*, all concur to make one wish this *Atkinson*, who is little less than the hero of the whole work, had been better provided for, than in such a match; especially, as it appears that 'this poor and humble swain' had entertained from his tenderest infancy, 'a plain, honest, modest, involuntary, delicate, heroic passion for the fair *Amelia*,' which he never declared to her till he apprehended himself to be on his death-bed, when he reveals the secret to her, and restores to her her picture, which he had secreted, through a species of felony, easily forgiven in love, which picture afterwards becomes the instrument of recovering Mr. *Booth* and his *Amelia* out of all their distresses. The 3d and 4th volumes are made up of the several difficulties, in which this otherwise happy pair are involved; partly through the criminal designs of false friends upon the fair *Amelia*, and partly through the misconduct of Mr. *Booth* himself, in many points of life; in which his errors of vivacity and inadvertence, appear rather the misguidances of his head, than of his heart, and are contrasted by the constancy of good-sense, and of every virtue which can heighten, and place the character of his heroine *Amelia* in the fairest light for praise and imitation. She is painted, in fine, as the model of female perfection, formed to give the greatest and justest idea of domestic happiness. She fills every character, in every scene, in every situation, where the tender, agreeable wife, the prudent fond mother, and the constant friend can have leave to shine.

The two episodes of the stories of Miss *Mathews*, and Mrs. *Bennet*, contribute a due share towards unravelling the plot of the history.

110. Pierre Clément

1 January 1752

From Lettre XCI, in *Cinq années littéraires* (The Hague, 1754), iii. 267–80.

Your reception of *Betsy*[1] was so unfavourable, Monsieur, that I am not sure whether I should send you *Amelia*. This is a new novel of our best craftsman, Mr. Fielding, whom you will surely not accuse of having no thoughts; for it is clear, if I am not mistaken, that he has seriously planned to make up four volumes. I acknowledge that the digressions appear long and frequent, but they are perhaps there to bring out the background of the picture, which had need of shadows. The erudition might appear to you at first as equally trivial and misplaced, but as one credits it to the ridiculous or semi-ridiculous characters, whom it weighs down excessively, it must form that kind of pleasantry which we call *humour*, of which you have no idea, nor I much more. As to details that are low, petty, and puerile, I would partially acknowledge the justice of your criticism; but you are of a delicacy so disdainful, you other Frenchmen, that to be pleased you have to have the grand, the noble, or at least the graceful. Nothing is too low in nature for a truly noble being, and it is with a pride far superior to yours that I dare admire the pictures of prison, tavern, and gibbet, of scoundrels deserving execution, gaolers deserving to hang, and magistrates to be pilloried, of which the

[1] Eliza Haywood, *The History of Betsy Thoughtless* (1751).

work I announce to you is formed. They are pictures from the hand of a master, for you must know that Mr. Fielding is a justice of the peace or district superintendent, that he has surprised Nature in *flagrante delicto,* has closely copied her, and there is no execrable object with which he is not familiar. . . . Compare his novel with a work serving as a history of the mores of the eighteenth century: both have the same end. If in each subordinate profession (for there are always enough portraits of people of the first rank) there happened to be someone who had enough talent, taste, and time to paint for us indiscriminately all that falls under his eyes, what a gallery would he form! what instruction for the little people and what amusement for the philosopher! Agreed, this may not be your favourite passtime; for myself, I would like to spend whole days at White's.[1] But pray do not judge the taste of our nation by mine; although no one can accuse me of singularity, I suspect I could find many people of a restive humour who do not value the manner of Mr. Fielding as much as I do; who would willingly strike out of his book all the digressions which break the interest, all the reflections that cool the sympathy, and all the details that appear to debase or that show the author (and above all the justice of the peace) a party to the humour which they find displaced. They would begin by suppressing the first five chapters, reduce the rest by half, and even after that reduction demand more. . . .

[He cursorily describes the characters—Amelia, Miss Bennet, Booth, James, Miss Matthews, Major Bath, Dr. Harrison, and Sergeant Atkinson; he alludes facetiously to Amelia's ruined nose, and concludes:]

All the same, read the book and do not believe all the slanders you have heard: one cannot deny Mr. Fielding much spirit, imagination, sensibility, and sprightliness.

---

[1] Coffee- and gambling-house in St. James's Street.

111. Lady Orrery, letter

6 January 1752

From a letter to Lord Orrery, *The Orrery Papers,* ii. 285–6.

MY DEAREST LORD,—I wrote a good many Letters last night in hopes of being able to goe on with Swift this day,[1] and writing to Garrick. but a horrid head Ach will not possibly allow me to goe thro this worke, indeed, I belive it was occasioned by reading so much of *Amelia* last night till it was very late, which I have finished, but cannot say it has given me equal pleasure with *Tom Jones* or *Joaseph*[2] *Andrews.* it certainly is his own history, the Love part foolishly fond *beneath the dignity of a man. Amelia* vastly good, but a little silly. I think she is dead many years in reality. the Prison and Baliff Sceans very well. the Catastrophy of recovering their fortune unnatural. Amelia's conduct in carrying her Children to *my Lord* foolish and indiscreet. Mrs. Atkinson's character neither uniform nor natural, the only good stroke in it making so learned a lady also a drunken Lady. Miss Mathews the most consistant character in the book. however, his observations on the abuse of laws, and his moral discourses are very well. but all together it is tedious.

✶   ✶   ✶

[1] Orrery's *Remarks on the Life and Writings of Dr. Jonathan Swift* (1752).
[2] As in the original.

112. 'C.D., F.R.S.', *The London Evening Post*

16–18 January 1752

Verses which were reprinted in the *General Advertiser*, 18 January.

To prop the tott'ring Credit of his own
H——l[1] roars out, *F——g*'s Spirit's dead and gone.
What hear we now, astonish'd Readers cry,
No Spirit in the Scenes of *Amely*!
Where Wit with Sense, Instruction with Delight,
Keeps pace; where Virtue shines in purest white:
Where keenest Satire plays the justest Part;
Stings deep, and only stings the guilty Heart;
No Spirit there! Quoth Clencher, by my troth,
He's thinking on his own dear Idol Froth.

[1] Dr. John Hill.

113. Mary Granville (Pendarves) Delany, letter

18 January 1752

From a letter to Mrs. Dewes, in *The Autobiography and Correspondence of Mary Granville: Mrs. Delany*, ed. Lady Llanover (1861), iii. 79.

---

*   *   *

We are reading Mr. Fielding's Amelia. Mrs. Don. and I don't like it at all; D.D. won't listen to it. It has more a moral design than either appears in Joseph Andrews or Tom Jones, but has not so much humour; it neither makes one laugh or cry, though there are some very dismal scenes described, but there is something wanting to make them touching. I shall be glad to have your opinion; some *few* people here like it. Our next important reading will be Betty Thoughtless;[1] I wish Richardson would publish his *good man*, and put all these frivolous authors out of countenance.

*   *   *

[1] By Mrs. Haywood: See No. 105.

114. [Henry Fielding], *The Covent-Garden Journal*

25 and 28 January 1752, i. 178–80, 186–7

Fielding summarizes the criticisms of Amelia—without very much exaggeration—and replies to them.

The page references in the title refer to the edition of G. E. Jensen (1915).

★　★　★

Proceedings at the Court of Censorial Enquiry, *Etc.*

(Amelia *was set to the Bar.*)

COUNSELLOR TOWN. May it please you, Mr. Censor, I am of Council in this Case, on the side of the Prosecution. The Book at the Bar is indicted upon the Statute of Dulness, a very antient Law, and too well known to need much expatiating upon. But it may be necessary to observe, *that that that* is Dulness in one Age, is not so in another, and what says that antient Sage, and Lawgiver, Horace;

> *Ætatis cujusque notandi sunt tibi mores.*
> *Every Writer is to observe the Manners of the Age.*[1]

I know the Word *ætatis* is, in this Place, by some Lawyers, understood in another Sense; but what I contend for, is, that it may very well be understood in that Sense that I have here given to it: and, accordingly, the same Horace lays it down as a Rule,

> *Et prodesse volunt, et delectare, poetæ.*
> *Poets desire to get Money, and to please their Readers.*[2]

For so I read the Law, and so I render it. A very good Law it is, and very wholesome to the Writers themselves.

Now the Humour, or Manners, of this Age are to laugh at every

---

[1] *Ars Poetica*, l. 156.
[2] ibid., l. 333 (slightly misquoted).

Thing, and the only Way to please them is to make them laugh; nor hath the Prisoner any Excuse, since it was so very easy to have done this in the present Case; what, indeed, more was necessary, than to have turned the Ridicule the other Way, and, in the Characters of Dr. Harrison, and Amelia herself, to have made a Jest of Religion, and the Clergy, of Virtue, and Innocence?

Here the Council was hastily stopt by the Censor, and desired to proceed to his Proofs.

TOWN. We shall prove then, to you, Sir, that the Book now at the Bar, is *very sad Stuff;* that Amelia herself is a *low* Character, a *Fool,* and a *Milksop;* that she is very apt to faint, and apt *to drink Water,* to prevent it. That she once *taps a Bottle of Wine, and drinks two Glasses.* That she *shews too much Kindness for her Children,* and is too apt *to forgive the Faults of her Husband.* That she exerts *no Manner of Spirit,* unless, perhaps, in supporting Afflictions. That *her concealing the* Knowledge of her Husband's Amour, when she knew he had discontinued it, was *low and poor.* That *her not abusing him,* for having lost his Money at Play, when she saw his Heart was already almost broke by it, *was contemptible Meanness.* That she *dresses her Husband's Supper; dresses her Children;* and *submits* to the Thoughts of every servile Office. That she once mentions THE DEVIL, and as often swears BY HER SOUL. Lastly, That she is a Beauty WITHOUT A NOSE, I say again, WITHOUT A NOSE. All this we shall prove by many Witnesses.

We shall likewise prove that Dr. Harrison is a very *low, dull, unnatural,* Character, and that his arresting Booth, *only because he had all imaginable Reason to think he was a Villain,* is unpardonable.

That Colonel Bath is a *foolish Character, very low, and ill-drawn.*

That the Scene of the Goal [*sic*] is *low and unmeaning,* and brought in by Head and Shoulders, without any Reason, or Design.

That the Abbé is supposed to *wear a Sword;* in short, not to descend to too many Particulars, which you will hear from the Mouths of the Witnesses, that the whole Book is a Heap of *sad Stuff, Dulness, and Nonsense;* that it contains no Wit, Humour, Knowledge of human Nature, or of the World; indeed, that the Fable, moral Character, Manners, Sentiments, and Diction, are all alike bad and contemptible.

All these Matters, Sir, we doubt not to prove to your Satisfaction, and then we doubt not but that you will do exemplary Justice to such intolerable sad Stuff, and, will pass such a Sentence as may be a dreadful Example to all future Books, how they dare stand up in Opposition to the Humour of the Age.

A great Noise was now heard in the Court, and much female Vociferation; when the Censor was informed, that it was a married Lady, one of the Witnesses against Amelia, who was scolding at her Husband for not making her Way through the Crowd.

Mr. TOWN then moved, that, as there were several Persons of great Fashion, who were to be Witnesses in this Cause, Room might be made for them by the Officers, which was ordered accordingly.

C. TOWN. Call Lady *Dilly Dally.*—(*She appeared*) Mr. Censor, we call this young Lady to the Character of Amelia, and she will give you an Account of all the low Behaviour I have opened.—Lady *Dilly,* your Ladyship knows the Prisoner at the Bar?

L. DILLY. I cannot say I ever saw the Creature before. (*At which there was a great Laugh*)

C. TOWN. I thought your Ladyship had said that Amelia was sad Stuff from Beginning to End.

L. DILLY. I believe I might say so.—Eh! I don't always remember what I say; but if I did say so, I was told it.—Oh! yes, now I remember very well, I did say so, and Dr. Dosewell, my Physician, told me so.— The Doctor said, in a great deal of Company, that the Book, I forget the Name of it, was a sad stupid Book, and that the Author had not a Bit of Wit, or Learning, or Sense, or any Thing else.

COURT. Mr. *Town,* you know this is only Hearsay, and not Evidence.—

C. TOWN. I do not contend for it. We shall call the Doctor himself by and by.—We will give your Ladyship no further Trouble.

L. DILLY.—I am heartily glad of it.—Mr. Censor, if you are the Judge, I beg, as you have brought me into this odious Place, you will see me safe out again.

Orders were then given to clear away the Crowd, which was very great, and Lady *Dilly* got safe to her Chair.

*   *   *

A Great Number of Beaus, Rakes, fine Ladies, and several formal Persons with bushy Wigs, and Canes at their Noses, pushed forward, and offered themselves as Witnesses against poor Amelia, when a grave Man stood up and begged to be heard; which the Court granted, and he spoke as follows.

'If you, Mr. Censor, are yourself a Parent, you will view me with Compassion when I declare I am the Father of this poor Girl the Prisoner at the Bar; nay, when I go farther, and avow, that of all my

Offspring she is my favourite Child. I can truly say that I bestowed a more than ordinary Pains in her Education; in which I will venture to affirm, I followed the Rules of all those who are acknowledged to have writ best on the Subject; and if her Conduct be fairly examined, she will be found to deviate very little from the strictest Observation of all those Rules; neither Homer nor Virgil pursued them with greater Care than myself, and the candid and learned Reader will see that the latter was the noble model, which I made use of on this Occasion.

'I do not think my Child is entirely free from Faults. I know nothing human that is so; but surely she doth not deserve the Rancour with which she hath been treated by the Public. However, it is not my Intention, at present, to make any Defence; but shall submit to a Compromise, which hath been always allowed in this Court in all Prosecutions for Dulness. I do, therefore, solemnly declare to you, Mr. Censor, that I will trouble the World no more with any Children of mine by the same Muse.'

This Declaration was received with a loud Huzza, by the greater Part of the Spectators; and being allowed by the Court, was presently entered of Record. Then Amelia was delivered to her Parent, and a Scene of great Tenderness passed between them, which gave much Satisfaction to many present; some of whom, however, blamed the old Gentleman for putting an End to the Cause, and several very grave and well looking Men, who knew the whole Merits, asserted, that the Lady ought to have been honourably acquitted.

Then the Court adjourned to Saturday, Feb. 1.

115. Sarah Chapone, letter

11 February 1752

From a letter to Elizabeth Carter, *The Works of Mrs. Chapone* (1807), i. 45–7.

★　　★　　★

Mr——tells me that you are a friend to Fielding's Amelia. I love the woman, but for the book—it must have merit, since Miss Carter and some few more good judges approve of it. Are not you angry with the author, for giving his favourite character such a lord and master? and is it quite natural that she should be so perfectly happy and pleased with such a wretch? A fellow without principles, or understanding, with no other merit in the world but a natural good temper, and whose violent love for his wife could not keep him from injuring her in the most essential points, and that in circumstances that render him utterly inexcusable. Can you forgive his amour with that dreadful, shocking monster, Miss Mathews? Are we to look upon these crimes as the failings of human nature, as Fielding seems to do, who takes his notions of human nature from the most depraved and corrupted part of it, and seems to think no characters natural, but such as are a disgrace to the human species? Don't you think Booth's sudden conversion a mere botch to save the author's credit as a moral writer? And is there not a tendency in all his works, to soften the deformity of vice, by placing characters in an amiable light, that are destitute of every virtue except good nature? Was not you tired with the two first volumes? What think you of Mrs. Bennet and her story? Pray let me have your sentiments at large on this book, for I am uneasy to know how it comes to pass that you like it, and I do not. The last volume pleased me very well; Doctor Harrison's character is admirable; the scene between Colonel James and his lady, excellent; that in which colonel James's challenge comes to the hands of Amelia is extremely affecting; the conversation between the Lord and Doctor Harrison, the doctor's letter, and the comments of the bucks upon it, I also admire very much. And now, I think, I have mentioned all that I can praise in the whole book; but it would take up more paper than I have left to point out one half of the pages that disgusted me.

*　　*　　*

116. Anne Donnellan, letter

11 February 1752

From a letter to Samuel Richardson, Barbauld, iv. 55–6.

*　　*　　*

I rejoice to find you proceed in the noble design of shewing the man of virtue in all the different circumstances of social life. But what can you mean by seeming uncertain whether you shall publish it? and how can you be so cruel to your own generation, as to think of leaving it to another? Is it that we do not want such a pattern, or that you imagine there are others can give it better? Will you leave us to Capt. Booth and Betty Thoughtless for our examples? As for poor Amelia, she is so great a fool we pity her, but cannot be humble enough to desire to imitate her. But pray, Sir, you that desire women should be learned, what do you say to Mrs. Atkinson? Must we suppose that if a woman knows a little Greek and Latin she must be a drunkard, and virago? Now, perhaps, you have not read this stuff, but I desire you will, and then I think your conscience must make you publish. Poor Fielding, I believe, designed to be good, but did not know how, and in the attempt lost his genius, low humour. Who the author of Betsy Thoughtless is I don't know, but his poetic justice I think very bad: he kills a good woman to make way for one of the worst, in my opinion, I ever read of; but I only mention these, to excite Sir Charles Grandison to rescue us out of their hands.

*　　*　　*

117. Thomas Edwards, letter

12 February 1752

From a letter to the Rev. Mr. Lawry, in 'Letter Book of Thomas Edwards,' Bodley MS. 1011, pp. 331–2.

★   ★   ★

This winter has been a very barren one, to me at lest [*sic*] of literary productions; I have seen nothing but Amelia, and that I do not half like; His Heroes are generally good-natured Fellows, but not honest men; and indeed I think, if Hogarth and he knew their own talents, they should keep to the Dutch manner of painting, and be contented to make people laugh, since what is really great seems to be above their powers. Somebody says, a great Poet must be a good man; I hope the observation is true, but I do not call all great Poets who write a great many verses; This however I think seems certain, that a man will but weakly describe passions and affections which he himself cannot feel; there will be a certain stiffness, as we see in copying a picture, which will make it fall vastly short of that freedom and nature which shews itself in a good original.

I think it scarce possible not to feel this difference between the Author I just now mentioned and my friend Mr Richardson whenever they attempt to describe either the great or the tender sentiments of the mind; the one we see every moment does *personam gerere*,[1] he is an Actor, and not a Garrick neither, the other is the thing itself.

★   ★   ★

[1] represent a character.

320

118. [Bonnell Thornton], *Have at You All: or The Drury-Lane Journal*

13 February 1752, pp. 102–7

A piece entitled 'A New Chapter in Amelia'. Casual, and some-times focused, criticism of *Amelia* and *The Covent-Garden Journal* runs through Thornton's *Drury-Lane Journal*; for example, he says he will employ the jargon of prison and sponging-houses, 'tho' I should be forced to attend the Thief-catcher's Office in *Covent-Garden*, or ransack *Amelia* for them' (No. 1, 16 January 1752, p. 5). The papers are essentially personal attacks on 'Justice Scribble', but in the first number he publishes a parody advertisement:

This Day is published,

(In four Volumes Duodecimo, with the help of Dedication, Introductory Chapters, long Digressions, short Repetitions, polite expletives of Conversation, genteel Dialogues, a wide Margin, and large Letter, Price but 12s.)

SHAMELIA, a Novel.[1]

Then followed a series of parodies that are sometimes revealing as criticism.

A NEW CHAPTER in AMELIA.

More witty than the rest, if the Reader has but sense enough to find out the Humour.

Amelia, finding her husband did not come home, sat herself down con-tented to her supper, which consisted of no other variety than a Welch rabbit, and of which I have told my reader she was particularly fond.

---

[1] The same idea appears in *Some Observations on the Writers of the Present Age* (1752), p. 30: claiming that he wishes to praise the art of printing, the author says, 'What I mean, is to celebrate that Art by which *Amelia* became four Volumes, and the Remains of Lord *Bolingbrooke* were lengthened into two.'

Her little family were squatted upon the hearth close by her knees, and knawing each of them an huge luncheon of bread and butter, with windows cut upon it, and strew'd with brown sugar. Poor Mrs. Atkinson, who had taken too large a sip of the Cherry Brandy bottle that evening, had loll'd herself back against her chair by the fireside, and sat snoring.

The disconsolate turtle was lamenting the long absence of her mate, when the old decrepit magistrate of the night went his rounds, and with an hearty bounce at the door proclaim'd it—past twelve o'clock, and a frosty morning. Booth was not yet return'd; and Amelia, who was sitting all the while upon tenter-hooks, had enough to do to quiet her babes, who incessantly worried her with, Mammy!—where's Pappy? —Mammy!—where's Pappy?—Mammy!—where's Pappy?

'He's coming presently,' cried the fond mother, 'he's but gone to buy a Dilly-cock for pappy's nown children to shy at.'—And she comforted them as well as she could, with singing *Dance over the Lady Lea*, and telling them merry stories about murder.

At length a very violent knocking was heard, which almost beat the door down, and made the house ring again: The children squall'd out: Mrs. Atkinson started, and endeavouring to get up, fell off her seat sideways: Amelia's gentle spirits were so much agitated, that if she had not gulp'd down some small oats, which she had warm'd in a tin cup at supper, she must infallibly have fainted away. As it was, she had no power to wag, but sat upright in her chair with both arms expanded, stiff and motionless, all the same as if she had been ty'd to a stake, or put into the ducking stool.

Little Betty burst open the door, and ran in, frighten'd out of her seven senses. 'La, Mistress,' says she, 'here's Master com'd home, as drunk as a piper; to be sure, he's in a woundy sad pickle, that sartain: he's all over of a gore of blood, and as nasty!—I wouldn't touch him with a pair of tongs.'

During this, there was a great rumbling upon the stairs; when presently Serjeant Atkinson led the staggering Booth in; and, as he held him out at arms length with one hand, pinch'd his own nostrils close together between his thumb and fore-finger with the other. Amelia was just going to have her old qualms again, but taking heart and another gulp of beer, she flew into her husband's arms, clasp'd him round the middle, and immediately fell a whimpering: nor did she perceive the nasty souse he had been swash'd in, till her delicate nose scented something about him not very savoury.

'Are you hurt, my dear, any wheres?' cried the tender Amelia. 'Hiccup,' says Booth, and what he had never been guilty of before, belch'd in her lovely face. She then clap'd him down upon a chair, and was going to wipe his mouth with her muckender: but what was her consternation, when she found his high-arch'd Roman Nose, that heretofore resembled the bridge of a fiddle, had been beat all to pieces! As herself had before lost the handle to her face, she now truly sympathis'd with him in their mutual want of snout.

But it was more than she could bear, when she came to search his breeches, and found nothing in them: for she had put a crooked shilling (the only one they had in the world, and which had been long kept for luck's sake) into his pocket, before he went out, that he might appear like a gentleman.

Atkinson by this time had rais'd his wife, who, in the tumble, got a great bump upon her nob, and was gone down to fetch some brown paper and vinegar. As soon as Mrs. Atkinson spy'd the queer figure Booth cut with his flatten'd proboscis, she set up an horse-laugh; and as she is an old dab at latin, especially when tipsy, she pour'd out the following scraps from Virgil and Horace.

'Monstr' horrend' inform' ingens, cui lumen ademptum!
Hoc magis esse velim, quàm pravo vivere naso
Spectandum nigris oculis, nigroque capillo.'

'Ha' done with your Nasos, and your Negroes, (quoth Amelia in a pet) and don't ye laugh at other people's haps'.—'Why, Madam, (replied Mrs. Atkinson, a little dumb-founded) sure a body may talk Greek, mayn't one, without'—here a hiccup opportunely cut the thread of her sentence. 'God bless you, poor woman! (cries Amelia, and lifted up her hands.)' 'God bless me! (says Mrs. Atkinson, snapping her up); God bless you; I have no more need of God's blessing than you—Madam!'

Little Betty, coming in at this instant with a pail of water, put a stop to the dispute, which other wise might have ended in the destruction of caps. Serjeant Atkinson was permitted to apply the plaister to his wife's forehead, which help'd to cool her brains. All hands were now aloft in assisting to sweeten poor Booth, who, after having puk'd awhile, recover'd his senses sufficiently to remember how he came in this condition.

The sum of it is this: Capt. Trent had carried him, by main force, to the nobleman's so often mentioned in this history, who ply'd him so with burgundy and champaigne, that Booth cross'd the streets all the way in reeling home. He had thought enough to know he could not muster up the dust to pay the hire of a chair, having dispos'd of his last and only hog to the footman at the door.—In his way he unfortunately stumbled against a tub, which the Nightmen had left standing in the middle of the street; knock'd his nozzle against the brim of it, and fairly (I should rather say, foully) tumbled into it: where he must have been smother'd in the ordure, had they not come to his assistance, and help'd him out. In this stinking condition he swagger'd home by himself, not being able to tell them where he lodg'd.

After they had put Booth to bed, the Serjeant and his crooked rib took themselves away, and retired to rest; Amelia did the same, as soon as she had disposed of her little nursery, who were sent down, and kept below stairs during what has been related in the conclusion of this chapter. She comforted herself with the old proverb, that——*luck was good luck*, as it indeed proved to Booth. But what the good fortune consequent to this accident was, the Reader, if he has any nose at all, may smell out in the next chapter.

N.B. We could have split this into innumerable breaks, according to the example of the original, which would have spun it into two pages more; but we chuse to crowd as much matter into our numbers we can, that nobody may complain they have not an exceeding good THREEPENNY-WORTH for their THREE-PENCE.

119. [Matthew Maty], review, *Journal Britannique*[1]

February 1752, vii. 123–46

The story of a married couple who, despite their virtue, are exposed to the most severe trials, and who in the thick of their setbacks never stop loving each other, makes the subject of this work. From this Mr. Fielding intends to make us see how much the pure pleasures of the conjugal union prevail over all other joys. He wishes to demonstrate the delicacy and, if I dare to say it, the severity of this union; that if true virtue is the foundation, true happiness follows. Under a thatched roof, dressed in rough homespun, even deprived of liberty, one can still be happy. The sweetest consolation is that which obtains innocence, the severest punishment is that which one finds in his heart. These truths are revealed in twenty treatises, but one yawns reading them, and few readers are tempted to do that while holding *Amelia*.

Perhaps I have said too much. Our country abounds in critics, and one blushes to be moved. Ashamed to have wept, one closes the book to condemn the author. The faults revolt, the sentiments escape. To a large extent we sacrifice the simple and useful for the graceful. Carping critics, frivolous petit-maîtres: I neither contest nor envy your taste. You know the rules; you are familiar with the great world; you decide wonderfully well the proprieties. The only thing you lack is well expressed by the old man of Terence: *Homo sum; humani nihil a me alienum puto.*[2]

Let us not push enthusiasm too far; let us agree ingenuously that in this work the faults are joined with beauties. I think I can say that some of the incidents are unnatural or badly brought about, that the denouement is neither well prepared for nor sufficiently explained, that there is not enough nobility or consistency in various characters, that the

[1] Translated from Maty's French. The passages Maty quotes from *Amelia* have been adjusted to Fielding's words when possible (Maty is, of course, citing the English version), but when the deviation is too great Maty's version has been followed.

[2] 'I am a man, and nothing in man's lot can be indifferent to me' (Terence, *Heauton Timorumenos*, I. 77).

remote digressions and displaced erudition uselessly lengthen the novel. But I like to pardon these errors in an author whose pen is no less chaste than spiritual, and who equally unveils Nature and ennobles humanity. 'The good-natured reader,' says Mr. Fielding himself, 'if his heart should be here affected, will be inclined to pardon many faults for the pleasure he will receive from a tender sensation: and for readers of a different stamp, the more faults they can discover, the more, I am convinced, they will be pleased' ['Dedication to Ralph Allen, Esq.'].

The citizen and the magistrate appear no less in this work than the philosopher and the Christian. The post occupied by Mr. Fielding puts him in a position to observe equally the faults of his compatriots and those of their laws. A perfect administration exists only in theory, and great advantages are purchased only by great inconveniences. In a country where liberty is the idol of the people, it is difficult to avoid license. In order to induce a nation so jealous of its rights to sacrifice some of them, it is well to demonstrate that he who inordinately fears a master is in every respect the slave, the victim of the vilest tyrants. Athens considered itself free but allowed the banishment of Aristides and the destruction of Socrates. Senseless people, know your tyrants, Anytus, Aristophanes, and the gross boor who could not write the names of the men he wished to banish.

Too many serious reflections could alienate the readers for whom this article is intended. From the promise of its title they expect adventures. The journalist ought to satisfy their curiosity. He should try to amuse them or move them, and, assembling the principal beauties of his original, reproduce what the author has already made, even if in place of four volumes he has been limited to a sheet.

A prison first reveals Captain Booth, the hero of this work. He is a brave officer who, as repayment for his services during the war, lacks bread during the peace. On his half pay he is reduced with his family to sinking into debt, skulking to avoid his creditors, and despite all his precautions, to spending part of his life in prison. Contempt for a constable and the partiality of a magistrate appointed to keep the law has at the moment lodged Booth in this sad place. He is absolutely without a penny and mingled with the scum of the human race. A self-seeking jailer, an atheist card sharp, and a bigotted robber are shown to advantage. The centre of the scene is occupied by a girl of twenty years who, among the charms of her sex, has preserved only her beauty. Victim of a fiery temperament, an excessive vanity, and neglected education, Miss Matthews has been seduced by a perfidious wretch, whom she has tried to punish with a blow of the knife; but the hand was too weak, the blow not deep enough. He was believed, however, to be dead of the wound, and his murderer was arrested. She congratulates herself on having done to death her perjurer and glories in her vengeance. One sees her successively weep in her first weakness, brave a punishment which seems to her inevitable, and rekindle a passion for the husband of Amelia. In general vice is more generous than virtue, and what is money to an amorous courtesan? Miss Matthews profusely provides for the needs of her dear Booth. She recounts to him her adventures, with that steadfastness which in certain souls appears to ennoble the crime; she hears the recital of his own adventures with the curiosity of a woman and the avidity of a rival. In each tender scene that he recounts she puts herself in the place of Amelia. Her sighs, her glances, some words of interruption give the husband an idea of her feelings. She does more (forgive me, Mr. Fielding, has virtue so little power over our sex?), by her advances and her kindnesses she catches him in momentary weaknesses. These weaknesses, joined with his passion for gaming, are the cause of Booth's principal misfortunes.

His wife is the beautiful and virtuous Amelia. He had begun to love her at the same time that a cruel accident had broken her nose. She had become the object of insults from her sex and disgust from ours. A lover who presents himself under such circumstances deserves to be well received, and Amelia becomes attached to him who cherishes her even without her nose. It is not made clear how she recovered a member so essential to a beautiful face; but apparently a clever surgeon fixed it because after her marriage there is hardly a man who does not become amorous with her or a woman who does not envy her. Judge to what all this leads and whether an indigent husband and a woman as lovable as wise have not much to suffer.

Colonel James, a friend of Booth, after having seen Amelia, and moreover being jealous of Miss Matthews, cannot forgive the captain for being more loved than he by his mistress and for possessing an incorruptible wife. His kindly feeling cannot hold up against two beautiful eyes. He is not the only one whom Amelia has subjugated. A young Lord, as hot in his emotions as inconstant in his attachments, finds in Amelia's resistance a goad to his love. Were she to surrender, a single day would complete his triumph. Ruses, solicitations, presents, all are tried, and all prove useless. Booth's wife, warned by a member of her own sex who has been the victim of this Lord's artifices, happily avoids the same snares. She does not, however, completely imitate the example of Marianne in returning to her M. de Climal his presents, which she has very innocently received for her children.[1] Dishonour to any one who casts a reproach upon our heroine. She really possesses great virtue, but, as M. Clément has said very prettily, 'virtue is never under suspicion.'

Amelia's, however, is almost brought to such a pass in another circumstance. It happens at a masquerade, where her husband wants to take her and where she foresees that she might meet her admirers. She gives her domino to her friend (the Lord's former victim), who by chance has her height and voice but under the mask effects a falsetto which serves as a disguise. Even her husband is fooled; intending to follow his wife, he thinks he sees her carrying on a very lively conversation with the Lord. What a sight for a husband who had until this moment been untroubled! On returning to their house he reveals his discontent. He asks many questions, and at her doubtful answers his discontent redoubles. 'Would to heaven,' cries Booth at last, 'you had not been there!' 'Since you wish it,' replies Amelia, 'it is sweet to me to be able to indulge you in your wish. You were deceived, I was not there' (Bk. X, Chap. 3). Her friend confirms the ruse and shows herself to him in the domino under which he had thought he saw his wife, and the scene concludes with their transports.

Now for the other side: Miss Matthews, who believed she had bought Booth and, after her departure from prison, appeared to be completely ignored by him, accidentally met him and furiously threatened to reveal their intrigue to his wife. 'No more delay,' she tells him, 'I await you this evening, or you are lost' (Bk. XI, Chap. 7). The trembling husband accepts the rendezvous for fear she will not hold her tongue and with the single intention of making a final break with her. This was the only way to keep her silent. The same evening Amelia (because for some time the unfortunate couple had been reduced to doing without servants) had prepared for her husband's supper two of his favourite dishes. It was to be a gala occasion with their children joining the party. The wife tells her dear Booth, who arrives home this evening at 8:30 before going to his rendezvous, of her plans for him (Bk. XI, Chap. 8). 'At least for this evening,' she tells him, 'banish sorrow, deliver us over to joy.' A sigh from Booth announces his refusal. 'I need not tell you how uneasy it makes me, or that I am as much disappointed as yourself; but I am engaged to sup abroad. I have

---

[1] The reference is to Marivaux's *Vie de Marianne*.

absolutely given my honour; and besides, it is on business of importance.' At these words the gaiety ceases to animate the cheeks of
Amelia. With a trembling voice she repeats, 'You are leaving me this
evening.'

Unfortunate wife, what rough blows are going to overwhelm you!
You await the return of your husband at 11 and in his place comes first
a letter from James. He reproaches Booth in the strongest terms for the
rendezvous which, against his word and despite all he owed to the most
lovable wife, he had accepted with Miss Matthews. To repay this injury
he wishes to cut his throat. The paper is read by Amelia. She cannot
withstand this note which tells her of a new infidelity of her husband
—at last indignation is her first reaction, and fear only follows after
with reason. 'It is too much, too much to bear,' she cries. 'Why
did I bring these little wretches into the world? why were these
innocents born to such a fate? . . . O my children! my children!
forgive me, my babes! Forgive me that I have brought you into such a
world as this! You are undone—my children are undone!' 'How undone, mamma? my sister and I don't care a farthing for being undone,'
replies one of them with the voice so well known to a mother. 'Don't
cry so upon our accounts—we are both very well. . . . But do pray
tell us. I am sure some accident hath happened to poor papa.' 'Mention
him no more, . . . your papa is—indeed he is a wicked man—he cares
not for any of us. O Heavens! is this the happiness I promised myself
this evening?' (Bk. XI, Chap. 9).

A new letter interrupts her agonies. From whom? from that husband
who, instead of being in the arms of Miss Matthews, has been seized at
the instigation of Amelia's amorous Lord. His expressions are most
touching. He reproaches himself (indeed it appears that in Booth's soul
unhappiness is the thermometer of prudence) for having hidden from
Amelia his first false step. 'Oh my dear! had I had resolution to confess
my crime to you, your forgiveness would, I am convinced, have cost
me only a few blushes, and I had now been happy in your arms. Fool
that I was, to leave you on such an account, and to add to a former
transgression a new one!—Yet, by Heavens! I mean not a transgression
of the like kind; for of that I am not nor ever will be guilty; and when
you know the true reason of my leaving you to-night I think you will
pity rather than upbraid me' (ibid.). Amelia calms herself; a confused
glimmer tells her that her husband is more unhappy than criminal. To
know him a prisoner is less terrible than to believe him guilty. The
circumstances certainly excused the first offence; the second would have

been voluntary. The first fault Amelia knew from a letter written by Miss Matthews to revenge herself on Booth.

In the morning Amelia runs to the prison. Booth kisses her with rapture, and after having recounted all his story he urges her to forgive him. 'Forgive you,' she says, 'I cannot now forgive you the fault you have confessed; and my reason is—because I have forgiven it long ago. Here is a letter from my rival who told me of your folly and made various other accusations which I have not cared to believe' (Bk. XII, Chap. 2). After this revelation, tears of tenderness and joy run from their eyes, their souls intermingle, and for some minutes they forget all their sorrows. Their situation was, however, deplorable, and there remained no other resource than the arrival and compassion of a virtuous clergyman named Dr. Harrison.

This honest man had the principal part in their marriage, and when during the absence of Booth and his wife at Gibraltar the will of Amelia's mother had deprived her of her inheritance, which an avid younger sister had seized, he had assisted them with his advice and, that which in a clergyman is least equivocal, with his money. Finally tired of Booth's frequent imprudences, which had stretched his patience and his purse, for some time he refused Amelia's solicitations. She melted him, however, and who would not be melted by Amelia! He consents to make a last effort, but on the condition that both retire immediately to his village and live under his eyes. Happily the clouds are suddenly dispersed, for at last the novel must end. A wretch, conducted almost dying into the place where Booth is confined, asks to speak to the clergyman who is visiting there. He reveals to him the fraud of Amelia's sister: the will was forged. One easily divines the sequel. The couple are put in possession of a considerable fortune, they leave London never to return, and I think they are still living in some English county.

I would be very sorry if one were to judge *Amelia* by my delineation. The hand of some clever translator will make it better known. That honour has been done Mr. Fielding's earlier novels, and I do not imagine that the lot of *Amelia* will be different from her elders.

I have already suggested that the work is not without faults, even considerable faults. It sins in various passages against the rules of art and taste. But one also finds beauties there! What truth in the descriptions! what finesse in the dialogue! what variety in the portraits! You ingenious authors, so admired by the French, narrate admirably. There are new things in your subjects; the incidents are bound to the action, nothing is forced in your attitudes. But will I never see anything but petit-maîtres and the same petits-maîtres; financiers, abbés, some prudes, and coquettes without end? The English nation would never accommodate itself to such conformity. She wants her characters more various than the adventures, and with Mr. Fielding only the jailers resemble each other.

Booth is a husband, virtuous and tender, but open to seduction, prone to give way under misfortune, and dominated by pride. James is an officer, mechanically generous and savage, incapable of delicacy and constraint, and always ready to sacrifice his friend to the desire to debauch his wife. He himself has a wife with whom he lives as all becoming husbands are obliged to live with the person who carries their name. His very cold and frivolous other-half has passion only for spectacles, finery, and 'society'. She hates her husband not precisely because he has mistresses but because they are not of her rank. Amelia, her old friend, she considers as she would a woman who lacks equipage. For Booth she feels something a bit stronger but not as strong as love. Her brother, by whom she is tenderly loved, is Major Bath, an impractical and captious man who draws his sword at the least suspicion of foible or offense to his dignity. Aside from his duelling he is a good man and even religious.

One cannot avoid loving the model pastor, Dr. Harrison, whose only zeal is to be charitable and who feels pleasure only in making others happy. This character is not extremely common, and it would be well to describe him at length. He is marvellously contrasted with another preacher, newly returned from the university and already full of the spirit of the church (Bk. IX, Chap. 10). Intolerant quibbler, full of prejudices, and swelled underneath his frock, he reveals himself in a simple conversation, and I would recognize him if I ever had the unhappiness to see him again. I do not know if his business displeases me more than Mrs. Bennet's. She is an irresolute character, but in whom pedantry, bitterness, and vanity dispute the terrain with a rather equivocal virtue. This virtue permits her who possesses it to obtain under a mask, and on involved conditions, from her corrupter whom she detests, a company for her second husband. Whether for reason or temperament, she has honoured with this title a certain Sergeant Atkinson, who becomes captain in the manner I have just described. This honest man appears throughout the body of the novel as a virtuous and simple companion attached to Booth by gratitude and zeal. One cannot avoid the suspicion that this crude man, brought up in the same village with Amelia, has conceived for her since his childhood the most lively and silent passion. The occasion comes, however, when he declares himself, and this is when an illness reduces him to the last extremity. The avowal of his sentiments produces in the person who has given rise to them, and to whom he reveals them, a fleeting emotion, and she receives tremblingly a portrait of her he had stolen years before. I hope that the honest sergeant, for whom this miniature was all his solace, put it under his wife's bedhead. Whatever the case, it is this portrait which Amelia is later forced to pawn in order to buy necessities, which action leads to the denouement. It is recognized at the pawn-broker's by the accomplice of her younger sister, excites his remorse, and leads to his confession.

I would end here what I proposed to say about this novel; but in re-reading it I found a passage to which I cannot refrain from drawing attention. It is in the middle of a conversation that Captain Booth has with a miserable author (Bk. VIII, Chap. 5). Booth is represented as an excellent man of letters and a man of very good sense; and quite a few readers have thought that Mr. Fielding had taken the portrait from no other original than himself. Does he sustain these, however, when on the subject of translations from Lucian he doubts that one has ever rendered a good translation in French of any of the Greek authors? 'To confess the truth,' he adds, 'I believe the French translators have generally consulted the Latin only; which, in some of the few Greek writers I have read, is intolerably bad. And as the English translators, for the most part, pursue the French, we may easily guess what spirit those copies of bad copies must preserve of the original.' To hazard such a criticism it would be necessary to be sure that it is well founded. I leave to the English the case of justifying their compatriots, and content myself with asking Mr. Fielding if he would turn his eyes to the French translations of Dacier, Tourreil, Massieu, Terrasson, Gédoyn, and many others that I could name.[1]

---

[1] André Dacier translated Horace; his wife Mme Dacier translated Aristophanes, Plautus, Terence, and Homer; Jacques de Tourreil translated Demosthenes; Guillaume Massieu, diverse Latin and Greek poets; Jean Terrasson, Homer; and Louis Gédoyn, Pausanius and Quintilian.

120. [William Kenrick], from *Fun:*

a Parodi-tragi-comical Satire

1752, Scene 3

As it was to have been perform'd at the Castle-tavern, Pater-Noster-row, on Thursday, February 13, 1752, but suppress'd, by special order from the Lord-mayor and Court of Aldermen.

In this parody on Macbeth the Weird Sisters circle about their cauldron, casting in contemporary novels, periodicals, and pamphlets. At length, to insure the charm's potency, the First Witch holds up *Amelia:* 'To add to these and make a pois'nous Stench, Here take 4 Ounces of a *noseless wench*.' During the course of the action Mountain (Hill) says to Drawcansir (Fielding): ' . . . she has undone thee, Drawcansir; she has ruin'd thee.' To which Drawcansir replies:

Dr.   Dost thou join Ruin with *Amelia's Name?*
       Doth she not come replete with Wealth and Honour?
Moun. O no *Drawcansir!* She has robb'd thy Name
       Of that high Rank and Lustre which it boasted;
       Has level'd thee with Men of common Fame,
       Has made thee a Picture for the Hand of Scorn
       To point her slow and moving Finger at.
       There's not a Boy, or Porter in the Streets,
       But casts the base *Amelia* in thy teeth.

★   ★   ★

121. Samuel Richardson, letter

21 February 1752

From a letter to Thomas Edwards, Forster MSS., XII. i. f. 41; Carroll, pp. 195–6.

★　　★　　★

Mr. Fielding has met with the Disapprobation you foresaw he would meet with, of his Amelia. He is every Paper he publishes under the Title of the Common Garden Journal, contributing to his own Over-throw. He has been over-matched in his own Way, by People whom he had despised, and thought he had Vogue enough, from the Success his spurious Brat Tom Jones so unaccountably met with, to write down. But who have turned his own Artillery against him, and beat him out of the Field. And made him even poorly in his Court of Criticism give up his Amelia, and promise to write no more on the like Subjects.[1]

★　　★　　★

[1] See the *Covent-Garden Journal*, 25 and 28 January 1752, above No. 114.

122. Samuel Richardson, letter

22 February 1752

A reply to Anne Donnellan's letter of 11 February (No. 116): see Carroll, pp. 198–9.

*   *   *

Will I leave you to Captain Booth? Cap. Booth, Madam, has done his own business. Mr. Fielding has over-written himself, or rather *under-written*; and in his own journal seems ashamed of his last piece; and has promised that the same Muse shall write no more for him. The piece, in short, is as dead as if it had been published forty years ago, as to sale.

You guess that I have not read Amelia. Indeed I have read but the first volume. I had intended to go through with it; but I found the characters and situations so wretchedly low and dirty, that I imagined I could not be interested for any one of them; and to read and not to care what became of the hero and heroine, is a task that I thought I would leave to those who had more leisure than I am blessed with.

Parson Young sat for Fielding's Parson Adams, a man he knew, and only made a little more absurd than he is known to be. The best story in the piece, is of himself and his first wife. In his Tom Jones, his hero is made a natural child, because his own first wife was such.[1] Tom Jones is Fielding, himself, hardened in some places, softened in others. His Lady Bellaston is an infamous woman of his former acquaintance. His Sophia is again his first wife. Booth, in his last piece, again himself; Amelia, even to her noselessness, is again his first wife. His brawls, his jarrs, his gaols, his spunging-houses, are all drawn from what he has seen and known. As I said (witness also his hamper plot) he has little or no invention: and admirably do you observe, that by several strokes in his Amelia he designed to be good, but knew not how, and lost his genius, low humour, in the attempt.

*   *   *

[1] These statements do not require comment. See, for example, Dudden, i. 142, or, for the subsequent statement about Lady Bellaston, Cross, ii. 171–2.

335

123. Samuel Richardson, letter

23 February 1752

From a letter to Lady Dorothy Bradshaigh, Carroll, pp. 198–9.

* * *

I have not been able to read any more than the first volume of Amelia. Poor Fielding! I could not help telling his sister, that I was equally surprised at and concerned for his continued lowness. Had your brother, said I, been born in a stable, or been a runner at a sponging-house, we should have thought him a genius, and wished he had had the advantage of a liberal education, and of being admitted into good company; but it is beyond my conception, that a man of family, and who had some learning, and who really is a writer, should descend so excessively low, in all his pieces. Who can care for any of his people? A person of honour asked me, the other day, what he could mean, by saying, in his Covent Garden Journal,[1] that he had followed Homer and Virgil, in his Amelia. I answered, that he was justified in saying so, because he must mean Cotton's Virgil Travestied; where the women are drabs, and the men scoundrels.[2]

* * *

[1] 25 and 28 January 1752.
[2] Charles Cotton, *Scarronides: or, Virgile Travestie* (1664).

124. From the Preface to *The Adventures of a Valet*

1752, I. iii–v.

AN unbounded Liberty has been given to Fancy in the Novels, Adventures, or by whatever other Names may be called the Exploits and Atchievements of our late created Heroes in the Fields of Gallantry and Fortune: Their ideal Actions have been well adapted to the Characters which have been produced as the Agents: Characters which could exist only in the Imagination of their Writers; and not there unless that Imagination were in a vitiated State.

WE find, that the Distemperature of the Fluids will so far affect the Appearance at least of external Objects, that, to a green-sickness Girl, her Apron shall appear ting'd with the Colour of her Complexion; and, to the Man in a Jaundice, a Shilling shall assume the Likeness of a Guinea. These Changes, though they seem to be existent in the Things before us, are, however, no where but in our own distemper'd Organs: They are but Appearances, supported by no Foundation in Reality; and, in the same Manner the Judgment, subject to a thousand Disorders (not the less real because yet unhonoured with Names) spreads its own Colours over the Objects that offer themselves to its Contemplation. The Man, who sees human Actions distorted, describes them as he sees them, and then wonders that others of less disturbed Minds see them as they really are, and in Consequence of that declare his Pictures wholly unlike the Originals.

IT will not look like Adulation to except the Authors of *Tom Jones* and *Clarissa* from this general Censure; nor would it have been needful indeed to have named their Works, if we had but said there were two such: But how deplorable a Thought, that in an Age in which there is so uncommon, so unequalled a Multiplicity of Writers in this Way, there should be only two worthy the Exception.

* * *

THE COVENT-GARDEN
JOURNAL

4 January—25 November 1752

---

125. [Bonnell Thornton], from *Have at You All:*
or *The Drury-Lane Journal*

5 March 1752, pp. 184–8

What follows is a sampling of the parodies of Fielding's *Covent-Garden Journal* perpetrated by Thornton.

The COVENT GARDEN JOURNAL EXTRAORDINARY.

NUMB. I.

Under this title will be publish'd every Thursday an Essay in the true DRAWCANSIRIAN Stile and Sentiment.

> *Omnibus hoc vitium est* ★ POTORIBUS *atque poetis.*[1]
> HORAT.

In my last Tuesday's paper I made a serio-comical dissertation about PERRY and CHAMPAIGNE, to which I resembled the several degrees of false and true Wit. I shall now carry on the allusion of writings to liquor, of both which I am acquainted with all the several sorts, having in my unsettled course of life tasted of them all.

As there are very few palates that can distinguish what wines are neat and unadulterated, so are there very few understandings that can judge for themselves in the true relish of sheer wit and humour. Therefore, as in all the city clubs of thorough-pac'd topers one, whose

---

★ *So I chuse to read it for the present.*
[1] 'This is the failing of all DRINKERS and poets.' Cf. *Satires*, I. iii. 1.

338

experience qualifies him for that important office, always acts as caterer or taster for the rest; I would also propose that somebody, who can READ at least, should be appointed prime Critic to the public, that they may not inadvertently swallow those unwholesome draughts, which are daily cram'd down their throats by the catch-penny Wit-merchants. For this province I can recommend no one so fitting as MYSELF, having, long dabbled in these commodities, and acquir'd a just relish of their true smack and flavour.

There is no VINEYARD so fertile as that of Novels: but our modern productions in this way, which pretend to be of the truly *British* growth, are compounded of an unnatural mixture and combination of ill tasted juices. Some are brought over to us in *French* casks; but when they are *translated* into our own vessels, all their original spirit is evaporated, and nothing remains but an insipid dull draught, and gross lees.

Our modern HISTORY WINES are all made at home, very little being exported from abroad, or fetch'd from the countries which they belong to: but I must particularly guard my reader against drinking, any of that vapid stuff, which is puff'd off to them under the name of BIRCH-WINE. There was likewise a quantity of this Brewage sub-scrib'd for, and carried about by a CART: but even the friends to THE *Pretender* had not stomachs to get it down.

Our Politics are a sort of HOT-POT or FLIP, made of vile spirits and sour Ale boil'd up together into a ferment, sweeten'd with the brown sugar of Property, and season'd with the spices of discontent. This is the old COUNTRY remedy against the gripes or the heart-burn, and is a favourite draught, that always go down glibly, with sailors, fox-hunters and old women.

Our controversial treatises (especially in divinity) are FOSTER'D upon us frequently as the only *salutary* liquors to be depended on. The Presbyterians regale us with their ELDER-WINE; The Roman Catholics would force the bitter stale drench of HOLY WATER upon us; but it always proves an emetic to the good people of England, who loath the sight of it, and have often cast it up again, whan prescrib'd against their wills: Sometimes we have the pleasant Composition of a BISHOP, given in a GRACE-CUP:—but generally these controversies are at best but a thin NEGUS or COOL TANKARD, made of bad materials, and have often the effects of COWSLIP WINE, which intoxicates, as soon as it gets up into the head, and fairly lays the drowsy drinker asleep.

Our Poetry partakes of so many different sorts of liquids, that it is difficult to ascertain the peculiar taste of each. The wit and humour of our comedies froth up in empty bubbles, like bottled small beer full of wind and pert briskness, which flys off as soon as pour'd out, and leaves nothing but a puffy, insipid, strengthless fluid behind. Our late Tragedies are a sort of HALF AND HALF, sometimes the mild, sometimes the stale being more prevalent. There is a deal of SPRUCE BEER retail'd out in Epigrams, Epithalamiums, Riddles, Acrostics, &c. tho', when you have taken a large swig of them, you may find yourself still as dry and empty as before.

The Libels, which are sold at every shop in town, are no better than common GIN, tho' disguis'd under various appellations of Ragged Sarah, Strip me naked, Aniseed, &c. and are indeed the nusance as well as the disgrace of the nation. It is not to be wonder'd at, that such poison should be vended, as with the ordinary vulgar it serves for meat and drink: but those of a more refin'd palate nauseate such inflaming distillations.

There are a number of brewers in the literary way, who serve the town with a tolerable commodity, which, like PORTER, always finds a sale among the general, and is sometimes admitted to the tables of the polite. Besides these, there are innumerable *Magazines*, where (in imitation of the immortal ASHLEY[1]) PRO BONO PUBLICO PUNCH may be had in small quantities; and the several Retailers profess to give you more in quantity, and at a cheaper rate, than the rest of their brethren. You have an odd mixture of sour, and sweet, and spirit; but their ingredients are generally smuggled, or stole, and are very vilely and miserably blended together.

Upon a chemical analysis of almost every writing, we find a very little salt, scarce any spirit, a great deal of phlegm, a fœtid oil, and all the rest a mere caput mortuum. There is a kind of SNAP-DRAGON, which I don't chuse to meddle with; but in which the Rivals of my Censorship have lately burnt their fingers, without having any *Reasons*.

I shall conclude with cautioning the purchaser (as I did before in BIBLIOPOLIUM and BIBITOPERRYUM) not to trust to the signs that are hung out of THE ALDERMAN'S ENTIRE BUTT Beer, or to an F. R. S. an S. T. P. an M. D. in the Advertisements, remembering that, as good wine needs no Bush, so a good Book has no occasion for a talking Title-page.

---

[1] J. Ashley, a well-known tavern-keeper on Ludgate Hill who had a reputation as a popularizer of punch.

126. [Bonnell Thornton], from *Have at You All: or The Drury-Lane Journal*

12 March 1752, pp. 211–14

The COVENT GARDEN JOURNAL EXTRAORDINARY.

NUMB. II.

—————————*Valeat res ludicra, si me*
Palma negata macrum, donata reducit optimum.

HORAT.[1]

In English.

Farewell the humourous prize, e're such a matter
Should make me leaner, or should make me fatter.

As there is a kind of natural sympathy between the author and his reader, I have observ'd that whenever I have been dosing over any of my compositions in the writing, the same soporific effect has been communicated to others in the perusing of them. I therefore give my customers this fair warning, that if they find themselves inclin'd to take a nap over this essay, they may not be surprised at it, as I own I was faily asleep myself, when I form'd the plan of it.

I was lolling in my elbow chair yesterday, and indulging an insensible vacation from thought, when the narcotic fumes of my morning pipe lull'd me into a gentle slumber. As I was just before plodding for matter to make up my next Journal, my imagination still busied itself in this employment. The paper methought lay before me, the pen was in my hand, and I was ready to give a loose to my invention:— but alas! in vain did I beat about for sense, in vain did I knock at my forehead, and found nobody at home.

Chagrin'd by this embarrassment I immediately invoked the Assistance of WIT, with whom I had conceiv'd myself a singular favourite. The Goddess appear'd before me; and the bright rays that darted from her countenance, as I had never been us'd to them, quite discomposed me with their dazzling lustre. I applied to her for a

[1] *Epistles*, II. i. 180–1.

brilliant sentiment, but she put me off with a pun; I ask'd her for a quaint expression, but she gave me a quibble; I snatch'd up what I thought a smart repartee, but upon examination I found it dwindled into a conundrum.

Being thus disappointed I had recourse to HUMOUR, with whom I had long before been intimate: I saw her indeed at a distance, but when I wanted to approach her, and endeavour'd to catch her in my arms, she flew from my embraces. To free herself from my pursuits, she flung down a packet upon the table, which upon opening contain'd nothing but an undigested mixture of mispellings, disposed in the form of blundering depositions and vulgar examinations.

I had but little room to hope for any favour from LEARNING, whom I never had much knowledge of, and had long ago dropt the slight acquaintance I had formerly commenc'd with him. But upon making my case known to him, he put into my hand a long string of Greek and Latin quotations with bald translations annex'd to them, and tack'd together without any regular connexion. These I laid by very carefully, determin'd to employ a number of them in every Journal, without regarding whether they were *à propos* to my subject or not.

SATIRE I perceiv'd very busily employ'd in sharpening her darts, and dipping the points of them in gall. I was stepping up to her to desire some of the keenest, when she levell'd her aim directly at myself, and forc'd me to skulk under the shield of AUTHORITY. As I had no hopes from that quarter, I betook myself to DEFAMATION, who furnish'd me with whole vollies of abuse, and foul language; with which I might occasionally bespatter my adversaries.

I would fain have courted CRITICISM to my party; but as JUDGMENT absolutely refus'd to come near me, the other would not stir with her. I was therefore glad to take up with CENSURE, who is blindfold, and falls indiscriminately on every one in her way, as she wants the guide of REASON, and never hearkens to the direction of JUSTICE.

When I had review'd my little stock of materials, I was under some doubt whether I had best proceed in my business of Journalist, being quite dishearten'd with the slight put upon me by those whom I vainly expected to have join'd me. While I was in this dilemma, IMPUDENCE with her brazen front and IGNORANCE with her leaden head came up to me: They encourag'd me to march on with intrepidity; and animated by their persuasions methought I was preparing to set forward, when immediately I found myself surrounded by a parti-colour'd train led by RIBALDRY, BUFFOONERY, SCURRILITY, and NONSENSE. These ragamuffins echoed the Name of SIR ALEXANDER DRAWCANSIR so loudly throughout the Regions of DULNESS, that the noise of it awoke me, and I recollected I had all the while been only in a dream.

127. [Bonnell Thornton], from *Have at You All: or The Drury-Lane Journal*

19 March 1752, pp. 236–7

The COVENT GARDEN JOURNAL EXTRAORDINARY.

NUMB. III.

★   ★   ★

We periodical writers of literary scraps, vulgarly call'd essays, have the advantage over the more voluminous composers of continued treatises: for after we have made our exit in our single shape, we can appear again in public in a collective body, as the SPECTATORS, &c. have done before us.—Sometimes an Author undergoes various metamorphoses; and tho' he be fairly knock'd o'the head in one form, yet he instantly revives again, and pushes his way forward in a new dress and figure. Thus the TATLER, when he had done chattering, became a GUARDIAN; thus MIST was turn'd into a FOG; and thus the pedantic STUDENT sunk into a prating Old WOMAN, or MIDWIFE.

I myself have experienc'd various changes in my state of Authorship: I once had a garret in GRUB-STREET, whence I publish'd a Journal, and gave a loose to my favourite *humour* in making puns upon Newspapers;—a sport that I first learn'd in my infancy, and shall be fond of to my extremest old age. Afterwards I commenced downright bully, and set up for a CHAMPION: I put on a fierce look and bold behaviour, assuming the tremendous name of HERCULES VINEGAR: But in my encounters I unhappily stumbled upon Party, which tript up my heels, and laid me *flat* in an instant.

Having once blunder'd into Politics 'twas the same thing to me, what cause I espous'd: so I e'en call'd myself honest JOHN TROTPLAID, and laid about me pellmell among the JACOBITES: I was also a TRUE PATRIOT every inch of me; till finding my genius rather qualified for a *worshipful* employment, I have since set up a REGISTER-OFFICE for Thieves, and conscious of my bullying capacity have now taken upon me the SIR-name of DRAWCANSIR. As I perceive my end is approaching, I have no other refuge than to sollicit an ACT OF PARLIAMENT for monopolizing News-papers, not for my own *Interest* to be sure, but solely and wholly for the *Good* of *Community*, which the *Energy of Benevolence* and the *Milk of Human Kindness* makes me always have so much at heart.

N.B. *In my next perhaps I may give an account of my exploits as* MANAGER *of a* PUPPET-SHOW.[1]

---

[1] See Martin C. Battestin, 'Fielding and "Master Punch" in Panton Street', *Philological Quarterly* (1966), xlv. 191–208.

AMELIA

128. Catherine Talbot, letter

14 March 1752

From a letter to Elizabeth Carter, *A Series of Letters* . . . i. 294.

*   *   *

I have not read Amelia yet, but have seen it read and commented upon much to my edification by that good Bishop of Gloucester,[1] who seldom misses spending two or three days of the week at this deanery. Judge then if it must not be an agreeable situation that gives us so much more of his company, and in a so much more comfortable way, than when we were nearer neighbours. I have been particularly delighted with some of our afternoons, when we have sat unmolested by my dressing room fire-side, he reading Amelia (and quarrelling excessively at the two first volumes) my mother and I reading or working, or following our own devices as it might happen, and every one mixing little interruptions of chat as things come into their heads; with not a single ring at the door to disturb us.

*   *   *

[1] Martin Benson.

129. Elizabeth Carter, letter

30 March 1752

From a letter to Catherine Talbot, *A Series of Letters* . . ., i.
295–6. A reply to Catherine Talbot's letter of 14 March (No. 128).

*　　*　　*

In favor of the Bishop of Gloucester's cold, his reading Amelia in
silence may be tolerated, but I am somewhat scandalized that since he
did not read it to you, you did not read it yourself. Methinks I long to
engage you on the side of this poor unfortunate book, which I am told
the fine folks are unanimous in pronouncing to be very sad stuff. The
Bishop of Gloucester's excessive sad quarrel with the two first volumes
I am determined to conclude proceeded from the effects of his cold.
How to account for Miss Mulso's[1] unmerciful severity to Amelia is
past my skill, as it does not appear but that she was in very good health
when she read the book.

*　　*　　*

[1] i.e. Hester Mulso, later Mrs. Chapone.

130. [Dr. John Kennedy], from *Some Remarks on the Life and Writings of Dr. J[ohn] H[ill]*

1751, pp. 59-61

This anti-Hill pamphlet, published in March 1752, was written in a series of letters, one of which, addressed to a friend in the country, turns to Fielding's *Amelia*.

*   *   *

You ask me for the Opinion of the Town, and my own of Mr. *Fielding*'s AMELIA. I must own to you, they are very different, if we are to form a Judgment of the Opinion of the Town by the Sale of the Work, which has not as yet gone thro' a second Edition.—For were I to take it from the Circle of my own Acquaintance, I should mention *Amelia* to you as a most finished Performance.—Hear the Sentiments of the judicious few.—It is, in Reality, as the Author says in his Dedication, calculated to promote Religion and Virtue. This one Circumstance, the most glorious that can animate the Soul of Man in the undertaking and perfecting any Work, has, instead of commanding the Applause, provoked the Censure of the Generality of its Readers. For, in short, our Youth, of both Sexes, have their Tastes so debauched with reading *Adventures, Intrigues,* &c. in an Age so abandoned, that even the Fair, unawed by that Timidity and Softness, which is so natural to their Sex, and which so effectually recommends them to ours, avow to the World their Guilt, and glory in acting over again, with a peculiar Gusto (in *Memoirs, Apologies,* &c.) those Scenes of Lewdness, which will justly render them infamous to all Posterity. A luscious Stile, high wrought Images, and glowing Colours, are requisite to palliate and set off the natural Deformity of Vice; and our late Master-pieces in this Way have actually given our Youth as wrong a Turn as ever Romance did to Don *Quixote*. It is this depraved Taste, and Mr. *Fielding*'s not complying with it, that has sunk the Reputation of the inestimable AMELIA; a Piece which entirely depends on the FORCE of native Virtue, without meanly stooping to be patronized by the Frailties of human Nature. It has all the Regularity and Beauties of epick, and all the Life of dramatick Poetry. Not one Character is superfluous or unconnected, but all contribute to shew, that Virtue will support itself against every Opposition, and that even a good Intention will carry a Man thro' Life, so as to make him at last happy.—Such a Fate attends each Performer, as we may justly expect from their respective Characters. Upon the whole it is, as I have told you before, a most finished Performance. But will, I am afraid, be attended with this Consequence, that as the worthy Author, consulted in this Piece, his own Disposition, and true Taste, more than that of the Age; its Fate, compared with the Success of those vile Pieces which disgrace the Press, will be a melancholy Caution to Writers, to apply rather to the vicious than virtuous Affections of Mankind.—What you take Notice of, as to AMELIA's Nose, was an Omission of the Author's which has occasioned a vast deal of *low wit*, and been a standing *Joke* here. I dare say it will be amended in any future Edition.

★ ★ ★

131. 'Criticulus'

The Gentleman's Magazine

March 1752, xxii. 102–3

Mr. URBAN,

Mr. Fielding's Amelia came lately into my hands, and I gave it a second perusal with great pleasure.

Tho' this novel has its imperfections, yet some of the characters are handled in so masterly a manner, virtue and vice meet with their due rewards, and it abounds with such noble reflections on the follies and vices, the perfections and imperfections of human nature, that he must be both a bad and ill natur'd reader, who is not by it agreeably entertain'd, instructed and improved.

His fair heroine's nose has, in my opinion, been too severely handled by some modern critics, whose writings will never make a sufficient recompence to the world, if Mr. *Fielding* adheres to what I hope he only said in his warmth and indignation of this injurious treatment, that he will never trouble the public with any more writings of this kind.

But the warmest advocate for Mr *Fielding* cannot justify the manifest anachronism of *Amelia*'s being with child at the siege of *Gibraltar,* and a blooming beauty at the time of the masquerades at *Ranelagh.* Neither will the author's friendship in recommending the Universal Register Office against *Cecil Street* in the *Strand,* (which has been but lately erected) where Mrs *Bennet* soon after her first marriage, and *Amelia* afterwards, apply for assistance, excuse as bad an anachronism.

The reader, I am persuaded, would have trusted the author's word for the genuineness of Miss *Matthew*'s letter, mention'd in *Vol.* ii. *p.* 169, had he not declared, 'That it was communicated to him by Mr *Booth* himself'; and would have been as pleas'd to receive 'the anecdotes of this lady' from Mr *Fielding*, as from 'Miss *Matthews*'s servant', and be as well satisfied of 'other materials of a private nature', tho' the author had not assur'd us that they 'were communicated to him by one of the clerks of the Universal Register Office'.   *Yours, &c.*

March 26, 1752.   CRITICULUS.

132. Catherine Talbot, letter

22 April 1752

From a letter to Elizabeth Carter, a reply to her letter of 30 March (No. 129). *A Series of Letters*. . ., i. 298.

*   *   *

At last we have begun *Amelia,* it is very entertaining. I do love Dr. Harrison and the good Serjeant; and Mrs. James's visit to Amelia has extremely diverted me. How many Mrs. James's in that good-for-nothing London! But Mr. Fielding's heroines are always silly loving runaway girls. Amelia makes an excellent wife, but why did she marry Booth?

*   *   *

133. Sarah Chapone, letter

27 May 1752

From a letter to Elizabeth Carter, *The Works of Mrs. Chapone*, i. 48–52.

*   *   *

I am extremely obliged to you for gratifying my curiosity with your reasons for speaking so favourably of Amelia, though, at the same time, I am not a little mortified to find that I cannot assent to all you say. I am afraid I have less mercy in my disposition than you, for I cannot think with so much lenity of the character of Booth, which, though plainly designed as an amiable one by the author, is in my opinion contemptible and wicked. 'Rather frail than wicked!' Dear Miss Carter! that is what I complain of, that Fielding contrives to gloss over gross and monstrous faults in such a manner that even his virtuous readers shall call them frailties. How bad may be the consequence of such representations to those who are interested in the deception, and glad to find that their favourite vices are kept in countenance by a character which is designed to engage the esteem and good wishes of the reader. Had I not reason to accuse the author of 'softening or hiding the deformity of vice,' when infidelity, adultery, gaming, and extravagance, (the three last accompanied with all the aggravation that the excellence of a wife and the distress of a young family could give them) are so gently reproved, even by Miss Carter? 'His amour with Miss Mathews,' you say, 'however blameable, was attended with some alleviating circumstances:' what these were I am unable to discover. I think none but an abandoned heart, incapable of the least delicacy, and lost to the love of virtue and abhorrence of vice, could have entertained any thoughts but of horror and detestation for that fiend of a woman, after hearing her story. Consider too the circumstances they were both in, Miss Mathews uncertain whether her life was not to atone for her crime; Booth in the deepest distress, his Amelia and her children left helpless and miserable; a gaol the scene of their amour! What a mind must that be, which, in such circumstances, could find itself under any temptation from the person of a woman whose crimes were so shocking, whose disposition so hateful, and whose shameless advances were so disgusting! how mean was his submitting to owe obligations to her! —Indeed I do think him a very wretched fellow, and I should not have cared sixpence had the book ended with his being hanged. In poetical justice I almost think he should have been so. Poor Amelia would have been rid of a good-for-nothing husband, whose folly and wickedness gave her continual distress. Doctor Harrison would have taken her and her children home with him, where I will suppose she spent her life in great tranquillity, after having recovered her fortune.—Have not I made a fine catastrophe? Now are you quite angry with me? I think I hear you call me 'cruel, bloody-minded wretch!' Well then, in complaisance to your tenderness, I will suffer him to live, but indeed I cannot suffer him to be a favoured character; I can't help despising him, and wondering that Amelia did not do so too. I agree with you entirely in what you say of the mixture of virtues and faults, which make up the generality of characters, and I am also apt to believe that the virtues have most commonly the predominant share; but if this is the case in real life, Mr. Fielding's representation of it is not just; for in most of his characters the vices preponderate. Doctor Harrison, Amelia, and the honest serjeant are indeed exceptions; Booth himself I cannot allow to be one, for I do not find that he had any virtues equivalent to his faults. Good nature, when it is merely constitutional, and has no principle to support it, can hardly be reckoned a virtue, and you see that in him it was not strong enough to keep him from injuring and distressing those he loved best, when temptation came in his way. His regard to his wife's honour may be attributed to his love; at best it is but a negative goodness, and only proves him not a monster. I cannot help believing that Fielding has a very low opinion of human nature, and that his writings tend to enforce it on his readers; and I own I am always offended with writers of that cast. What end can it serve to persuade men they are Yahoos, but to make them act agreeably to that character, and despair of attaining a better! Is it not the common plea of wicked men that they follow nature? whereas they have taken pains to debauch and corrupt their nature, and have by degrees reconciled it to crimes that simple, uncorrupted nature would start at.

★   ★   ★

FIELDING'S 'NEW SPECIES OF WRITING'

---

134. Francis Coventry, Epistle Dedicatory . . .

1752

. . . 'To Henry Fielding, Esq.', *The History of Pompey the Little or, The Life and Adventures of a Lap-Dog*, 3rd ed. (1752), pp. iii–xii.

Coventry, who may have been the author of the *Essay on the New Species of Writing* (Duddon, ii. 728), also referred to Fielding in the first edition of *Pompey the Little* (1751), remarking that he is writing what 'one of my contemporaries declares to be an epic poem in prose' (i. 1) and including praise of that 'great master of human nature, the ingenious author of *Tom Jones*, who justly styles himself king of biographers' (ii. 1).

SIR,

MY design being to speak a word or two in behalf of novel-writing, I know not to whom I can address myself with so much propriety as to yourself, who unquestionably stand foremost in this species of composition.

To convey instruction in a pleasant manner, and mix entertainment with it, is certainly a commendable undertaking, perhaps more likely to be attended with success than graver precepts; and even where amusement is the chief thing consulted, there is some little merit in making people laugh, when it is done without giving offence to religion, or virtue, or good manners. If the laugh be not raised at the expence of innocence or decency, good humour bids us indulge it, and we cannot well laugh too often.

CAN one help wondering therefore at the contempt, with which

353

many people affect to talk of this sort of composition? they seem to think it degrades the dignity of their understandings, to be found with a novel in their hands, and take great pains to let you know that they never read them. They are people of too great importance, it seems, to spend their time in so idle a manner, and much too wise to be amused.

Now, tho' many reasons may be given for this ridiculous and affected disdain, I believe a very principal one, is the pride and pedantry of learned men, who are willing to monopolize reading to themselves, and therefore fastidiously decry all books that are on a level with common understandings, as empty, trifling and impertinent.

Thus the grave metaphysician for example, who after working night and day perhaps for several years, sends forth at last a profound treatise, where *A.* and *B.* seem to contain some very deep mysterious meaning; grows indignant to think that every little paltry scribbler, who paints only the characters of the age, the manners of the times, and the working of the passions, should presume to equal him in glory.

The politician too, who shakes his head in coffee-houses, and produces now and then, from his fund of observations, a grave, sober, political pamphlet on the good of the nation; looks down with contempt on all such idle compositions, as lives and romances, which contain no strokes of satire at the ministry, no unmannerly reflections upon *Hannover,* nor any thing concerning the balance of power on the continent. These gentlemen and their readers join all to a man in depreciating works of humour: or if they ever vouchsafe to speak in their praise, the commendation never rises higher than, 'yes, 'tis well enough for such a sort of a thing;' after which the grave observator retires to his news-paper, and there, according to the general estimation, employs his time *to the best advantage.*

But besides these, there is another set, who never read any modern books at all. They, wise men, are so deep in the learned languages, that they can pay no regard to what has been published within these last thousand years. The world is grown old; mens geniusses are degenerated; the writers of this age are too contemptible for their notice, and they have no hopes of any better to succeed them. Yet these gentlemen of profound erudition will contentedly read any trash, that is disguised in a learned language, and the worst ribaldry of *Aristophanes,* shall be critiqued and commented on by men, who turn up their noses at *Gulliver* or *Joseph Andrews.*

But if this contempt for books of amusement be carried a little too far, as I suspect it is, even among men of science and learning, what shall be said to some of the greatest triflers of the times, who affect to talk the same language? these surely have no right to express any disdain of what is at least equal to their understandings. Scholars and men of learning have a reason to give; their application to severe studies may have destroyed their relish for works of a lighter cast, and consequently it cannot be expected that they should approve what they do not understand. But as for beaux, rakes, petit-maîtres and fine ladies, whose lives are spent in doing the things which novels record, I do not see why they should be indulged in affecting a contempt of them. People, whose most earnest business is to dress and play at cards, are not so importantly employed, but that they may find leisure now and then to read a novel. Yet these are as forward as any to despise them; and I once heard a very fine lady, condemning some highly finished conversations in one of your works, sir, for this curious reason—'because,' said she, ' 'tis such sort of stuff as passes every day between me and my own maid.'

I DO not pretend to apply any thing here said in behalf of books of amusement, to the following little work, of which I ask your patronage: I am sensible how very imperfect it is in all its parts, and how unworthy to be ranked in that class of writings, which I am now defending. But I desire to be understood in general or more particularly with an eye to your works, which I take to be master-pieces and complete models in their kind. They are, I think, worthy the attention of the greatest and wisest men, and if any body is ashamed of reading them, or can read them without entertainment and instruction, I heartily pity their understandings.

THE late editor of Mr. *Pope*'s works, in a very ingenious note, wherein he traces the progress of romance-writing, justly observes, that this species of composition is now brought to maturity by Mr. *De Marivaux* in *France*, and Mr. *Fielding* in *England*.[1]

I HAVE but one objection to make to this remark, which is, that the name of Mr. *De Marivaux* stands foremost of the two; a superiority I can by no means allow him. Mr. *Marivaux* is indeed a very amiable, elegant, witty and penetrating writer. The reflections he scatters up and down his *Marianne* are highly judicious, *recherchées*, and infinitely agreeable. But not to mention that he never finishes his works, which greatly disappoints his readers, I think, his *characters* fall infinitely short of those we find in the performances of his *English* contemporary. They are neither so original, so ludicrous, so well distinguished, nor so happily

---

[1] See No. 103.

contrasted as your own: and as the characters of a novel principally determine its merit, I must be allowed to esteem my countryman the greater author.

THERE is another celebrated novel writer,[1] of the same kingdom, now living, who in the choice and diversity of his characters, perhaps exceeds his rival Mr. *Marivaux*, and would deserve greater commendation, if the extreme libertinism of his plans, and too wanton drawings of nature, did not take off from the other merit of his works; tho' at the same time it must be confessed, that his genius and knowledge of mankind are very extensive. But with all due respect for the parts of these two able *Frenchmen*, I will venture to say they have their superior, and whoever has read the works of Mr. *Fielding*, cannot be at a loss to determine who that superior is. Few books of this kind have ever been written with a spirit equal to *Joseph Andrews*, and no story that I know of, was ever invented with more happiness, or conducted with more art and management than that of *Tom Jones*.

As to the following little piece, sir, it pretends to a very small degree of merit. 'Tis the first essay of a young author, and perhaps may be the last. A very hasty and unfinished edition of it was published last winter, which meeting with a more favourable reception than its writer had any reason to expect, he has since been tempted to revise and improve it, in hopes of rendering it a little more worthy of his readers regard. With these alterations he now begs leave, sir, to desire your acceptance of it; he can hardly hope for your approbation; but whatever be its fate, he is proud in this public manner to declare himself

Your constant reader,
and sincere admirer.

[1] i.e. Crébillon *fils*.

135. [Arthur Murphy], letter

1753

From a letter prefixed to Christopher Smart's *The Hilliad*. For Murphy's authorship see J. P. Emery, *Modern Language Notes* (1946), lxi. 162–5, and Arthur Sherbo, *New Essays by Arthur Murphy* (1963), 169 and 172 (text).

Murphy is discussing the attack on Fielding by Dr. John Hill, and, by way of contrast, Fielding's work:

*　　*　　*

Upon the commencement of the Covent-Garden Journal, Mr. Fielding declared an humorous war against this writer, which was intended to be carried with an amicable pleasantry, in order to contribute to the entertainment of the town. It is recent in every bodies memory, how the INSPECTOR behaved upon that occasion. Conscious that there was not an atom of humour in his composition, he had recourse to his usual shifts, and instantly disclosed a private conversation; by which he reduced himself to the alternative mentioned by Mr. POPE; 'and if he lies not, must at least betray.'[1] Through all Mr. Fielding's inimitable comic Romances, we perceive no such thing as personal malice, no private character dragged into light; but every stroke is copied from the volume which nature has unfolded to him; every scene of life is by him represented in its natural colours, and every species of folly or humour is ridiculed with the most exquisite touches. A genius like this is perhaps more useful to mankind, than any class of writers; he serves to dispel all gloom from our minds, to work off our ill-humours by the gay sensations excited by a well directed pleasantry, and in a vein of mirth he leads his readers into the knowledge of human nature; the

[1] *Epistle to Dr. Arbuthnot*, l. 298; read 'lye'.

most useful and pleasing science we can apply to. And yet so deserving an author has been most grossly treated by this wild Essayist,[1] and, not to multiply instances, has he not attempted to raise tumults and divisions in our theatres, contrary to all decency and common sense, and contrary to the practice of all polite writers, whose chief aim has ever been to cherish harmony and good manners, and to diffuse through all ranks of people a just refinement of taste in all our public entertainments?

*   *   *

136. [Christopher Smart], from *The Hilliad*

1753, p. 44

At the end of *The Hilliad* Smart shows Hill as the 'arch-dunce'—

While with joint force o'er humour's droll domain,
Cervantes, Fielding, Lucian, Swift, shall reign.[2]

[1] i.e. Hill.
[2] Cf. Fielding's listing of these in the *Covent-Garden Journal* No. 10, 4 February 1752, and Smart's assertion in *The Midwife*, ii. 101, that as a wit Fielding belonged in the company of Lucian, Swift, Butler, and Erasmus. Murphy also frequently links combinations of these names.

137. Lady Mary Wortley Montagu, recalled by Lady Louisa Stuart

undated

'Introductory Anecdotes', *Letters and Works of Lady Mary Wortley Montagu* (1861), i. 106–7.

Lady Mary Wortley had a great regard for Fielding; she pitied his misfortunes, excused his failings, and warmly admired his best writings; above all Tom Jones, in her own copy of which she wrote *Ne plus ultra*. Nevertheless, she frankly said she was sorry he did not himself perceive that he had made Tom Jones a scoundrel; alluding to the adventure with Lady Bellaston. She would indeed have seldom passed a wrong judgment on what she read, if her natural good taste had taken its way unbiased; but where personal enmity or party prejudice stepped in, they too frequently drove it blinded before them. A book is a book, no matter who wrote it; in fair criticism it has a right to stand upon its own proper ground, and should no more be condemned for the sins of its author, than commended for his virtues.

*　　*　　*

138. Allan Ramsay, *A Letter to the Right Honourable . . .*

1753

From *A Letter to the Right Honourable the Earl of——Concerning the Affair of Elizabeth Canning*. By a Clergyman (1753), pp. 3–4, 16–17.

Fielding had published his pamphlet *A Clear State of the Case of Elizabeth Canning* in March 1753.

Ramsay's initial generalizations about Fielding may be more rhetorical concession than criticism, but together with his later comment on *Tom Jones*, they suggest something of his own opinion.

★   ★   ★

Your Lordship knows the value I set upon every thing that is written by that author [i.e. Fielding], who has succeeded so well in every subject he has undertaken, either of business or pleasantry; and I with great reason expected one or other of these from the twelvepenny worth I saw advertised. And, perhaps there are none of his performances that more discover the ingenuity of the man of wit, the distinctness of the lawyer, or the politeness and candour of the gentleman.

But while I admired the stile and composition of this pamphlet, and the ingenious, and at the same time unadorned method, in which Mr. *Fielding* defended the cause of *Canning,* I could not help being surprized to find upon what slight grounds he and many other sensible men, had founded their belief of her veracity; and that they should be satisfied with evidence that seems to be in no manner adequate to the nature of the facts meant to be proved by it: especially when a life is concerned, of which our laws and customs are in most cases extremely tender.

★   ★   ★

[*Tom Jones* is the highest type of] an artful story, . . . where the incidents are so various, and yet so consistent with themselves, and with nature, that the more the reader is acquainted with nature, the more he is deceived into a belief of its being true; and is with difficulty recall'd from that belief by the author's confession from time to time of its being all a fiction.

★   ★   ★

139. William Whitehead, *The World* No. 19

10 May 1753

From an Epistle 'To Mr. Fitz-Adam', *British Essayists*, ed. A. Chalmers (Boston, 1856), xxii. 181, 183. Also reprinted in Whitehead's *Plays and Poems* (1774), ii. 313, 315. In 1762, after he was made Poet Laureate, he again commented on Fielding:

> 'Tis our own fault if *Fielding*'s lash *we* feel
> Or, like French wits, begin with the Bastile.

(Plays and Poems, ii. 296)

The present race of romance-writers run universally into a different extreme [from idealizing fantasy]. They spend the little art they are masters of in weaving into intricacies the more familiar and more comical adventures of a Jack Slap, or a Betty Sallet. These, though they endeavour to copy after a very great original, I choose to call our writers below nature; because very few of them have as yet found out their master's peculiar art of writing upon low subjects without writing in a low manner.

*   *   *

Here, therefore, Mr. Fitz-Adam, you should interpose your authority, and forbid your readers, whom I will suppose to be all persons who can read, even to attempt to open any novel, or romance, unlicensed by you; unless it should happen to be stamped Richardson or Fielding.

*   *   *

AMELIA AND THE
DOMESTIC NOVEL

140. Friedrich Melchior,
Baron Grimm, letter

1 August 1753

Correspondance Littéraire, ii. 267–8.
Discussing Smollett's *Peregrine Pickle* ('which has in its own country the reputation of being the worst English novel; a reputation which it merits and which it has completely upheld in France'), and *Pompey the Little* ('a bad novel about a bitch'), Baron Grimm turns to Fielding's *Amelia*.

*   *   *

The English have a kind of domestic novel that is completely unknown to the French. I speak of the novels of an excellent author in that genre, Mr. Fielding, who has just produced a new novel in English called *Amelia*. This writer, who doubtless deserves a distinguished place among the authors who have added glory to England, is a great and original painter, always truthful and sometimes as sublime as Molière. His *Tom Jones or the Foundling, Charlotte Summers, the Fortunate Parish Girl* [sic], above all his *Joseph Andrews and Parson Adams*, are the most excellent works of the kind, full of strokes of genius. At first it seems astonishing that the French, who have many good novels in their language, have never painted their domestic customs; but when one reflects a bit, he finds that if there are no representations in this genre, it is not the fault of the painter but of his models. For when he paints our *petits maîtres* and *petites maîtresses* he has almost exhausted the subject, and put all the national character [*le national*] it is possible to put in a French novel. Such are the works of M. Crébillon fils, which one can properly call the domestic novels of our nation.

*   *   *

141. [Jane Collier], from *An Essay on the Art of Ingeniously Tormenting*

1753, pp. 228-30

Near the end of her ironic tract on tormenting, Mrs. Collier delivers a peroration to her 'scholars'.

*   *   *

I know that many learned and good men have taken pains to undermine this our noble art [i.e. of tormenting], by laying down rules, and giving exemplars, in order to teach mankind to give no offence to any one, and, instead of being a torment, to be as great a help and comfort to their friends, as it is in their power to be. But with infinite pleasure do I perceive, either that they are not much read, or, at least, that they have not the power of rooting from the human breast, that growing sprig of mischief there implanted with our birth; and generally, as we come to years of discretion, flourishing like a green palm-tree: yet, to shew my great candour and generosity to these my mortal (or rather moral) foes, I will endeavour, as far as my poor recommendation will go, to forward the sale of their books, even among my own pupils. For if, my good scholars, you will guard your minds against the doctrines they intend to teach; if you will consider them as mere amusements; you have my leave to peruse them. Or rather, if you will only remember to observe my orders, in acting in direct opposition to all that a Swift, an Addison, a Richardson, a Fielding, or any other good ethical writer intended to teach, you may (by referring sometimes to these my rules, as helps to your memory) become as profound adepts in this Art, as any of the readers of Mr. Hoyle are in the science of whist.

*   *   *

142. Miss Smythies of Colchester
From *The Stage-Coach*
1753, i. 71

This novel, by a disciple of Richardson, introduces a discussion among its characters of the subject of novels.

*　　*　　*

The conversation turned upon the prevailing taste for novels. Mr. Manly said he had never read any thing of that kind, but the works of Cervantes, till lately he had been persuaded to pursue Clarissa, and some of the Covent-Garden justice's performances; and though he formerly had thought such fictions below his notice, he was now not ashamed to aver, there were some, which, if attended to, and not run over meerly to kill time, were capable of yielding profit with amusement, particularly those he had mention'd.

*　　*　　*

143. From *Critical Remarks on Sir Charles Grandison* . . .

1754

Critical Remarks on Sir Charles Grandison, Clarissa, and Pamela (1754), pp. 18–20. For a useful introduction and facsimile text, see Alan D. McKillop's edition, Augustan Reprint Society, publication No. 21 (1950). The author also alludes to Fielding's *Shamela* and/or *Joseph Andrews* with some sympathy: 'The fine, or rather the *naughty gentleman*, in your Pamela, to whom Mr. Fielding very properly gives the sirname of Booby, is indeed one of the greatest bubbles, and blunderers that one can meet withal' (p. 21). The anonymous author, addressing himself to Richardson, turns to a comparison of the 'good man' in Richardson and in Fielding.

In Grandison, you have endeavoured to give an example of universal goodness and benevolence. But I am afraid you have strained and stretched that character too far; you have furnished him with too great a variety of accomplishments, some of them destructive, at least not so consistent with the principal and most shining virtue. *The man is every thing*, as Lucy or Harriet says; which no man ever was, or will be. Homer in the Odyssey, and in the character of Euemaeus, has given an example of universal benevolence; but then he represents him an entire rustic, living constantly in the country, shunning all public concourse of men, the court especially, and never going thither, but when obliged to supply the riotous luxury and extravagance of the suitors. Mr. Fielding has imitated these circumstances, as far as was consistent with our manners, in the character of Allworthy, and has with admirable judgment denied him an university education, made him a great lover of retirement, seldom absent from his country seat, never at the metropolis but when called by business, and constantly leaving it, when that was over. . . . Should we now consider the matter a little more deeply, we shall find a reason in nature for the practice of these just painters of men and manners [i.e. Fielding and Sarah Fielding in David Simple]. A human creature, in a simple unimproved state, is naturally generous and benevolent; but when he comes abroad into the world, and observes the universal depravity of morals, and the narrow selfishness that every where prevail, according to his particular temper or circumstances, he is either contaminated by the example, or contracts a misanthropical disposition, and hates or despises the greatest part of his species. There may be, and no doubt there are, men who have seen the world, who have been conversant, even in courts, during their whole lives, who yet have retained and exercised humane and benevolent dispositions; but such characters are very rare, and, for the reasons above specified, never can be poetically probable. Such, Sir, is your Grandison; he seems never to have enjoyed retirement, to have been abroad almost all his life-time, to have seen all the courts in Europe, and been conversant, with the great, rich, and powerful, in all nations. You represent him likewise to be a man universally learned, and tell us, at the same time, in capital letters, that SIR CH. GRAND. is a CHRISTIAN; and that too, in the strictest and most bigotted sense of the world; for he refuses the woman he loves, for a difference in religious principles. This, in my humble opinion, is likewise an inconsistency, for universal learning naturally leads to scepticism, and the most useful, as well as solid branch of human knowledge, consists in knowing how little can be known. There are several other inconsistencies in his character, particularly in some of his duelling stories; besides, at any rate, his benevolence has something showy and ostentatious in it; nothing in short of that graceful and beautiful nature which appears in Fielding's Allworthy.

★　　　★　　　★

144. Sarah Fielding, from *The Cry* . . .

1754

The Cry: A New Dramatic Fable (1754), iii. 121–4, by Sarah
Fielding and probably Jane and Margaret Collier.
This work contains many scattered references to *Joseph Andrews*,
Tom Jones, and 'an ingenious author' (i.e. Fielding), and alludes in
its artificial structure to what its authors evidently take to be a
characteristic of Fielding's 'new species of writing'. In the following passage the authors are responding to criticism that labels
heroes like Don Quixote and Parson Adams 'ridiculous'. *The Cry*
was published in March 1754, which precluded the possibility
that Sarah Fielding was answering Murphy's account of Parson
Adams in the *Gray's-Inn Journal*, 6 September 1754 (No. 147
below). Ramsay's *Essay on Ridicule* (1753, p. 78n.) or, earlier,
Whitehead's *On Ridicule* (1743, in *Plays and Poems*, ii. 91–104)
might have elicited this response.

* * *

To travel through a whole work only to laugh at the chief companion allotted us, is an insupportable burthen. And we should imagine
that the reading of that incomparable piece of humour left us by
Cervantes, can give but little pleasure to those persons who can extract
no other entertainment or emolument from it than laughing at *Don
Quixote's* reveries, and sympathizing in the malicious joy of [his
tormentors] . . . and that strong and beautiful representation of
human nature, exhibited in *Don Quixote's* madness in one point, and
extraordinary good sense in every other, is indeed very much thrown
away on such readers as consider him only as the object of their mirth.

Nor less understood is the character of parson *Adams* in *Joseph Andrews* by those persons, who, fixing their thoughts on the hounds trailing the bacon in his pocket (with some oddnesses in his behaviour, and peculiarities in his dress) think proper to overlook the noble simplicity of his mind, with the other innumerable beauties in his character; which, to those who can understand *the word to the wise*, are placed in the most conspicuous view.

That the ridiculers of parson *Adams* are designed to be the proper objects of ridicule (and not that innocent man himself) is a truth which the author hath in many places set in the most glaring light. And lest his meaning should be perversely misunderstood, he hath fully displayed his own sentiments on that head, by writing a whole scene, in which such laughers are properly treated, and their *characters truly depicted. But those who think continual laughter, or rather sneering, to be one of the necessary ingredients of life, need not be at the trouble of travelling out of their depths to find objects of their merriment: they may spare themselves the pains of going abroad after food for scorn; as they may be bless'd with a plenteous harvest ever mature and fit for reaping on their own estates, without being beholden to any of their neighbours.

The greatest men, 'tis true, may have some oddnesses and peculiarities, which are indeed food for mirth and pleasantry: but the honest laughs which they create in the judicious and benevolent mind are such, as their own candor (if they are truly great men) will readily excuse; and their good-humour, if they have any, will then induce them to join the mirthful chorus: and the result must be the charm of universal chearfulness and innocent mirth. We are very apt to do as manifest an injury to comic writers, as we do to the characters they represent; and because they here and there properly embellish their pictures with risible figures, we want to turn the whole into farce, by desiring to see nothing but the grotesque: we expect in every page to meet with such jests as shall distort our features into a broad grin; otherwise, let them paint the most agreeable images of human nature, let them ever so accurately search the inmost recesses of the human heart, there is a general outcry set up against them, that they are spiritless and dull.

But indignation at the malicious rather than ignorant absurdities which we have heard vented on honest parson *Adams*, hath led us into a much wider digression than we at first intended. . . .

* *Joseph Andrews*, book iii. chap. 7. The characters are an old half-pay officer, a dull poet, a scraping fiddler, and a lame *German* dancing master.

145. [Arthur Murphy]
From *The Gray's-Inn Journal*
7 July 1753, No. 38, i. 240–3

The *Gray's-Inn Journal* began as a feature of the *Craftsman*, 21 October 1752, and ran to forty-nine weekly issues; on 29 September 1753 Murphy began to issue it as a separate publication in folio, and the fifty-two weekly numbers that followed were freshly numbered. The essays from both series were brought together and consecutively renumbered, revised, and sometimes augmented with new essays, in the collected edition of 1756. Since the *Craftsman* essays have not survived in their original form, the text of the collected edition is reproduced.

Murphy frequently alludes to Fielding in the *Gray's-Inn Journal*, e.g. in No. 16, 3 February 1752, he remarks that '*Fielding* will ever be a faithful Guide to the Adventurer in comic Romance', and in No. 20, 3 March 1752, he brackets Fielding and Hogarth. As these show, in general he repeats what Fielding has already said himself.

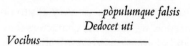

―――――――*pòpulumque falsis*
Dedocet uti
Vocibus―――――――――

HOR.[1]

It has been long since recommended to the Tribe of Criticks, to adjust and settle their Ideas, in a clear and regular Order, by fixing the distinct Meaning annexed to each Term they make use of in conveying their Remarks. If this Advice was properly adhered to, it would cut Matters very short in all Debates, which arise upon Points of Literature; and would enable those, who aspire to the Province of Criticism, to pass their Judgement with Precision. But the Reverse of this is frequently the Case, and I shall at present single out two Expressions, from a Multitude of others, which appear to me to be used in a vague, random

[1] '[Virtue] teaches the people not to use false words.' *Odes*, II. ii. 19–21.

Manner, the determinate Meaning of either not being sufficiently ascertained.

The Terms, I mean, are an HUMOURIST and a MAN OF HUMOUR. They are thought, by what I find, synonymous by many People, which must be the Source of numberless Mistakes. To define each, may be, perhaps, Matter of some Difficulty; but if I understand them right, the Reader is welcome to what Light I can give him into the Matter.

An HUMOURIST, I take to be, one under the Influence of some remarkable Oddity, or unaccountable Whim, which has taken such strong Possession of the Mind, and has so insinuated itself into all its Operations, that it mixes with the common Train of his Ideas, and thereby gives such a Cast to his Way of thinking, that every Thing strikes him in a different Light from the rest of his Fellow-Creatures, and of Consequence, every Thing he does, is also in an extravagant Manner.

I have not been able to investigate, in any Historian, the first Appearance of this Species of Men in this Kingdom. Whether it was in the Nature of the *Aborigines*, or first Inhabitants of this Island; or whether it made its Inroad among us, with that general Conflux of different Nations, which landed here, is a Point not very easy to determine. One Thing is clear, that they are of a long Standing among us, and indeed they thrive with such large Increase in this our Soil, that there is room to apprehend, the whole Nation will shortly become a Nation of odd Fellows.

Besides the many Extravagancies, which this Set of Men are addicted to, they have all a strange Notion, that they must have their own Way. Mr. *Congreve* has observed,[1] that there is a Proverb by which they are, in a great Measure, governed. *He that will have a May-pole, shall have a May-pole.* They are entirely attached to the Gratification of their own particular Bent; their Imaginations have contracted such whimsical Habits, that they see Things through a Medium, to which Men of a more reasonable Turn, are Strangers; and thence it results, that wild and fantastick Opinions are delivered upon all Topics, and their Conduct is nothing but a Series of Inconsistencies.

The Person, who falls into this Way of thinking, is properly speaking an HUMOURIST, and *Quidquid vult, valde vult*, should be the Motto of every one of them; they being all inflexible in Pursuit of their Inclinations. It is a trite Remark, that the Spirit of Liberty and Independency, which is diffused throughout this Kingdom, contributes very much to

[1] In 'Concerning Humour in Comedy' (1695), J. E. Spingarm, ed., *Critical Essays of the Seventeenth Century* (1908), iii. 252.

feed this odd Turn, and to promote its Growth. I have mixed frequently in the Meetings of *Humourists*, in order to animadvert upon their Ways; and have always observed, that none of them will suffer themselves to be controuled, for this excellent Reason; because, 'D—mn my Blood, I can club my Reckoning as well as any Man, and I have been an House-keeper, Man and Boy these thirty or forty Years; and I pay my Rent, and so a Fig for King G——.' ——Thus, while the HUMOURIST has his Property secured to him, by the salutary Laws of our noble Constitution, he will enjoy his Independency; to give a Proof of which, he thinks it essential to have a Value for no Man; and to please himself, though at the Expence of his Company, is his darling Delight.

It is to the Observation of these Oddities, that we owe the MAN OF HUMOUR; and hence is deducible a Definition, or rather Description of his Character. He is one who *Eyes Natures Walks*, as Mr. *Pope* finely phrases it, and *catches the Manners living, as they rise*.[1] He sees the Foibles, which have taken Root in the Man, and the many motly Circumstances, which adhere to him. He looks, as it were, into his very mind, perceives there the Jaundice, through which every Thing passes; and from whence all Objects derive their Hue; he sees the Imagination tinged with this strange Dye, and all the Affections of the Soul discoloured by it. He views such Traces formed in his Brain, that it is rendered quite different, from that of any other human Creature; and thus the MAN OF HUMOUR perceives the secret and internal Springs of Action, which lead on the HUMOURIST; he cannot help smiling to see the Operations of his Soul so extravagant, and being acquainted with the latent Cause of those odd Appearances which disclose themselves upon all Occasions, he afterwards represents them to the World in true and lively Colours.

Thus may the two Characters in Question, be described, though they have been so much mistaken by many People. The Confusion, I apprehend, is owing to the vague Use of the Word HUMOUR, which is promiscuously applied to both. It is common to say of the HUMOURIST, he has his Humour, or it is his Humour, and of the humourous Man, we assert, that he has a great Fund of Humour. In both Cases, the Phrase carries with it a different Sense, denoting in the former Instance, the Foible or Whim, which operates upon the Man's Conduct, and in the latter signifying that Pleasantry, which represents the odd Fellow in a diverting Light. The Poverty of our Language has introduced this ambiguous Use of the Word, but if People would be careful to acquire

[1] *Essay on Man*, I. 13–14.

Perspicuity in their Ideas, and the Terms they express them by, it would prevent much Perplexity and Confusion.

For Instance, it would be absurd in any Critic, to call the inimitable Mr. *Fielding* an HUMOURIST, but he who would pronounce him to be a Man of exquisite Humour, would, I believe, express something more pertinent to the Point. In like Manner, Mr *Hogarth* has exhibited in his Pieces, with the most masterly Strokes of his Pencil, an whole Set of *Humourists*, and the ingenious Artist, who thus enchants our Eye, is undoubtedly a MAN OF HUMOUR.

★   ★   ★

146. [Arthur Murphy]
From *The Gray's-Inn Journal* No. 39

22 June 1754

The text used is that of the first printing; in the collected edition of 1756 this essay was renumbered 86 and redated 8 June 1754 (ii. 214–16). The essay is presented as a feigned letter regarding Parnassus as a parliament (alluding to the General Election of 1754).

★   ★   ★

The *New Interest* exulted greatly upon their Conquest in the last Election, and in order to compleat their Triumph, proceed further into the Regions of *Humour* and *Ridicule*. *Homer* was here again put up by *Aristotle*, who urged the *Margites* as a sufficient Claim; but the Writings of that Estate being lost, he was obliged to decline the Poll. After this an Advertisement was published, desiring the Votes and Interest of all the true Sons of Merriment for *Aristophanes, Menander, Plautus,* and *Terence*, who had just lost their Election in another Place; *Lucian* set up upon his own Interest. The *Moderns* declared *Cervantes, Rablais, Swift* and *Butler* joint Candidates, being all Gentlemen heartily attached to true Wit and Humour. Votes were also sollicited for several other Personages; Monsieur *la Sage, Scarroon, Marivaux,* and *Addison* were strongly recommended; but the latter being returned in Conjunction with *Terence* and *le Sage* for the Borough of POLITE-MIRTH, Sir *Richard Steel* appeared on the Hustings and withdrew his Friend's Name. *Swift* mixed with the lower Sort of People; joked with the Women about their Dressing Posteriors and republished his Account of the strange Man just arrived in Town. *Rablais* contributed a good deal to the general Mirth; *Cervantes* occasionally gave vent to a Vein of low Humour, but *Lucian* could not make himself universally understood, and many of his Turns did not allude to modern-practiced Life. *Scarroon* got together a Company of Strollers, and exhibited Entertainments in Booths with great Success. *Ward, Concanon,* and *Tom Brown* offered themselves on this Occasion, but were rejected with Contempt. At length the Books were closed, and *Lucian, Cervantes, Butler,* and *Swift* were declared duly elected. At which the Managers for the *New Interest* were highly inflamed; they lodged a Petition in Favour of *Rablais,* but such a Vein of Extravagance run through the Whole, and some Passages were worked up into such a Strain of unintelligible Frolic, that it was generally supposed it would be given against him. However, his friends were determined to bring him in for an inferior Borough, and *Scarroon* and *Marivaux* were also assured of their Election. Whenever *Fielding* shall take Possession of his Estate in this Part of *Parnassus,* there is a Borough ready to elect him.

147. [Arthur Murphy]
From *The Gray's-Inn Journal* No. 49

31 August 1754

The text used is that of the first printing; in the collected edition of 1756 the essay was renumbered 96 and redated 17 August 1754 (ii. 276–81). In this essay Murphy discusses definitions of the ridiculous, at one point turning to Shaftesbury's definition of ridicule as a test of truth:

★   ★   ★

The Dispute that subsisted among the learned for a considerable Time and is perhaps not yet determined, *viz.* Whether Ridicule is a Test of Truth, is, in my humble Opinion, extremely idle and frivolous; the Faculty of Reason, which compares our Ideas, and sustains or rejects the various Affirmations concerning them, being the sole Judge of Truth, however complicated the Means may be by which it gains its End. I have often wondered, that neither *Aristotle, Tully*, nor *Quintilian*, have given a just and adequate Definition of Ridicule. To say that it consist [*sic*] in raising our Laughter, at some Turpitude, is a very insufficient Account of the Matter. Mr. *Fielding*, in his Preface to his *Joseph Andrews*, has thrown some Light upon the Matter, but as he places the Source of it in Affectation, he appears to me not to have taken a comprehensive Survey of his Subject. I apprehend the Ridiculous may be formed, where there is no Affectation at the Bottom, and his Parson *Adams* I take to be an Instance of this Assertion.

The best and most accurate Definition I have ever met with of the Ridiculous is in a note of Doctor *Akenside*'s to his excellent Poem *on the Pleasures of Imagination*. '*That, says he, which makes Objects ridiculous is some Ground of Admiration or Esteem connected with other more general Circumstances, comparatively worthless or deformed; or it is some Circumstances of Turpitude or Deformity connected with what is in General excellent*

375

or beautiful; the inconsistent Properties existing either in the Objects them-
selves, or in the Apprehension of the Person to whom they relate, implying
Sentiment or Design, and exciting no acute or vehement Emotion of the
Heart.'[1] . . . .

The Emotions here intended are Laughter and Contempt, and these
it is the Business of Comedy to excite, by making striking Exhibitions
of inconsistent Circumstances, blended together in such a thwarting
Assemblage, that a gay Contempt irresistably shall take Possession of
us. . . .

148. [Arthur Murphy]
From *The Gray's-Inn Journal* No. 50

6 September 1754

The text again is of the first edition; in the collected edition of 1756
the essay is renumbered 97 and redated 23 August 1754 (ii. 283–5).

Angustis hunc addere rebus honorem,   Virg.
Ampullas & Sesquipedalia verba.   Hor.[2]

HAVING in my last offered some cursory Remarks upon RIDICULE,
I shall in this Day's Paper take Notice of a Species of Writing, which on
Account of some Affinity between them, is often supposed to be the
same with the Ridiculous; and yet, upon an attentive View of the
Matter, it appears to be a Mode of Composition introduced by Men of
Genius in order to fall in with that Propensity to Laughter, which pre-
vails with all Mankind in general. What I here intend is *Burlesque*; and,

---

[1] Note on Bk. III, l. 248.

[2] 'To add this dignity to ordinary subjects.' *Georgics*, III. 290. 'Bombast and fifty-cent
words.' *The Art of Poetry*, l. 97.

in my humble opinion, to mark its Boundaries, its Procedure and Extent, will be no improper Subject among these Essays, which only pretend now and then to glance so much Light upon Matters of this Nature, as may serve to illustrate them to the unlearned.

It must be remembered, that as the *ridiculous* consists in a Coalition of Circumstances repugnant to each other in their own Natures, but yet whimsically blended together in any Object, any human Action or Passion, to call forth this Inconsistency to public View, and to shew the heterogeneous Assemblage, in such a Manner as to provoke the Mind to laugh at it with Contempt, is to exert the rare and excellent talent of *Ridicule*, and as this is attended when well executed, with fine consequential Effects, the Lovers of *Burlesque* will not wait to discover a real Incongruity, but by the Force of their own Imaginations they create it for themselves, and by obtruding Circumstances which perhaps do not belong to the Object, they are frequently very successful in rendering Things apparently ridiculous, which to an attentive Eye may not wear the motly Livery, however it may serve the Purposes of Mirth to invest it with it. In order to explain more fully, what is here insisted on, it may not be improper to lay before the Reader an Instance or two of the *Ridiculous*, and also of *Burlesque*, which may in some Measure serve to render this Matter still more intelligible and clear.

When *Fielding*'s Parson *Adams* being in Distress at an Inn, retires very gravely with a *London* Bookseller to raise Money upon some Manuscript Sermons, I believe the dissonant Circumstances in this Case strike very forcibly, and our Laughter is still urged with greater Impetuosity, when, after having travelled a great many Miles from his own Place of Abode towards *London*, with no other Business upon Earth, but to dispose of these Sermons, we hear the Parson not being able to find them, very gravely say, '*I protest I believe I left them behind me.*' When the same Personage assures us, that he is very rich, and then adds, that he does not say it by way of boasting or complying with worldly vanity, but to shew that he can live well on the Road, and, to confirm this, produces half a Guinea, the Difference between his Opinion and the small value of the Piece, and this too from a Clergyman, a Scholar, and in many Things a Man of excellent Understanding, produces an Emotion of Laughter attended in this Instance with a Contempt for *Adam*'s Want of Knowledge of the World. In like manner, when *Don Quixote* very gravely says, that he has seen the Sea, and that it is much larger than the River at *La Mancha*, we cannot help laughing at a Man who has formed his Ideas of Things by what he has seen at his own native Place, and to find an insignificant River compared to the Sea, presents such a re-pugnant Conjunction of Images, as must necessarily operate upon our risible Faculties.

These Instances, which have first, among a Thousand, offered them-selves to my Memory, are true Instances of the *Ridiculous*, nothing here being obtruded upon our Imaginations, but in *Burlesque* there are many adventitious Ideas called up, in order to form a motly Concurrence of thwarting Images, and so produce the same Effect with the really *Ridiculous*. As for Instance, if any Object which comes before the *Burlesque* Writer, be low in its own Nature, he immediately bethinks himself of conferring on it a mock Dignity, in which it begins to look big, like the Champion at a Coronation, who boldly challenges all Mankind when he knows no Body will fight him. I have ever been highly pleased with a Touch of this Kind in a Note to Mr. *Fielding's Tom Thumb*, where mentioning something of the Soul of Man, he gravely tells us, '*Plato is of this Opinion, and so is—Mr. Banks.*'[1] The Stroke in the *Beggar's Opera* is of the same Nature—'*There is nothing so merry as a great Man in Distress*'.[2] In this Case the great Disproportion between the two Objects strikes our Imagination, and our Laughter bursts out at that which is, without Foundation, set in Competition.

✶   ✶   ✶

[1] *The Tragedy of Tragedies*, I. ii. note 13.
[2] Cf. III. xv, where Lucy says, 'There is nothing moves one so much as a great man in distress.' In the 1756 edition *'merry'* was changed to 'moving'.

149. Lady Mary Wortley Montagu, letter

23 July 1754

From a letter to the Countess of Bute, *Letters and Works of Lady Mary Wortley Montagu*, ii. 279–80. Text collated with Halsband's transcript in *Philological Quarterly* (1966) xlv. 154.

★   ★   ★

H. Fielding has given a true picture of himself and his first wife, in the characters of Mr. and Mrs. Booth, some compliments to his own figure excepted; and, I am persuaded, several of the incidents he mentions are real matters of fact. I wonder he does not perceive Tom Jones and Mr. Booth are sorry scoundrels. All these sort of books have the same fault, which I cannot easily pardon, being very mischievous. They place a merit in extravagant passions, and encourage young people to hope for impossible events to draw them out of the misery they chose to plunge themselves into, expecting legacies from unknown relations, and generous benefactors to distressed virtue, as much out of nature as fairy treasures. Fielding has really a fund of true humor, and was to be pitied at his first entrance into the world, having no choice (as he said himself) but to be a hackney writer or a hackney coachman. His genius deserved a better fate; but I cannot help blaming that continued indiscretion, to give it the softest name, that has run through his life, and I am afraid still remains. I guessed R. Random to be his, though without his name. I cannot think Fadom [Ferdinand Fathom] wrote by the same hand, it is every way so much below it.

★   ★   ★

150. 'From Joseph Addison to the Author of Tom Jones'

1754

Letter XVI in *Admonitions from the Dead in Epistles to the Living* (1754), pp. 215–28.

On the Qualifications of modern Writers, and the Art of Writing.

There is a Time when Men the most readily receive Information, and it is generally when the Season in which it could be of Use is at an End. Perhaps if I were ask'd in what Instance this was most obvious, and least to be overcome, the Answer would be among those who write. That I think you worthy Information, is the Reason of my writing to you at this Time. That I supposed it would be vain to attempt conveying that Information, so as to make it regarded, while you was actually employing yourself in this Manner, is the Reason that I did not give it sooner. If People will not repent of their Sins, while they have Spirit and Strength to keep in the Course of them, even tho' one rose from the Dead; yet it is possible that they may, on the lesser Consideration of receiving Intelligence from them, be convinc'd of their Follies, when they have already declin'd the Use of them.

It is for many Years that I have look'd upon you, among a Multitude of Men, who, because they could make Letters, supposed they were able to write, as one of another Stamp and Character; who ought to be inform'd of your own Importance; but who, as it would have been impossible to have made you sensible that your Faults were Faults, while they were so pleasing to you, would only have been spoil'd by that Information. Now you have done: or, for that will answer the same Purpose, now you believe you have done, you may attend with Impartiality. Having no longer any Tongue, you may be the more distinct of Ear; and after seeing what is, and what is not in your Power, you may be more useful to the World in one Pamphlet, than hitherto in forty Volumes.

It has grieved me to see so much Power to do good as you have possess'd, employ'd to so little Purpose as you have employ'd it. For tho' there are few of your Writings that have been plan'd with a different Intent, and perhaps not any, unless at Times when your Necessities inspir'd them, I think the Defect of that which ought to be the End of all Writing is too evident in most, not to say all of them, when there appears any thing that has the Face of Morality, it seems to have fallen in your Way by Chance, rather than to have been an original Part of the Design; and when I read those Things, they bring to my Mind certain Answers often made before you, on a different Occasion: when Persons being asked how they came by Things, we did not expect to find in their Possession, answer, that *they found them in the Street*.

Wit, the most dangerous Weapon in the Hands of an ill-natur'd, or ill Man, that could be put into them, you possess, or have possessed in a Degree superior to all your Cotemporaries. But it were well if you had apply'd it to those Purposes which it would so happily have answer'd in the Hands of a good, or good-natur'd Person. I am not about to censure you in Wantonness; so shall not produce from your several Works, Instances of the Manner in which you have used this Talent: but for the future, when you write, (for I know you must write,) direct the Artillery against Vice; Folly does not deserve it, while the other is so frequent. Do this, and the Remains shall be of more Use to the World, nay, and of more Honour to yourself, than the full Power of it. Men will place more value in the little Brook, retir'd at length within the Confines of its natural and narrow Margin, while it cherishes all Things in its Course; than they did upon the full Torrent when, swell'd by melted Snows and continu'd Rains, all its Magnificence was mischievous.

Ridicule, tho' one of the lowest Parts of what deserves the Name of Wit; nay, Humour, which, if there be a yet lower, is that lowest, may be rendered useful; No Man has possessed it more perfectly than you have done. Nature joined in you the Spirit of the late *Rabelais*, and of the early *Lucian*: but you have not employed them as they did. She has given you, with the Humour, a double Portion of the Indelicacy of the *Frenchman*, and with the Wit of the *Greek*, a Tenfold Freedom where Restraint was necessary. If you have misapplied your Wit, you have trifled away these lesser Talents; and I believe it were well if no Account were call'd for. But as there are in this Place no Omissions, do that which is yet in your Power; bury the ill Use you have made of them, under a better.

Severity you have possessed in the same superior Degree; but it were to be wish'd you had made of this, as of your other Talents, an Use that would be pleasing to you in the Recollection. If a Man were to be pick'd up out of all the World to hunt another down to Death and Desperation, you are the foremost: but what should we say of that Dog, who having Power to tear the Wolf, worried the Sheep?

I hope you will hereafter use this better. There are Men who deserve all your Severity, but they have yet escaped it: there are those who deserve your Approbation; be generous, and declare it. But hereafter use more Discretion in your Praise, and less Bitterness in your Severity. When you would wound, the Dagger must be carried in the Thought, not in the Hand; and you may learn from every common Reader, that ill Language, as it is below Wit, so is it understood never to be connected with it, but always to be employed in its Place.

As I would have you put to a more proper Use those Things which you possess, so I would wish you to avoid making Pretences to such as you have not. Too much Force laid upon any one thing, that is in itself valuable, makes the Judicious doubt whether you have it. For it savours of Affectation. If God and Religion are in your Heart, you are so much the better, and the happier Man; but unless they are in your Practice also, they have no Business to be upon your Tongue. All Affectation hurts an Author in the Eye of those whose Praise is worth deserving, but of all kinds that most which has Respect to Things most sacred.

Believe that you may err, and carrying that modest Opinion always with you, never be positive. The Antients, with whom few People are more acquainted than you are, had scarce an Expression in their common Conversation that amounted to absolute Affirmation: and instead of that positive Oath which is so constantly expected, and so readily given in our Courts of Justice, they hardly expected more at their most solemn Tribunals, and on the most important Occasions, than the Witnesses serious Attestation that such or such was his Belief of the Matter. Whether he had Reason for that Belief, others were to judge. I think that in those Days, false Evidence was rare; you are a good Judge whether it be more or less rare now. But I named this not for others, but for yourself. As you know, and as I doubt not approve their Custom, imitate it; and where at least you have not absolute Knowledge, speak with Reserve. The Credit the World is ready to pay to what you say, ought to have Weight to inspire you doubly with this Caution: and your Reputation will be concerned, for there is nothing that reflects so much upon a Man's Judgement as to have been very positive in a Thing in which it after appears he was wrong. When Circumstances seem the most convincing, it is possible all may be false which they are advanced to prove, because they also may be feigned as well as real; and he who cannot know the Heart, cannot be assur'd in any thing that is otherwise. This single Consideration ought to stamp a Character of Uncertainty upon every thing that has not been in all Parts the Object of our own Senses; and what we conceive as uncertain, we have no Right to speak of as if sure. Get the better of that false Pride, which has its Origin in the Sense we entertain of our own superior Discernment, and you will not then find it difficult to speak on these Occasions with the necessary Reserve. I shall acknowledge to you freely, that very few Men have more Right to assume to themselves upon a more than ordinary Discernment than you have, but none has a Right that ought to lead him to the Insolence of Certainty; none can while he is mortal, nor is it expected of any.

There is therefore no Derogation in speaking with some Degree of Doubt; and, far from taking from, it adds to the Character of the Person, who so speaks, or writes, which ever Way the Event falls out. If it be according to the Opinion, none supposes that was the less certain in the Breast of him who spoke with Diffidence, while what he spoke has been found Truth: this is the Consequence, if all be right; and if it fall out otherwise, all Imputation is avoided: Friends will have no Occasion to shake their Heads, nor Enemies Opportunity to triumph. He who spoke with that Uncertainty, which became a Person who might err, will never be accused for having err'd; but what he deliver'd as his Opinion will be weighed as an Opinion, and if he entertain'd it fairly, and with Candour, it will be allowed to have had Reason: whereas, had the Event been otherwise, it would have been call'd a modest Way of proposing what the Person knew to be certain.

If there be any thing which deserves to be admitted as an additional Consideration to the speaking doubtfully of *Things*; it is the speaking candidly of *Men*: and above all other Men, of those who also write. I know how natural Envy is to those who see a Superior in their own Way; and I know how prevalent that false Ambition often is, which, when a Man is acknowledged to be the first in his Way, cannot rest unless he be alone. Of all Persons of the present Time, you have the least Temptation to the first of these Faults; and you will not be in Danger of falling into it, because you are sufficiently sensible that you have no such Occasion: as to the other, I am afraid I have distinguished in you somewhat too much of it. Let us reason concerning this fairly.

You are allowed to be, in your Way, the first Writer of your Age and Nation; and you have not a Desire to be allowed more; since you have not attempted to go out of that Way, in which you have succeeded so happily. What then is your Ambition? Is it, that none should do well in any other Road? That is extravagant; and I cannot charge any thing of it upon you. Was Archbishop *Tillotson* the less a Preacher, because Sir *Isaac Newton* was reverenced for the Mathematicks? or had the Laurels of *Pope* the less Lustre, because *Bolingbroke* exceeds in Prose? certainly not: and yet it is not impossible, that one of these, tho' there is only one who can be suspected of it, might have looked with ill Eyes upon another. But I acquit you generally of this Fault: if you have ever fallen into it, the World has not perceived it: and if you ever should again, be wary how you write. There is a Way of doing Hurt, without seeming to intend it. This is mean. But this is, for the Person who attempts it much better than that, which beside that it is certain to miss its Aim, will not fail to throw upon him who offered the Insult, all the Shame he meant to lay upon the other.

I must be more express with you upon the other Head, else I shall act less candidly. 'Tis certain, that while you are allowed to excel others, you are not satisfied with the Praise, unless you can make it be thought that they cannot do well. If generous Minds condemn that Envy which wishes Ill to those who are above us in our own Way; much more do they condemn that Spirit; which directs its ill Designs against those whom it ought to pity.

But let us suppose that among those who have attempted to make themselves conspicuous for their Genius, during that Time when yours was in its fullest Glory, some have had more than the Desire of doing this: nay, let us suppose, what perhaps is more than the Truth, that many of them have been possess'd of Genius and Abilities, enough to attract the Attention and Command, in some Degree, the Approbation, of the World; tho' weak, and little, in Comparison of yours. Was it your Interest to take from these the little Laurels they had obtained, even if it were in your Power to do it? No. Is it not better to excel there where many succeed, than to be alone the Person who have attempted? Assuredly it is: and so long as that Superiority is allowed to you, the greater is their Merit who have attempted, and the higher does it carry your Triumph.

This is undoubtedly the Case. But supposing your Interest, for I now talk to you on no other Principle, lay in the taking from these the scanty Reputation they had some Way or other obtained, in Spite of your Preeminence: does it appear to you, that violent Censure is the Way to effect this? Be assur'd it is not. No good was ever done to the very worst Cause, by Violence: many a good one has been lost by it; and, if we descend to the Particulars, and consider what may be the natural Effect of Scurrility, and ill Language, we shall find, that in the Pamphlet, as in the Street, it reverts upon the Person who utters it, without any Injury to him against whom 'twas levelled. This is only contemptible, when used by those who have no other Weapons; but when it takes the Place of Wit; and when all that decent Reproof, which, if there be Occasion for it, is in your Power, gives Way to it, there rises as much Indignation in the Breasts of those who read it: and he who writes, is hated as much as he is despised.

Severity of Satyr, even if it be carried to the Height without this Stain, yet is, of all Things, that for which a judicious Writer would least wish to be prais'd. Because those who prais'd, would at the same Time dread him; and Men naturally hate what they fear. No one is secure from these Arrows; and as they often fly in the Dark, there is always Suspicion, that they may come unprovoked; because the Hand may be unseen that draws the Bow. Caprice may break a Friendship, which no Fault on their own Part would have ever destroyed; and they may always fear this Caprice, and fear also the Person whom it may from a Friend convert into our Enemy. He who can make so terrible an Use of the Trifles he has heard, and that imperfectly, of a Stranger, how will he swell the Account against him whose Secrets he has known? What is there he will not divulge of these? and what is there he will not add? and of all that he can add, What is there that will not be believed? Men are ill-natur'd too often, and those who are inclin'd to think the worst, will receive all as Truth, because there is some Pretence for supposing he who writes has known it all.

This is the Light in which every Man will see the Satyrist, who, with the Power of wounding, possesses that Badness of Heart which will give him Pleasure in doing it. All will dread him, and he can never be assur'd that those with whom he is in the most perfect Intimacy, do not in their Hearts detest him. We see farther, who are out of the World, than you do who are in it; and, believe a friendly Shade, who tells you that this has been the Case with many, who have thought themselves happy in their Friendships; and this has been the Case with you. I shall not particularise your Friends, thro' Fear; but they make too great a Part of those you call by that general Name: of these, there is not one whom you may not convert into such as you now take him to be;

and all that is wanting to this, is your own Choice to have it so.

Were you less capable of writing, or were it probable you should discontinue writing, this had been unnecessary, but as you have Talents, and are so accustomed to the employing them that you will not wholly leave off doing it, I have said all this to you, partly for your own Sake, and partly for the Sake of the World. 'Tis in your Power to be more your own Friend; and 'tis your duty to be so to others. Use your Talents, for they were given you for that Purpose; and, if you have at any Time abused the Intent with which they were given, atone for the Fault, by the Manner in which you shall now employ them. Farewell.

THE JOURNAL OF A VOYAGE
TO LISBON

25 February 1755[1]

---

151. Unsigned notice, *The London Magazine*

February 1755, xxiv. 54–6

There has just appeared a Posthumous Work of the late Mr. Fielding, called
A Journal of a Voyage to Lisbon; *which is far from doing discredit to his
Memory: It contains many Circumstances that must give it an extraordinary
Relish to Persons of Benevolence and Humanity; and is such a Specimen of
the Strength even of an expiring Genius, that our Readers will excuse our
giving them an Extract from it; wherein he is describing the Inconveniencies
he endured on Shipboard, and his own depressed State of Health, which
encreased the Mortifications he went thro'. It seems to have been published for
the Benefit of his Children, which, as the Dedication to the Publick, says,*
'will no doubt be a Motive to encourage its Circulation through the
Kingdom.'

[Quotation of *Journal*, Henley, xvi. 200–2]

---

[1] This is the earlier, 'edited' version of the *Journal*. Andrew Millar did not publish the
longer original text until early December 1755.

THE JOURNAL AND ANSWER
TO BOLINGBROKE

152. Unsigned notice
The Gentleman's Magazine
March 1755, xxv. 129

This journal contains an account of the adventures and distresses of the author and his family, in a journey from *Fordham* to *Rotherhithe*, on board the ship; thence to the isle of *Wight*, and on shore there, while they were wind bound, at a paltry alehouse, where, as the best room, they chose to dine in a barn. The captain, the seamen, the landlady and her husband, and several other characters, which the particular circumstances of his situation brought under his notice, are described, with that humour in which he is confessed to have excelled every other writer of his age. But this little book would be very valuable for the instruction which it contains, if the entertainment was wanting; the remarks upon his own situation, upon the manners of others, upon many intollerable inconveniences which arise either from the defect of our laws, or the ignorance of those by whom they should be executed, deserve the attention not of individuals only but of the public.

★   ★   ★

[Quotation on the importance of English fisheries, Henley, xvi. 263–6[1]]
The fragment of an answer to *Bolinbroke*, however short, will strongly incline every man who has a taste for wit, and a love of truth, to wish it was longer.

[1] In a later issue (Jan. 1756, xxvi. 22), the *Gentleman's Magazine* speaks again of the 'important truths' regarding English fisheries 'advanced by Mr. *Fielding* in his Voyage to *Lisbon*'.

153. Unsigned notice, *The Monthly Review*

March 1755, xii. 234–5

As this publication is intended to be of service to the widow and children of the very ingenious author, it would be inhumanity to search it for imperfections; but there is another powerful reason for its exemption from criticism; which we shall give in the words of the editor.[1]—'If in this little work there should appear any traces of a weakened and decayed life, let the reader's imagination place before his eyes a true picture, in that of a hand trembling in almost its latest hour, of a body emaciated with pains, yet struggling for our entertainment; and let this affecting picture open each tender heart, and call forth a melting tear, to blot out whatever failings may be found in a work begun in pain, and finished almost at the same period with life.'—

This narrative, tho' not greatly abounding with incidents, we have perused with some pleasure. The reflections interspersed in it, are worthy of a writer, than whom few, if any, have been more justly celebrated for a thorough insight into human nature: tho', as the editor remarks, 'it must be acknowledged, that a lamp almost burnt out, does not give so steady and uniform a light, as when it blazes in its full vigour; but yet it is well known, that by its wavering, as if struggling against its own dissolution, it sometimes darts a ray as bright as ever'.—We are given to understand, that Mr. *Fielding* hath left behind him some other pieces, which, we hope, will follow this last written, tho' first published, posthumous volume of an author, who long hath been, and will continue to be, the delight of his readers. The fragment annexed to this journal of Mr. *Fielding*'s, entitled *A comment on Lord* Bolingbroke's *essays*, is a small introductory sketch, of only twenty-seven pages; in which the author shews himself in a new and advantageous light; so that we cannot but think it a misfortune to the public, that he did not live to prosecute and finish his design.

[1] i.e. John Fielding.

154. Horace Walpole, letter

27 March 1755

From a letter to Richard Bentley, *Letters of Horace Walpole*, ed. Paget Toynbee (1903), iii. 294.

★   ★   ★

You will receive, some time or other, or the French for you, the following books: a fourth volume of Dodsley's *Collection of Poems*,[1] the worst tome of the four; three volumes of *Worlds*;[2] Fielding's Travels, or rather an account how his dropsy was treated and teased by an inn-keeper's wife in the Isle of Wight.

★   ★   ★

[1] The enlarged 1755 edition of Robert Dodsley's *A Collection of Poems by Several Hands*.
[2] i.e. *The World*, to which Walpole himself occasionally contributed.

155. Unsigned letter

31 March 1755

This letter, possibly by Margaret Collier to Samuel Richardson, is to be found in J. Paul de Castro, 'Henry Fielding's Last Voyage', *The Library* (1917), viii. 157–9.

Ryde in ye Isle of Wight March 31st 1755.

We had the curiosity at this place to visit the landlord and landlady whom Mr. F. has thought worthy so much of notice, and given so large a place to, in his late book, and of whom he tells us, the description is lowered instead of being heightened, recommending us to that of the Furies for an idea of the woman; but I must confess the sight of her, having as he observes many symptoms of a deep jaundice in her look, rais'd in my mind nothing but compassion; and in her behaviour we saw yet less of the character of those infernal deities. We ask'd them if they remembred [*sic*] Mr. F., they told us he had lodg'd with them, and had given them a great deal of trouble, and that they thought Mr. F. the strangest man in the world, whom it was impossible to please: The chamber he lodged in here was the best I ever saw in a house of the size and sort, nor did it want very sufficient and decent furniture, there were two good beds in it, and a handsome looking-glass, which Mr. F. had a napkin put over, that he might not be struck with his own figure, while he was exaggerating that of others: in his room he cook'd his victuals, dressing as much as he could of it by a chamber fire; and making the sauce himself. Here sending one day for the landlord to keep him company, while his own were gone out, and he enquiring of his health and expressing his wishes for the amendment of it, he saluted the stoic with imprecations, bad him not talk of his health, but confine himself to the subject of husbandry, which was what he wanted to talk to him about: now whatever means Mr. F. had used to try the temper of the woman, whom he pronounced it impossible to please, he certainly put to the proof that of the man, whom he honestly confesses it impossible to displease. We found the circumstances of their dining in a barn a fiction, there was no such barn with a pleasant view to the fields, nor dined they out of the house. The venison so miraculously receiv'd on their coming to a place, whither they were by accident driven; was not in fact so great a miracle as it appears in the story, for Mr. F's servant was dispatch'd to Southampton to buy it, and paid half a guinea for it, but whom it was bought of remains a secret to this day, and very happily for the seller it does so. Fortune indeed must have been a very cunning goddess and attended very closely the steps of our author; to have found him at casting anchor with a present of a buck ready for his acceptance; the circumstances then relating to the venison we were convinced were wholly misrepresented.

As to the old woman, I believe she was naturally afflicted with too much gall, and now indeed was plainly dying under the overflowing of it, and consequently demanded great allowances on that score; but I am surprized that so great an observer of the humours of the lower class of people, had never discovered that the circumstance of paying them, will not always make them amends for the trouble you give them: I have seen those who have been very poor, and yet rather than be put out of their way would forego the profitts that would attend doing what they did not like, or were not used to: and Mr. F. was certainly under great obligations to any body that would admit him into their house, whom disease had render'd offensive to more senses than one: indeed our author appears under as great infirmities as the old woman, or any old woman whatever, and lays great claim from others of that charitable allowance, which a man of sound mind and body would have made for this poor creature. In this house he pass'd the last days he saw in his native land, in abusing the people to whom he was under some obligation, and yet not confining his invectives to them only—in ransacking every place for the means to gratify his depraved appetite, in tormenting himself, and all about him: afraid to see his own figure, unwilling to correct himself, he exposed that of others, and railed at their Faults.—

N.B. Tho' Mr. F. has printed the bills that were made him at the Inn, he paid them no more than he chose.—

156. Thomas Edwards, letter

28 May 1755

From a letter to Samuel Richardson, Forster MS. XII, f. 141. Reprinted in A. D. McKillop, *Samuel Richardson* (1936), p. 176; cf. Barbauld, iii. 125.

★　　★　　★

I have lately read over with much indignation Fielding's last piece, called his Voyage to Lisbon. That a man, who had led such a life as he had, should trifle in that manner when immediate death was before his eyes is amazing; but his impudence, in attributing that to your works[1] which is the true character of his own which are the reverse of yours, is what puts me beyond all patience. It seems to me as if conscious that the world would not join with Warburton in transferring the palm from your's to his desertless head,[2] he envied the reputation which you have so justly gained in that way of writing. From this book I am confirmed in what his other books had fully persuaded me of, that with all his parade of pretences to virtuous and humane affections, the fellow had no heart. And so—his knell is knoll'd.

★　　★　　★

[1] In the Preface, Fielding had humorously referred to 'the conduct of authors, who often fill a whole sheet with their own praises, to which they sometimes set their own real names, and sometimes a fictitious one' (Henley, xvi. 185). Edwards had briefly commented on the same point in a letter to Daniel Wray, 23 May 1755 (Bodley MS. 1012, p. 208): 'Fielding's Voyage is the arrantest catch-penny that ever was published; I am amazed that a man who felt himself dying by inches could be so idly employed; but his insolent censure of Mr. Richardson is unpardonable because it is highly unjust.' In another letter to Wray, of 16 June (Bodley MS. 1012, p. 212), he adds: 'Fielding's malevolence against our friend was the more unpardonable as the Good Man had once by his interposition saved his bones and at the very last by his correspondence at Lisbon had procured him accommodations which he could not otherwise have had.'

[2] A reference to Warburton's note on Fielding in his edition of Pope (see above, No. 103).

157. Lady Mary Wortley Montagu, letter

22 September [1755]

From a letter to the Countess of Bute, *Letters and Works of Lady Mary Wortley Montagu*, ii. 282-3.

*　　*　　*

I am sorry for H. Fielding's death, not only as I shall read no more of his writings, but I believe he lost more than others, as no man enjoyed life more than he did, though few had less reason to do so, the highest of his preferment being raking in the lowest sinks of vice and misery. I should think it a nobler and less nauseous employment to be one of the staff-officers that conduct the nocturnal weddings. His happy constitution (even when he had, with great pains, half demolished it) made him forget everything when he was before a venison pasty, or over a flask of champagne; and I am persuaded he has known more happy moments than any prince upon earth. His natural spirits gave him rapture with his cook-maid, and cheerfulness when he was fluxing in a garret. There was a great similitude between his character and that of Sir Richard Steele. He had the advantage both in learning and, in my opinion, genius: they both agreed in wanting money in spite of all their friends, and would have wanted it, if their hereditary lands had been as extensive as their imagination; yet each of them [was] so formed for happiness, it is pity he was not immortal. . . .

The most edifying part of the Journey to Lisbon, is the history of the kitten: I was the more touched by it, having a few days before found one, in deplorable circumstances, in a neighbouring vineyard. I did not only relieve her present wants with some excellent milk, but had her put into a clean basket, and brought to my own house, where she has lived ever since very comfortably.

I desire to have Fielding's posthumous works, with his Memoirs of Jonathan Wild, and Journey to the Next World: also the Memoirs of Verocand, a man of pleasure, and those of a Young Lady. You will call all this trash, trumpery, &c.

*　　*　　*

394

158. Margaret Collier, letter

3 October 1755

From a letter to Samuel Richardson, Barbauld, ii. 77–8.

★   ★   ★

I was sadly vexed, at my first coming, at a report which had prevailed here, of my being the author of Mr. Fielding's last work, 'The Voyage to Lisbon:' the reason which was given for supposing it mine, was to the last degree mortifying, (viz. that it was so very bad a performance, and fell so far short of his other works, it must needs be the person *with him* who wrote it. . . .

FIELDING'S UNDERSTANDING
OF HUMAN NATURE

159. Samuel Richardson, letter

7 December 1756

From a letter to Sarah Fielding, Carroll, p. 330.

*   *   *

I amuse myself as well as I can with reading. I have just gone through your two vols. of Letters.[1] Have reperused them with great pleasure, and found many new beauties in them. What a knowledge of the human heart! Well might a critical judge of writing say, as he did to me, that your late brother's knowledge of it was not (fine writer as he was) comparable to your's. His was but as the knowledge of the outside of a clock-work machine, while your's was that of all the finer springs and movements of the inside.

*   *   *

[1] i.e. *Familiar Letters Between the Principal Characters in David Simple* (1747).

160. [Arthur Murphy], *The Literary Magazine* No. 11

15 February–15 March 1757, p. 78

From a review of Samuel Foote's *The Author*; reprinted in *New Essays by Arthur Murphy*, ed. Arthur Sherbo (1963), 119–20.

★   ★   ★

The primary intention of farce is, and ever ought to be, to promote laughter by scenes of pleasantry. It does not from hence follow that an author has a right to pursue every whimsical caprice that enters into his imagination, or that he is licenced to indulge himself in a frolicsome deviation from nature. Farce is to Comedy what the *caricatura* is to the just and regular designs of portrait-painting: a feature may allowably be exaggerated beyond its due proportion; a cast may be given to the eye; the nose may be represented shapeless, defects may be heightened into enormities, and the drapery may be so fantastically imagined as to give a burlesque appearance to the whole form; but in the general air of the countenance and the figure, there must be still a regard to nature, and some touches of resemblance must be preserved to shew that it is not a non-existence, a mere creature of the writer's over-heated imagination. The same rule will hold good with regard to the exhibition of farcical personages. Foibles may be enlarged, and even imaginary circumstances may be obtruded, in order to season the ridicule as highly as possible, and to give a kind of grotesque attitude to the portraiture. These touches of bizarre imitation sometimes occur in scenes of comedy, where exactness and truth are more in demand: and we likewise find something of this stile in picturing the manners of the comic romance, which is to comedy, what the sublime epic is to tragedy.

This distinction is as old as *Aristotle*, and would in all probability be felt by every reader, had not the *Margites* of *Homer* unfortunately perished.[1] For instances of farcical imitation there is no necessity of pointing out the *Bobadil* of *Johnson*, the Sir *Joseph Wittol* and *Nol Bluff* of *Congreve*,[2] together with many personages of *Shakespeare*. In the mock epic we may reasonably presume that there are many strokes of this over-charged painting in the *Don Quixote* of *Cervantes*, and in *Scarron*'s comic romance. In the only writer of deserved estimation in this way among ourselves, it is not difficult to remember lineaments extended beyond their boundaries, without turning over the pages of *Joseph Andrews* and *Tom Jones* for the example; though in general it must be said of Mr. *Fielding* that the strokes of his brush are correct and reserved. If this liberty is taken in compositions of the highest comic, a farce writer may surely be allowed to 'outstep the modesty of nature,'[3] in order to impress the signatures of ridicule more strongly on the mind, and thereby more powerfully to answer the primary intention of his work, which is raise a laugh.

$$\star \qquad \star \qquad \star$$

[1] Cf. the preface to *Joseph Andrews*.
[2] Ben Jonson, *Every Man in his Humour*; Congreve, *The Old Bachelor*.
[3] *Hamlet*, III. ii. 19.

161. Thomas Barrett Lennard, twenty-sixth Baron Dacre, letter

May 1757

From a letter to Sanderson Miller, in *An Eighteenth-Century Correspondence* (1910), p. 366.

Sanderson Miller, the architect, had been one of the party at Radway Grange who heard parts of the unpublished *Tom Jones* read by Fielding. In 1757 Lord Dacre sent him a prescription for curing 'the Blew Devils', which included the advice:

Let no thing induce you now to Read too serious or abstracted Books: Don Quixote is better for you than all of them put together, or Gil Blas or Tom Jones or Joseph Andrews: In all this *Experto Crede*.

* * *

162. Horace Walpole

1759

From *The Parish Register of Twickenham* (1759), in Austin Dobson, *Horace Walpole* (1927), p. 178.
'Twit'nam,' writes Walpole, is the place.

Where Fielding met his bunter muse,
And, as they quaff'd the fiery juice,
Droll Nature stamp'd each lucky hit
With inimaginable wit[1]

★　　★　　★

[1] In 1752 Fielding took a farm called Fordhook in Ealing, which remained his summer residence for the rest of his life (Cross, ii. 289–90).

163. Oliver Goldsmith, *The Bee*

10 November 1759

From an essay 'On Education', *Collected Works of Oliver Goldsmith*, ed. Arthur Friedman (1965), i. 461.

Discussing the importance of frugality in the education of a boy, Goldsmith makes an allusion to Fielding that reflects Johnson's view in *Rambler* No. 4 (see above, No. 92).

★　　★　　★

Instead, therefore, of romances, which praise young men of spirit, who go through a variety of adventures, and at last conclude a life of dissipation, folly, and extravagance in riches and matrimony, there should be some men of wit employed to compose books that might equally interest the passions of our youth, where such an one might be praised for having resisted allurements when young, and how he at last became lord mayor; how he was married to a lady of great sense, fortune, and beauty; to be as explicit as possible, the old story of Whittington, were his cat left out, might be more serviceable to the tender mind, than either Tom Jones, Joseph Andrews, or an hundred others, where frugality is the only good quality the hero is not possessed of.[1]

★　　★　　★

[1] Fielding may also have been in Goldsmith's mind when he said much the same of romances in *The Citizen of the World*, Letter LXXXIII (originally published 15 Oct. 1750; *Collected Works*, ii. 340–1).

164. [Elizabeth Montagu], 'Plutarch, Charon, and a modern Bookseller'

1760

Dialogue XXVIII in George, Lord Lyttelton, *Dialogues of the Dead* (1760), pp. 318–19.

Discussing the novels of Richardson, and especially *Sir Charles Grandison*, in which the protagonist is 'a noble Pattern of every private Virtue, with sentiments so exalted as to render him equal to every public Duty', Plutarch asks, 'Are there no other Authors who write in this manner?'

BOOKSELLER

Yes, we have another writer of these imaginary Histories; One who has not long since descended to these regions; his Name is Fielding, and his works, as I have heard the best judges say, have a true spirit of Comedy, and an exact representation of Nature, with fine moral touches. He has not indeed given lessons of pure and consummate Virtue, but he has exposed Vice and Meanness with all the powers of ridicule; and we have some other good *Wits* who have exerted their Talents to the Purposes you approve. Monsieur de Marivaux and some other French writers have also proceeded much upon the same Plan, with a spirit and elegance which give their works no mean rank among the *Belles Lettres*. I will own that, when there is wit and elegance enough in a Book to make it sell, *it is not the worse for good morals.*

★   ★   ★

165. Tobias Smollett, from *Continuation of the Complete History of England*

1761, iv. 127

The genius of Cervantes was transfused into the novels of Fielding, who painted the characters, and ridiculed the follies of life with equal strength, humour and propriety.

166. Arthur Murphy, *Essay*

25 March 1762

From 'An Essay on the Life and Genius of Henry Fielding, Esq.', in *The Works of Henry Fielding, Esq.: with the Life of the Author* (1762), i. 5–49.

The most interesting of the reviews of Murphy's edition is the *Critical Review*'s (July 1762, xiv. 1–21), in which the reviewer calls Fielding the 'neglected slave of an ungrateful people, who admired without rewarding his genius'—words that sound like Smollett (cf. No. 165). The reviewer's only disagreement with Murphy is that the latter prefers *Tom Jones* to *Joseph Andrews*, which the reviewer believes, though not so intricate and regular in 'fable', contains more humour and 'natural painting'. A long summary as published in the *Monthly Review* (May 1762), xxvi. 364–75; (Appendix, Jan.–June), 481–94; and (July), xxvii, 49–56. The *Gentleman's* and the *London* only mentioned the publication.

Murphy's commentary on Fielding's work begins (p. 11) after a short biographical sketch. Further biographical passages are omitted.

His first dramatic piece soon after adventured into the world, and was called *Love in several Masques*. It immediately succeeded the *Provoked Husband*, a play, which, as our author observes, for the continued space of twenty-eight nights received as great and as just applauses, as ever were bestowed on the English stage. '*These*, says Mr. Fielding, *were difficulties, which seemed rather to require the superior force of a Wycherley or a Congreve than a raw and unexperienced pen (for I believe I may boast that none ever appeared so early upon the stage.)*'[1] Notwithstanding these obstacles, the play, we find, was favourably received: and considering that it was his first attempt, it had, no doubt, the marks of a promising genius. His second play, the *Temple Beau*, appeared the year after, and contains a great deal of spirit and real humour. Perhaps in those days,

---

[1] *Love in Several Masques*, Preface.

when audiences were in the era of delicate and higher comedy, the success of this piece was not very remarkable; but surely pieces of no very superior merit have drawn crowded houses within our own memory, and have been attended with a brilliancy of success; not but it must be acknowledged that the picture of a Temple Rake since exhibited by the late Dr. Hoadly in the Suspicious Husband,[1] has more of what the *Italians* call FORTUNATO, than can be allowed to the careless and hasty pencil of Mr. *Fielding*. It would lead a great way from the intention of this essay should we attempt to analyze the several dramatic compositions of this author; and indeed, as he confessedly did not attain to pre-eminence in this branch of writing, at least was unequal to his other productions, it may be sufficient to observe that from the year 1727 to the end of 1736, almost all his plays and farces were written, not above two or three having appeared since that time; so that he produced about eighteen theatrical performances, plays and farces included, before he was quite thirty years old. No selection has been made of those pieces, but they are all printed together in this edition, that the public might have the *entire theatre* of Henry Fielding. For though it must be acknowledged that in the whole collection, there are few plays likely to make any considerable figure on the stage here-after, yet they are worthy of being preserved, being the works of a genius, who in his wildest and most inaccurate productions, yet occasionally displays the talents of a master. Though in the plan of his pieces he is not always regular, yet is he often happy in his diction and style; and in every groupe, that he has exhibited, there are to be seen particular delineations that will amply recompense the attention bestowed upon them. The comedy of the *Miser*, which he has mostly taken from Moliere, has maintained its ground upon the stage, ever since it was first performed, and has the value of a copy from a great painter by an eminent hand. If the comedy of *Pasquin* were restored to the stage, it would, perhaps, be a more favourite entertainment with our audiences than the much admired *Rehearsal*; a more rational one it certainly would be, as it would undoubtedly be better understood. The Rehearsal at present seems to be received rather from prescription than any real delight it affords: it was the work of a noble wit, and the object of its satire was one of the greatest geniuses of this nation, the immortal Dryden. These two circumstances gave the play a wonderful eclat on its first appearance; and the wit and humour of the parodies were undoubtedly very high-flavoured. But has it not lost its relish at

[1] Benjamin Hoadly, *The Suspicious Husband* (1747).

present? and does not the whole appear a wild *caricature* which very few can refer to any original objects? However, its traditional fame still procures for it a fashionable prejudice in its favour; and for the sake of having the favourite actor, who performs the part of *Bayes*, continually before the eye, we crowd to it still, whenever it is acted, and we laugh, and applaud, and roar and 'wonder with a foolish face of praise.' What Mr. Dryden has said concerning this celebrated performance, is but a mild judgment from one, who might have used more exasperated language. 'I have answered not the Rehearsal,' says he, 'because I knew the author sat to himself, when he drew the picture, and was the very Bayes of his own farce. Because also I know that my betters were more concerned than I was in that satire: and, lastly, because Mr. Smith and Mr. Johnson, the main pillars of it, were two such languishing gentlemen in their conversation, that I could liken them to nothing but their own relations, those noble characters of men of wit and pleasure about the town.'[1]

But sense survived when merry jests were past,[2] as his generous rival has sung since; and Dryden is now the admiration of his country. The Pasquin of *Fielding* came from the pen of an author in indigence, or, as the late *Colly Cibber* has contumeliously called him, a broken wit;[3] and, therefore, though its success was considerable, it never shone forth with a lustre equal to its merit; and yet it is a composition that would have done honour to the Athenian stage, when the Middle Comedy, under the authority of the laws, made use of fictitious names to satyrise vice and folly, however dignified by honours and employments. But the middle comedy did not flourish long at Athens; the archness of its aim, and the poignancy of its satire, soon became offensive to the officers of state; a law was made to prohibit those oblique strokes of wit, and the comic muse was restrained from all indulgencies of personal satire, however humourously drawn, under the appearance of imaginary characters. The same fate attended the use of the middle comedy in England; and it is said that the wit and humour of our modern *Aristophanes*, Mr. Fielding, whose quarry in some of his pieces, particularly the *Historical Register*, was higher game than in prudence he should have chosen, were principal instruments in provoking that law, under which the British theatre has groaned ever since. But the minister was sore,

---

[1] *A Discourse concerning the Original and Progress of Satire,* in *Essays of John Dryden,* ed. W. P. Ker (1900), ii. 21–2.

[2] Pope, *Essay on Criticism,* 1. 460.

[3] See No. 35 above.

and in his resentment he struck too deep a blow. Had he considered that by the bill, which afterwards passed into a law, he was entailing slavery on the muses, and that a time might come, when all dramatic genius should thereby be led a vassal in the train of the managers of the theatre, to be graciously fostered, or haughtily oppressed, according to their caprice and prejudice; perhaps then, as he was of himself of a large and comprehensive understanding, and possessed besides the virtues of humanity, he might have been contented with milder restrictions, and not have made the remedy almost worse than the disease. But licentiousness was to be retrenched; and liberty received a stab in the operation: luxuriant branches, that were extravagant in their growth were to be lopped away, and to make short work of it, the woodman in a fit of anger applied his axe to the root of the tree. The tree, it is true, is not quite fallen to the ground; but it is grown sapless, withered and unproductive; its annual fruits want the high flavour, which they might have in a more generous nursery; no wood-notes wild are heard from its branches, and it is exactly in the state described by Lucan;

Trunco, non frondibus efficit umbram.[1]

But it may be asked, are the players to be judges of the king's ministers? Shall grimace and mimicry attack the most exalted characters; and must the great officers of state be, at the mercy of the actors, exhibited on a public stage? Why no;—except in a coronation, I think, his majesty's servants should not be made ridiculous; and the dangerous tendency of this buffooning kind of humour is strongly marked by a learned writer,[*] when he observes that 'this weapon, in the dissolute times of Charles II. completed the ruin of the best minister of that age. The historians tell us, that Chancellor Hyde was brought into his majesty's contempt by this court argument. They mimicked his walk and gesture, with a fire shovel and bellows for the mace and purse. Thus it being the representation, and not the object represented, which strikes the fancy, vice and virtue must fall indifferently before it.'

If such were the effects of private mimicry, public drolls would undoubtedly be found of more pernicious consequence. Away with them therefore; they are illiberal, they are unworthy; let licentiousness be banished from the theatres, but let the liberty of the free-born Muse be immortal! The true idea of liberty consists in the free and unlimited power of doing whatever shall not injure the civil and religious

---

[1] 'It makes shade not with its leaves but with its trunk.' *Civil War*, I. 140.
[*] The author [William Warburton] of the Divine Legation of Moses [1738-41].

institutions of the state, nor be deemed invasive of the peace and welfare of our fellow-subjects; but dramatic authors are so circumstanced at present, that this invaluable blessing is withdrawn from them; the muses are enslaved in a land of liberty, and thus at least should excuse the poets of the age for not rising to nobler heights, till the weight is taken off, which now depresses their strongest efforts. It must be allowed, that in restraining the licentiousness of the theatre our legislature very wisely imitated the good sense of the Athenian magistracy, who by law interdicted the freedoms of the MIDDLE COMEDY; but it is to be wished that they had also imitated the moderation of the Greek law-givers, who, when they resolved to give a check to indecorum, yet left a free and unbounded scope to the *New Comedy*, which consisted in agreeable and lively representations of manners, passions, virtues, vices, and follies, from the general volume of nature, without giving to any part of the transcript the peculiar marks or singularities of any individual. Thus poets were only hindered from being libellers, but were left in full possession of useful and general satire, and all avenues of access to the public were generously thrown open to them. As we have at present the happiness of living in a reign, when majesty condescends to look with a favourable aspect on the liberal arts, many are sanguine enough to entertain hopes that the Muse may be released from her fetters, and restored to the free exercise of the amiable part of her province. When a bee has been deprived of its noxious sting, it may be safely permitted to rove at large among all the flowers of a garden; and it will be no inconsiderable addition to the lustre of the crown, if, with an AUGUSTAN REIGN of equity, moderation, victory, and wisdom, which every Briton promises himself, there be also revived an AUGUSTAN AGE OF LETTERS.

Though the foregoing observations may appear digressive from the main design of this essay, yet as the subject is important, and took its rise in a great measure from the writings of Mr. Fielding, to advert awhile to the consequences which flowed to the community from his actions, cannot be deemed altogether impertinent. It is only like going out of the way a little to trace a rivulet in its progress, to mark its windings, to observe whether it bestows fertility on the neighbouring meadows, and then returning to the straight road, to pursue the regular track of the journey.

In the comedy called *Rape upon Rape*, or, *the Coffee-house Politician*, we have an admirable draught of a character very common in this country, namely, a man who is smitten with an insatiable thirst for news, and concerns himself more about the balance of power than of his books. The folly of these statesmen out of place is there exhibited with a masterly ridicule; and indeed in all the plays of our author however in some respects deficient, there are strokes of humour and half-length paintings not excelled by some of the ablest artists. The farces written by Mr. Fielding were almost all of them very successful, and many of them are still acted every winter with a continuance of approbation. They were generally the production of two or three mornings, so great was his facility in writing; and to this day, they bear frequent repetition, at least as well as any other pieces of the kind. It need not be observed, in justification of their being preserved in this collection of more important works, that farce is deemed by our best critics an appendage of the theatre as well as pieces of a higher nature. A learned and excellent critic* has given it a full consideration, in his *Dissertation on the several Provinces of the Drama* [1753]. 'The representations,' says he, 'of common nature may either be taken accurately, so as to reflect a *faithful and exact image* of their original, which alone is *that* I would call COMEDY; or they may be forced and overcharged above the simple and just proportions of *nature*; as when the excesses of a *few* are given for *standing* characters, when not the man (in *general*) but the *passion* is described; or when, in the draught of the man, the leading *feature* is extended beyond measure; and in these cases, the representation holds of the province of farce.'

These remarks, from the pen of so accurate and sensible a writer, will evince that our author's farces very justly make a part of this edition. The mock tragedy of TOM THUMB is replete with as fine parody as, perhaps, has ever been written: the LOTTERY, the INTRIGUING CHAMBERMAID, and the VIRGIN UNMASKED, besides the real entertainment they afford, had on their first appearance, this additional merit, that they served to make early discoveries of that true comic genius which was then dawning forth in Mrs. Clive, which has since unfolded itself to a fulness of perfection, and continues to this day to be one of the truest ornaments of the stage. As this excellent actress received great advantages from the opportunities Mr. Fielding's pen afforded her, so he, in his turn, reaped the fruits of success from her abilities, and accordingly we find him acknowledging it in a very handsome letter addressed to her, and prefixed to the INTRIGUING CHAMBERMAID: such a testimony of her merit, as it conduced to advance her progress, so it now will serve to perpetuate her fame, being enrolled in the records of a genius, whose works will be long admired.

* The Rev Mr Hurd.

'*I cannot help reflecting,*' says our author, '*that the town has one obligation to me, who made the first discovery of your great capacity, and brought you earlier forward on the theatre than the ignorance of some, and the envy of others, would have otherwise permitted. I shall not here dwell on anything so well known as your theatrical merit, which one of the finest judges, and the greatest man of his age, hath acknowledged to exceed in humour that of your predecessors in his time.*' If this remark, was true thirty years ago, it may be added to her honour, that she hath not been eclipsed by any who have entered into the service of the comic muse since that time.

As this Essay promises to treat of the genius, as well as the life of Henry Fielding, it may not be improper to pause here for an inquiry into his talents, though we are not arrived at that period of his life, when they displayed themselves in their full warmth and splendor. And here it is necessary to caution the reader not to confine his idea of what is intended by the word *genius* to any one single faculty of the mind; because it is observable that many mistakes have arisen, even among writers of penetrating judgement, and well versed in critical learning, by hastily attaching themselves to an imperfect notion of this term so common in literary dissertations. That invention is the first great leading talent of a poet has been a point long since determined, because it is principally owing to that faculty of the mind that he is able to create, and be as it were a MAKER, which is implied in his original title given to him by the consent of Greece. But surely there are many other powers of the mind, as fully essential to constitute a fine poet and therefore, in order to give the true character of any author's abilities, it should seem necessary to come to a right understanding of what is meant by GENIUS, and to analyse and arrange its several qualities. This once adjusted, it might prove no unpleasing task to examine what are the specific qualities of any poet in particular, to point out the talents of which he seems to have the freest command, or in the use of which he seems, as it were, to be left-handed. In this plain fair-dealing way the true and real value of an author will be easily ascertained; whereas in the more confined method of investigation, which establishes, at the outset, one giant-quality, and finding the object of the enquiry deficient in that, immediately proceeds to undervalue him in the whole, there seems to be danger of not trying his cause upon a full and equitable hearing. Thus, I think, a late celebrated poet is likely to suffer an unjust sentence from a gentleman, who has already obliged the public with the first volume of an Essay on his Life and Genius.

[Digression on Pope and Warton's *Essay*, pp. 16–19.]

It may be observed by the reader, that in pursuing the foregoing train of reflections, sight has been lost of HENRY FIELDING: but it never was intended, in this little tract, to observe the rules of strict biography. Besides, men of genius, like the arts they practice, have a connexion with each other, and are in a manner linked together by certain ties of affinity; *habent quoddam commune vinculum, & quasi cognatione quadam inter se continentur*.[1] Moreover, it was expedient, for the true delineation of an eminent writer's character, to remove difficulties out of the way, and to explain the terms of art which critics make use of. And thus having shown the different provinces of INVENTION, we may now arrive at a juster idea of what is meant, when we talk of an author's GENIUS.

He may be truly said to be a GENIUS, who possessed the leading faculties of the mind in their vigour, and can exercise them with warmth and spirit upon whatever subject he chuses. The imagination (in order to form a writer of eminence) must, in particular, be very quick and susceptible, or, as a fine poet has expressed it, it must be *feelingly alive all o'er*, that it may receive the strongest impressions either from the objects of nature, the works of art, or the actions and manners of men; for it is in proportion as this power of the mind is wrought upon, that the author feels in his own breast those fine sensations, which it is his business to impart to others, and that he is able to describe things in so lively a manner, as to make them, as it were, present to us, and of consequence to give what turn he pleases to our affections. The JUDGEMENT also must be clear and strong, that the proper parts of a story or description may be selected, that the disposition of the various members of a work may be such, as to give a lucid order to the whole, and that such expression may be made use of as shall not only serve to convey the intended ideas, but shall convey them forcibly, and with that decorum of stile which the art of composition requires; so that simplicity shall not be impoverished into meanness, nor dignity be incumbered with a load of finery, and affected ornament. Invention must also concur, that new scenery may be opened to the fancy, or at least that new lights may be thrown upon the prospects of nature; that the sphere of our ideas may be enlarged, or a new assemblage may be formed of them, either in the way of fable or illustration so that if the author does not disclose original traces of thinking, by presenting to us objects unseen before, he may at least delight by the novelty of their combination, and the points of view in which he offers them. The power of the mind, moreover,

[1] Cicero, *Pro Archia Poeta*, I. 2.

which exerts itself in what Mr. Locke calls the association of ideas, must be quick, vigorous, and warm, because it is from thence that language receives its animated figures, its bold translation of phrases from one idea to another, the *Verbum ardens*, the glowing metaphorical expression, which constitutes the richness and boldness of his imagery; and from thence likewise springs the readiness of ennobling a sentiment of description with the pomp of sublime comparison, or striking it deeper on the mind by the aptness of witty allusion. Perhaps what we call genius, might be still more minutely analysed; but these are its principal efficient qualities; and in proportion as these, or any of these, shall be found deficient in an author, so many degrees shall he be removed from the first rank and character of a writer. To bring these remarks home to the late Mr. Fielding, an estimate of him may be justly formed, by enquiring how far these various talents may be attributed to him; or, if he failed in any, what that faculty was, and what discount he must suffer for it. But though it will appear, perhaps, that, when he attained that period of life in which his mind was come to its full growth, he enjoyed every one of these qualifications, in great strength and vigour; yet, in order to give the true character of his talents, to mark the distinguishing specific qualities of his genius, we must look into the temper of the man, and see what bias it gave to his understanding; for when abilities are possessed in an eminent degree by several men, it is the peculiarity of habit that must discriminate them from each other.

A love of imitation very soon prevailed in Mr. Fielding's mind. By Imitation the reader will not understand that illegitimate kind, which consists in mimicking singularities of person, feature, voice or manner; but that higher species of representation, which delights in just and faithful copies of human life. So early as when he was at Leyden, a propensity this way began to exert its emotions, and even made some efforts towards a comedy in the sketch of Don Quixote in England. When he left that place, and settled in London, a variety of characters could not fail to attract his notice, and of course to strengthen his favourite inclination. It has been already observed in this essay, that distress and disappointments betrayed him into occasional fits of peevishness, and satyric humour. The eagerness of creditors, and the fallacy of dissembling friends, would for a while sour his temper; his feelings were acute, and naturally fixed his attention to those objects from whence his uneasiness sprung; of course he became, very early in life, an observer of men and manners. Shrewd and piercing in his discernment, he saw the latent sources of human actions, and he could trace the various incongruities of conduct arising from them. As the study of man is delightful in itself, affording a variety of discoveries, and particularly interesting to the heart, it is no wonder that he should feel delight from it; and what we delight in soon grows into a habit. The various ruling passions of men, their foibles, their oddities, and their humours, engaged his attention; and from these principles he loved to account for the consequences which appeared in their behaviour. The inconsistencies that flow from vanity, from affectation, from hypocrisy, from pretended friendship, and in short, all the dissonant qualities, which are often blended together by the folly of men, could not fail to strike a person who had so fine a sense of ridicule. A quick perception in this way, perhaps, affords as much real pleasure as the exercise of any other faculty of the mind; and accordingly, we find that the ridiculous is predominant through all our author's writings, and he never seems so happy, as when he is developing a character made up of motley and repugnant properties, and shews you a man of specious pretences, turning out in the end the very reverse of what he would appear. To search out and to describe objects of this kind, seems to have been the favourite bent of Mr. Fielding's mind, as indeed it was of Theophrastus, Molière, and others; like a vortex it drew in all his faculties, which were so happily employed in descriptions of the manners, that upon the whole he must be pronounced an admirable COMIC GENIUS.

When I call our author a COMIC GENIUS, I would be understood in the largest acceptation of the phrase, implying humorous and pleasant imitation of men and manners, whether it be in the way of fabulous narration, or dramatic composition. In the former species of writing, lay the excellence of Mr. Fielding: but in dramatic imitation he must be allowed to fall short of the great masters in that art; and how this hath happened to a COMIC GENIUS, to one eminently possessed of the talents requisite in the humorous provinces of the drama, will appear at the first blush of the question something unaccountable. But several causes concurred to produce this effect. In the first place, without a tincture of delicacy running through an entire piece, and giving to good sense an air of urbanity and politeness, it appears to me that no comedy will ever be of that kind, which Horace says, will be particularly desired, and seen, will be advertised again. I know that the influence of a favourite performer may for a time uphold a middling production; but when a *Wilks* leaves the stage, even a *Sir Harry Wildair* will be thrown by neglected.[1] The idea of delicacy in writing, I find

[1] Robert Wilks (1665–1732), the famous comedian. George Farquhar, *Sir Harry Wildair* (1701).

so well explained in an ingenious essay on that subject, now on the table before me, that I shall transcribe the passage. '*Delicacy*', says this polite author, '*is good sense; but good sense refined; which produces an inviolable attachment to decorum, and sanctity as well as elegance of manners, with a clear discernment and warm sensibility of whatever is pure, regular, and polite; and, at the same time, an abhorrence of whatever is gross, rustic, or impure; of unnatural, effeminate, and overwrought ornaments of every kind. It is, in short, the graceful and the beautiful added to the just and the good*'.[1] By snatching the grace here defined and described, the late Colly Cibber has been able in a few of his plays to vie with, and almost outstrip, the greatest wits of this country; and, by not adverting to this embellishment, this liberal air of expression, if I may so call it, Mr. Fielding, with strong observation upon life, and excellent discernment of the humorous and the ridiculous, in short, with a great COMIC GENIUS, has been rather unsuccessful in COMEDY. There seems to me little or no room to doubt but that this want of refinement, which we here complain of, was principally owing to the woundings which every fresh disappointment gave him, before he was yet well disciplined in the school of life, and hackney'd in the ways of men; for in a more advanced period, when he did not write *recentibus odiis*, with his uneasiness just beginning to fester, but with a calmer and more dispassionate temper, we perceive him giving all the graces of description to incidents and passions, which in his youth he would have dashed out with a rougher hand. An ingenious writer,* to whom we have already referred, has passed a judgment upon *Ben Jonson,* which, though Fielding did not attain the same dramatic eminence, may be justly applied to him. 'His taste for ridicule was strong, but indelicate, which made him not over-curious in the choice of his topicks. And lastly, his *style* in picturing his characters, tho' masterly, was without that elegance of hand, which is required to correct and allay the force of so bold a colouring. Thus the byass of his nature leading him to Plautus, rather than Terence, for his model, it is not to be wondered that his wit is too frequently caustic; his raillery coarse; and his humour excessive.' Perhaps the asperity of Fielding's muse was not a little encouraged by the practice of two great wits, who had fallen into the same vein before him; I mean *Wycherley* and *Congreve,* who were in general painters of harsh features, attached more to subjects of deformity than grace; whose drawings of women are ever a

---

[1] Nathaniel Lancaster, *Plan of an Essay on Delicacy* (1748), reprinted in *Fugitive Pieces* (1761), i. 2.

* Mr Hurd.

sort of *Harlot's Progress*, and whose men, for the most part lay violent hands upon deeds and settlements, and generally deserve informations in the king's bench. These two celebrated writers were not fond of copying the amiable part of human life, they had not learned the secret of giving the softer graces of composition to their tablature, by contrasting the fair and beautiful in characters and manners to the vicious and irregular, and thereby rendering their pieces more exact imitations of nature. By making Congreve his model, it is no wonder that our author contracted this vicious turn, and became faulty in that part of his art, which the painters would call DESIGN. In his style, he derived an error from the same source: he sometimes forgot that humour and ridicule were the two principal ingredients of comedy; and, like his master, he frequently aimed at decorations of wit, which do not appear to make part of the *ground*, but seem rather to be embroidered upon it. It has been observed,* that the plays of *Congreve appear not to be legitimate comedies, but strings of repartees and sallies of wit, the most poignant and polite indeed, but unnatural and ill-placed*. If we except the *Old Batchelor*, *Foresight*, and *Sir Sampson Legend*, there will hardly, perhaps, be found a character in this lively writer exempt from this general censure. The frequent surprises of allusion, and the quickness and vivacity of those sudden turns, which abound in Mr. Congreve, breaking out where you least expected them, as if a train of wit had been laid all around, put one in mind of those fire-works in a water-piece, which used formerly to be played off at *Cuper's Gardens*; no sooner one tube, charged with powder, raised itself above the surface, and vented itself in various forms and evolutions of fire, but instantly another and another was lighted up; and the pleasure of the spectators arose from seeing secret artificial mines blazing out of an element, in which such machinery could not be expected. The same kind of entertainment our author aimed at, too frequently in his comedies; and as in this he bore a similitude to *Wycherley* and *Congreve*, so he also frequently resembled them in the indelicacy, and sometimes the downright obscenity of his raillery; a vice introduced, or at least pampered by the wits of Charles II. the dregs of it, till very lately, not being quite purged away. There is another circumstance respecting the drama, in which *Fielding's* judgment seems to have failed him: the strength of his genius certainly lay in fabulous narration, and he did not sufficiently consider that some incidents of a story, which, when related, may be worked up into a deal of pleasantry and humour, are apt, when thrown into action, to excite sensations incompatible with

* See the Adventurer [No. 133, 12 February 1754 (Joseph Warton)].

humour and ridicule. I will venture to say, that if he had resolved to shape the business and characters of his last comedy (*the Wedding Day*) into the form of a novel, there is not one scene in the piece, which, in his hands, would not have been very susceptible of ornament: but as they are arranged at present in dramatic order, there are few of them from which the taste and good sense of an audience ought not, with propriety, to revolt. When *Virgil* is preparing the catastrophe of his *Dido*, the critics have never objected to him, that he describes the nurse with a motherly and officious care tottering along the apartments:

Illa gradum studio celerabat anili[1]

But woe to the tragic poet, that should offer to present the same circumstance to the eye of an audience! The *Tom Jones* of our author, and the *Gil Blas* of *Le Sage*, still continue to yield universal delight to their respective readers; but two late attempts to dramatise them,[2] if I may so call it, have demonstrated that the characters and incidents of those applauded performances, which, when figured to us by the imagination only, are found so agreeable and interesting, lose much of their comic force and beauty, when they are attempted to be realised to us on the stage. There are objects and parts of nature, which the rules of composition will allow to be described, but not actually to be produced on the scene, because they are attended with some concomitant circumstances, which in the narrative are overlooked, but, when shown to view, press too hardly on the mind, and become indelicate.

Segnius irritant animos demissa per aurem
Quam quæ sunt oculis subjecta fidelibus, & quæ
Ipse sibi tradit spectator.—[3]

To these causes of our author's failure in the province of the drama, may be added that sovereign contempt he always entertained for the understandings of the generality of mankind. It was in vain to tell him that a particular scene was dangerous on account of its coarseness, or because it retarded the general business with feeble efforts of wit; he doubted the discernment of his auditors, and so thought himself secured by their stupidity, if not by his own humour and vivacity. A very re-

[1] 'She was hurrying her steps with the eagerness of an old woman'. *Aeneid,* IV. 641.
[2] George Colman's *The Jealous Wife* was produced in the winter and spring of 1761; Edward Moore's *Gil Blas* was first performed in February 1751.
[3] 'The things that we hear about are less exciting to the mind than those that we see with our own eyes, and which the spectator makes himself aware of.' Horace, *The Art of Poetry,* ll. 180–2.

markable instance of this disposition appeared, when the comedy of the Wedding Day was put into rehearsal. An actor, who was principally concerned in the piece, and, though young, was then, by the advantage of happy requisites, an early favourite of the public, told Mr. Fielding he was apprehensive that the audience would make free with him in a particular passage; adding, that a repulse might so flurry his spirits as to disconcert him for the rest of the night, and therefore begged that it might be omitted. 'No, d—mn 'em!' replied the bard, 'if the scene is not a good one, let them find *that* out.' Accordingly the play was brought on without alteration, and, just as had been foreseen, the disapprobation of the house was provoked at the passage before objected to; and the performer, alarmed and uneasy at the hisses he had met with, retired into the green-room, where the author was indulging his genius, and solacing himself with a bottle of champagne. He had by this time drank pretty plentifully; and cocking his eye at the actor, while streams of tobacco trickled down from the corner of his mouth, *What's the matter, Garrick?* says he, *what are they hissing now?* Why, the scene that I begged you to retrench; I knew it would not do, and they have so frightened me, that I shall not be able to collect myself again the whole night. *Oh! d—mn 'em*, replies the author, *they* HAVE *found it out; have they?*—

If we add to the foregoing remarks an observation of his own, namely, that he left off writing for the stage, when he ought to have begun; and together with this consider his extreme hurry and dispatch, we shall be able fully to account for his not bearing a more distinguished place in the rank of dramatic writers. It is apparent, that in the frame and constitution of his genius there was no defect, but some faculty or other was suffered to lie dormant, and the rest of course were exerted with less efficacy: at one time we see his wit superceding all his other talents; at another his invention runs riot, and multiplies incidents and characters in a manner repugnant to all the received laws of the drama. Generally his judgment was very little consulted. And indeed, how could it be otherwise? When he had contracted to bring on a play, or a farce, it is well known by many of his friends now living, that he would go home rather late from a tavern, and would, the next morning, deliver a scene to the players written upon the papers, which had wrapped the tobacco, in which he so much delighted.

Notwithstanding the inaccuracies, which have arisen from this method of proceeding, there is not a play in the whole collection which is not remarkable for some degree of merit very striking in its kind; in general, there prevails a fine idea of character; occasionally, we see the true comic both of situation and sentiment; and always, we find a strong knowledge of life, delivered indeed with a caustic wit, but often zested with fine infusions of the ridiculous: so that, upon the whole, the plays and farces of our author are well worthy of a place in this general edition of his works; and the reader, who peruses them attentively, will not only carry away with him many useful discoveries of the foibles, affectations, and humours of mankind, but will also agree with me that inferior productions are now successful upon the stage.

★　　★　　★

A large number of fugitive political tracts, which had their value when the incidents were actually passing on the great scene of business, came from his pen: the periodical paper, called the Champion, owing its chief support to his abilities; and tho' his essays in that collection, cannot now be so ascertained, as to perpetuate them in this edition of his works, yet the reputation arising to him at the time of publication was not inconsiderable. It does not appear that he ever wrote much poetry: with such talents as he possessed, it cannot be supposed that he was unqualified to acquit himself handsomely in that art; but correct versification probably required more pains and time than his exigencies would allow. In the preface to his Miscellanies he tells us, that his poetical pieces were mostly written when he was very young, and were productions of the heart rather than of the head. He adds, that this branch of writing is what he very little pretended to, and was very little his pursuit. Accordingly, out of this edition, which is intended to consist entirely of pieces more highly finished than works of mere amusement generally are, his verses are all discarded: but as a specimen of his ability in this way, it is judged proper to preserve, in this Essay on his Life and Genius, one short piece, which the reader will not find unentertaining.

[Reproduces 'An Epistle to the Right Honourable Sir Robert Walpole.']

This piece, it appears, was written in the year 1730 and it shows at once our author's early acquaintance with distress, and the firmness of mind, which he supported under it. Of his other works (I mean such as were written before his genius was come to its full growth) an account will naturally be expected in this place; and fortunately he has spoken of them himself, in the discourse prefixed to his Miscellanies, (which is not reprinted in the body of this edition) in terms so modest and sensible that I am sure the reader will dispense with any other criticism or analysis of them.

'The Essay on Conversation,' says Mr. Fielding, 'was designed to ridicule out of society, one of the most pernicious evils which attends it, *viz.* pampering the gross appetites of selfishness and ill-nature, with the shame and disquietude of others; whereas true good-breeding consists in contributing to the satisfaction and happiness of all about us.'

'The Essay on the *Knowledge of the Characters of Men* exposes a second great evil, namely hypocrisy: the bane of all virtue, morality and goodness; and may serve to arm the honest, undesigning, open-hearted man, who is generally the prey of this monster, against it.'

The *Journey from this World to the Next*, it should seem, provoked the dull, short-sighted, and malignant enemies of our author to charge him with an intention to subvert the settled notions of mankind in philosophy and religion: for he assures us, in form, that he did not intend, in this allegorical piece, 'to oppose any prevailing system, or to erect a new one of his own. With greater justice,' he adds, 'that he might be arraigned of ignorance, for having, in the relation which he has put into the mouth of *Julian*, whom they call the Apostate, done many violences to history, and mixed truth and falsehood with much freedom. But he professed fiction, and though he chose some facts out of history, to embellish his work, and fix a chronology to it, he has not, however, confined himself to nice exactness, having often ante-dated, and sometimes post-dated the matter, which he found in the Spanish history, and transplanted into his work.' The reader will find a great deal of true humour in many passages of this production; and the surprise with which he has made Mr. Addison hear of the *Eleusinian Mysteries,* in the sixth Æneid, is a well turned compliment to the learned author who has, with so much elegance and ability, traced out the analogy between Virgil's system and those memorable rites.[1]

With regard to the History of *Jonathan Wild*, his design, he tells us, was not 'to enter the lists with that excellent historian, who, from authentic papers and records, &c. hath given so satisfactory an account of this great man; nor yet to contend with the memoirs of the ordinary of Newgate, which generally contain a more particular relation of what the heroes are to suffer in the next world, than of what they did in this. The history of Jonathan Wild is rather a narrative of such actions, as he might have performed, or would, or should have performed, than what he really did; and may in reality as well suit any other such great

[1] i.e. Warburton, in his *Divine Legation of Moses* (1738), Bk. ii, Sect. 4

man as the person himself whose name it bears. As it is not a very faithful portrait of *Jonathan Wild*, so neither is it intended to represent the features of any other person; roguery, and not a rogue, is the subject; so that any particular application will be unfair in the reader, especially if he knows much of the great world, since he must then be acquainted with more than one, on whom he can fix the resemblance.'

Our author proceeds to give a further account of this work in a strain which shews, however conversant he might be in the characters of men, that he did not suffer a gloomy misanthropy to take such possession of him, as to make him entertain depreciating ideas of mankind in general, without exceptions in favour of a great part of the species. Though the passage be long, I shall here transcribe it, as it will prove subservient to two purposes: it will throw a proper light upon the history of *Jonathan Wild*, and it will do honour to Mr. Fielding's sentiments.

[Quotes Henley, xii. 242-6, as follows: 'I solemnly protest . . . till virtue disdains them both.']

Thus hath our author developed the design, with which he wrote the history of *Jonathan Wild*; a noble purpose surely, and of the highest importance to society. A satire like this, which at once strips off the spurious ornaments of hypocracy, and shews the genuine beauty of the moral character, will be always worthy of the attention of the reader, who desires to rise wiser or better from the book he peruses; not to mention that this performance hath in many places such seasonings of humour, that it cannot fail to be a very high entertainment to all, who have a taste for exhibitions of the absurd and ridiculous in human life. But though the merit of the Life of *Jonathan Wild* be very considerable yet it must be allowed to be very short of that higher order of composition which our author attained in his other pieces of invention. Hitherto he seems but preluding, as it were, to some great work, in which all the component parts of his genius were to be seen in their full and vigorous exertion; in which his *imagination* was to strike us by the most lively and just colouring, his *wit* to enliven by the happiest allusions, his *invention* to enrich with the greatest variety of character and incident, and his *judgment* to charm not only by the propriety and grace of particular parts, but by the order, harmony, and congruity of the whole: to this high excellence he made strong approaches in the *Joseph Andrews*; and in the *Tom Jones* he has fairly borne away the palm.

In the progress of Henry Fielding's talents there seem to have been three remarkable periods; one, when his genius broke forth at once with an effulgence superior to all the rays of light it had before emitted, like the sun in his morning glory, without the ardour and the blaze which afterwards attend him; the second, when it was displayed with collected force, and a fulness of perfection, like the sun in meridian majesty, with all his highest warmth and splendour; and the third, when the same genius, grown more cool and temperate, still continued to cheer and enliven, but showed at the same time that it was tending to its decline, like the same sun, abating from his ardor, but still gilding the western hemisphere.

To these three epochs of our author's genius, the reader will be before-hand with me in observing that there is an exact correspondence in the *Joseph Andrews*, *Tom Jones*, and *Amelia*. Joseph Andrews, as the preface to the work informs us, was intended for an imitation of the stile and manner of *Cervantes*: and how delightfully he has copied the humour, the gravity, and the fine ridicule of his master, they can witness who are acquainted with both writers. The truth is, Fielding, in this performance, was employed in the very province for which his talents were peculiarly and happily formed; namely, the fabulous narration of some imagined action, which did occur, or might probably have occurred in human life. Nothing could be more happily conceived than the character of Parson Adams for the principal personage of the work; the humanity, and benevolence of affection, the goodness of heart, and the zeal for virtue, which come from him upon all occasions, attach us to Mr. Adams in the most endearing manner; his excellent talents, his erudition, and his real acquirements of knowledge in classical antiquity, and the sacred writings, together with his honesty, command our esteem and respect; while his simplicity and innocence in the ways of men provoke our smiles by the contrast they bear to his real intellectual character, and conduce to make him in the highest manner the object of mirth, without degrading him in our estimation, by the many ridiculous embarrassments to which they every now and then make him liable; and to crown the whole, that habitual absence of mind, which is his predominant foible, and which never fails to give a tinge to whatever he is about, makes the honest clergyman almost a rival of the renowned *Don Quixote*; the adventures he is led into, in consequence of this infirmity, assuming something of the romantic air which accompanies the knight errant, and the circumstances of his forgetfulness tending as strongly to excite our laughter as the mistakes of the Spanish hero. I will venture to say, that when *Don Quixote* mistakes the barber's basin for *Mambrino's* helmet, no reader ever found the situation more ridiculous and truly comic than Parson Adams's travelling to London to sell a set of sermons, and actually *snapping his fingers and taking two or three turns round the room in exstacy,* when introduced to a bookseller in order to make an immediate bargain; and then immediately after, not being able to find those same sermons, when he exclaims, 'I profess, I believe I left them behind me.' There are many touches in the conduct of this character, which occasion the most exquisite merriment; and I believe it will not be found too bold an assertion, if we say that the celebrated character of an absent man, by La Bruyere, is extremely short of that true and just resemblance to nature with which our author has delineated the features of Adams; the former indeed is carried to an agreeable extravagance, but the latter has the fine lights and shades of probability. It will not be improper here to mention that the Rev. Mr. Young, a learned and much esteemed friend of Mr. Fielding's, sat for this picture. Mr. Young was remarkable for his intimate acquaintance with the Greek authors, and had as passionate a veneration of Æschylus as Parson Adams; the overflowings of his benevolence were as strong, and his fits of *reverie* were as frequent, and occurred too upon the most interesting occasions. Of this last observation, a singular instance is given by a gentleman who served, during the last war in Flanders, in the very same regiment to which Mr. Young was chaplain. On a fine summer's evening, he thought proper to indulge himself in his love of a solitary walk; and accordingly he sallied forth from his tent: the beauties of the hemisphere and the landskip round him pressed warmly on his imagination; his heart overflowed with benevolence to all God's creatures, and gratitude to the Supreme Dispenser of that emanation of glory, which covered the face of things. It is very possible that a passage in his dearly beloved Æschylus occurred to his memory on this occasion, and seduced his thoughts into a profound meditation. Whatever was the object of his reflections, certain it is that something did powerfully seize his imagination, so as to preclude all attention to things that lay immediately before him; and, in that deep fit of absence, Mr. Young proceeded on his journey, till he arrived very quietly and calmly in the enemy's camp, where he was, with difficulty, brought to a recollection of himself by the repetition of *Qui va la?* from the soldiers upon duty. The officer, who commanded, finding that he had strayed thither in the undesigning simplicity of his heart, and seeing an innate goodness in his prisoner, which commanded his respect, very politely gave him leave to pursue his contemplations home again. Such was the gentleman from whom the idea of Parson Adams was derived; how it is interwoven into the History of Joseph Andrews, and how sustained with unabating pleasantry to the conclusion, need not be mentioned here, as it is sufficiently felt and acknowledged. The whole work indeed abounds with situations of the truly comic kind; the incidents and characters are unfolded with fine turns of surprise; and it is among the few works of invention, produced by the English writers, which will always continue in request. But still it is but the sun-rise of our author's genius. The hint, it seems, was suggested to him by the success of the late Mr. *Richardson's* history of Pamela Andrews: Joseph is here represented as her brother, and he boasts the same virtue and continency which are the characteristics of his sister. In the plan of the work, Mr. Fielding did not form to himself a circle wide enough for the abundance of his imagination; the main action was too trivial and unimportant to admit of the variety of characters and events which the reader generally looks for in such productions: the attainment of perfection in this kind of writing was in reserve for Mr. Fielding in a future work.

Soon after the publication of Joseph Andrews, the last comedy, which came from this writer's pen, was exhibited on the stage, intitled *the Wedding Day:* and, as we have already observed, it was attended with an indifferent share of success.

★   ★   ★

He engaged in two periodical papers successively, with a laudable and spirited design of rendering service to his country. The first of these was called the *True Patriot*, which was set on foot during the late rebellion, and was conducive to the excitement of loyalty, and a love for the constitution in the breasts of his countrymen. A project of the same kind had been executed in the year 1715, when the nation laboured under the same difficulties, by the celebrated Mr. *Addison*, who afterwards rose to be secretary of state. The *Freeholder* by that elegant writer contains, no doubt, many seasonable animadversions, and a delicate vein of wit and raillery: but it may be pronounced with safety, that in the *True Patriot* there was displayed a solid knowledge of the British laws and government, together with occasional sallies of humour, which would have made no inconsiderable figure in the political compositions of an *Addison* or a *Swift*. The *Jacobite* Journal was calculated to discredit the shattered remains of an unsuccessful party, and, by a well applied raillery and ridicule to bring the sentiments of the disaffected into contempt, and thereby efface them not only from the conversation, but the minds of men. . . .

Our author by this time attained the age of forty-three; and being incessantly pursued by reiterated attacks of gout, he was wholly rendered incapable of pursuing the business of a barrister any longer. He was obliged therefore to accept an office, which seldom fails of being hateful to the populace, and of course liable to many injurious imputations namely, an acting magistrate in the commission of the peace for *Middlesex.* That he was not inattentive to the calls of his duty, and that, on the contrary, he laboured to be a useful citizen, is evident from the many tracts he published, relating to several of the penal laws, and to the vices and mal-practices which those laws were intended to restrain. Under this head will be found several valuable pieces; particularly a Charge to the Grand Jury, delivered at Westminster on the 29th of June, 1749. In this little work, the history of grand juries from their origin, and the wise intention of them for the cognizance of abuse, and the safety of the subject, are thought to be traced with no small skill and accuracy. The pamphlet on the *Increase and Cause of Robberies,* has been held in high estimation by some eminent persons who have administered justice in Westminster Hall, and still continue to serve their country in a legislative capacity. It has been already observed, that he left behind him two volumes of Crown Law; and it will not be improper to mention in this place a pamphlet, entitled, A Proposal for the Maintenance of the Poor; which, though it is not reprinted in this collection, not being deemed of a colour with works of invention and genius, yet it does honour to our author as a magistrate, as it could not be produced without intense application, and an ardent zeal for the service of the community.

Amidst these severe exercises of his understanding, and all the laborious duties of his office, his invention could not lie still; but he found leisure to amuse himself, and afterwards the world, with the History of *Tom Jones.* And now we are arrived at the second grand epoch of Mr. Fielding's genius, when all his faculties were in perfect unison, and conspired to produce a complete work. If we consider *Tom Jones* in the same light in which the ablest critics have examined the *Iliad,* the *Æneid,* and the *Paradise Lost,* namely, with a view to the fable, the manners, the sentiments, and the stile, we shall find it standing the test of the severest criticism, and indeed bearing away the envied praise of a complete performance. In the first place, the action has that unity, which is the boast of the great models of composition; it turns upon a single event, attended with many circumstances, and many subordinate incidents, which seem, in the progress of the work, to perplex, to entangle, and to involve the whole in difficulties, and lead on the reader's imagination, with an eagerness of curiosity, through scenes of prodigious variety, till at length the different intricacies and complications of the fable are explained after the same gradual manner in which they had been worked up to a crisis: incident arises out of incident; the seeds of every thing that shoots up, are laid with a judicious hand, and whatever occurs in the latter part of the story, seems naturally to grow out of those passages which preceded; so that, upon the whole, the business with great propriety and probability works itself up into various embarrassments, and then afterwards, by a regular series of events, clears itself from all impediments, and brings itself inevitably to a conclusion; like a river, which, in its progress, foams amongst fragments of rocks, and for a while seems pent up by unsurmountable oppositions; then angrily dashes for a while, then plunges under ground into caverns, and runs a subterraneous course, till at length it breaks out again, meanders round the country, and with a clear, placid stream flows gently into the ocean. By this artful management, our author has given us the perfection of fable; which, as the writers upon the subject have justly observed, consists in such obstacles to retard the final issue of the whole, as shall at least, in their consequences, accelerate the catastrophe, and bring it evidently and necessarily to that period only, which, in the nature of things, could arise from it; so that the action could not remain in suspense any longer, but must naturally close and determine itself. It may be proper to add, that no fable whatever affords, in its solution, such artful states of suspense, such beautiful turns of surprise, such unexpected incidents, and such sudden discoveries, sometimes apparently embarrassing, but always promising the catastrophe, and eventually promoting the completion of the whole. *Vida*, the celebrated critic of Italy, has transmitted down to us, in his Art of Poetry, a very beautiful idea of a well-concerted fable, when he represents the reader of it in the situation of a traveller to a distant town, who, when he perceives but a faint shadowy glimmering of its walls, its spires, and its edifices, pursues his journey with more alacrity than when he cannot see any appearances to notify the place to which he is tending, but is obliged to pursue a melancholy and forlorn road through a depth of vallies, without any object to flatter or to raise his expectation.

> Haud aliter, longinqua petit qui fortè viator
> Mænia, si positas altis in collibus arces

Nunc etiam dubias oculis videt, incipit ultro
Lætior ire viam, placidumque urgere laborem,
Quam cum nusquam ullæ cernuntur quas adit arces,
Obscurum sed iter tendit convallibus imis.[1]

In the execution of this plan, thus regular and uniform, what a variety of humorous scenes of life, of descriptions, and characters has our author found means to incorporate with the principal action; and this too, without distracting the reader's attention with objects foreign to his subject, or weakening the general interest by a multiplicity of episodical events? Still observing the grand essential rule of unity in the design, I believe, no author has introduced a greater diversity of characters, or displayed them more fully, or in more various attitudes. *Allworthy* is the most amiable picture in the world of a man who does honour to his species: in his own heart he finds constant propensities to the most benevolent and generous actions, and his understanding conducts him with discretion in the performance of whatever his goodness suggests to him. And though it is apparent that the author laboured this portrait *con amore*, and meant to offer it to mankind as a just object of imitation, he has soberly restrained himself within the bounds of probability, nay, it may be said, of strict truth; as, in the general opinion, he is supposed to have copied here the features of a worthy character still in being. Nothing can be more entertaining than WESTERN; his rustic manners, his natural undisciplined honesty, his half-enlightened understanding, with the self-pleasing shrewdness which accompanies it, and the bias of his mind to mistaken politicks, are all delineated with precision and fine humour. The sisters of those two gentlemen are aptly introduced, and give rise to many agreeable scenes. *Tom Jones* will at all times be a fine lesson to young men of good tendencies to virtue, who yet suffer the impetuosity of their passions to hurry them away. *Thwackum* and *Square* are excellently opposed to each other; the former is a well drawn picture of a *divine*, who is neglectful of the moral part of his character, and ostentatiously talks of religion and grace; the latter is a strong ridicule of those, who have high ideas of the dignity of our nature, and of the native beauty of virtue, without owning any obligations of conduct from religion. But grace, without practical goodness, and the moral fitness of things, are shown, with a fine vein of ridicule, to be but weak principles of action. In short, all the characters down to Partridge, and even to a maid or an hostler at an inn, are drawn with truth and humour: and indeed they abound so

[1] II. 150–5.

much, and are so often brought forward in a dramatic manner, that every thing may be said to be here in action; every thing has MANNERS; and the very manners which belong to it in human life. They look, they act, they speak to our imaginations just as they appear to us in the world. The SENTIMENTS which they utter, are peculiarly annexed to their habits, passions, and ideas; which is what poetical propriety requires; and, to the honour of the author, it must be said, that, whenever he addresses us in person, he is always in the interests of virtue and religion, and inspires, in a strain of moral reflection, a true love of goodness and honour, with a just detestation of imposture, hypocrisy, and all specious pretences to uprightness.

There is, perhaps, no province of the comic muse that requires so great a variety of stile as this kind of description of men and manners, in which Mr. Fielding so much delighted. The laws of the mock-epic, in which this species of writing is properly included demand, that, when trivial things are to be represented with a burlesque air, the language should be raised into a sort of tumour of dignity, that by the contrast between the ideas and the pomp in which they are exhibited, they may appear the more ridiculous to our imaginations. Of our author's talent in this way, there are instances in almost every chapter; and were we to assign a particular example, we should refer to the relation of a battle in the *Homerican style*. On the other hand, when matters, in appearance, of higher moment, but, in reality, attended with incongruous circumstances, are to be set forth in the garb of ridicule, which they deserve, it is necessary that the language should be proportionably lowered, and that the metaphors and epithets made use of be transferred from things of a meaner nature, that so the false importance of the object described may fall into a gay contempt. The first specimen of this manner that occurs to me is in the *Jonathan Wild*: 'For my own part,' says he, 'I confess I look on this death of hanging to be as proper for a hero as any other; and I solemnly declare, that had Alexander the Great been hanged, it would not in the least have diminished my respect of his memory.' [IV. xiii] A better example of what is here intended might, no doubt, be chosen, as things of this nature may be found almost every where in Tom Jones, or Joseph Andrews; but the quotation here made will serve to illustrate, and this is sufficient. The mock-epic has likewise frequent occasion for the gravest irony, for florid description, for the true sublime, for the pathetic, for clear and perspicuous narrative, for poignant satire, and generous panegyric. For all these different modes of eloquence, Mr. Fielding's genius was most happily versatile, and his power in all of them is so conspicuous, that he may justly be said to have had the rare skill, required by Horace, of giving to each part of his work its true and proper colouring.

——*Servare vices, operumquè colores.*[1]

In this consists the specific quality of fine writing: and thus our author being confessedly eminent in all the great essentials of composition, in fable, character, sentiment, and elocution; and as these could not be all united in so high an assemblage, without a rich invention, a fine imagination, an enlightened judgment, and a lively wit, we may fairly here decide his character, and pronounce him the ENGLISH CERVANTES.

It may be added, that in many parts of the *Tom Jones* we find our author possessed the softer graces of character-painting, and of description; many situations and sentiments are touched with a delicate hand, and throughout the work he seems to feel as much delight in describing the amiable part of human nature, as in his early days he had in exaggerating the strong and harsh features of turpitude and deformity. This circumstance breathes an air of philanthropy through his work, and renders it an *image of truth*, as the Roman orator calls a comedy.[2] And hence it arose, from this *truth of character* which prevails in Tom Jones, in conjunction with the other qualities of the writer, above set forth, that the suffrage of the most learned critic* of this nation was given to our author, when he says, 'Mons. de Marivaux, in France, and Mr. Fielding in England stand the foremost among those, who have given a faithful and chaste copy of *life and manners*, and by enriching their romance with the best part of the comic art, may be said to have brought it to perfection.' Such a favourable decision from so able a judge, will do honour to Mr. Fielding with posterity; and the excellent genius of the person, with whom he has paralleled him, will reflect the truest prase on the author, who was capable of being his illustrious rival.

Marivaux possessed rare and fine talents; he was an attentive observer of mankind, and the transcripts he made from thence are the *image of truth*. At his reception into the French Academy, he was told in an elegant speech, made by the Archbishop of *Sens*, that the celebrated La Bruyére seemed to be revived in him, and to retrace with his pencil those admirable portraits of men and manners, which formerly un-

---

1 'To preserve the nuances and colours of the work.' *The Art of Poetry*, l. 86.
2 Cicero, as reported in *De Comoedia*, V. i.
* Dr Warburton. [See No. 103.]

masked so many characters, and exposed their vanity and affectation. *Marivaux* seems never so happy as when he is reprobating the false pretences of assumed characters: the dissimulation of friends, the policy of the ambitious, and the littleness and arrogance of the great, the insolence of wealth, the arts of the courtezan, the impertinence of foppery, the refined foibles of the fair sex, the dissipation of youth, the gravity of false-importance, the subtleties of hypocrisy and exterior religion, together with all the delicacies of real honour, and the sentiments of true virtue, are delineated by him in a lively and striking manner. He was not contented merely to copy their appearances; he went still deeper, and searched for all the internal movements of their passions, with a curiosity that is always penetrating, but sometimes appears over-solicitous, and, as the critic expresses it, *ultrà perfectum trahi*.[1] It is not intended by this to insinuate that he exceeds the bounds of truth; but occasionally he seems to refine, till the traces grow minute and almost imperceptible. He is a painter, who labours his portraits with a careful; and scrupulous hand; he attaches himself to them with affection; knows not when to give over, *nescivit quod bene cessit, relinquere*, but continues touching and retouching, till his *traits* become so delicate, that they at length are without efficacy, and the attention of the connoisseur is tired, before the diligence of the artist is wearied. But this refinement of *Marivaux* is apologized for by the remark of the ethic poet, who observes that this kind of inquiry is

> Like following life through insects we dissect;
> We lose it in the moment we detect.[2]

If therefore he sometimes seems over curious, it is the nature of the subject that allures him, and, in general, he greatly recompenses us for the unwillingness he shews to quit his work, by the valuable illustrations he gives it, and the delicacy with which he marks all the finer features of the mind. His diction, it must not be dissembled, is sometimes, but not often, far-fetched and strained; and it was even objected to him in the speech already mentioned of the *Archbishop of Sens*, that his choice of words was not always pure and legitimate. Each phrase, and often each word, is a sentence; but he was apt to be hazardous and daring in his metaphors, which was observed to him, lest his example and the connivance of the Academy, which sits in a kind of legislative

---

[1] 'Over-perfect'. Cf. Horace, *Satires*, I. x. 69–70.
[2] Pope, *Epistle to Cobham*, ll. 29–30 (misquoted).

capacity upon works of taste, should occasion a vicious imitation of the particulars in which he was deemed defective. This criticism *Marivaux* has somewhere attempted to answer, by observing that he always writes more like a man than an author, and endeavours to convey his ideas to his readers in the same light they struck his own imagination, which had great fecundity, warmth, and vivacity. The *Paysan Parvenu* seems to be the *Joseph Andrews* of this author; and the *Marianne* his higher work, or his *Tom Jones*. They are both, in a very exquisite degree, amusing and instructive. They are not written, indeed, upon any of the laws of composition promulged by *Aristotle*, and expounded by his followers: his romances begin regularly with the birth and parentage of the principal person, and proceed in a narrative of events, including indeed great variety, and artfully raising and suspending our expectation: they are rather to be called *fictitious biography*, than a comic fable, consisting of a *beginning*, a *middle*, and *end*, where one principal action is offered to the imagination, in its process is involved in difficulties, and rises gradually into tumult and perplexity, till, in a manner unexpected, it works itself clear, and comes by natural but unforseen incidents, to a termination.

In this last mentioned particular, *Fielding* boasts a manifest superiority over *Marivaux*. Uniformity amidst variety is justly allowed in all works of invention to be the prime source of beauty, and it is the peculiar excellence of *Tom Jones*. The author, for the most part, is more readily satisfied in his drawings of character than the French writer; the strong specific qualities of his personages he sets forth with a few masterly strokes, but the nicer and more subtle workings of the mind he is not so anxious to investigate; when the passions are agitated, he can give us their conflicts, and their various transitions, but he does not always point out the secret cause that sets them in motion, or, in the poet's language, 'the small pebble that stirs the peaceful lake.'[1] Fielding was more attached to the *manners* than to the *heart*: in descriptions of the former he is admirable; in unfolding the latter he is not equal to *Marivaux*. In the management of his story, he piques and awakens curiosity more strongly than his rival of France; when he interests and excites our affections, he sometimes operates more by the force of situation, than by the tender pathetic of sentiment, for which the author of *Marianne* is remarkable; not that it must be imagined that Fielding wanted these qualities; we have already said the reverse of him; but in these particulars *Marivaux* has the preference. In point of stile, he is

[1] Pope, *Essay on Man*, IV. 364.

more unexceptionable than *Marivaux*, the critics never having objected to him that his figures are forced or unnatural; and in humour the praise of pre-eminence is entirely his. *Marivaux* was determined to have an air of originality, and therefore disdained to form himself upon any eminent mode of preceding writers; *Fielding* considered the rules of composition as delivered by the great philosophic critic; and finding that Homer had written a work entitled *Margites*, which bore the same relation to *comedy*, that the *Iliad* or *Odyssey* does to tragedy, he meditated a plan★ conformable to the principles of a well-arranged fable. Were the *Margites* still extant, it would perhaps be found to have the same proportion to this work of our author, as the sublime epic has to the *Télémaque* of *Fénelon*. This was a noble vehicle for humorous description; and to insure his success in it, with great judgment, he fixed his eye upon the stile and manner of *Cervantes*, as *Virgil* had before done in respect to *Homer*. To this excellent model, he added all the advantages he could deduce from *Scarron* and *Swift*; few or no sprinklings of *Rabelais* being to be found in him. His own strong discernment of the foibles of mankind, and his quick sense of the ridiculous being thus improved, by a careful attention to the works of the great masters of their art, it is no wonder that he has been able to raise himself to the top of the *comic character*, to be admired by readers with the most lively sensations of mirth, and by novel-writers *with a despair that he should ever be emulated with success.*

Thus we have traced our author in his progress to the time when the vigour of his mind was in its full growth of perfection; from this period it sunk, but by slow degrees, into a decline; *Amelia*, which succeeded *Tom Jones* in about four years, has indeed the marks of genius, but of a genius beginning to fall into its decay. The author's invention in this performance does not appear to have lost its fertility: his judgment too seems as strong as ever; but the warmth of imagination is abated; and in his landskips or his scenes of life, Mr. Fielding is no longer the colourist he was before. The personages of the piece delight too much in narrative, and their characters have not those touches of singularity, those specific differences, which are so beautifully marked in our author's former works: of course, the humour, which consists in happy delineations of the caprices and predominant foibles of the human mind, loses here its high flavour and relish. And yet *Amelia* holds the same proportion to *Tom Jones*, that the *Odyssey* of *Homer* bears, in the estimation of *Longinus*, to the *Iliad*. A fine vein of morality runs through the whole;

★ Vide the preface to Joseph Andrews.

many of the situations are affecting and tender; the sentiments are delicate; and upon the whole, it is the Odyssey, the moral and pathetic work of Henry Fielding.

★　　★　　★

AMELIA IN FRANCE

---

167. Friedrich Melchior, Baron Grimm, letter

June 1762

Correspondance Littéraire, v. 99. See also v. 273, where Grimm briefly alludes to Fielding and his sister Sarah.

Finally the third novel [with *The Life and Adventures of Joe Thompson* and Mrs. Sheridan's *Sidney Bidulph*] is *Amelia*, translated from the English of Mr. Fielding by Mme. Riccoboni; but only the first part has appeared. We must await the rest to know what sort of a thing it will be: for Mme. Riccoboni has radically changed and shortened it. You know from his own works how light his style is, how lively and agreeable. There are longueurs and bad things in Mr. Fielding's original, but there are also very fine things.

★　　★　　★

168. Unsigned review, *L'Année littéraire*

3 July 1762

A review of the French translation of *Amelia*, Lettre VII, *L'Année littéraire* (1762), iv. 145–75.

Sir, Mme. Riccoboni has already translated two parts of this novel by Mr. Fielding, and published them. The new version of which I inform you is complete. The translator, in his 'Advertisement,' rendering justice to the talents of his rival, demonstrates that she has deviated from her original. This is what led our interpreter to present Mr. Fielding's *Amelia* as he composed it, and in the simple style which seemed the best for conveying the recital of facts which were altogether commonplace in themselves. He inserts the details of passages from the English version that Mme. Riccoboni has excised or totally mutilated. 'Mr. Fielding,' he says, 'has divided his work into 12 books, and the books into chapters; these offer as many natural resting places as the reader needs to catch his breath, and easily find himself again without losing the thread of the narrative. However, Mme. Riccoboni has removed all these divisions, and her narrative goes so swiftly that the reader is obliged to follow without pause to the very end of each part. I do not know whether the public will be pleased with this alteration. She has changed even the names of many of the most interesting characters in the book. I do not see very well her reason for doing so; but it appears to me that Booth is a better name than Fenton, and this applies to others also. Only the name Amelia is preserved.' I would follow our translator in all the reproaches he makes against Mme. Riccoboni. They seem to me well founded. I accept for that matter the end of his 'Advertisement': 'If this book presented in its entirety, as I present it and Mr. Fielding thought fit to publish it, proves pleasing to the public, my object will have been fulfilled; in any case, there will be two Amelias, the one French, and the other in the English taste; the reader will be able to choose for himself.'

[Plot summary follows.]

*   *   *

This work of Mr. Fielding is not unworthy of the pen of that illustrious author. *Amelia* presents passages worthy of *Tom Jones*; characters that are various, well conceived and well carried out; a great knowledge of the world and of men; pointed criticism, sometimes powerful and energetic; moments of interest drawn from nature itself. But one can also recall insupportable languors, clumsy pleasantries, displaced details, above all a monotony that sheds a general coldness over this production. Mrs. Bennet ceases to interest after we learn that she had the baseness to take an annuity from the Noble Lord; she is also stained by her second marriage. She should have felt it necessary to pass her life in tears for having caused the death of her husband. Why make the Lord kinsman of that infamous Ellison? The action, in short, is drowned in a heap of distractions. The translator seems to have been perhaps too faithful to his original. It is true that it is a simple English picture, doubtless preferable to these translations, where, employing the French spirit, one totally loses sight of his model. Despite all these faults, *Amelia* excites the curiosity of the reader, and his interest is retained through many passages. . . .

JONATHAN WILD IN FRANCE

169. Unsigned review, *L'Année littéraire*

23 February 1763

A review of the French translation of *Jonathan Wild, L'Année littéraire* (1763), ii. 26–7.

Mr. Fielding has been immortalized by his novels *Joseph Andrews* and *Tom Jones*; today we kiss all the traces of his steps. The new work that has just been translated is well below those works of this author just mentioned. Little action, many reflections, above all a general tincture of bad taste and detestable pleasantries. . . . I do not speak of the main character who may be odious only to us French. We do not like to follow for two volumes a hero of roguish and wicked actions who ends on the gallows. The *Vie de Cartouche*, no matter how much art is put into its presentation, will be a disgusting book and will fall from our hands.[1] But these pictures are less revolting to the English, who love nature wherever they find it. The character of Jonathan is admirable in all its proportions; he is guided with an art that honors the genius of his author. His opposite, Heartfree, is no less well handled in his kind.

[1] A remark of the Empress Catherine II of Russia has been recorded that probably refers to the French translation: 'If I ever write a comedy I shall certainly not take the *Mariage de Figaro* as a model, for, after *Jonathan Wild*, I have never found myself in such bad company' (K. Waliszewski, *The Romance of an Empress*, 1905, p. 337).

170. Christopher Smart
'Epitaph on Henry Fielding, Esq.'

1763

In *Poems on Several Occasions* (1763), pp. 13–14. For other versions
of the poem, see the *St. James's Magazine* (July 1763), ii. 312, and
the *London Magazine* (August 1763), xxxii. 441.

The master of the GREEK and ROMAN page,
The lively scorner of a venal age,
Who made the publick laugh, at publick vice,
Or drew from sparkling eyes the pearl of price;
Student of nature, reader of mankind,
In whom the patron, and the bard were join'd;
As free to give the plaudit, as assert,
And faithful in the practise of desert.
Hence pow'r consign'd the laws to his command,
And put the scales of Justice in his hand,
To stand protector of the Orphan race,
And find the female penitent a place.
From toils like these, too much for age to bear,
From pain, from sickness, and a world of care;
From children, and a widow in her bloom,
From shores remote, and from a foreign tomb,
Call'd by the WORD of LIFE, thou shalt appear,
To *please* and *profit* in a higher sphere,
Where endless hope, imperishable gain,
Are what the scriptures *teach* and *entertain*.

THE FATHERS

171. Unsigned notice, *The St. James's Chronicle*

1 December 1778

Last Night a Comedy called *The Fathers*, or *The Good-natured Man*, was performed for the first Time at this Theatre. It was written by the late *Henry Fielding*, one of the first Geniuses that ever adorned this Island. Like Persons of that Order, in all Communities, where Abilities and Virtues are not the Instruments of Success, he was often involved in Difficulties, and has left a Family, for whose Advantage this Play is performed. This precludes all Censure of its Irregularities and Defects. Indeed this Reason is not necessary in the Case of the present Comedy. The opposite Dispositions of two Fathers, whose Families are inclined to unite, are delineated so exactly from Nature; the Sentiments of the Piece are so genuine; and then Dialogue so easy and witty, that it cannot fail of pleasing, if it be fairly and properly kept on the Theatre.

The Comedy is not made the most of; the Strength of the House being reserved to insure the Success of more favourite Writers.

172. Samuel Johnson, in conversation

From James Boswell, *Life of Johnson*, ed. G. B. Hill and L. F. Powell (1934), ii. 48–9 (Spring 1768); 173–5 (6 April 1772); iii. 43 (12 April 1776).

*   *   *

'Sir, (contained he,) there is all the difference in the world between characters of nature and characters of manners; and *there* is the difference between the characters of Fielding and those of Richardson. Characters of manners are very entertaining; but they are to be understood, by a more superficial observer, than characters of nature, where a man must dive into the recesses of the human heart.'

It always appeared to me that he estimated the compositions of Richardson too highly, and that he had an unreasonable prejudice against Fielding. In comparing those two writers, he used this expression; 'that there was as great a difference between them as between a man who knew how a watch was made, and a man who could tell the hour by looking on the dial-plate.' This was a short and figurative state of his distinction between drawing characters of nature and characters only of manners. But I cannot help being of opinion, that the neat watches of Fielding are as well constructed as the large clocks of Richardson, and that his dial-plates are brighter. Fielding's characters, though they do not expand themselves so widely in dissertation, are as just pictures of human nature, and I will venture to say, have more striking features, and nicer touches of the pencil; and though Johnson used to quote with approbation a saying of Richardson's, 'that the virtues of Fielding's heroes were the vices of a truly good man', I will venture to add, that the moral tendency of Fielding's writings, though it does not encourage a strained and rarely possible virtue, is ever favourable to honour and honesty, and cherishes the benevolent and generous affections. He who is as good as Fielding would make him, is an amiable member of society, and may be led on by more regulated instructors, to a higher state of ethical perfection.

*   *   *

Fielding being mentioned, Johnson exclaimed, 'he was a blockhead'; and upon my expressing my astonishment at so strange an assertion, he said, 'What I mean by his being a blockhead is that he was a barren rascal.' BOSWELL. 'Will you not allow, Sir, that he draws very natural pictures of human life?' JOHNSON. 'Why, Sir, it is of very low life. Richardson used to say, that had he not known who Fielding was, he should have believed he was an ostler. Sir, there is more knowledge of the heart in one letter of Richardson's, than in all "Tom Jones". I, indeed, never read "Joseph Andrews".' ERSKINE. 'Surely, Sir, Richardson is very tedious.' JOHNSON. 'Why, Sir, if you were to read Richardson for the story, your impatience would be so much fretted that you would hang yourself. But you must read him for the sentiment, and consider the story as only giving occasion to the sentiment.'—I have already given my opinion of Fielding; but I cannot refrain from repeating here my wonder at Johnson's excessive and unaccountable depreciation of one of the best writers that England has produced. 'Tom Jones' has stood the test of publick opinion with such success, as to have established its great merit, both for the story, the sentiments, and the manners, and also the varieties of diction, so as to leave no doubt of its having an animated truth of execution throughout.

*   *   *

[Johnson] said, that for general improvement, a man should read whatever his immediate inclination prompts him to; though, to be sure, if a man has a science to learn, he must regularly and resolutely advance. He added, 'what we read with inclination makes a much stronger impression. If we read without inclination, half the mind is employed in fixing the attention; so there is but one half to be employed on what we read.' He told us, he read Fielding's 'Amelia' through without stopping. He said, 'if a man begins to read in the middle of a book, and feels an inclination to go on, let him not quit it, to go to the beginning. He may, perhaps, not feel again the inclination.'

*   *   *

439

173. George, Lord Lyttelton, in conversation

sometime before 1773

In James Beattie, *Dissertations Moral and Critical* (1783), 571 n.

The great Lord Lyttelton, after mentioning several particulars of Pope, Swift, and other wits of that time, when I asked some question relating to the Author of Tom Jones, began his answer with these words, 'Henry Fielding, I assure you, had more wit and more humour than all the persons we have been speaking of put together.' This testimony of his Lordship, who was intimately acquainted with Fielding, ought not to be forgotten.

174. Madame du Deffand, letter

14 July 1773

From a letter to Horace Walpole, *The Yale Edition of Horace Walpole's Correspondence*, ed. W. S. Lewis (1937–65), v. 383.

---

*   *   *

Je viens de relire *Tom Jones*, dont le commencement et la fin m'ont charmée. Je n'aime que les romans qui peignent les caractères, bons et mauvais. C'est là où l'on trouve de vraies leçons de morale; et si on peut tirer quelque fruit de la lecture, c'est de ces livres-là; ils me font beaucoup d'impression; vos auteurs [sont] excellents dans ce genre, et les nôtres ne s'en doutent point. J'en sais bien la raison, c'est que nous n'avons point de caractère. Nous n'avons que plus ou moins d'éducation, et que nous sommes par conséquent imitateurs et singes les uns des autres.[1]

*   *   *

[1] I have just reread *Tom Jones*, which charms me from beginning to end. I like only those novels that paint characters, both good and bad. That is where true moral lessons are to be found; and if one can reap any benefit from reading, it is from books like these; they make a very great impression on me; your authors are excellent in that genre, and ours are innocent of such things. I know the reason, it is that we have no 'character'. We have only more or less education, and consequently we are only imitators and apes of each other. (Cf. Desfontaines' opinion to the same effect, above, No. 49.)

175. Horace Walpole, letter

3 August 1773

From a letter to Madame du Deffand, *Yale Walpole*, v. 390.

. . . Je n'accorde pas, comme vous, le même mérite à nos romans. *Tom Jones* me fit un plaisir bien mince: il y a du burlesque, et ce que j'aime encore moins, les moeurs du vulgaire. Je conviens que c'est fort naturel, mais le naturel qui n'admet pas du goût me touche peu. Je trouve que c'est le goût qui assure tout, et qui fait le charme de tout ce qui regarde la société. Scarron peut être aussi naturel que Mme de Sévigné, mais quelle différence! mille mères peuvent sentir autant qu'elle; c'est le goût qui la sépare du commun des mères. Nos romans sont grossiers. Dans *Gil Blas* il s'agit très souvent de valets, et de telle engeance, mais jamais, non jamais ils ne dégoûtent. Dans les romans de Fielding, il y a des curés de campagne qui sont de vrais cochons.—Je n'aime pas lire ce que je n'aimerais pas entendre.[1]

⋆　　⋆　　⋆

[1] I do not accord the same merit as you to our novels. *Tom Jones* gives me a very slight pleasure indeed: it is full of burlesque and, what I like even less, the behavior of the vulgar. I realize that this is very 'natural', but the natural imitated without taste does not interest me. I find that it is taste that distinguishes everything, and that gives charm to what we think of as society. Scarron could be as natural as Mme. de Sévigné, but what a difference! a thousand mothers can feel as she does; it is taste that separates her from the commonality of mothers. Our novels are coarse. In *Gil Blas* there are many knaves and such, but never, no never do they disgust me. In the novels of Fielding, there are country parsons who are real scoundrels.—I do not like to read what I would not like to hear.

176. Samuel Johnson, in conversation

c. 1780

From Hannah More, letter to a sister, 1780, *Memoirs of the Life and Correspondence of Mrs. Hannah More* (1834), i. 168.

I never saw Johnson really angry with me but once; and his displeasure did him so much honour that I loved him the better for it. I alluded rather flippantly, I fear, to some witty passage in Tom Jones: he replied, 'I am shocked to hear you quote from so vicious a book. I am sorry to hear you have read it: a confession which no modest lady should ever make. I scarcely know a more corrupt work.' I thanked him for his correction; assured him I thought full as ill of it now as he did, and had only read it at an age when I was more subject to be caught by the wit, than able to discern the mischief. Of Joseph Andrews I declared my decided abhorrence. He went so far as to refuse to Fielding the great talents which are ascribed to him, and broke out into a noble panegyric on his competitor, Richardson; who, he said, was as superior to him in talents as in virtue; and whom he pronounced to be the greatest genius that had shed its lustre on this path of literature.

★　　★　　★

177. James Harris, 'Philological Inquiries'

1781

In *Works* (1781), iii. 163–4.

*   *   *

His JOSEPH ANDREWS and TOM JONES may be called *Master-pieces* in the COMIC EPOPEE, which none since have equalled, tho' multitudes have imitated; and which he was peculiarly qualified to write in the manner he did, both from his *Life*, his *Learning*, and his *Genius*.

Had his *Life* been *less irregular* (for irregular it was, and spent in a promiscuous intercourse with persons of *all* ranks) his *Pictures of Human kind* had neither been so *various*, nor so *natural*.

Had he possest less of *Literature*, he could not have infused such a spirit of *Classical Elegance*.

Had his Genius been less fertile in *Wit and Humour*, he could not have maintained that *uninterrupted Pleasantry*, which never suffers his Reader to feel fatigue.

*   *   *

178. Samuel Johnson, in conversation

sometime before 1784

In Hester Lynch Piozzi, *Anecdotes of the Late Samuel Johnson, LL.D.* (1786), reprinted in *Johnsonian Miscellanies*, ed. G. B. Hill (1897), i. 297.

---

*　　*　　*

[Johnson's] attention to veracity was without equal or example: and when I mentioned Clarissa as a perfect character; 'On the contrary (said he), you may observe there is always something which she prefers to truth. Fielding's Amelia was the most pleasing heroine of all the romances (he said); but that vile broken nose never cured, ruined the sale of perhaps the only book, which being printed off betimes one morning, a new edition was called for before night.'

179. Horace Walpole

26 June 1785

From a letter to John Pinkerton, *Yale Walpole*, xvi. 270.

---

*　　*　　*

Fielding had as much humour perhaps as Addison, but having no idea of grace, is perpetually disgusting. His innkeepers and parsons are the grossest of their profession, and his gentlemen are awkward when they should be at their ease.

*　　*　　*

180. Sir John Hawkins, from *The Works of Samuel Johnson*

1787, i. 214–15

*   *   *

At the head of these [writers of fiction] we must, for many reasons, place Henry Fielding, one of the most motley of literary characters. This man was, in his early life, a writer of comedies and farces, very few of which are now remembered; after that, a practising barrister with scarce any business; then an anti-ministerial writer, and quickly after, a creature of the duke of Newcastle, who gave him a nominal qualification of 100*l.* a year, and set him up as a trading-justice, in which disreputable station he died. He was the author of a romance, intitled 'The history of Joseph Andrews,' and of another, 'The Foundling, or the history of Tom Jones,' a book seemingly intended to sap the foundation of that morality which it is the duty of parents and all public instructors to inculcate in the minds of young people, by teaching that virtue upon principle is imposture, that generous qualities alone constitute true worth, and that a young man may love and be loved, and at the same time associate with the loosest women. His morality, in respect that it resolves virtue into good affections, in contradiction to moral obligation and a sense of duty, is that of lord Shaftesbury vulgarised, and is a system of excellent use in palliating the vices most injurious to society. He was the inventor of that cant-phrase, goodness of heart, which is every day used as a substitute for probity, and means little more than the virtue of a horse or a dog; in short, he has done more towards corrupting the rising generation than any writer we know of.

Select Index

I

Names of authors, periodicals, and anonymous works quoted from or cited:

II

Authors compared or related to Fielding:

III

Individual works by Fielding:

IV

Selected topics of Fielding criticism: